FROM "MASTER"* STORYTELLER JACK OLSEN

COLD KILL

"A story as interesting as it is bizarre."
—*San Diego Tribune*

"Brutal. . . . But the violence is tempered with background and psychology that make the story more complex than most." —*Tulsa Daily World*

"Fascinating and horrifying. . . . True-crime veteran author Olsen moves beyond the cold facts of the case to recreate a vivid portrait of a twisted and bizarre relationship between two social misfits . . . a raw, chilling, terrible true story." —*Lincoln Journal*

"Jack Olsen . . . can write a mean tale."
—*The Sacramento Union*

"Shattering reading . . . Olsen has another winner this time." —*Publishers Weekly*

"*Cold Kill* shows Olsen still a master of murder."
—*Seattle Post-Intelligencer*

* *Detroit Free Press*

BOOKS BY JACK OLSEN

COLD KILL

The True Story of a Murderous Love

JACK OLSEN

A DELL BOOK

Publisher's Note
This is a true story, told from the perspective of various people involved as events unfolded. The reader should remember, of course, that an individual's perception of events and circumstances is shaped by what he or she knows or believes at any given moment. Perception and reality are not always the same.

Published by
Dell Publishing
a division of
The Bantam Doubleday Dell Publishing Group, Inc.
666 Fifth Avenue
New York, New York 10103

For information address: Atheneum, a division of Macmillan Publishing Company, New York, New York.

The trademark Dell ® is registered in the U.S. Patent and Trademark Office.

ISBN: 0-440-20212-4

Reprinted by arrangement with Atheneum, a division of Macmillan Publishing Company

Printed in the United States of America

Published simultaneously in Canada

December 1988

10 9 8 7 6 5 4 3 2 1

KRI

1980

1

The first time David saw her, she was huddled at a table in the student union, peering through strings of brownish hair. He thought, Who's the new girl and why is she hiding? When he saw that his old girlfriend Jamie Campbell was sitting at the same table, he walked over.

Jamie smiled; the others seemed indifferent. It didn't upset him. He was used to indifference.

Jamie looked as striking as ever, a Texas Jodie Foster with the lean angularity of a model. Their romance had been short, platonic; he'd always hated to force himself on a woman. Lately she'd avoided him. He figured it was because of the scene with the maid. He'd called the Mexican woman *"pinche idiota"* and *"pinche puta"* and got himself barred from Jamie's parents' fancy house. Well, he thought as he unfolded his paper napkin, she *is* a fucking idiot and she *is* a fucking whore. Kept insisting that Jamie wasn't home when he knew damn well she was. A goddamn servant!

He said "Hi" in his thin voice and waited for an introduction to the newcomer. In the strained silence she sat on her crossed legs and sucked on a cigarette. When he smiled, she seemed to shrivel like a salted slug.

He thought, She doesn't know dick about make-up. She'd accented her cheeks with big round splotches of tomato aspic suitable for a circus clown. Her fake eyelashes were a half-inch long. She was about five five or five six, with big breasts, thighs that spread the fibers of her jeans, and a backside shaped like South America. He tried not to show his disapproval. Back in the Marines, he'd trained himself to view fat as the enemy. Before every trip to the mess hall, he imagined slitting his skin with an electric knife and trimming off the ugly sheets of fat. He'd dieted down to a lean 155 and stayed there. Showed what a guy could do if he learned to control his appetite.

Jamie broke the silence. "David, this is my sister, Cindy Ray."

"Hi, Cindy," he said softly. "How ya doing?"

She didn't react.

He remembered telling Jamie that he was partial to brunettes with strong bone structure and French or Latin features, classical beauties like Katharine Hepburn, Natalie Wood, Jane Seymour. Jamie had said, "Then you'd *love* my sister Cindy. She looks like that—but she's crazy! And she's driven a couple of psychiatrists crazy."

So this was the crazy sister. The last he'd heard, she was studying art somewhere. What the hell was she doing here at Crooker Center? And why was she so . . . out of it?

He waved his palm in front of her face. "Hello hello," he said in his best Star Trek voice. *"Earth to Cindy."*

She responded so weakly that he couldn't make out the words. It was like meeting a backward five-year-old. He wanted to yell, "Speak up!" She didn't smile. Her eyes appeared colorless, but when she opened them wide, they turned out to be hazel with a hint of amber, slightly tilted and exotic-looking. He'd always liked the Mediterranean look. Her waist nipped in a few inches, giving her a semblance of a shape. She had full lips and a straight nose with a cute bulb at the tip, and her long hair looked as though it might brighten to an attractive bronze if she ever washed it. He imagined her thirty pounds lighter, and sighed.

He muttered a few words to his old friend Jamie and then left the University of St. Thomas for the day. He wasn't enrolled, though he often ate at the student union. He was studying photography at the University of Houston and tending bar part-time. When he looked back, Cindy Ray was staring at the floor.

A few days later he spotted her alone at the same place. He'd just finished working out on a Nautilus and was deep into plans for improving himself with physical manifestations of positive energy, after the teachings of B. F. Skinner and others.

"Hi!" he said. He wondered if she would remember him.

"Oh," she said, looking up through her hair. "Hi."

"How's it going?"

She answered, but he had to ask her to repeat. "Okay," she said.

He sat and began to talk. At first she barely responded. When he made a joke, she smiled or sighed; he couldn't always tell which. He thought, She'll never win Miss Congeniality. But after a while he was surprised to detect a sense of humor and some intelligence. He thought, Well, all right! There's a real person here!

Close up, her impossibly long chestnut eyelashes turned out to be real. Fat or not, she was pretty. She looked like a worthwhile candidate for the self-improvement techniques he was learning. On impulse, he lifted her hair off her face. "C'mon now," he said in the firm tone he used on his pit bulls, "sit up straight! That's it! *There!* See how nice that feels?"

A faint smile rewarded him. "Look," he said, "you could be a fairly attractive person. Just lose some weight. Start dressing decently. Straighten out your posture. With a little less make-up, you could be an attractive girl."

She smiled and mumbled.

"Look at yourself," he went on. "How much do you weigh?"

"One eighty," she said in a waiflike voice.

He squeezed her thigh. "Well, look at that!" he said enthusiastically. "That's solid, ya know? That's not just a big blob of lard." He waited for his compliment to take effect, then added, "You don't look one eighty. You're not sloppy or flabby. You're proportionate. You've still got muscle tone."

He left her smiling. As he walked toward class, he thought, Unconditional positive regard—it works every time. Too bad she's such a tub.

The next time they ran into each other, she seemed more open. When he commented on how little she resembled her sister Jamie, she said, "Oh, that's because I'm illegitimate." She explained that her father had sired her in Italy during World War II and had sworn the family to secrecy.

"Oh?" David said. He thought, This is 1980. If she was born during World War II, she has to be . . . thirty-five or forty. But she isn't even thirty. He decided she must be kidding. Women teased him a lot. He never took offense. It was better than being ignored.

That night he was drawing a draft beer for a customer when the phone rang in the bar and a sexy voice asked for David.

"This is David," he said.

"Hi! It's Cindy Ray." He was surprised. What happened to her shyness? "You know something, David?" she said in a bright, upbeat voice. "You're cute. You really are."

He said, "Thank ya. I'm flattered."

She said, "I'd like to go on a date with you sometime."

He thought, Well, good grief, it's nice to be wanted, but . . . she's a blimp. He said, "Well, uh . . . sure."

She said, "Well, good-by then, David," and hung up.

2

Jamie Lee Campbell watched as her sister Cindy put down the phone and said, "He's really gross."

"Who?" Jamie asked.

"David West. He looks like a pig. Have you ever watched him eat?"

"Yeah," Jamie answered. In her Houston accent it became a two-syllable word.

"He looks just like a dog or something, doesn't he?"

"Yeah."

"You know," Cindy mused, "somebody like that will do anything you tell 'em."

Jamie asked why she'd just asked him for a date if she found him so unappealing. "Well," her older sister answered, "he'd be like a dog. He'd be easy to train."

Jamie thought, This conversation is a little too damn typical. Ever since Cindy had left her latest husband and come back home to her parents, she'd seemed crazier than ever. A few days ago she'd attacked Jamie and their mother in the driveway, forcing Jamie to jump into the Chevy Suburban just ahead of a roundhouse punch. When Cindy turned to hit her tiny mother, Jamie decided to squash her flat with the oversized station wagon, but before she could get it in gear, Cindy yelled "Bitch!" and ran.

Soon after that scene their father had told Jamie in his mellifluous lawyer's voice that her grades at the University of St. Thomas weren't up to the Campbell family's standards. Jamie ran upstairs in tears, and Cindy told her, "We'd be a lot better off without Daddy. I think I should kill him and I have an idea how to do it."

Jamie blinked and said, "You're crazy."

"No I'm not. It would work. I'd dress up like a man and I'd wear men's shoes or heavy boots and I'd leave footprints around a window and some Marlboro cigarettes and it would really look like a man did it. I'd wear gloves, too."

"You're *crazy.*"

Jamie listened to a few more lunacies and ran out of their shared bedroom. Her mother was standing just outside the door. The look on her face showed that she'd heard.

Jamie phoned her oldest sister in Austin for guidance. Michelle wasn't home, but her best friend heard the story and told Jamie to report Cindy to the police.

Maybe I should have, Jamie thought as she pondered her latest problems with her older sister. How could anyone cope with Cindy and still make good grades? Every morning Jamie drove the two of them to the midtown campus. At twenty-five Cindy still hadn't learned to drive.

The commute was always a bummer. Cindy griped constantly, threatened to quit St. Thomas, and bitched about Jamie's driving. Sometimes she lobbed cigarette butts into her sister's straight brown hair. One morning she yanked at the steering wheel and almost caused a wreck. Several times she ordered Jamie to pull over and stop, and once she jumped out while the car was moving.

Jamie was reluctant to complain to her parents because she doubted that it would do any good. It had always been accepted that Cindy was the family's eccentric *artiste* and lived in a different world. She lied constantly, turning sister against sister and friend against friend, but she was such a skillful liar that she was able to manipulate the same victims again and again. Especially her parents. Ever since childhood she'd been deceiving and hurting James and Virginia, and in return they forgave her, welcomed her back after her frequent escapades, excused her destructive fantasies and her vicious mind games. But the strain was beginning to show. Recently Virginia Campbell had confided, "You know, Jamie, Cindy's the only person I know who can just walk across the room and make me feel like a nervous wreck." Jamie had felt like adding, Hey, Mom, try driving her to school!

At last Jamie summoned the courage to approach her father. "I know Cindy has to get to school, but I can't drive her anymore. She tried to jump out of the car again. She's gonna get us killed."

"Jamie, she cain't drive herself," James Campbell said in his educated country-boy accent. He was a rangy man, six four, over two hundred pounds, with warm brown eyes and lots of laugh wrinkles.

"But Daddy," she said, "Cindy chose not to learn to drive."

"If you don't want to help your sister," he said after a while, "I'll have to take back your car." Jamie knew better than to argue.

The next day she came home from school to find a Buick Regal parked in the driveway. Her mother explained happily, "Daddy got it for Cindy. All she has to do is learn to drive. We'll pay for the lessons."

That night Jamie heard Cindy yell at her father to send the Buick back. She said she would never, *never* learn to drive and they'd better get that through their heads. The car was gone in the morning.

3

David West was upending a Belhaven Scottish Ale in a campus bar when he noticed Jamie and Cindy Campbell and offered to drive them home in his custom Ford van. The Good Times was a ten-thousand-dollar black beauty with captain's chairs in back and a navigator's seat for Tiger, his latest pit bull. He gunned the engine and steered toward the West Loop, the most heavily traveled stretch of freeway in the world. They drove past the Galleria with its glittering shops and rich Mexican customers who paid cash, and rolled into the green hush of the Memorial section with its giant oaks, pecans and pine trees.

Inside the van the sisters progressed from minor disagreement to shrieks. By the time they reached the Campbell house on Memorial Drive, they'd almost come to blows. David was happy to get away.

Each time he ran into Cynthia Campbell Ray after that, she seemed less repellent. She was still a blimp, but how many women had ever asked him for a date? He had to give her bonus points for that.

Gradually he got her to laugh at his Star Trek impressions and jokes. She had a disarming modesty, referring to herself as "dumpy nerdy Elmo." After a while he began to suspect that they shared the same problem: self-hatred. He admitted that he despised his looks. "I've got a face like a pig," he said. "I always think of myself as shorter than I am and weaker than I am and uglier than I am."

She replied, "You're really very nice-looking, for a male chauvinist." They both laughed.

She did a sketch of him in her notebook—*zip, zap, zip* and it was finished. He'd inherited artistic talent from his mother, but he took one look at the drawing and realized he could never match her skill. It was enough to make him throw away his Niji pens.

He was surprised when she announced that she was dropping out of school. "Why?" he asked.

"It's Mother and Daddy," she said. "My grades are much
better than Jamie's, so they said they won't let her drive me
anymore."

He didn't understand how Cindy's grades could be better
than Jamie's. She never carried books and hardly ever went
to class. But it wasn't his nature to question what women
told him; he was content just to be in their company. "What
kind of reason is that?" he asked gently. "Your mom and
dad oughta be happy for you."

Cindy said, "They're always messing with my head. They
say I'm not a good person. They ignore me. They're so
mean."

He thought, You never know what goes on behind the
walls of those fancy homes with the Grecian columns and all
that bullshit. Look at "Dallas" and "Dynasty." "Why
would they be mean to you?" he wondered out loud.

"They hate me. The whole family hates me."

"Why?"

Her lower lip wobbled and her voice rose to a squeak.
"They gave Jamie a car, but they won't even buy me an old
junker."

Despite her size, she seemed fragile. "That's terrible!" he
said. How could anyone hurt this pathetic creature? What
kind of parents would tell their own flesh and blood that
they hated her?

He tried to remember the Campbells from the two or
three visits he'd made before his banishment over the *pinche
puta.* Cecelia West had brought him up to be hypercritical—
all those hours sitting in front of the TV listening to her
eviscerate actors, plots, sets, wardrobes. As his mother's son,
he wasn't impressed by Cindy's parents or their home. The
front yard was a tangle of unpruned bushes and shrubs under a thick growth of crape myrtle, magnolias and oaks. The
lawn was a battleground for weeds and thick-bladed St. Au-
gustine grass. The ragged stumps of two dead palms flanked
the entrance to a worn driveway. It seemed to David that
the owner lacked pride.

The house resembled a bunker—blocky, cold, faced with

tan flagstone. Jamie had told him that it was built in the twenties by a steelman. The pull-up entrance to the basement was a slab of dimpled steel suitable for a light cruiser. The backyard was dominated by a water tank that looked borrowed from a factory. Anyone with taste would have torn the house down and started over. The place stood out in the fancy Memorial section for the wrong reasons.

Inside, it looked as though the family had just moved in. The walls were mostly blank except for the obligatory set of Texas longhorns, a few *primitivo* paintings by Mrs. Campbell, and a plaster of paris relief of the Three Musketeers with tinny swords sticking out—"like something you'd buy in Tijuana," he told his mother later. The floor was covered in faded blue carpet with bare spots the size of dinner plates. Wherever he looked, there seemed to be another antiquated console TV; apparently the Campbells bought heavily at garage sales and never held one of their own. He couldn't understand why people with enough money to live in a four-hundred-thousand-dollar home couldn't decorate it better.

Poor Cindy, he thought as she stood before him wringing her plump hands. "What'll you do now?" he asked. "Take the bus?"

"It's too far. And I don't have the money."

"Your Mom and Dad won't give you bus fare?"

"Oh, no." She said it flatly, hopelessly.

"What'll you *do?*"

"I'll just have to drop out."

He thought, That's unfair! Everybody's a millionaire on that stretch of Memorial Drive. This is . . . sick!

He felt a touch of his old rage about the mistreatment of females. All his life he'd defended women, loved them, pedestalized them, asked nothing but a little affection in return. In the end, they always left. Except his mom, of course.

"Listen, Cindy," he said, touching the soft arm, "I've got this house in the Montrose. It's not much, but you can have a room of your own. You can walk to school from there." He had no ulterior motive. She was a woman and a victim.

But she jerked away as though he'd dropped his pants. *"No!"* he said. "Listen, I know it sounds like I'm trying to

maneuver you, but believe me—I won't lay a finger on you."
She still looked dubious. "For one thing," he added, "you're
too fat."

She seemed to be thinking it over. "You won't, uh . . .
bother me?"

"I give you my word. No strings attached." A man's word
was everything. It was the most important lesson his father
had taught him. DuVal West would rather lose out on a
business deal—and sometimes had—than tell the smallest
lie. It placed him at a disadvantage in the marketplace.

Cindy turned away, then looked back narrow-eyed. "Let
me tell you one thing," she said. Her voice had dropped
several notes. "If you bother me, I'll be gone." There wasn't
the slightest doubt that she meant every word.

So did he. A woman who weighed 180 pounds had nothing to fear from David West.

4

Jamie was relieved that she didn't have to drive Cindy to
school anymore, but her sister's live-in arrangement with
David West had come a little too late for her own peace of
mind. The problem was that Cindy was still on campus and
West still dropped around to visit. As far as Jamie was concerned, that made the University of St. Thomas an overpop-
ulated area.

Sometimes she wished Cindy had never decided to go to
college. As a child she'd had to be dragged to school,
flunked two grades, dropped out at sixteen, later inveigled a
high school equivalency degree with her father's help. After
a couple of unhappy marriages, she'd taken a commercial-
art course and landed a job as Woolco store artist. On the
second day she'd quit and announced that she was enrolling
at St. Thomas to become an actress. As usual, the indulgent
parents had patted her on the head and let her have her way.

Jamie was aggravated that Cindy had brought David West
back into her life. She'd met him two years earlier in a politi-

cal-science class, a wimpy-looking guy with a scraggly reddish beard that didn't quite cover a weak chin. A pronounced overbite gave him a rabbity look. She'd studied his
face for several days before realizing that his left eye was
grayish-blue and his right was yellowish-brown. His voice
was reedy, treble. He had dimples, a matched pair of cow-
licks in blow-dried brown hair, and a heraldic eagle tattooed
on his upper arm. She was surprised to learn that he was an
ex-Marine on the GI Bill. He didn't look tough enough.

On Christmas Eve, 1978, he'd called her at home to say
he was lonely. She felt sorry for him: he'd always seemed
short on friends, slouching around with his pit bulls and
trying to entice people into his van. He took her to a movie
and spent most of the evening griping about his parents. He
told her that he'd inherited a hundred thousand dollars from
an oil-rich aunt in Tulsa, and his mother had invested most
of it in a rotting old duplex that was draining him dry. He
described his father as an emotionally constipated intellectual who paid more attention to his dog and his jazz records
than to his wife and son. At the time Jamie had said to
herself, It's hard to relax around this guy. He sounds too
much like Cindy.

She'd run into him a few more times in her first year at St.
Thomas. He was the one the other guys sent for beer. He
wasn't important enough to be liked or disliked. When he
managed to find an audience, he put people to sleep with
run-on stories. He was impervious to a bored expression or a
subtle put-down. He pestered women long after they'd
shaken him off. "Doesn't he notice how rude I am?" said a
woman who dated him once. "Why's he still calling?"

It seemed to Jamie that he didn't realize how his words
came across to others. He told a group of students at
Crooker Center that he admired the Romans for "perpetuat-
ing the health of their race. When they had a deformed
baby, they'd lay it on the hillside." He said openly that the
retarded should be sterilized. He professed to abhor Nazism
but believed in breeding for a master race. "What could be
wrong about trying to make the next generation bigger and
stronger and healthier? If I can say, 'I want to order my kid,
I want him to be like so-and-so,' and then I fill out a little

form and they go *ding-ding-ding beep-beep,* mess with the little chromosomes and give me a six-foot-two genius with blue eyes and blond hair, well, what the hell is wrong with that?"

She hadn't been surprised to learn that, despite his thin voice and innocent look, he had a mean streak. Their mutual friend Jane Armistead was with him when he bumped a gas-station attendant with his car and then cursed him for getting in the way. In the ensuing fight West was slashed in the ear with a scraper, leaving a scar.

Students shared stories about his violence. One day at Crooker Center he even told one on himself, with much gesturing and relish. "I was stopped at a light and I saw an old guy in the van behind me pounding on a girl about eighteen. I jumped out of my van and said, 'Hey, man, you wanna fucking hit somebody, hit me!'

"The girl goes, 'It's okay, it's *okay!* He's my father.'

"I go, 'My dying ass it's okay! Come on outa there, motherfucker!' I slapped him through the open window, grabbed him by his tie, and jerked him hard.

"He goes, 'All right, goddamn it, pull over there, punkie!'

"We park around the corner and he gets out. He's forty-six, forty-eight and about two fifty. He used his weight and got on top of me. He was beating the piss outa me. I tried to kick him in the groin, but I couldn't quite reach. Some teachers came along and broke it up just in time."

Jamie had repeated the story to her mother, and Virginia Campbell had commented, "It sounds like your friend has an authority problem."

An authority problem, yes, but Jamie wondered what else lay beneath his wimpy exterior. He didn't even follow his own code of behavior. He orated about chivalry and honor but acted proud to be a dirty fighter. *I tried to kick him in the groin.* . . . What kind of chivalry was that?

After a few casual dates Jamie had cut him off; he'd begun to act as though she belonged to him. He phoned three or four times a day. At last she stopped answering. "Jamie," Virginia Campbell said, "you can't just ignore the boy."

"Mother," she said, "the guy is weird. I don't want to see him anymore."

"Well, honey, he just keeps calling. You've got to do something."

For a while Jamie had used the maid as a buffer till West lost his temper and cursed Maria out in Spanish. After his banning from the house, he'd seemed on his way out of the Campbells' lives. But no such luck, Jamie thought. Two years later he's weaseled his way back through Cindy.

One day Jamie asked her sister, "What on earth do you see in that West?"

Cindy said, "I think he'll be good for beating people up."

5

"Everybody thinks we're sleeping together," Cindy said in her little-girl voice.

David looked at her fleshy arms and thought, Fat chance. But he would never hurt her feelings. She was so vulnerable. You had to watch every word.

It was October 1980, and he'd installed her in a spare bedroom and treated her exactly as he'd promised. They shared a bathroom but dressed and undressed privately. Sitting around his living room, they laughed about the impression they were giving their evil-minded friends.

Even though he wasn't charging her for room or board, David found himself apologizing for the surroundings. He couldn't forget that she'd been brought up in Memorial. While he'd been away in the Marines, the Montrose of his childhood had changed. He hadn't been home a week when a pasty-faced fruit in a yellow convertible chirped kisses at him till David bashed in his door with a hunk of concrete.

He still couldn't believe the changes in the neighborhood where he'd grown up in a comfortable two-story house shaded by a sweet gum, camphor trees and a giant pecan. The respectable old shops were failing one by one, the vacancies quickly filled by palm readers, enterprises like the Bangkok Oriental Modeling Studio, callgirl operations, titty

bars like the Booby Rock, and limited-clientele clubs for
biker gays, transvestites, and friendly old fruits, each club
barred to the others. "There used to be a few hippies around
Kipling," David complained to a friend, "but now it's sissy
motherfuckers walking up and down. I thought that was
against the law. Those perverts sit out in front of my mom's
house!" It was the unkindest cut. He didn't believe that the
sweet gum and camphor trees in his front yard should shade
deviates.

When he'd fully realized that Houston's demographics
weren't going to change back, he bought a .38 Colt
Diamondback and slid it under the front seat of his car.
Sometimes he carried a military knife for good measure. He
might be surrounded by degenerates, but he was ready for
the next pervert who took him for one.

Cindy didn't seem to mind his neighborhood or his house.
There was plenty of room in the duplex, but there was no
heat. The topless toilet flushed from inside the tank. The
roof leaked. Windows had been replaced with cardboard
and foil. Corroded air conditioners produced mostly noise.
The bare wood walls smelled like scorched clothes in the
summer and mold in winter. The decaying foundations
housed mice and rats. It galled him that the place was in this
kind of condition *after* he'd sunk seventeen thousand dollars
of his inheritance into improvements. And before that
there'd been a thirty-one-thousand-dollar down payment.
He figured he would be paying on the goddamn house till
the twenty-first century. No wonder he sometimes felt like
wringing his mother's neck for manipulating him into buying the old dump.

Cindy settled in without a word of complaint. She
thanked him for freeing her from her cruel parents and
wicked sisters. He was surprised to find that there was at
least one sugar daddy in her life, a short, bald, fat, fiftyish
restaurateur who wore gold chains and pinky rings. When
he came around, David graciously posed as her brother. "He
never makes advances," Cindy said of her elderly friend. "I
like that in a man."

He also detected a taste for what he thought of as "the
romantic mondo-bizarro." She had a love affair with a Japa-

nese-French student named Robert who kept babbling to
David that he and Cindy were telepathic. Like his father,
David scorned the spiritual. "Goddamn it, Cindy," he
warned her, "that guy's feeding you full of mystical garbage
and you already got enough of a problem with reality as it is,
ya know? If you were like my mom and used the mystical
stuff for fun and games, it'd be different. But you're starting
to believe all this bullshit about spirits and mind reading
when what you need is an injection of reality." The romance
with Robert ended soon after.

He only wished she weren't fat, so he could try a few
moves. His sex life had always been minimal. He dated an
old girlfriend or two and made an occasional barroom score.
He liked to back his women into a corner, stare intently with
his dichromatic eyes and display his erudition. *Bismarck was
the father of his country ya know? So was Garibaldi. . . .
Nietzsche's a hell of a lot more relevant than you think. . . .*
He bridled at interruptions, even from waiters. "Don't you
see the lady and I are talking?" he would say in his treble
voice. "Where's your manners?"

He permitted no deprecation of females, even females he
didn't know. He despised yellowbellies who wouldn't protect their women. To him there was no greater responsibility. He just wished he had a few more to champion with his
ready fists.

For an ex-Marine, he was woefully short on fighting finesse. He windmilled into his opponents, substituting fury
for art. He believed in knocking sense into the less intellectually advantaged. Fighting, he told his friend John Lee, was
an educational opportunity. The idea was to teach some asshole a lesson and win. "I used to duke it out, hit the other
guy, let him get up," he explained. "Fuck that! Nobody
fights like that anymore. That's from the sixties. When you
get an advantage, press it!"

Cindy seemed admiring of him in all his roles—host, ad-
viser, security guard, pedagogue. In turn, he basked in her
admiration and soon began viewing her as an acceptable
specimen of womanhood—not the tall Aryan breeder he'd

always hoped to marry, but not the unappealing slab she'd seemed at first, either.

At night the roommates watched TV, a lifelong habit of both. David sat on the old black Naugahyde convertible sofa, reproducing the sounds of "Star Trek" with his pliant mouth. Cindy sat shoeless and cross-legged on the floor, praising his performances. He kidded her about her favorite romantic movies and she ragged him about his shoot-'em-ups and sci-fi epics. She displayed a fine singing voice with a lovely sustained vibrato. She continued to dazzle him with her skill at drawing. One day she sketched an idealized self-portrait and deliberately left a lower corner unfinished. He thought, God, Cindy, that's you! Beautiful but unfinished. . . .

He gradually realized that they had more in common than he'd thought. They were both sensitive, imaginative, witty, bright. Both dreamed of old-fashioned love; the idea of a great romance had always been more important to David than sex. Both had a flair for the histrionic; she was still studying drama at St. Thomas and his family had a history of interest in the stage. And both thought they'd been victimized as children and didn't mind talking about it.

But in moments of candor he had to admit that her main asset was her pathetic reliance on his encouragement and help. She was touchingly thankful for every compliment, each small kindness. For one of the few times in his life, he was made to feel wanted. And appreciated. No one except his mother had ever appreciated him so much. It was a trip.

He deduced that she had an abnormal need for support simply because of her long history of failures. He'd learned in his psychology courses that failure can feed on itself. She didn't even know how to drive and refused to learn how. Of course! he said to himself. She knows she'll fail.

He decided she needed a record of accomplishment to start rebuilding her ego. He bought her a three-hundred-dollar Austrian Puch so she could get around the Montrose like his mother. But when she fell off the bike on a slope, she ran to a bush and cowered in fear. After that, the Puch gathered dust.

He continued trying to program her, and he soon learned

that negative criticism didn't work. She cringed like a kicked dog. One night he came home from work and complained, "Cindy, there's grease on the dishes. You didn't use the scrubber." She hadn't touched the dishes since. He told himself that he should have remembered how she'd stopped sweeping after he'd pointed out a leftover mote.

He drew on his old behaviorism textbooks and substituted praise for criticism. "Look," he said, propping her in front of a mirror, "you've got good bone structure, great cheeks, full lips, pretty eyes. Okay, you're overweight, but you've got a flat belly and a small waist. Just exercise and diet and follow good nutrition. Feel good about yourself. Hold yourself upright. You'll be great!"

In her childlike voice, she said she'd suffered abuse as a fat little girl. "The other girls said they'd pop me like a balloon." He could see that she didn't think it was the least bit funny. "I don't know how to lose weight," she said. "I tried, but . . . I can't."

He said, "Will you just listen to me and do what I tell you?"

"I—I guess." She sounded threatened. That's okay, he thought. It's a start.

He taught her a set of basic exercises—leg raises, side bends, trunk twisters, squats—and beat time as she creaked through them morning and night. He introduced her to his Marine Corps diet, the one that had worked when he'd been a chubby perimeter guard—no starches, no grease, no sweets, no fats. Just V-8 and skim milk, lean meat, fish, chicken and greens. He taught her how to do her face, how to get in a car, how to hold a cigarette. He lectured her on posture, made her balance a book on her head and walk across the room.

He showered her with unconditional positive regard and ordered her to lighten up on herself. "Cindy," he said, "can't you see what you're doing? These other people—your parents, your sisters—to hell with them! You're letting them do a number on you. Stand up for yourself. The only reason you're a victim is because you allow it. Don't accept anything unquestioningly and don't allow *anybody* to do your thinking for you." He paused for effect. "Not even me."

As she looked up from the floor, he said, "And remember: you're a *good* person. If you were a bad person, you wouldn't be in my house."

For the first few weeks there was no visible progress. He knew that she'd been taught to think of herself as a wart on the ass of mankind, and he hadn't expected overnight results. Then one day she announced she'd lost five pounds. She began holding her head higher and paying attention to her clothes. She took pains with her make-up, the way he'd taught her, and soon she began to look better.

It was time to show her to Mom.

6

Cecelia watched her son's new friend in action for a few minutes and said to herself, This one can't be real. The overweight woman was a ham actress.

If there was one thing Cecelia West knew after sixty-four years, it was acting. In the 1950s, when David was an infant, she'd worked on wardrobes at Houston's famous Alley Theatre. Her shy husband DuVal even had taken a role in *The Skin of Our Teeth* before retreating backstage to handle the lights. The stage had preoccupied husband and wife for years. They'd tried to adapt the novel *Emma* for the stage, but it was one of many marital projects that fizzled. "DuVal wanted to make the hero so *unpleasant*," Cecelia complained in her punched-up style of speech. "So *severe*, rigid. He *magnified* the man's defects."

DuVal replied in his gravelly voice that the problem lay more with Jane Austen's skill than his own lack of it. "She wrote subtleties and nuances that couldn't be captured on the stage." The argument had waxed and waned for years.

Cecelia was glad her husband wasn't home when David dragged his latest loser into her kitchen. He introduced her as "my friend Cindy Ray" and added that she was Jamie Campbell's sister. Cecelia remembered Jamie as one of David's college friends, a tall child who'd spent a year in Switzerland and hadn't learned a thing, not even a little French. Or sophistication.

Her first impression of Cindy Ray was equally negative. She looked like an overweight Daisy Mae, unkempt, barely holding together. She had gorgeous long lashes and batted her eyes like an ingenue, but her fake smile wouldn't have worked in a reform school production of *Peter Pan*.

Cecelia's family went back two hundred years in the United States and she knew her etiquette. She smiled courteously and said, "Nice to meet you."

Cindy Ray peeped through her lashes, looked down shyly and murmured "Hello."

Cecelia thought, My Lord, She's trying to do Shirley Temple. Next she'll be scratching the rug with her toe.

That night Cecelia got on the phone and shared her perceptions with her son. She'd never been reluctant to critique his girlfriends, and he'd always valued her opinions. "Something's wrong with your latest," she said. "She really can't be like that."

"Yes she is," David insisted. His opinion doesn't mean a hell of a lot, Cecelia said to herself. In many ways David was like his father, decent and ethical to a fault, but father and son were hopeless at the practical business of judging others. Sometimes she wanted to shake DuVal by his bony shoulders and say, My god, man, you're descended from lawyers and judges going back to the Huguenots. Didn't you inherit a *little* judgment?

Cecelia decided that she would draw her own conclusions about her son's new friend. But the woman certainly wasn't off to a good start.

A few days later Cindy Ray edged shyly into Cecelia's kitchen and asked, "Is that how you do that?"

"Yep. That's how it's done." She was slicing potatoes.

"I never learned things like that," the little voice said. "Our Mexican maid wouldn't teach me."

Cecelia thought, It isn't as though I'm preparing beef Wellington, for God's sake.

David took a seat at the table and Cindy assembled her-

self at his feet. Cecelia liked people who sat on floors; she'd
spent half her own life looking up at others. One of her
many physical ailments was a damaged coccyx that hurt
when she stood. Then arthritis had arrived to go with her
thyroid problem, her high blood pressure, her mastectomy,
the lost muscle tissue in her upper arm, her inverted womb
and other miseries.

The three of them chatted for a while, and Cindy began to
open up. She explained that she wore long-sleeved shirts to
cover her scars; men had beaten her often. Cecelia saw that
the lovely hazel eyes were speckled with rust-colored clots,
and the woman seemed hard of hearing. Cindy explained
that an eardrum had been ruptured in one of the beatings.

Cecelia thought, How sad. She had a tender spot for battered wives, although she'd never been one herself.

The conversation swung to the subject of cosmetics and
personal hygiene. Cindy said she'd never used deodorants or
antiperspirants and didn't know one from the other. My
God, Cecelia thought, have you lived in a tent?

When David wandered off to talk to his father, Cindy
poked at the brushpile atop her head and said, "I can't do
anything with my hair anymore. It's gotten so tangled."

"Have you tried a comb?" Cecelia asked.

"I can't. My scalp's too sensitive."

Cecelia was an expert on hair. Once hers had been as
thick and red as Maureen O'Hara's. It was still a luxuriant
mound of curly waves, but a stroke ten years before had
caused some whitish-gray patches. She wished she had fine
young hair like Cindy's to fuss with in front of the mirror.
"Here," she said, pulling a comb from her purse, "let me
try."

"My scalp's so sensitive," Cindy said.

"I won't hurt you."

The child sat on the floor as Cecelia started at the ends
and cleared an inch at a time. The scalp was red and raw.
"What on earth have you been using?" she asked.

"A metal brush with prongs."

"You've damaged yourself."

"Oh?"

Cecelia thought, She doesn't know how to slice potatoes

or use deodorant, and when she combs her hair she slashes her scalp. Didn't anybody train this poor child? What kind of a mother did she have?

A few tangles had to be sliced out with scissors. "Don't worry," Cecelia said. "It'll grow in thicker than ever."

"It *will?*" Cindy said. She sounded surprised to learn that human hair grew. Again Cecelia wondered if she was putting on an act, but she decided not. David had insisted that she was always the same. How pathetic, Cecelia thought. I wonder what froze her in this eternal state of childhood.

A few weeks later Cecelia mounted her adult-sized tricycle and rode through the heart of the Montrose, parting shoals of gays with her squeeze-bulb horn. She'd toured the decaying neighborhood at a steady four miles an hour for thirty years, outlasting three trikes. When David was a baby she'd put a pillow in the basket and pedaled him all the way to her mother's house in West University Place.

Her latest model was a blue three-speed Schwinn ("S'winn" in Cecelia's rich Gulf Coast accent) with a deep metal grocery basket, silver fenders and an air pump for the tires that kept going flat. In a black moment Cecelia complained that a tricycle was "subconsciously all the freedom that DuVal wants me to have," but it was also true that she'd never learned to drive a car. DuVal had tried to teach her and given up. It just made her too damn nervous.

At busy Westheimer Road she rested, a rounding woman barely five feet tall, with hazel-green eyes, a straight nose and a firmer chin than her son's. How convenient, she thought, that David's house was so close, the result of her own strategic planning. "What you did," he'd once complained, "is you went out on your tricycle, shopping for a house for me. Now what kind of methodology is that? You did it that way 'cause you wanted me in range, ya know? Didn't you know I'd be surrounded by faggots?"

But he always seemed glad to see her, proud to show her off in skater bars like Warren's, where she carried on animated conversations with members of the Urban Animals about their costumes and bizarre way of life. It was a point of pride with Cecelia that she could converse with all kinds,

even androgynes with pinpoint pupils and rings in their
noses.

When Cecelia arrived at David's house, some of his tacky
friends were there—the drifters and bikers and skaters who
(as she'd once complained to her husband) "magnify certain
aspects of his personality that don't need magnifying." They
were freeloading as usual; thousands of dollars of her son's
inheritance had passed through the tubes of red-eyed young
men with names like "Mad Military Mike." They talked like
cesspools and drank like sump pumps. Cecelia was unintimi-
dated. Before her stroke she'd worked sixteen years as an
artist on the *Houston Post,* and she could knock back a Bud
with anyone.

Favoring her bad knee, she trudged up the creaky wooden
stairs to the second-floor landing. A barefooted Cindy Ray
opened the door and said, "Guess what? My hair's growing
out underneath, and I don't have any tangles." The poor
woman did look more presentable. Her hair gleamed and
curved gently over her shoulders. There was a little more
space between her waistline and her nicely defined bust. Cecelia thought, Why, she's like an adolescent, stretching up
and out. Maybe there's hope.

David gave his mom a squeeze. They'd been close since
the day he popped into the world, a cuddly, warm infant,
sunny and gregarious. Thirteen years before that blessed
birth, the newborn daughter of Cecelia's first marriage had
taken one look at her and screamed, but when they brought
David in from the nursery, he'd smiled sweetly at her. She'd
mothered and fathered him while DuVal stayed behind his
barricades of books and records. She'd taught her only son
how to throw a football, build a fire, shoot an arrow, ride a
bike, play marbles. She fought his school battles, took him
camping, walked him to Boy Scout meetings and dancing
school, bought him his first rifle and showed him how to
shoot it.

It was true that this damn house had come between them
for a while. He said he resented the way she'd maneuvered
him, but as trustee of his legacy she'd tried to make the best
investment. When one of his friends complained that the
house had been her idea, her own personal fantasy, she

snapped, "That house isn't anybody's fantasy! It's an in-
come-producing property." But there was no denying that
the house had forced David to return to Houston after his
discharge from the Marine Corps, instead of remaining in
Southern California as he'd planned.

From the beginning he'd insisted on treating the place like
a barracks. He installed four Marine buddies and supported
them with his inheritance. Not one lick of work got done,
and the house lost value in the middle of a housing boom.
Cecelia spent thousands of dollars from his legacy on tools
to convert the place into a plantation-type home with balcony porches and wide staircases and high-ceilinged rooms
and glittering chandeliers, all done in an architectural line
that "soars upwards to catch some of the breezes," as she'd
described it to one of her friends. She'd redesigned the place
to the last square inch and sketched it in filigreed works of
art suitable for framing. She reckoned that the finished product would command upwards of two hundred thousand dollars, a tidy 100 percent profit after expenses. But instead of
improving the place, David sold off the tools or let his guests
steal them. It was enough to make a mother give up.

David poured drinks while Cecelia popped a Bud Light
and lit a Carlton 100 menthol. Vexed by a taciturn husband,
she looked forward to these sessions with her son and his
rowdy friends. Soon she was in the middle of an energetic
game of reminiscence. The subject: who could recall the earliest childhood scene?

At first Cindy refused to play, but after a few drinks she
loosened up. "My first memory was standing in a hall in our
house," she began haltingly from her position on the floor.
"I was about fifteen months old. I stood up, holding onto the
wall. Then I turned loose and started walking. My mother
was standing in the doorway watching me, and I took one
step and another step toward her and I was so proud and
happy—and she calmly put her foot out and tripped me."

Cecelia thought, Is this more acting, or a case of creative
memory? It seemed downright bestial. If it were true, then
the mother must have been crazy or under terrible stress.
Cecelia knew about stress. The daughter of her tragic first

marriage had given her nightmares of stress and strain. So had Cecelia's own jealous sister. So had her beloved mother, the country doctor's spoiled child, a perpetual infant in adult clothing. Cecelia could feel her mother cutting the blood out of her with angry swipes at her back, shoulders and arms, the switch whining as it sliced through the air.

But . . . a mother tripping her own infant?

Cindy sat impassively on David's worn old rug, her arms folded as though she expected a blue norther to come howling through the room any minute. Well, Cecelia thought, she's damaged goods, sure as hell. *Something* was done to her.

Against her better judgment, she began to feel sorry for the child.

1981

7

By January 1981, three months after Cindy had come under his protectorate, David was proud that she was down to 150 pounds. Her waist was narrowing, her bust firming, her high cheekbones emerging prettily. Another three months, David thought, and she'll be Sophia Loren. There was already a resemblance.

Every day he grew more excited about his progress as combination guru, father, brother and drill instructor. On Saturday mornings he took long hot baths, talking to his friends on the telephone while his pale skin turned pink and the steam cleared his sinuses. Then, freshly bathed and scented, he called his class to order.

She sat on the floor while he repeated the lessons he'd learned at home and in ninth-grade military school: Roman history, Greek democracy, the threat of communism, World War II, Nazi nationalism, French colonialism. "The great thing about Bismarck," he told her as she stared up at him with big innocent eyes, "is that he made Germany one country instead of, ya know, a whole bunch of little bitty principalities and duchies and baronies."

Occasionally he got too far ahead and had to back up. Like him she'd quit high school, but unlike him she hadn't had the benefit of erudite conversation at the dinner table. Caesar, Lawrence of Arabia, George Bernard Shaw, Albert Einstein—they were only names to her. He would say, "As Alexander the Great put it," and her face would cloud. He reminded himself to minimize the classical references.

Sometimes he would lose his patience and say, "Come on, Cindy. I know you're not stupid." She would fall back as though slapped. It made him feel ashamed. It wasn't her fault she'd been brought up in ignorance. A girl doesn't bring up herself.

For a while she bought supplemental textbooks, but he noticed that they stayed shut. He wondered if she was interested in being smart or *looking* smart. Or was she just trying to please the instructor? He gave her the benefit of the doubt and pressed on.

One night they started dancing spontaneously in his living room. For all her weight, she was light on her bare feet. But when he tried to whirl her around at a bar a few nights later, she said, "No. Not here." He decided it was because she was being watched.

He began to feel more comfortable about their public appearances. As the fat melted off, other men stared. David glared back; he realized that his possessiveness was showing, an old failing, but women were naïve and Cindy especially so. She needed a protector. It made him feel like somebody. He thought, What a great technique I've developed. If you can't attract a beautiful woman, create one. It's "I Dream of Jeannie." He joked to himself about franchising his system.

After they'd been together for three months, David began to realize that sex was inevitable, despite her earlier warnings. She still insisted that she was "a good girl" whenever he broached the subject, but he detected a physical interest in her motions and her eyes. Sometimes she stared longingly and turned away, retreating to her frightened-child mode. He hinted, entreated, argued, trying to break through her guard. When he tried to kiss her in his usual gentlemanly manner, she said, "It's no use, David. I don't think of you that way."

"What way?"

"The, uh, sexual way."

"Well, hey, Cindy, what's the matter with sex?"

She made a disagreeable face and said, "Sex is bad, David."

"Sex isn't bad," he pressed. "It just depends, ya know? If there's two people that care about each other, and if you're not having a bunch of babies, and if there's no disease or mental anguish involved, there's nothing wrong with sex."

She still disagreed. For a few weeks it was two steps forward and one back. She would yield a small favor, then turn him away. "Wow!" he asked her one night. "What's the thing?"

She reminded him that she was a good girl.

"Whattaya mean you're a good girl? What's good and what's bad? We're not talking the same language." He flashed on an idea. "Cindy, have you been raped?"

She turned away, as though she didn't want to answer. Then she whispered, "Yes." He couldn't bear to ask her more.

For another month Joan of Arc defended the battlements. On a chilly mid-February night he walked into her room and found her naked in bed. Her breasts were big, but not so big that they sagged. Her narrowing waistline accentuated flaring hips. He thought, She's a Rubens, a Velasquez. No, I created her. She's a West!

"Look," he said as she covered up, "you're interested in me sexually and I know it. And I'm interested in you and you know it. So . . . ?" She looked frightened. He softened his tone and poured out every argument old and new: "You can't suppress it anymore . . . You can't hide it. . . . We both have to acknowledge it. . . ." After an hour or so she gave in.

They stayed in bed for two days. Once he said, "Let's stop for a snack."

"No!" she said.

He adapted to her pattern early. She didn't like vaginal intercourse, but she was enthusiastically oral. When he insisted on penetration, she couldn't handle it unless she took on the personality of a little girl and called him "Daddy." Then she became frenzied and hypersensitive. She moaned "Daddy, Daddy, Daddy, Daddy" as she climaxed again and again.

When he came home from work, he would find her on his black couch, eyes glazed, waiting. He thought, She makes up for every frigid bitch I've ever known. She's sexual dynamite, terrific, scary. He wondered if she had a hormonal imbalance. If she does, he thought, it's my good luck. Goddamn, she's a gold mine!

She taught him positions she said she'd learned from one of her husbands, not the ignorant hillbilly who'd fathered her sons but the kinky one with the big imagination. When they weren't in bed, she brought David treats, rubbed his back and sang to him in her pure clear voice. After one especially energetic night she asked if she could wash his feet with her hair, like Mary Magdalene with Jesus. He was embarrassed but touched. He was being worshiped, and all he'd ever wanted was love.

Gradually he eased her into his circle of friends. He introduced her to Dave Garrett, a Marine Corps buddy who was running a tattoo parlor, and his childhood companions John Lee and Chuck Montgomery. David and Chuck liked to clown, and soon she was joining in, rapping, telling jokes. It was a side of her that he'd never seen—Cindy as entertainer. Sometimes her repartee was so fast-paced that even a professional comic like Montgomery had trouble keeping up as she fired plays on words, riddles, spasms of wit to match the spasms of sex at home. David wondered if he had a closet genius on his hands. He kept thinking, What's the catch? *What is the catch?*

They got drunk at a downtown bar called La Carafe, a dungeon of a place bathed in reddish tones from a glass grape-light fixture and frequented by skaters like the Urban Animals. At midnight Cindy propped herself up on the end of the thick wooden bar and began reciting Shakespeare: "Behold the light spreads glimmer on the icy face of dawn. Faith, let us away, and ne'er to the sullen prince his evil deeds portend. . . ."

On she went, her voice projecting to every corner. Holy shit, David thought, she's into it! We're all into it! "Forsooth, sweet prince," she called out, "on this dank night the goblins seek the fardels of the knave." Slowly she extended her arm, palm up, wrist bent like a ballerina's. "Behold!" she said in a throbbing voice that reminded him of Katharine Hepburn's. "A vision! And its name is . . . Giselle."

She made a fluttering gesture with her hand and curtsied to the floor, her lovely face flushed, as the drinkers applauded and stomped. David was goggle-eyed. He'd read some Shakespeare, but he was ashamed to admit he couldn't place the play. It wasn't the first time lately that the pupil had upstaged the master. He didn't mind. He was happy for her. She was a tribute to both of them.

On the way home she giggled and admitted she'd faked the lines. He thought, My God, the woman's amazing!

As the days went on, she began telling him about her parents. He was predisposed to dislike them both. He already knew that James Campbell lacked fairness; you didn't banish someone from your house just because of an argument with a goddamn servant. He remembered Mrs. Campbell as a small woman in the shape of a parenthesis, caused by a bone disease called scoliosis. Deformed people grossed him out. He'd learned in one of his psych courses that behind their friendly posturings they often harbored deep resentments. He remembered Mrs. Campbell scuttling up to him and whining, "Well, he*lo*, David! How're *yew*?" He'd tried his best to smile.

It didn't surprise him when Cindy described the grimmest of childhoods. Her mother had favored the three sisters, Betty, Michelle and the spoiled baby Jamie. Cindy's clothes were usually hand-me-downs. The other girls had allowances but she had to earn her own money.

Cindy said that her mother had always told her, "Silence is golden." If Cindy kept on talking, Virginia would say, "Shut up! Get in the other room! I don't want to see your face." If the child didn't move out, she was slapped. When a favorite uncle praised Cindy's singing voice, the mother dragged her away and never let her return to his house. Sometimes she was locked in a closet, and when she would beg to come out, her mother would taunt her in a singsong white-trash voice, "Cindy, you're not *loud* enough. Ah cain't *hear* yewwww!"

Cindy said that she would bang on the door till her knuckles bled, while her mother yelled, "Harder! *Harder!* You've got to knock harder!" It seemed there was no end to the cruelties. Sometimes, she said, her mother forced her to douche while she watched. Poor Cindy, David thought. What a family.

"When I was three," she told him, "we all went swimming in a lake, and I stepped in a hole and went under. I kicked up and went under again, up and down, up and down. I was facing the shore, but I couldn't get enough air to call for help. My mother sat there and watched me with a little smile. It was like, 'Die, bitch!' A man accidentally stepped on my body and brought me to shore. They had to pump the water out."

David worked up some theories to explain such outrageous behavior. He decided that Cindy was just too damned talented, too bright, too attractive to mesh with the rest of the Campbells. He'd seen pictures of the older sisters, Betty and Michelle, and he'd seen the rest of the Campbells in the flesh, and they just weren't in Cindy's class before *or* after her transformation. She didn't even look like a Campbell except for the bulb at the end of her nose. No wonder she thought she'd been conceived in Italy. She was everything that her humpbacked mother and dough-faced sisters could never be.

Cindy emphasized that the family situation was unchanged now that she was an adult. Her sisters got the money and the attention, even though the two older ones had moved to Austin. The mother still clung to every nickel. Sometimes Virginia would give Cindy a dollar or two, but only after saying, "Beg for it, bitch!"

She seemed curiously ambivalent about her father. She insisted that James Campbell was a clever lawyer—bright, witty, highly respected. Plainly, she held him in awe, but David noticed that she never described him as loving, sweet, kind or good. "Whatever Daddy says goes!" Cindy said. "He is . . . strict!" Yeah, David thought, but is he a nice guy? A good father?

She said she'd run away at twelve to live with a kindly old lady in Tulsa. Then she'd moved to a rooming house operated by a strange man who kept his dead cat in the freezer, its face in a rictus of agony. He also stored pornography under his bed. When she'd fled back to Houston, her father had thrown her into the state mental hospital.

David couldn't believe it. He said, "Mr. Moneybags lives on a two-acre estate on Memorial, he coulda sent you to the best hospital in Houston—and he puts you in a snake pit?"

"For my own good," Cindy said quickly. "It was just a threat. He brought me home after a few days. He said, 'If you go public with this, I'll say you're crazy. If you run

away again or make me look bad, I'll send you back.' I ran
away a lot after that, but he never sent me back."

After a while David thought he recognized a pattern.
Cindy had elevated her father to a godlike status. It was
called the Electra complex. He noticed that she never questioned anything James Campbell said or did. And she didn't
run to him with complaints about her mother's abuse because, she said, she didn't want to tear the family apart. It
was poor reasoning, but it was thoroughly decent behavior.

One night as they sat in his living room in their customary
positions of master and serf, she admitted that she'd seen
psychiatrists and they'd all made advances. She said they
were just like every man she'd ever known. Except David, of
course.

She began talking faster. "That's why I've never been able
to hold a job. Guys hit on me and I can't handle it." Her
lower lip stuck out and she looked as though she were going
to cry.

He tried to think of a distraction. Since meeting his parents, she'd seemed interested in his illustrious ancestry, the
judges, politicians, lawyers and frontiersmen on both sides
of the family. He held her hand as he explained that his
father's ancestors had settled in Virginia in the 1600s. "Did
I tell you that Dad went to West Point?" he asked. "He
never talks about it. Never talks about much of anything. He
just kinda keeps to himself."

Cindy nodded. After a while he realized that she wasn't
listening. "They always hit on me," she mumbled. He took
her to bed.

His old friend Chuck Montgomery turned them all onto
nighttime jobs at a new club called the Lone Star Comedy
Shop, located in a one-time topless joint on Telephone Road.
It was a marginal operation, subsisting on the energy and
talent of young amateurs and postdated checks. The plan
was for David to tend bar, Chuck to manage and perform,
and Cindy to serve drinks.

David also handled the lights, cued the laughs and polished glasses while Cindy hid in a corner in her waitress's
outfit and tossed down drinks to settle her nerves. One night

she laughed raucously, insulted a customer and ended up wallowing on the floor issuing guttural threats. David tried to coax her to the car. "Come on, Cindy," he said. "Let's go!"

She belched. "Come *on!*" he said, yanking at her arm. "Get up and quit acting like a pig."

Montgomery performed over the noise. "I went to a store on the East Side and told a guy I wanted a mop. He says, 'You wan' a mop of Houston? A mop of Texas?"

Cindy bellowed, "I'm not such a pig that I'd fuck *you!*"

David was embarrassed and confused. Was this *his* Cindy? He realized that he'd now heard four distinct voices: her ordinary voice, pleasant and mellow; her little-girl voice; her older-girl voice, softly shy like Marilyn Monroe's, and now this bull-dagger bellowing. He wondered what was going on. Was she one of those multiple personalities that he'd read about? No, he decided. She was just good old histrionic Cindy. She'd had a little too much to drink, that was all.

By the time he got her outside, the owner had arrived. Not long afterward the two of them were fired.

He decided that she needed a steady job, something she hadn't managed in all her twenty-six years. He talked ABM Security into hiring them both as part-time building guards, David on a post and Cindy at a reception desk in the lobby. That way they could continue with their schooling and he could keep an eye on her progress.

She looked slender and lovely in her rent-a-cop jacket and suit. After the first night she told him she couldn't go on.

"Why?" he asked.

"That shift leader won't let me alone."

"You mean he hit on you?"

She nodded. "He made my skin crawl."

"Well, Cindy, what could the man do to you in the lobby of a building?"

"He could rape me."

He thought about it for a few seconds. He hated the idea of that slimy little creep bothering his woman, but Cindy needed to learn to handle men. "For Christ's sake," he said, "you gotta stop being so touchy. I mean, goddamn it, you gotta face reality, ya know? Shit, everybody that's interested in having sex with you isn't a rapist!"

She looked doubtful. "Look, Cindy," he said, "you gotta learn to handle this situation 'cause it's gonna keep coming up. Attractive girls get hit on all the damn time. They learn how to handle it. But you—you only got two speeds, ya know? You either get scared and run, or you turn on 'em— 'Get away from me, you fucking pervert!' Now try to remember these three responses, okay? 'Drop dead, buddy, I'm not interested.' Or 'Go take a hike,' or 'Why don't you go wring out your chicken, ya know?' "

He made her repeat them back. Now she was ready for the business world.

She walked off the job the next day.

8

On the first clear day after a week of intermittent rain, the three good companions cleaved the clamshell-colored puddles in David's little gray car. From her seat of honor in front, Cecelia was reminiscing about her family in her dramatically lyrical style. Like her husband, she was descended from French Huguenots, though more recent ones, and her ancestors hadn't been landlocked like DuVal's. Cecelia's people were blockade runners, explorers, boatsmen, shipwrights, seldom farther than sniffing distance from the sea.

She turned sideways as she approached the climax of one of her favorite family stories. Cindy was leaning forward, caught up in the same excitement that once had held Cecelia at her father's feet. "And just then," Cecelia intoned, "a man came galloping madly along on a foam-flecked horse, yelling and pointing toward Galveston Bay, and they looked and here was this wall of water coming toward them, a tidal wave, and they could see boats and horses and cows and trees, all sorts of things living and dead, in the curl of this giant wave . . ."

When Cecelia spoke, she had no intention of being ig-

nored. Friends said it was hard to believe that she'd been a
wardrobe mistress and not a star at the Alley Theatre. She
arched her short fingers, accented key phrases, lengthened
her vowels for effect. She'd always had command of her
audiences, except (she thought ruefully) when the audience
was her husband DuVal. A friend once said that she
sounded like Helen Hayes playing Amanda Wingfield. She
said "rawther" for "rather" and so did her son David, but
they weren't putting on airs. No one on the Simmons side of
the family had ever pronounced the word otherwise. Her
speech was rich in image and metaphor and style. David had
loved her stories from the beginning.

Just as Cecelia reached the end of the tale about her telegrapher father's adventures, David pulled up in front of a
small apartment building on quiet Kingston. Cindy explained that her father had recently bought the property as
an investment and she wanted to show it off. "There's four
units," she said proudly, "and one is mine." A light always
seemed to come into her eye when she mentioned her father.
Once she'd told Cecelia, "I'm Daddy's little girl, you
know." It sounded like an odd claim for a grown woman,
but Cecelia had refrained from passing judgment.

To the older woman's practiced eye the brick building
looked rundown and the apartments barely big enough to be
livable. As they drove off, Cecelia said, "I can show you how
to make a lot of improvements, Cindy. Did David ever tell
you what his place looked like when we first bought it? The
wallpaper pattern was from a Mexican curio shop. There
was a basket painted in coarse gold cross-hatching, and out
of it poured fruit—the most garishly purple plums, the most
violently, luridly red apples, grapes as green as the Erin Isle,
and some in lavender purple. All over the walls! *Ugggh!*"

As Cecelia completed her word picture, Cindy clapped
her hands together and smiled. So many of her movements
are infantile, Cecelia thought, but she brings them off with
grace. Maybe she's not so phony after all.

That night on the phone, Cecelia confided to her son,
"Cindy's taken to me like a kitten to a hot-water bottle."

* * *

After a few more meetings, Cecelia was surprised to learn how much she and Cindy had in common. Both were outcasts as children, adored strong fathers, discounted their mothers, clashed with their siblings and made disappointing marriages. Both were morbidly fearful of everything from sexual abuse to learning to drive. Both were artistic, superstitious, reclusive, fascinated by costumes and design, and obsessed with physical ailments and problems, especially their own. "Ya know, Mom," David said one day, "Cindy's an exaggerated version of you." Cecelia thought, Three months ago I would have been insulted.

She could see that Cindy was still trying to gain her parents' love. She phoned and visited, brought them presents, complimented them, tried to get their attention. "My father's a wonderful man," she told Cecelia one day, then added, "I mean, I *ought* to think he's wonderful. I *ought* to realize what a grand man he is—how forceful, how authoritative. I *ought* to feel lucky for it." She paused and frowned. "Shouldn't I?"

Cecelia thought, The poor thing will never be whole till she realizes that whatever happened to her as a child wasn't her fault. It was *their* fault! Cindy clung to the infantile idea that her life would change completely if her parents would just decide to love her. Cecelia tried to explain that there were profound injustices and cruelties in every family; you accepted them and went on. She felt so sad for Cindy, and sometimes the two new friends shared tears. Especially when Cindy began reminiscing.

As a small child, she related, her mother had locked her in closets while she took the other sisters on shopping trips. If the frightened child soiled herself, she was beaten. When Cindy was seven, Virginia Campbell began chaining her to the bathroom fixtures and leaving her there for hours. Once a mean old yardman peered through the window at her nakedness while she tried to hide her tiny body behind the toilet.

Both parents consistently ignored Cindy and showered gifts on the other daughters. The only kindness she knew as a child came from her paternal "big grandmother," whom

she was forbidden to see. One Christmas her only presents
were three dolls from the grandmother. The other sisters
dismembered them.

When she was eleven, Cindy said, her big grandmother
noticed that she had no clothes of her own and bought her
five dresses. Encouraged by the mother, the oldest sister cut
them up—"not a piece left as big as a hand," Cindy insisted.
Even Jamie, the baby of the family, joined in the cruelty.
"Jamie was like my baby," Cindy said. "I took care of her. I
dressed her, bathed her, fed her. I thought she would love
me, but she turned out just like the others."

For a time Cecelia held her opinion in abeyance. Blood
ran hot between family members; daughters told fanciful
stories about mothers, husbands lied about wives, memories
became twisted and skewed. Cecelia had seen it with her
own people. She believed in tarot cards and Ouija boards,
but she didn't believe in monsters, and she wondered if
Cindy might not have been responsible for some of her own
unhappiness. There were times when the sob story wore
thin. "Cindy's a moaner and groaner," Cecelia complained
to DuVal, "and, you know, after a while you get kind of
tired of that."

The stories turned darker, almost too hard for Cecelia to
bear. "When I was little, I had appendicitis," Cindy said,
"and Mother and Daddy wouldn't do anything about it till
it was real bad. A few days after I got home from the hospital, Daddy got angry with me. He held me on my bed. He
took off his belt. He beat my incision with the big brass
buckle."

Cecelia gasped. It couldn't be true. Why was the child
exaggerating? For sympathy?

Cindy tugged her jeans a few inches down and showed a
keloid scar about five inches long. "I can't even wear a bath-
ing suit," she said. To Cecelia the scar resembled a grotesque
pair of flesh-colored lips. She covered her mouth with her
palm and thought about the great lawyer James Campbell.
Cindy had described him often enough: six four, strong,
heavily built, big-boned. It would have been so simple for
him to hold her down. She thought, This is sick, sadistic.
And maybe something worse. . . .

The child returned a few days later, and Cecelia went straight to the point. "I've been thinking about your family," she said, "and I'll tell you how it would look to any decent person." She knew her words would shock, but as a physician's granddaughter she intended them as a cauterization.

She took a deep breath and said, "Cindy, I think your father abused you for his own sexual satisfaction. And I think your mother knew and approved of it. And I think . . . it's despicable."

Cindy looked surprised but offered no comment. Cecelia decided not to push.

That evening she phoned her son. "David," she said, "are you sure Cindy isn't having to pay her father for that new apartment on Kingston?"

"Mom, she doesn't have any money."

Cecelia lowered her voice. "I wasn't talking about money, David. Listen, I think Cindy was raped as a child. I'd bet on it. And I think it was her father."

He asked, "How do you know?"

"The signs are there."

"You think something's still going on?"

"It might be."

There was a long silence. She imagined her son pulling himself together, frowning and shaking his head. Well, who the hell wouldn't be shocked?

"Okay, Mom," he said in a shaky voice. "I'll ask her about it."

9

David had been to Africa and Europe, had seen and heard and done more than many men his age, but he was unprepared for the story that Cindy spun that night. No wonder she called him Daddy when they made love. No wonder men freaked her out. He almost wished his mother had left the can of worms unopened.

The talk began when he described Cecelia's suspicions. Cindy was quiet for a while, then admitted that she'd been raped. "As a kid?" he asked.

She nodded.

"Who was he?" he demanded.

She stammered and finally said, "My father."

The first word that came to his mind was "incest." Oh, God, he thought, Mom was right. He felt violated. He wanted to mash James Campbell's face. He wanted to take his pit bull out to the house on Memorial and put him on the pervert's throat.

It didn't take long to worm out the rest of the story. She said it started when she was twelve. She was standing in front of her mirror brushing her hair. Her father came up behind her and told her she was pretty, "a good girl." He held her by the shoulders, pressed against her, and began stroking her breasts.

David said, "That's enough."

But Cindy didn't seem to want to stop. She told how her father had eased her onto the bed. She said the pain was almost unbearable. She went on and on through tears. Several times she interrupted herself to say, "But I'm a good girl!"

At last David saw the connection. When she had sex with her father, she was being a good girl, but he'd instilled in her that sex with others was evil. That's why she called David "Daddy." Then it was tolerable.

"Of course you're a good girl, Cindy," he said, stroking her hair. "You're a victim."

He thought, I should report this to the cops right now. I should just pick up the phone and turn the motherfucker in. But who would listen? Campbell's a prominent lawyer. He knows underworld characters, politicians, cops. He's got judges in his pocket. And I'm just a nobody from the Montrose. They'd laugh themselves hoarse if I called. . . .

Later he thought, Mom sure knows human nature. From his earliest days she'd seen to it that he knew all about rape.

She'd sensitized him to women's problems by describing some of her own with her usual vividness. One of her stories still gave him bad dreams. "I was walking in the shadows on a freezing December night," she'd told him when he was ten, "and a car slid out of the shadows and blocked my way. The driver was masturbating violently. He'd wrapped that part of himself in pieces of bloody white cloth. It was dripping with blood, and he was mumbling weird sounds, incantations. He chased me but I got away . . ."

David thought, No wonder she had that filthy Campbell's number.

Now that the secret was out, Cindy kept wanting to talk about it, but David shut her down. The subject was too goddamn painful. She told him that her mother had known what was happening from the beginning and regarded her as a rival, not a daughter. She trembled as she spoke, broke into sobs, reached out for him. But what could he do? He was as upset as she was.

"Don't!" he said one day when she started in again. "Goddamn it, Cindy, I get the point."

"No," she said, "you don't." She lowered her face and her voice. "Daddy is my son Michael's father."

At first he didn't comprehend. Then he couldn't help but look dubious. "Come on, Cindy," he said.

"Anybody can tell," she said quickly. "You've seen how smart he is." David had met her two young sons. They lived in the Memorial home with the *pinche puta* maid and the elder Campbells. Cindy had unloaded them on her parents five or six years before.

"Michael looks like Daddy because he's *from* Daddy," Cindy went on. "Little Matthew's from my first husband, that dumb hick." David remembered Michael, a strapping kid, bright, quick. It was true; he resembled his grandfather. No, David thought, James Campbell is not his grandfather —James Campbell is his *father*. No, he's both! God, it gets worse and worse.

Cindy sobbed as she told how confused she'd been when she'd matured and discovered that she had an abnormally strong sex drive. David thought, Yes, of *course!* You must have always had a hormonal imbalance, and your father took advantage of it. There were no words to describe a betrayal like that.

Cindy admitted that the shame of bearing a child by her father had turned her to female sex partners two or three times. "I had to trust somebody," she said. "If I was having sex with a man, it could only be Daddy. Otherwise I wasn't being a good girl." She reached over and gripped his arm. "But David, I never preferred women to men. They just made me feel . . . safer."

He understood. She asked if he could ever forgive her, and he said there was nothing to forgive. But he also told her that he'd heard as much as he could stand. He was torn with rage and pain and jealousy. He felt insulted and diminished by the incestuous rapist who'd treated him like a naughty child and banned him from the house. And there wasn't a goddamn thing he could do about it. The insults would stand forever.

10

Her father fondly replied, "Ah, my dear, I wish you would not make matches and foretel things, for whatever you say always comes to pass."
—JANE AUSTEN, *Emma*

David said, "Cindy doesn't want to see you, Mom. She knows you're the one who figured out what her father did. She's ashamed."

A week passed, and then David led the reluctant victim into the house. In the voice of a three-year-old she asked Cecelia, "Are you still speaking to me?"

"Why, of course," Cecelia said. "Dear, no one's blaming you for what happened."

"You're . . . not?" She seemed surprised.

Cecelia thought, This is even worse than I imagined.

After a while David made a discreet exit, and Cecelia got out the tarot cards to take Cindy's mind off her troubles. The two women shared an interest in reincarnation, telepathy, witches, ghosts. But unlike Cindy, Cecelia tried to temper her mysticism with reality. She owned four books on tarot but preferred her own system of interpretation. For a long time she'd been aware that the cards were lying about her while telling the truth about others. She warned Cindy that you couldn't take tarot as literal truth.

Cecelia chanted as she shuffled the dog-eared deck with the fifteenth-century design on the backs. The cards revealed that Cindy had been wise to reveal her past. They showed that she was a moral person; it was her father who was evil. The cards said she would soon solve her problems and go on to a happy life. She seemed relieved.

After the cards were put away, Cindy said, "When I was ten or eleven, I had a teacher who guessed what you guessed. I'd been making straight A's, but after Daddy started on me, my grades fell off and I had crying spells, and this teacher made an excuse to drive me home one day and brought it up in the car. I was too ashamed to say anything."

Cecelia thought, Ashamed? You should have been outraged! You should have shouted, My father's raping me! *My father's raping me!* But instead she took the shame on her own shoulders. Apparently those dreadful parents had victimized the child for years. And yet she'd grown beyond her background into a gentle creature, diffident and lovely. You had to respect her courage.

To Cecelia's pleasure and surprise, DuVal invited Cindy to hear some of their old theater albums in the big front room. The Wests hadn't done much entertaining at home since 1973, when DuVal had been fired for inventing a gadget that made him redundant. The shock had caused him to sit in the same chair and smoke five packs of Carltons a day, his dark blue eyes staring through his thick glasses. Over the months the tar and smoke had laid an amber patina over everything in the room, including an unsigned Tur-

ner and Cecelia's most prized oil. It didn't do any good to
open the shutters to let in air and light; DuVal always
slammed them shut. It was then that he'd begun to build
barricades of books around his favorite chair.

Improvement had been slow; there'd been years when Cecelia doubted that he would ever again welcome an outsider
to his sanctum. But he seemed to approve of Cindy. My
God, Cecelia thought, there's hope for us yet.

Both Wests had known from the beginning that Cindy
loved the stage. She'd always talked about becoming an actress, and when the sibilant voice of Boris Karloff as Captain
Hook boomed from the old Kenwood speakers, she clapped
her hands and giggled. Cecelia thought, That's exactly the
way a five-year-old would react!

DuVal played *Medea,* and when the record was over,
Cindy recited passages from the "Women of Corinth"
speech in a voice surprisingly like Judith Anderson's. She
stopped abruptly when she saw that the Wests were paying
attention. "I didn't mean to take up your time," she said.

DuVal said, "Cindy, don't apologize all the time."

"I'm sorry," Cindy said.

The only way to save this poor child, Cecelia thought, is
to clear the cobwebs from her mind. Going into detail about
her father's acts won't be easy, but it's necessary for her
mental health. She's kept his foul secret for so many years
that it's rotting her soul.

Gently Cecelia pried out the details. She'd lived through a
Dickens novel of miseries herself and didn't cry easily, but
as Cindy spoke, first in a trickle and then in a torrent, the
older woman often choked back sobs. It was worse than
Dickensian, worse than anything in Gogol or Dostoyevski.
It was grotesque.

Of course you had to overlook the small inconsistencies.
Cecelia had learned by now that there was a kernel of truth
in everything Cindy said, but the child was imaginative and
more than a little mixed up. She would make a statement,
repeat it later in altered form, then add a third version or
return to the first. It seemed to depend on her mood. If her

mood was black, her facts turned black. Well, why not, Cecelia thought, after what she's been through?

Cindy said that she'd had to defend herself against her father from just after her tenth birthday. The earliest acts had taken place in the family's small brick home in the Montrose. "After that first time, Daddy moved me into a room by myself, away from my sisters," she said. "Until then I'd always shared a room with Jamie. But now I was alone and couldn't defend myself."

She lit a cigarette and resumed. "Nobody else suspected a thing, but I knew what he wanted. I locked the door that night, but I had to open it to go to school in the morning. When I got back from school, Daddy had broken the lock. All the locks inside the house were the same, so I worked the pins out of the hinges and switched doors. That night he smashed it down. I pleaded and pleaded, but he—he raped me again."

Cecelia sighed. The story sounded like fiction, but it seemed much too bizarre to be made up. It rang with authentic detail—pins, hinges, locks. How would Cindy know about things like that? Cecelia asked, "What about your mother, your sisters? Didn't they hear anything?"

"No." The child bit her lip hard. "They didn't see or hear a thing."

Cecelia realized the truth but held her tongue. Of course they'd heard. Once Cindy had pointed out the brick house on West Gray where the incest had started. In a small place like that, how could the others not have heard? Didn't Virginia notice that James was leaving her bed every night? Didn't the sisters hear Cindy's pleading? They'd *chosen* not to hear; that was the obscene truth of the matter. Mistreatment of Cindy was a habit in that sick family. Hadn't the mother tried to let her drown? Chained her to the toilet? Hadn't the sisters cut up her books and torn her dolls apart? *Why not let Daddy have a little fun? It's only Cindy. . . .*

She said that the incest had continued for years. She'd been forced to find a husband to legitimize her father's child. She married and divorced a West Virginia hillbilly, became pregnant by her father again and found another husband, but this one, she claimed, mistreated her. Cecelia wasn't surprised. She knew about men.

The horror stories unfolded for days. Cecelia thought it revolting that Virginia Campbell still regarded Cindy as a rival instead of a daughter. She'd always mistreated the poor child, but after the incest she'd turned the screws tighter till Cindy's only hope was to run back to the sweet motherly woman who'd cared for her as a runaway in Tulsa. But even that hadn't worked out, Cindy explained. The woman's daughter had grown jealous, told lies about Cindy and forced her to return to Houston and her father's sick embrace. So here she was, back in the nest of snakes, still trying to tough it out.

Cecelia decided it was time for more than words. This shattered child needed love, sympathy, care. She needed to be lifted out of herself, distracted from her memories and pains. Cecelia's relationship with her own grown daughter was shaky as usual, and she didn't mind taking on a new maternal responsibility. At least this child was appreciative. She asked, "Honey, what can we do to have a little fun?"

"Fun?" Cindy asked. "You can't have fun in Houston without a lot of money."

"Oh? Where'd you get that idea?"

"Well, David and I go to the Comedy Workshop, but we have to pay for drinks. Or we go to Rudyard's and play the jukebox. Or we go out to eat. Whatever we do, it costs thirty or forty dollars."

Yes, Cecelia thought, and that's another reason why David is about to lose his house. She said, "We can have fun in Houston without spending that kind of money. Have you ever been to the zoo?"

"The . . . zoo?" The child looked wide-eyed. It was as though she'd never heard of the zoo in Hermann Park. In her tiniest voice, she said, "Oh, I wouldn't want to see animals in cages."

"They're not all in cages," Cecelia said in the firm tone that she used to correct misstatements. "Come on. There's a bus that goes right to the entrance."

It turned out that Cindy had never been to a zoo. Never! She was enchanted by the bird house. She laughed with joy as they walked past glassed-in cages set off by dioramas. A large enclosed jungle looked like Yucatán. Bright red birds flew from plant to plant like sparks. At the Mayan Temple, she insisted on running her fingers over every stroke by the ancient artisans. "I can't believe I'm in Texas," she said. Cecelia thought, You've lived here all your life, and your parents never brought you here. Why, David's been here a dozen times!

That night she called her son to report on the successful outing. "I could hardly get her to move on," she said. "We barely had time for the sea lions before the thunder clouds rolled in. We got drenched waiting for DuVal to come get us. David, she was so happy that she stood in that hurricane and talked about ninety miles a minute. She kept saying, 'Oh, how lovely it was!' That's the kind of child she is."

11

By the spring of 1981 Cindy had been living with David for six months, and for the first time in his life he wasn't lonely. He'd always yearned for a romance with all the grace notes, tender and sweet. Maybe it was naïve, but Cindy seemed to share his feelings. They'd become so close that he could almost read her thoughts.

She'd slimmed to 130 pounds and a 24-inch waist. Gone were the thunder thighs and the facial pouches. As she shrank, she improved in other ways. Her self-esteem climbed and her thought processes sharpened. She retained some of her old paranoia, especially around men, but he was sure it would subside. She began taking his hints about personal hygiene, although she still seemed to prefer perfume to baths. He liked to walk into Rud's with her on his arm and his latest pit bull, Max, on a leash. It made him feel like one of the rising young men in *Downtown* or the *Houstonian*.

Their sex life fell short of perfect, but only a fool would have complained. She seemed to feel that penetration was dirty except by her father: she wasn't being "a good girl" if

she accepted anyone else. David didn't pressure her: there
was time. Besides, she'd become so sensitized to him that he
could look at her in a certain way and she would climax,
even in public. She writhed a little, rolled her eyes upward,
and—*boom!* Another Cindy miracle.

He hated to think how close he came to missing out. He'd
always taken his girlfriends home to meet Mom, and Cecelia
had impossibly high standards. She'd counseled him over
and over that his women had to be attractive, intelligent,
moral and, above all, well-bred. He'd gone a year or two
without meeting a female who qualified. "Basically my life's
been one disappointed romance after another," he told
Cindy in a night of confessions and reminiscence. "I was a
nerdy little kid with a big head and a skinny neck and no
muscles and I didn't know how to deal with women. All
heart and no snap, ya know?"

Now he was glad he'd been forced to wait. He'd never
wanted just any old marriage. His parents had spent thirty
years in an endurance contest of eccentric indifference. But
David was never indifferent toward his women. He idolized
them, showered them with attention, treated them with
politesse. Unlike most of the men he knew, he was sexually
patient. He refused to think of sex as getting his ashes
hauled or his rocks off. He figured he got his share, though
not from anyone he would marry. But he was courteous
even to whores and pickups—"sleazy bitches," as he called
them in private. What the hell, they were still females, and
females had always been victims. He'd learned that from his
mother. And now he was loved by Cindy, the perfect example.

After she dropped out of St. Thomas, the new lovers were
together constantly. With their weak scholastic backgrounds, they'd both accepted the fact that college would
take more time and effort than they could put in.

His inheritance was dwindling—just about all he had left
were his thirty-three country acres at Iola. Although he was
afraid of heights, he'd taken a job as an ironworker's helper,
riding the beams with a bunch of good ol' boys from
Splendora, Texas. Downtown Houston was in the final

stages of transforming itself into a contemporary museum of high-rise mirrored-glass buildings, the wonder of the architectural world. Within a few weeks he learned why his job paid $16.50 an hour to start; two men fell to their deaths and another was critically injured. Each morning he rode the open elevator seventy stories up, stepped onto a four-inch steel beam, and tried to remember what his dad and military school teachers and Marine officers had taught him about fear. "It's normal to be afraid," he kept telling himself. "Bravery's just a matter of discipline." It didn't keep him from trembling when he looked down.

At home he threw himself into sitcom domesticity. After a shift on the high iron, it seemed like heaven to climb his creaky stairs, accept a frosty beer from Cindy, and ask, "How was your day?" He embraced every ideal of the yuppily married. They weren't clichés to him; they were his dreams. He thought of Cindy as his princess and jumped at each chance to prove his love and fidelity.

One day his first-floor tenant, Jim Daggett, shouted up the staircase, "I just about got in a fight with those drunken assholes next door. They were making cracks to my wife."

David told him to mellow out and drank a few bottles of home brew with his boss Ron Westphal. Then he led Cindy and Ron toward Rudyard's British Pub down the street. Holding fresh bottles, the three friends strolled past the house where the loud-mouthed drunks still sprawled on a brick porch. One of them grabbed his crotch and yelled, "Hey, baby, I got somethin' for ya!"

David flung his bottle against the wall above their heads, yelled "motherfucker!" and charged. Two of the men ran inside. He knocked the mouthy one off the porch, straddled his body and gouged at his eyes, then began slugging him on his face and head.

"Stop!" Westphal yelled. "Dave, stop. *Stop!*"

David lifted up. The drunk's face was covered with blood. "You okay?" David asked. "I didn't kill ya, did I, buddy?" When the victim didn't move, he giggled nervously. He hadn't intended to destroy the guy.

After a few minutes an arm moved. "He's all right,"

David said. "Let's get out of here." He felt Cindy grip his arm as they left.

At Rud's she listened big-eyed as he explained: "Somebody had to stand up to those assholes. They act nasty because they can get away with it. It's like . . . it's like their mamas didn't spank 'em, so it's my turn. It's like they have an attitude problem, and along comes the white knight, Don Quixote. I can't take credit for it. It's just, ya know, something I have to do."

A few days later he drove around the corner at Waugh Drive and saw Cindy pointing out their upstairs window at a white Ford. When the car moved off, Cindy ran outside and gasped, "David, David! That guy's driven past ten times!"

David slid his .38 Colt Diamondback from under the seat of his car. "Come on inside," he said. "We'll watch from the windows."

After a few minutes the car returned. David ran down the stairs and squared off in a shooting stance in the middle of Vermont Street. When the car was about fifty yards away, he fired two rounds.

The car lurched and stopped, then spurted around the corner.

David liked the way Cindy hugged him hard. He said, "That asshole won't be back."

It wasn't long before he lost his temper again. He was behind on his $350 monthly mortgage payments, and the bank threatened foreclosure. For once Cecelia balked at his demand for money, and the two of them drifted into her dining room arguing. When she refused to cosign a check, he grabbed her by the shoulders, slammed her to the floor and yelled, "Goddamn it, sign this right now!"

A voice spoke in a familiar low-key drone. "She can't sign anything. Can't you see she hit the cabinet? She's stunned."

He looked up. DuVal was tall, thin, a little bent, a healthy man but not nearly as strong as his son. David had faced him down twice by the time he was sixteen, dared him to fight, *begged* him. DuVal had explained later that intelligent human beings didn't decide things by force, and fathers didn't fight sons. But David would have felt better if DuVal had whipped his ass.

This time he ignored his father and stormed out the door. A few hours later, full of contrition, he phoned the house. "Dad," he said, "that was the stupidest thing I've ever done." Waves of remorse flowed over him when he heard that Cecelia had cracked the sheathing on a rib and was nursing a knot in the back of her head. He rushed to the old house on Kipling and begged her forgiveness. While he was there, she signed the check.

As spring passed into summer, he slowly began to realize what was bothering him. He'd always assumed that he would get over his shock about Cindy's affair with her father, but instead he found himself obsessed with the subject. In his mind's eye he saw the two bodies fiercely entangled, sweating, father and daughter grunting like hogs. The mental picture was so vivid that he sometimes felt pain in his abdomen, his head, his heart. He lay in bed unable to sleep, anguished by the thought that even though the incest had started as the bully-rape of a child, the affair had continued for years. How did he know it wasn't still going on? He destroyed his peace of mind with questions. Did she moan? Did she have the same hot orgasms she had with him? The thought was too much to bear.

He'd learned to live with most of her sexual history. No longer was he bothered by the thought of her first fumbling lovers, the drifters she'd met on the road, the two ex-husbands, the common-law marriage that ended just before they met at St. Thomas, the dirty old man she'd dated when she first moved into his house. But he couldn't get over the affair with her father because she wouldn't stop yelling "Daddy" when they made love.

For a while he lived on the hope that she would learn to accept him as himself instead of a stand-in. He thought, Maybe she means it as a compliment. I'm her new "daddy." She's invested that passion in me and I should feel good about it. But he didn't. Why did she switch to the teeny-tiny voice when she called him Daddy? It made him feel like a pervert, a child abuser.

The next time it happened, he jerked away and said, "See? See? See what your father's done to you?"

"No!" she insisted. "My daddy's a good man!" She said the incest was her fault: Daddy was wonderful; she was a bad person. He thought, Sick! It's fucking *sick!* And she's trying to draw me into her sickness. . . .

He asked her to quit yammering about the subject. The goddamn incest was ancient history, and anyway her versions had begun to differ suspiciously. Once or twice he wondered if it was all bullshit, but he figured the contradictions came from trauma; no one remembered horror scenes the same way twice. She corrected her original story to say that her first husband, Michael Ray, had fathered her son Matthew but that the older boy, Michael, was her father's. Then she said that James Campbell was father of both. "Cindy," David said, "you're not making sense. Weren't you living in Oklahoma when Matthew was conceived?"

She seemed upset that he would doubt her. He thought, Well, shit, I'm just gonna lay off. She's all mixed up, and she's got enough mental problems already.

The next time she mentioned the incest, he said, "Cindy, if somebody was doing all this shit to me, I'd fucking kill 'em."

He expected her to look alarmed, but her expression didn't change. "Uh, I don't know how," she muttered.

He wanted to shock her into dropping the subject forever. "Look," he said, "when you decide to do something like that, all you gotta do is just do it, ya know? If the reasons are right, if it's justifiable and unavoidable, then it's just a matter of mechanics. You just . . . *do it!*"

She didn't comment, and he turned away. He thought, I didn't exactly mean it the bloodthirsty way it sounded, but I didn't *not* mean it either. James and Virginia Campbell were a living torment to both of them, and apparently there was no end to it. Whenever the subject began to die, Cindy would visit the house on Memorial or the Campbell law office and return to him in tears. Her parents hated her and showed it in every way. *Awful people!* He would feel much better if they were gone.

12

Jamie Campbell was happy that her parents had finally seen her point about Cindy. They usually gave their daughters what they wanted, and Jamie wanted to bail out of Houston for Knoxville, Tennessee, home of some student friends she'd met in Switzerland. There were good schools in Knoxville, including the University of Tennessee, and best of all, it was a thousand miles from Cindy.

Jamie had had enough. She'd been the prime target of Cindy's cruelty for years, the victim of her lies and exaggerations and lunatic moods. Jamie wasn't sure why Cindy had singled her out; maybe it was plain old sibling rivalry, some Freudian thing involving the way she'd preempted Cindy as the baby of the family. The reason didn't matter. Her memories of life in their shared bedroom were so painful that she'd managed to block some out. She wished she could block them all.

Cindy had kept her little sister in a state of fright by insisting that the old house on Memorial Drive was haunted. "Jamie, look!" Cindy would whisper, shaking her awake. "It's a black nun!"

"I—I . . . don't see anything," Jamie would say.

"In the shadows! She's dressed in black. That's why you can't see her."

After a few seconds, the chanting would begin: *"Om ah! Om ah whah! Om ah! Om ah whah!. . . ."* Jamie wanted to run to her mother, but Cindy wouldn't let her.

When Cindy was nine and Jamie five, Cindy capped a long string of cruelties by trying to choke her in the upstairs bathroom. When Jamie broke free, Cindy warned, "If you tell, I'll say you tried to strangle me first." Jamie hid the bruises.

Cindy insisted to Jamie that James Campbell disliked his four daughters. Sometimes she said that he loved Cindy but despised Jamie, Betty and Michelle. "Daddy told me himself," she would taunt Jamie. "And he especially hates *you!*"

The child ran off and cried, still too young to realize that Cindy enjoyed setting one family member against another.

Once Cindy declared that she was the reincarnation of Marie Antoinette and began sketching eerily detailed pictures of the clothes of the French court. She used her Ouija board to confirm that she was the Cinderella of the Campbell family, the mistreated outcast. As a child Jamie wondered where the Ouija board got such ideas. Cindy had always come in for more personal attention and loving care than the other daughters, but no amount seemed to satisfy her. She created demon stories about their mother, whom she called "that selfish bitch." Once Cindy described a series of injustices that ended with her being chained to a toilet fixture, but Jamie knew that she was making it up because they'd seen the same sequence in a TV movie a few days earlier. She wondered what compelled Cindy to lie about the kindest mother in the world.

As Jamie packed for Tennessee, she remembered how the Campbells' life had always revolved around Cindy's needs. When she had her appendectomy, her parents abruptly cancelled plans to attend Betty's confirmation, an important event in the Catholic family. The appendix proved to be oversized and off-line, and the doctors made an unusually large incision. Cindy liked to show the scar as one more sign of mistreatment.

Jamie remembered the gloom that enveloped the old house the first time Cindy ran away: Daddy driving up and down the dark streets calling her name, the vigils by the phone, mother's drawn face. Cindy had put the family through the same ordeal again and again. She used the threat of leaving as a club, conned them out of money, ran with criminals and dopers. She made impassioned telephone calls for return air fare from places like Chicago and Denver, then spent the money and called for more. The system always worked. Her parents were *so* gullible.

The other sisters often wondered why their parents didn't just disown the problem child. The answer was always the same. "We love Cindy," their saintly mother explained, "and not just when she's good."

Years later, when James and Virginia decided to take

teenaged Jamie and oldest sister Michelle to Europe, Cindy
had raged, "Well, I'm going, too!"

Her mother had said, "Well, honey, who'll take care of
Michael and Matthew?" At the time Cindy was jobless:
she'd just left her second husband and returned to the family
home with two infant sons. She fussed and flustered and
finally announced, "The next time anybody in this family
goes to Europe, it better be me!"

Now Jamie thought, To Cindy it's always been herself
first and the world second. She remembered the Christmas
when Cindy had headed to Foley's department store to ex-
change her gifts for cash. "Well, why not?" she explained.
"They're mine."

Lately there'd been signs that the parental patience was
running out. Well-meaning friends had suggested that Cindy
needed control, not handouts. James Campbell seemed to
agree. When Cindy cadged money these days, it was always
from her mother. She and her father barely spoke. Jamie
thought, Cindy won't take that forever. She's got the
meanest temper in the world. The situation was getting
scarier every day.

Well, Jamie thought, whatever's gonna happen, I won't be
here to see it. Thank god for that. She finished packing and
headed north.

13

"God*damn!*" David said with a self-congratulatory grin.
"When I met you, you were a blob. Look at you now!"

All through the steamy summer of 1981, he'd worked
hard on his masterpiece and she'd worked hard on herself.
Now she weighed 127 pounds and had a 22-inch waist. True,
those enticing large-nippled breasts had diminished by a few
sizes, but so had the rest of her—the porky thighs, the
satchel ass, the flabby upper arms with the cellulite dimples.
She'd even lost weight in her face. There was a new Cindy
Ray in the world, and she was all his.

Or was she? She'd begun to question his control, his direction. In some ways, he thought, she's acting like a rebellious
teen. Maybe that's normal. If so, it's also normal for her
primary caretaker to be pissed about it. And he was. He
didn't like the way she'd embarrassed him in front of his
ironworker boss Ron Westphal the other day, pigging out on
two giant hamburgers, a large Coke and a bag of potato
chips just when he'd been bragging about the diet-control
systems he'd taught her. "See?" David told his friend dis-
gustedly. "Goddamn it, she lost all that weight and looky
here—she's started putting it on again."

Nor had she earned a dime since walking off her job as a
rent-a-cop. He knew that her metamorphosis would be incomplete and maybe even reverse itself if she didn't assume
the responsibilities of an adult. Otherwise, what was the
point of dissolving the flab? She was a spectacular-looking
woman; employers would bust their humps to find a place
for her. But when he nagged her about it, she produced lame
excuses. "I don't know how to look for work," she would
say. Or "I'm afraid." Nebulous bullshit. She could get a
good job as a commercial artist. "Show your portfolio," he
told her. "People'll go, 'God, you're great!' "

When she refused, he erupted. "Goddamn it, Cindy, all
you do is wallow around the house. Why don't you get up
and smell the fucking coffee!"

"You're picking on me," she whined. "It's not fair. *You
stop picking on me!*"

He had the panicky feeling that they were on the
downcurve of their romance and he would wind up a loser
again. He'd given Cindy everything, emotionally and physically, but he'd learned from junior high school on that it
didn't matter. They left anyway. He wished he could discuss
the problem with his friends, but they were under the impression that things were fine, and he was too proud to say
otherwise. He decided that the best course was to back off,
indulge her a little, avoid inflaming her paranoia. Maybe this
love would be different.

Day after day, she pushed his patience to new limits. He
wondered, Will the garbage reach the ceiling before she car-
ries it out? Didn't that humpbacked Virginia Campbell

teach her how to clean her room? Make a bed? Did some kind of goddamn slave pick up after her or what? She wore her clothes for weeks and then dropped them on the floor as though some Watusi were following her with a palm leaf. His spider monkey Enoch, companion of his lonely high school days, had been more fastidious.

Her personal hygiene, never a priority, was also slipping. She slunk from mirror to mirror ahead of clouds of cologne that barely masked her B.O. She didn't change her clothes as often, and had to be reminded that he wasn't her personal washerwoman. She left trails of rubble, always had two or three open packs of cigarettes lying about and a butt or two smoldering in the ashtrays. She would sip from a can of beer, go to the kitchen and open a second, set it down half-full and carry a third into the bathroom.

She had no idea how to shop; frequently he had to return items she'd bought at the market. His pit bull almost died after she fed him pure caviar. When she was told that Max couldn't excrete salt, she apologized and said she would be sure to get salt-free caviar the next time.

At work on the high iron he got in a fight with a two-hundred-pound Chinese ironworker and came home in a foul mood. "Listen," he snapped, "why don't you start doing some of the chores around here? I mean, I'm feeding ya, I'm housing ya. At least you can clean up."

She said, "I forgot," then "I'm too tired," and finally "I was doing something else." The same goddamn excuses you'd hear from a four-year-old.

For a while he took his mind off his problems by working up a comedy act with his friend Chuck Montgomery. They'd pipedreamed for years about performing together, but David was too crowd-shy to take the idea seriously. This time Chuck insisted. He said that no one could make crazy sound effects like his old friend Dave. With his usual misgivings about himself, David agreed to try.

They opened on amateur night at the Comix Annex, part of Houston's Comedy Workshop, a storefront night club with the elegance of a retread shop. David had been in the place many times, hanging out with Cindy and Chuck. He remembered the night Jamie Campbell had taken a turn onstage: no threat to Joan Rivers, but not half bad for a nineteen-year-old.

The stage was an elevated platform that looked about to collapse; one of the other comics got an easy laugh by referring to it as "a postage stamp on steroids." David looked around the adjoining "green room" nervously. A graffito said, "Give to mental health or I'll kill you." It was late summer and the room was a furnace; the only ventilation came from holes in the wall where frustrated comics had rammed their fists. A bare light bulb hung from the ceiling. David thought, If this was a shotgun shack in the Fourth Ward, it'd be condemned. In a corner another amateur held his nose and repeated his opening lines in a high metallic voice: "Attention K-Mart shoppers. For the next half hour our ladies' pants will be half off . . ."

The first appearance of Montgomery & West was mercifully short. Chuck did the lines and David did the sounds:

"Before I became a comedian, I was a police officer. One day I was walking my beat (*clop, clop, clop*) when I noticed these bright lights above me. I looked up and saw a flying saucer (*hmmmmmm*), and all of a sudden this teleporter beam came out of the flying saucer and pulled me up (*whir-whir-whirrrrrr*). The doors opened (*creeeeeeeak*) and closed (*clank*). I looked around, and everywhere I looked, I saw computers (*whum-whum-whummmmmm*). All of a sudden I met this little guy, and he started talking to me in a strange language (*chirp, cheep, choop, cheep—skreeeee*). And I couldn't understand a word he said till he put on a language translator helmet which allowed us to speak in the common language of all law enforcement officers (*oink, oink, oink*). . . ."

To David's surprise, there was applause. But after nine or ten more performances at the Comix Annex, his stage fright showed no signs of abating, and he decided on early retirement.

As he drove back home on the last night of his comedy career, Cindy commented that it wouldn't be hard to perform; in fact, she would like to try. *"You?"* David said. "You'd be scared shitless."

"No, I wouldn't," she insisted. "I know all the comics by now. I feel at home there. And I'm a natural comedian anyway."

"Who'll write your routine?"

"I'll wing it. You've heard me, David. I'm good!"

Yes, she was, but only in intimate settings—David and a few close friends—and only after several drinks. The rest of the time she was too scared to talk, let alone perform. He hoped she wasn't serious.

But she was. For days they argued about her plans. David didn't want her to bomb in front of a crowd and lose what little confidence she'd developed. And he also didn't want to expose her to a bunch of randy comics when she still couldn't handle the advances of the Safeway bag boy.

"You gotta understand," he told her in his most earnest voice. "In some ways you're ready to move ahead and in others you're not. You don't have the wisdom yet. You don't have the snap to understand that these people at the Comix Annex may like you as a person, yes, but some of 'em are gonna put the moves on you."

"They won't!" she said. "They're good guys."

He thought, What's being a good guy have to do with a stiff dick? "Good friends can hit on you, Cindy. And you can't handle it." He was thinking about the security job she'd quit.

"You're just jealous," she said. She tossed her honey-colored hair, and David thought what a target she'd be at the Workshop. All those fast-talking dudes! How the hell could he keep up with them? He'd hung around the place for two years and most of them still thought of him as Chuck Montgomery's stooge, a sound-effects geek, and barely said hello.

Cindy said, "You're so goddamn possessive, David." He thought, The old Cindy never would have talked to me like this. She'd have listened obediently, brought me a cold beer and rubbed my feet. At the moment he wasn't sure he liked his creation, but he loved her and didn't intend to lose her to some jack-off comic with a line of shit.

"Look, Cindy," he said, "a long time ago I told you to think for yourself."

"Yeah," she interrupted, "and when I do, you tell me I'm wrong."

"I *want* you to think for yourself," he insisted. "But you think you're ready to take on the world, ya know? You're questioning my judgment and using poor judgment yourself. At any rate, you can't deal with men. You can't hold a job. You can't even keep the kitchen clean. *Cindy, you're not ready!*"

She said evenly, "You're the one that's holding me down."

When he came home from work the next evening, she was gone. He slumped into his sofa and thought, She'll be back. She's helpless out there. But *where the hell did she go?* Did she take off with . . . some guy? The thought kept him awake.

Two days later he was frantic. His mom reported that she'd heard nothing. He phoned the Campbell home and the goddamn wetback maid answered the phone. *"Dónde* Cindy?" he yelled into the mouthpiece. The old *pinche puta* hung up.

He looked in their favorite bars, peeked into classrooms at St. Thomas, looked behind trees in parks. He didn't know where to turn. He couldn't remember the names of any of her friends. She hadn't had many.

At last she phoned. "I'm staying with Gwen," she said. "I didn't want you to worry." He thought, Gwen . . . Sampson? I might have known. He remembered her as a flip, fat blonde who worked in her mother's insurance office and did artsy-fartsy sculpture on the side. Cindy had introduced her at St. Thomas as her old art teacher.

"I had to leave," Cindy said over the phone. "I was freaking out."

"Freaking out?" David yelped. "Over what?" He was thoroughly pissed. If it freaked her out to live in his house rent-free and eat his food and let him turn her whole goddamn life around, well, fuck her.

"Over your possessiveness," Cindy said.

"Yeah? Well, that's fine!" He hung up. And felt lousy.

14

Gwen Sampson wished she knew what the hell was going on. She was a good-natured woman, fond of jokes and wisecracks, but the latest developments in her life weren't funny. Her former art student Cindy Ray had moved into her house, and everyone in Gwen's family was climbing walls.

She'd always wondered what the hell C. Ray had ever seen in D. West. The guy was a schlump for all seasons, chauvinistic, pushy and *dull.* He could take a two-line joke and stretch it till your chin touched the floor. He wasn't good-looking, but then Cindy never dated good-looking boys. She bragged that he was the son of two college professors, but he certainly wasn't very bright himself. He was insanely jealous and pushed her around. Gee, Gwen thought, what a great catch!

There'd always been something unreal about the relationship. She remembered the day she and Cindy had run into West at Hamburgers by Gourmet, and afterward Cindy had confided, "He makes me sick. I just hate him! When I eat with him, I can't get the food down 'cause I have to look at his face."

Gwen had asked, "Then why eat with him?"

"Because I'm hungry."

After that Cindy never missed an opportunity to dump on West and call him "Pigface." And then moved in with him! Gwen thought, Sometimes good old Cindy doesn't make a lick of sense.

The two friends talked a lot about sex, and soon after moving into the house on Vermont, Cindy had confided to Gwen that she couldn't stand male-superior intercourse with West because it represented giving in. Oral sex, she said, gave her control. Also, she said, she would rather look at his tink than his face. Gwen asked, "But Cindy, why do it at all if you feel that way?"

"I need a place to stay," Cindy answered. Gwen remembered that Cindy had recompensed more than one sugar daddy with sex. She seemed completely relaxed about such transactions. Gwen thought, I could never do anything like that myself, but why be judgmental?

And now the romance with West had gone *phffft* and the slender new Cindy was lolling around Gwen's living room watching TV. She seemed morose, but she'd always gone from mood to mood. Gwen was sure this one would change with the tides or the moon.

Don wasn't as patient. He'd disliked Cindy from the start and made no effort to hide it. Gwen thought, Oh, God, one more coffin nail in our marriage. But that wasn't the only problem Cindy caused. Gwen's fifteen-year-old son Jeffery was sexually precocious, and she picked up on the undercurrents between him and the houseguest. Cindy wasn't always careful about covering herself in front of Jeffery and his five-year-old half-brother John.

So when Cindy announced that she was returning to West, Gwen was quietly pleased.

A few days after the departure Cindy phoned to say that she was selling everything she owned to raise money for a nose job. "I have that double cartilage at the end," she said, "and if I don't get it fixed, I'll end up looking like Karl Malden."

Gwen thought, There's nothing wrong with her nose, but if a nose job makes her feel better about herself, why not? She drove to the garage sale and bought rattan chairs and a desk. A glaring West stood on the front porch with arms folded, not offering to help carry the heavy pieces. When Gwen went near, he called her a cow and a whore.

15

Sometimes David wondered why he'd been so nice about taking Cindy back. She sure as hell wasn't acting grateful. She stuffed her face like a sumo wrestler and sucked up his booze as soon as he opened the bottle. All she could talk about was her goddamn nose job.

After the garage sale he decided she needed a jolt. "Come on, Cindy," he said. "Show some *snap!* Stand up for yourself!" He knew he was messing with her head, but he'd messed with it before. Maybe she would listen to him this time.

But instead she continued to drink heavily and make scenes. At a party a group of men swarmed her décolletage as David mingled with friends and tried to keep her in sight. When he noticed that she wasn't fending the men off, he sidled over and said, "Hi!" She didn't even acknowledge him.

He walked across the room and fell into an intense conversation about one of his favorite subjects. What people didn't understand about the Nazis, he explained, was that their means were bad but their aims made a lot of sense.

A tall, skinny dude piped up that Hitler tried to make too many decisions that should have been left to God. David thought, God, huh? Which one are you talking about, man? The Catholic God, the Baptist God, the Methodist-Episcopal God, Allah, Mohammed, Buddha, Yahweh, Jehovah, the Holy Roller God, the Christian Science God, the airplane god in New Guinea? There were a thousand of them. But he stayed quiet. The existence of God wasn't usually a fruitful subject of discussion at a typical Montrose party.

He decided to make Cindy jealous and slid away to talk to another woman. When he turned to catch Cindy's reaction, she was gone. He searched the house and parking lot. He heard tittering in a back bedroom and tried to enter. Someone was holding the door. He kicked it open and entered a darkened room that smelled of marijuana. When his eyes adjusted, he saw Cindy on the bed, surrounded by men.

"What the fuck's going on?" he asked.

"Nothing," she said in her baby voice.

"Come on!" he said, and dragged her home.

He knew her problem all too well: she had too much time on her hands and too little self-confidence. If some asshole paid her a compliment, she slobbered all over him in her Italian accent.

"Goddamn it, Cindy," he told her, "get your shit together! Get a job! If you can't support yourself, you're just gonna be clinging onto somebody always, ya know? Unless I get stinkin' rich, I want a working wife. The way things are now, it's too goddamn parasitic. It's eating us both alive."

At home she insisted that she needed privacy. As part of a negotiated truce, he moved her downstairs to the empty apartment. He hoped the arrangement would be short-lived. Sex came to a halt, but they still ate and hung out together. His hopes stayed high. Time was with him. She had to come around.

16

"He beats me every day, Gwen," the meek voice said, "and I can't get the movers to come, and I don't know *what* to do. Oh, Gwen, you're my best friend. Can't you help me?"

Gwen Sampson thought how crazy it had been for Cindy to return to a man she hated and how crazy it had been to think that the no-good S.O.B. would stop pounding her bones. But it was also crazy to think that Gwen Sampson, a respectable woman of sound mind, would intervene. As she'd told her husband, "David West is *not* rowing with both oars in the water." After hearing Cindy's horror stories about him, it was scary enough just to live in the same city.

But Cindy was her friend. "What do you want me to do?" Gwen asked, trying to sound as noncommittal as possible.

"Gwen, if you could just come over here and help me pack. Oh, please! We could get all my stuff in your van."

"What's Attila gonna be doing?"

"David? Oh, he's working."

Despite misgivings, Gwen drove her VW van to West's house. The two women loaded hurriedly and hauled the stuff to Cindy's new apartment on Kingston. "Don't you *ever* tell that psycho I helped you," Gwen said as she left.

"Don't worry. I won't."

That night she got a phone call. "Where's Cindy?" a tense male voice asked.

"I don't—"

"Goddamn it, you know where she is!"

"Yes," Gwen answered, "but I don't intend to tell you."

The ensuing tirade included the repeated use of the phrase "whore cow" and threats that she'd better cooperate or "I'll be over there." She was proud that she stood her ground.

As she drove toward her job as manager of the Billie Funk Insurance Agency, owned by her mother, Gwen ruminated on how she'd ever become involved with two such characters as Cindy Ray and David West. Maybe, she decided, I attract oddballs. She was pleased to be an Aquarian ("You will have many strange and colorful characters in your repertoire of friends") and something of a hedonist. She had wispy blond hair, small feet, a large body, kewpie lips and an impish Barbara Eden face. Sometimes she presented a flighty schoolgirl image, but she could be as determined as the marathoners who ran past her small house in the flats of southwest Houston. She'd learned a few things in her thirty-three years, and the main one was tolerance. She'd had polio as a child and recovered to carve out a life as wife, mother, sculptor, teacher, and now insurance person.

Gwen and Cindy had met two years ago at the Houston School of Commercial Art. As a student, Cindy had been a disappointment, her talent lost in a crushing lack of confidence. How odd, Gwen thought, that we became such good friends. It certainly wasn't my idea.

She remembered their first meeting, back in 1978. Forty students attended the private school, eight of them in Gwen's classes on color theory and production. The new girl was attractive, chunky but not fat, with heavy-lidded eyes made up like Elizabeth Taylor's and chestnut hair worn down. She was dressed in jeans and sweat shirt, the uniform of the era. And she seemed almost mute.

Within a few days it became clear that no amount of teaching would enable Cindy Ray to mix a flesh tone in acrylics. Gwen thought, That's downright peculiar. She does eye shadow perfectly. "Think of it as make-up," she advised the new student. "If you can do make-up, you can do a flesh tone."

But Cindy Ray couldn't. "Okay, then," Gwen said patiently, "let's try something else. Mix it on your arm."

"On my . . . arm?" The voice was barely audible.

"Yep. Right . . . *there!*" Gwen touched the inside of the student's bare forearm. "And keep mixing till you can't tell your skin from the paint."

The advice brought a shy smile. That's nice, Gwen thought. I sure don't teach for the money.

Cindy Ray was always behind in her schoolwork and seldom completed a project. She would produce a lovely sketch or painting and leave a corner undone. Gwen discussed the problem with the other teachers. Ray had been in the school for six months and had turned in two or three assignments; she said she was "reworking" the others. Her problem seemed rooted in fear of failure and criticism. A public school would have provided psychological counseling or dumped her, but the small art school was underfunded. So far she'd been "walked through" each course by indulgent teachers. Gwen became the latest.

The other students gossiped about her. She called herself "Gabriela" and spoke in foreign accents. She had a Mae West voice and a cheerleader's bellow and a couple of other voices that came and went for no apparent reason. She could be likable and made a few close friends, but she found excuses to dump every one, often for reasons that made no sense. For weeks she and another female were seen together. "Then . . . *chung!*" Gwen told her husband. "The Ray girl dropped her. She told somebody the girl attacked her. If it's true, I guess you can't blame her." But was it true? Some of the students claimed that Cindy lied a lot.

During a break Gwen heard someone reciting Shakespeare to applause. The voice broke into an operatic aria that climbed so high Gwen feared for the windows. She stepped into the hall to take a look just as a figure in jeans and sweat shirt came cancanning out a door ahead of a howling line of students.

Everyone trooped back to the classroom. Cindy entered with head down, avoiding the instructor's eyes as usual. Gwen asked, "What was that note you sang? G above high H?" Cindy looked embarrassed and didn't reply. Gwen thought, How interesting! There's two personalities in there. She's center-stage or in the dumps. And there's nothing in between!

After class Gwen felt someone watching. She looked up and saw Cindy Ray standing at the door. "Yes?" Gwen asked.

The student batted her big hazel eyes and watched silently.

Gwen tried again. "Did you have a question?"

"Uh . . . no."

Gwen thought, Then go away, please. I'm trying to grade these papers. In a few minutes she got her wish.

After four or five more days of staring sessions, Gwen asked, "What do you need? Don't you have a home?" When there was no answer, she said "Get away!" and threw a small brush. It missed.

Gwen wondered what she'd done to earn such slavish devotion. It was like feeding a puppy and not being able to get rid of it. Or was this . . . something else? After a few weeks she decided that the child was just lonely, or maybe troubled. Gwen relaxed and asked her in.

The odd relationship continued for a year, never extending beyond the short meetings after class. Cindy seemed mesmerized by her teacher. She would help with the chores, sit at Gwen's feet, and sometimes manage a word or two. Gwen thought, No harm done. But she kept her at arm's length.

Late in 1979 Gwen had quit teaching to work at home as a free-lance commercial artist. She installed a darkroom and bought an eighteen-inch camera. One of her first visitors was Cindy. "Hi!" she said when Gwen answered her knock. "How are you?" She seemed relaxed.

"I'm . . . fine," Gwen said, surprised. "How are you? What's, uh, going on?"

"Well, I came to visit."

Gwen hadn't seen the girl for several months. "Come on in," she said politely. "How'd you get here?"

"I took the bus to Willowbend."

Gwen thought, If she still lives down near NASA, she had

to take two bus rides to get here and then walk several blocks. What the hell made her go to all that trouble?

"I'm working in my darkroom," Gwen said.

"Fine!" Cindy said. She sauntered into the tiny room, kicked off an uncomfortable-looking pair of wooden shoes with high stacked heels, and sat on a stool in the corner. The room smelled of developer; wet prints hung on a thin rope; the only light came from a small red bulb. Cindy reminisced about school days and caught up on Gwen's life. They shared a six-pack and at the end of the afternoon were giggling about Cindy's odd behavior at art school. "I just like you, Gwen," she explained.

"Well, I like you, too," Gwen said. "You come back anytime, hear?"

It was the beginning of two years of darkroom socializing. Cindy always brought a gift—a framed butterfly, a conch shell, an art magazine, something that hadn't cost a lot but took some trouble. Gwen figured it was one more example of her low self-esteem—"You don't like me for myself, so I have to bring you something." Or maybe it was just the old apple for the teacher.

One day Gwen said, "You don't have to bring me things, Cindy."

"Well, I drink your beer, I eat your food."

"It doesn't matter. I pretty much run an open house. Jeffery and John are always bringing people over to eat. You're welcome for yourself."

Three days later Cindy arrived with a polished geode for the mantelpiece. Gwen gave up trying to change her.

She'd begun to think of Cindy as a little sister, and she wondered how Cindy saw her—as mother figure, confessor or what? After a while it didn't matter. The two women laughed at each other's drolleries, exchanged intimate secrets, chugged Coors Light, and frequently lost track of time in the little red-tinted room.

Gwen's husband disapproved of the friendship and said so. She wondered if he just disliked Cindy or if it was because he'd come home for dinner several times to find the two of them lit up like Roman candles. Gwen couldn't disavow her friend. She thought, How many characters like Cindy will I ever know?

"She's the funniest woman alive, Don," Gwen told her husband. "She's silly, she's crazy, she makes me laugh." She didn't tell him about the imitations that flowed like a one-woman show at the Alley Theatre. Sometimes Cindy was Gabriela with an Anna Magnani accent or Marie Antoinette sounding like Pepe Le Pew or Juliet bemoaning events in Verona. She did a full-voiced Maggie in *Cat on a Hot Tin Roof,* and when her Maggie lusted aloud for Brick, the "wow-*oooooh!*" peeled the wallpaper. She also did a deadly impression of Jackie O. as Marilyn Monroe as Shirley Temple. Gwen had to put aside her layouts to compose herself.

The two overweight women shared a love of Hollywood, TV, the theater, musicals, celebrities, anything with glitter and style. Cindy had a strong voice and Gwen had perfect pitch but no voice to go with it; they teamed up on songs from old Broadway musicals—"A kiss on the hand may be so con-ti-nental"—while waiting for photographs to come up. Gwen worried about the neighbors as the two of them belted out "Square-shaped or pear-shaped. . . ." Then they padded to the kitchen for another Coors.

In those carefree days before David West came on the scene, Gwen had realized that Cindy was different, but she hadn't thought of her as abnormal. She told a friend later: "That was a time when I wondered if there was a real Gwen underneath. So I could understand the actress in Cindy, the impressionist, the woman who seemed to have every voice except her own. And anyway, she's an artist. Artists are supposed to be weird, aren't we?"

One day Cindy brought a Ouija board and demonstrated its uses. Underneath a religious streak she seemed obsessed with anything scary. She said she'd learned voodoo from the family maid, Maria. "When I was a little girl," she said, "Maria would put pins in dolls. She had a special Madame Alexander doll that she dressed in an old gown and worked as a medium. At night I would hear Maria singing eerie tunes out the window of her apartment in back."

Gwen was puzzled. They'd discussed Maria before, and her impression was that the maid had been with the family for only the last three or four years. But maybe she'd gotten it wrong. It wasn't important. Cindy embroidered, exaggerated, even lied. So what?

Cindy said the Memorial house was haunted.

"Gee, I'd love to go inside," Gwen said.

"No! I wouldn't want you harmed. Or upset."

"By what?"

"Noises, bumps, screams, moans. Things move around in that house, Gwen. One night Jamie and I saw our grandfather clock float down the stairs."

"Where was it in the morning?"

"Back where it belonged."

Several times Gwen drove Cindy home, but she never invited Gwen inside. From the tree-shaded road the place looked like a miniature bastille. Cindy said a rich pervert had decorated it with sick signs and symbols. The shower door, she said, was etched with erotic nudes. She said it was like Stephen King's *The Shining*.

The Campbell family history turned out to be equally disquieting, at least in Cindy's version. Her father was an Italian gentleman and her mother's people were dirt farmers. "Daddy had to marry her because he got her pregnant," she went on. "But he never loved her."

"Campbell" didn't sound Latin to Gwen, but perhaps the family had Anglicized it. She didn't ask. She considered herself no more inquisitive than she was judgmental. Anyway, there were a few Mediterranean aspects to Cindy's features. Giotto did faces like hers, and so did Bernini.

Once the subject of the Campbell family life began to unfold, it seemed unending. Hour after hour in the cramped darkroom, the Broadway shows and comic impressions were forgotten as Cindy narrated the tragedy. She cowered in the corner as she told about her retarded sister Jamie who required care around the clock. She said her sister Betty was a dope addict with brain burnout. She insisted that her oldest sister Michelle was a lesbian and so was the mother, "the old hunchback." She claimed that her mother was jealous because the father loved Cindy. Her mother beat her and locked her in a closet. She asked Gwen to guess which of the four Campbell daughters had been written out of the parents' will.

"You?" Gwen asked unbelievingly.

"Me."

"But . . . *why?*"

"Because the others are my parents' favorites."

That was one of the reasons she'd never been able to hold a job, Cindy explained, or make a success of anything. She'd been so victimized as a child that she'd lost all confidence in herself. "Oh, Gwen," she said through tears, "I'll never amount to a thing."

Gwen was moved. "You can do it, Cindy," she said. "I got a job and I'm kind of a flake, so it *can be done.* Hey, you can have a bad childhood and still turn out okay."

About three months after the darkroom sessions had begun, Cindy climbed up on her favorite stool and said without preamble, "My son Michael is my father's child, ya know?"

In the red glow, Gwen took a deep breath and murmured a flat "Okay." She thought, Gee, sexual abuse is all the rage these days.

Cindy's voice lowered as she confessed to mixed feelings about the situation. Sometimes she found it hard to say no to her father because affection was in such short supply in the Campbell household. She said she sympathized with him because he had no other sex life. "He hates my mother," she explained. "He can't stand going to bed with the old hunchback."

The cronies absorbed two six-packs discussing the situation. "It's not the end of the world, Cindy, you know?" Gwen said gently.

Cindy said her father still made passes and so she had to stay away from the house where her own two sons were being raised. She didn't seem to mind. She never talked about the boys, what they ate or didn't eat, toilet training, problems at school, the things that mothers talk about. There didn't seem to be any bonding between her and her sons; it was as though they'd come from another body.

Cindy said she'd been married four times. Gwen had heard about the hillbilly, the abusive socialite and the carpenter, but she wondered who the fourth had been. Cindy said that the specter of her father had wrecked every marriage. She called her current common-law husband "Moe the Schmo"—she seemed to have a harsh nickname for everyone.

"Why do you put up with it?" Gwen asked. "I'd take a baseball bat and equalize."

Cindy stayed late one afternoon and begged a ride home. As Gwen steered onto the Southwest Freeway a car full of Mexican workers pulled close. "Hey, baby," Cindy yelled, "you want a leetle?"

The workers yelled *"Ay, mamacita!"* as Cindy did bumps and grinds through the window. The Mexican driver almost ran them off the road. Oh, God, Gwen thought, what does this mean? Is the woman repressed or what?

In the fall of 1980 Gwen watched with satisfaction as Cindy's stars seemed to be improving. She left Moe the Schmo, moved back in with her family and her sons, and enrolled in drama classes at the University of St. Thomas. She told Gwen that she was in love with a divine French-Japanese boy. "You'll got to meet R*obair!*" she insisted. They sneaked up to his room in the men's dorm and Gwen looked away as the lovers held hands on the bed and spoke quietly. She thought, How tender, how sweet. How many more sides are there to my friend? Soon afterward, that romance went the way of the others. Gwen didn't ask why.

After Robert, Cindy resumed her complaints that she couldn't function in social situations; she didn't know what to say to men and they made her a nervous wreck. Maybe, she said, it had something to do with her father.

Gwen invited her to parties, but Cindy didn't show; her size was ballooning and she said she hated to be seen. Gwen sponsored an educational visit to a females-only strip joint called La Bare on the theory that a "girls' night out" might help build her confidence. Two undressed dancers zeroed in on Cindy, flicking their oiled torsos and their skinny little butts, but she remained on her best behavior.

A few weeks after the successful outing, Gwen settled her own two sons in bed and went off to pick up Cindy for another expedition, this time to a notorious meat rack near the Galleria. The place featured dancing, a bar, and swarms of cologned old men with busy hands. As she parked her VW van, Gwen thought, What the hell, this'll be educational for both of us.

They'd hardly passed through the door before a man asked Gwen for a dance. "No," she said nervously.

They sat at a table and ordered beers. Two olive-skinned men in tight-fitting suits approached, bowing and rolling their r's. Gwen blurted out, "I've already got my drink. I'm just here to, uh, look."

"Hey," Cindy screeched "look at this! I can unbutton it right here! How do you like 'em, baby?" She thrust out her bust and leered. My God, Gwen thought, she's acting like a whore!

One of the men caressed Cindy's plump hand and said, "Hi! How arrrrre you?"

Cindy said in a sultry voice, "I know what you want, big boy!" Gwen thought, Where is she getting her lines? She sounds like the vamp in a thirties movie. Gwen looked around for the back door.

The Arab started to crawl up Cindy's backbone. Gwen said, "I'm leaving. Let's go. Let's, uh—*eat!* I'll pay for it."

Cindy turned to the man and said, "Take a hike, creep." Gwen thought, It's the same old Cindy: top speed or no speed. But she was glad to get away.

They went to a restaurant not far from the Campbell home on Memorial, where Cindy flirted with a scruffy-looking man in the end booth. The stranger brought over his cup of coffee. Gwen thought, Oh, god, if anybody sees me. A married woman with two kids. . . .

On the way home she reminded herself not to take Cindy out again. It was too painful, too embarrassing, and there was too much potential for scandal. But mostly Gwen was thinking, I thought I understood her, *but I don't.*

17

"Why do you suppose that child wants a nose job?" Cecelia asked.

DuVal said he didn't know. His face was hidden, as usual. He'd recently bought thicker glasses but still had to hold books close to his eyes. Lately he'd turned to big-print books, but choices were limited. He said, "There's a lot of things I don't understand about Cindy."

Cecelia was worried about the operation. She'd had her own problems with surgeons. A nose job was supposed to be simple and safe, but anything could happen when one person carved on another.

Lately Cindy hadn't been showing up often, and when she did, she griped about David. "He's trying to run my life," she complained. "He's too demanding, too strong. He makes me feel I can't do anything on my own."

Well, yes, Cecelia conceded to herself, David can be overbearing. But he's got so many compensating qualities. The tarot cards had predicted a marriage. She still thought it would be a good match.

A few days before the operation, Cecelia asked, "What in hell do you need with a new nose?"

Cindy claimed that she needed confidence for her career in comedy, and what could engender more confidence than a petite new nose? Her sister Jamie had had rhinoplasty, and so had her mother (and almost bled to death, Cindy admitted). It was only fair that she be accorded the same treatment, but of course at the hands of a much more skilled and expensive surgeon.

The underlying problem, Cecelia realized after Cindy had left, was that the child didn't see herself with any clarity at all. She was proud of her Oriental-style fingernails and long eyelashes and ashamed of everything else. Her neat little waist was *urp*. Her high bustline was *urp*. Her nose was double *urp*. To Cecelia, Cindy's nose seemed fairly straight and not nearly as wide and long as its owner imagined. Yes, there was a slight crease down the middle and the Campbell bulb on the end, but neither was unusually prominent. Cecelia had seen similar noses on movie stars. The problem was easily solved with a little shading on each side and some care with the lighting.

She shuddered when she thought how much money would be going into Cindy's cosmetic surgery—four or five thousand dollars, according to David. From his reports, her garage sale had been a modest success. Cindy had rounded up everything she'd stored from her three marriages: clothes, dishes, silverware, gewgaws, plus the Puch bike and several other items David had bought her. She'd come up a few thousand short for the operation, and her father had agreed to kick in the rest. How odd, Cecelia thought, that Campbell would help. Maybe he's trying to win her back now that she's committed to David. Nothing was too evil for a man like him.

When Cindy came around to display her new nose, Cecelia saw immediately that the surgeon had made it too retroussé, too Bob Hopish. He'd broken it and lowered the bridge; all he should have done was slim the tip. But she didn't comment. If Cindy thought it was attractive, maybe that was benefit enough. Cecelia watched as the child tilted the hand mirror and preened like a courtesan.

The scars were still livid when Cindy began babbling about her glorious future as a comic actress. "I'm heading straight for the Comix Annex," she said cheerfully.

Cecelia thought, I hope you're ready.

18

David was glad when Cindy returned to his ground-floor apartment. It would have been better if she'd come upstairs with him, but he would soon talk her into that.

The griping started on her first day back. She complained

that there were rats downstairs; it was spooky; it wasn't sealed properly; who knew what diseased, disgusting, *creepy* things were getting in? David was afraid she was just looking for an excuse to leave.

A week later she told him she intended to move back into the apartment her father had bought her on Kingston. She declined his offer of help and told him her parents would take care of the moving costs. He thought, Those scumbags? It seemed like an added affront.

She said it might be okay if they dated once in a while. After she left, he cried.

19

Cecelia wasn't quite sure what was going on between David and Cindy. She saw less and less of them, and David wasn't talking. Then one day Cindy called to say that he'd agreed to take the two women to a Sunday movie.

They were waiting to make a left turn off Montrose when the car was rammed from behind. The Capri jerked ahead a few feet as David yelled, "Son of a bitch!"

Cecelia turned and saw the scowling face of a middle-aged driver. As she watched, the man seemed to be preparing to ram them again.

"What'd we *do?*" she asked her son.

"Nothing," David said as he steered the car across two lanes of oncoming traffic and slid to the curb on Kipling. "I cut him off a little, that's all."

The madman caromed off a parked car and bumped the Capri again. David jumped out and aimed a karate kick at the driver's door.

Cecelia heard a noise and turned to look at Cindy. Her pupils had dilated so widely that her eyes looked almost black. She was thrashing back and forth on the seat. "Don't hit me again," she wailed as she covered her face. *"Mama, don't hit me again!"*

It was like dealing with an epileptic. She kept trying to

launch herself into the front seat and Cecelia kept shoving her back.

The Capri was hit again, so hard that it rose a few inches into the air. David resumed his karate attack as Cindy squeaked, "Just tell me what I've done wrong, Mama. *Please, tell me what I've done wrong!*"

Cecelia grabbed her as she tried to wriggle through a window. "I don't know what I've done wrong," the child yelled as Cecelia held her by the T-shirt, "but I won't do it again. Please, Mama, please! *Mama, Mama, don't hit me again!*"

When the other driver finally fled, David jumped back in the Capri as though to give chase. Cecelia said, "Never mind him. Let's get her home fast."

On the short drive Cindy curled into a ball, shaking, quivering, still pleading with her "mama" in the same strange voice. She didn't appear to recognize the two Wests. Cecelia held her tight and repeated, "It's okay, baby, it's okay." She led her into the house and poured her a beer. For five or ten minutes Cindy's lovely eyes stayed big and dark. Then she seemed to relax a little. It was hours before she was herself again, and then she refused to discuss what had happened.

20

At thirty comedian Steve Epstein had a close-cropped reddish beard and thinning curly hair. He was always being told that he looked like a rabbi, but in fact he was a widely traveled "road rat" or "road dog" and one of the few paid performers at the Comedy Workshop. Like the other comics, "Eppie" paid his dues in small clubs across the South while waiting to become the next Robert Klein.

He knew David West only slightly and, like most of the other habitués of the Comedy Workshop, tended to define him by what he wasn't. He wasn't exactly a nerd and he wasn't exactly a wimp. He wasn't big or menacing, but Eppie felt that it wouldn't be wise to cross him. He wasn't loud and didn't wear a Stetson or drive a pickup, and yet he came off as a good ol' boy. He also seemed malleable, impressionable, pleasant, basically shy. And he had one brown and one blue eye—the stuff of comedy, though none of the performers had the poor taste to exploit it.

West's glamorous friend Cindy appeared to be another story. She was so far out of the good ol' boy's league that some took him for her chauffeur or, at best, her brother. When she began appearing at the Comix Annex alone, Eppie was quick to show his admiration, and she seemed receptive. At the close of business early one morning, she said, "I don't have my car. Could you take me home?"

He drove her to a quadruplex on Kingston, a few blocks from the Montrose. A stench pervaded the hallway outside her second-floor apartment. Eppie decided that something was dead. She didn't ask him in.

After that she began showing up at the club nightly, drenched in scent. He wondered if it had anything to do with the smell at the apartment. He drove her home again and they groped in the hall. She seemed direct and honest, almost blunt. "Don't!" she said at one point, and cocked her heavy purse behind her ear.

No problem, Eppie thought—for now. He made it plain that he was open to her favorite subjects: telepathy, reincarnation, metempsychosis, witches, ghosts. He'd always been intrigued by weirdly beautiful women. Sometimes this one seemed psychic. She told how she'd watched his body language the first night and noticed his interest in her. He thought, How well I remember.

He soon discovered that she had a scary side. She picked up on his thoughts and voiced them immediately. She was as plain-spoken as a five-year-old. She would stare at his face and blurt out, "Right now you're thinking of grabbing my breast." Or "You don't like me tonight." He'd heard that paranoiacs were like that: idiot savants of the facial twitch and the raised eyebrow.

He was intrigued till he began to realize that she was trying to draw him into her private game. She seemed to need a prince; one night it was Eppie, another night it was West, then someone else. If you weren't her prince, you were a sex fiend trying to get into her pants. When he saw that she was committed to some kind of strange personal fantasy, he quit her cold.

21

Steve Moore had to make a decision. The new performer was young and beautiful, and the Comedy Workshop badly needed a female comic. He thought, To book or not to book. That is the question.

As artistic director, Moore was the man who decided whose act was ready. His dark good looks and wavy black hair gave him a pronounced Latin look, despite his name. He wore five-hundred-dollar suits, drove fast cars and was a Workshop hero for his hip monologues: "I like good lower-class Christian men who just want to work five hours a day, go home, molest the stepdaughter, watch TV, and fall asleep on a generic beer."

He kidded homosexuals and they loved it: "The Montrose is San Francisco with humidity. I think gays are a resource. I mean, a couple of gay men move into a rotting log and in a month it's a condominium." Like all good comics, he wasn't afraid to kid himself: "I'm terrible at sports. I was the only kid ever cut from the Special Olympics. . . ."

Every night the artistic director was reminded that comedy clubs like the Workshop attracted social misfits—the disenfranchised, faces on "wanted" posters, blank-faced dudes with bloody boots. Drifters were attracted by the laid-back camaraderie. "We're a family," Moore explained to newcomers. "We share material, help write bits, give support and encouragement. We also punch each other out, scream, break windows and don't talk for months. Right—*a family!* If a guy's phone is cut off, we chip in. If he can't make his next gig, somebody makes it for him. We're the last commune from the sixties."

Once in a while a bad-ass insinuated himself into the family. "We try to head them off," Moore said. But they weren't always successful.

At first the small-voiced woman hadn't seemed a threat to the club's image. She'd introduced herself to Moore as a friend of David West, whom the artistic director remembered as a quiet guy drinking beer on the back bench and applauding every act. For a few weeks he'd done a Star Trek variation with Chuck Montgomery. Showed a lot of promise. Then he'd quit.

When Cindy Ray insisted that she wanted to work up an act of her own, Moore auditioned her and thought, No. Never. . . .

Now she was showing up nightly, begging for advice and acting heartbreakingly grateful when she got it. She told Moore she was broke and hungry, thoroughly disarming him. He'd always felt that Houston was a hard-edged place for the poor.

The Ray woman kept trying to work up an act. He thought, She's never gonna make it, but she's persistent. Against his better judgment he gave her a few original ideas, helped her with her delivery, taught her some tricks to overcome her shyness. Steve Epstein had dated her for a while and was high on her talent. "She's great!" Eppie insisted. "She's different, she's interesting, she's nuts. She'd be good for the club."

Her first amateur night appearance confirmed Moore's original diagnosis. She rambled, got lost, forgot punch lines and ignored every idea they'd discussed. When she went off, the crowd howled with relief. Backstage she acted as though she'd been a hit. "No, no," Moore told her. "You don't understand, Cindy. You can't just go out and talk fast. You've got to work on a routine."

She tried again, this time with body English and a low-cut dress. Another bomb. She wouldn't quit. One night she came offstage and told Moore, "The men usually like me, but tonight they didn't. Wasn't I pretty enough?"

He said, "Looks are no advantage, Cindy."

"Aren't I sexy?" She whirled and displayed her hourglass

figure. That was one of the problems, Moore thought. Everybody's looking at her ass.

"It's better for a comic to be fat and ugly," he told her. "People have to be comfortable to laugh. They're not comfortable looking at you. The women in the audience don't want the competition, and the men are thinking, 'Why's a beauty like this fooling around with comedy?' "

"What can I do?"

He found her a silly hat and a shoe with a broken heel. Anything to take the edge off her sexiness. But she still looked great. And she still bombed.

The good friends Moore and Epstein discussed the problem. Eppie said, "I was wrong. She's not a comedian."

"Let's try to be positive," Moore said. The club still needed a female comic. "She's wild. She's—"

"—dirty, disgusting."

"Yeah," the artistic director admitted. "She'll say anything. She appeals to people who like car wrecks."

"All comedians are a little nuts," Eppie said. "She's got the nuts part down good."

"Did you hear her yell at that guy, 'Do you want to fuck me?' "

"Great moments in comedy."

They decided to ease her out.

22

Gwen Sampson was glad to hear that Cindy's life had turned around, but she missed the old hen parties in her darkroom. The two cronies were meeting less and less these days. Cindy said she hardly had a second to spare, even for "my best pal in the world."

"As long as you're happy," Gwen said. She'd never been one to pressure her friends.

Through the early months of 1981, Gwen had watched the metamorphosis with joy. Cindy's weight had always jumped up and down, but now she was positively *svelte*. Her

waist looked like an adolescent's. New planes and angles
appeared on her face. She attributed the improvement to
diet and vitamins. She made no mention of David West and
Gwen didn't ask about him. That 24-carat jerk was the last
person on earth she wanted to discuss.

For the first time since the two women had met back in
1978, Cindy seemed involved in a career. "Oh, Gwen," she
said, "I'm working at the Comix Annex and everybody just
loves me. God, I'm an overnight hit!"

Gwen thought back on the musical comedy sessions in
her darkroom. How could this clever kid be anything but a
hit?

"It's so great doing things on my own," Cindy went on,
"not being led around by my nose. Those comics, they're
bright, they're hip. I learn something new every night. And
. . . you know what?"

"What?"

"They say I can go all the way. Gwen, can you imagine
me on 'Carson'?"

"Of course I can. When can I come see you?"

Cindy paused. "Oh, uh, pretty soon. Okay? I love you so
much, you might make me nervous. I'll let you know when
it's okay."

Gwen waited and waited. No invitation came.

23

"Oh, David, *please!*" the female voice said. "I'm at the club,
and nobody'll drive me to my apartment."

He was instantly awake, so excited he almost dropped the
phone. She hadn't called in two weeks. "Wait right there!"
he ordered. It was 2 A.M. and he was due on the high iron at
dawn. It didn't matter. Nothing mattered. Cindy had called.

On the way from the Comix Annex to her new place on
Kingston, she acted as though nothing had changed between
them. He thought, What a great night! A hot dry wind had
blown from the hill country all day, and the temperature

was still in the eighties. Every star was out and the air was
as light as the desert air in Morocco.

She asked him in and handed him a cold beer. In a brief
conversation she promised that she would always be his
loyal friend. She offered her full red lips in a good-night kiss,
but he didn't take advantage. He didn't want to risk losing
this second chance by coming on too strong. It was a time
for patience and finesse.

Driving back to Vermont Street he thought about the Annex. Those motor-mouth comics were putting the moves on
her—you could take that as a given. But her Joan of Arc
attitude would hold them off for months, maybe years, and
by that time she'd be Mrs. David DuVal West. The Saturday
tutorials would become permanent. He would teach her
about Sisyphus and George S. Patton, Hannibal crossing the
Alps, the siege of Troy. This time he'd throw in Jane Austen.

In the next few weeks he tried to learn more about her
nighttime activities, but she provided no clues. She let him
take her shopping, buy her drinks, lend her money, but she
gave away no useful information. All he knew was that she
spent a hell of a lot of time at the Comix Annex. She admitted that she intended to do an act as "Gabriela." He'd heard
her use the name in her half-drunken Italian shticks. She
asked him to stay away from the club because she still
needed space.

"Well, hell, Cindy," he said, "I'm the one that took you to
the Comedy Workshop in the first place, ya know? These are
my friends." She stood her ground, said he could meet her at
the club and drive her home, nothing more. If he took one
peek inside while she was onstage, they would be finished.

He followed orders for a few weeks. She seemed on a
constant high, and he didn't know what to make of it. She
showed a renewed interest in Latinos and spoke in an Italian
accent even when she wasn't drinking. On the way to her
apartment one night, she raved about Steve Moore, how
protective he was, how masculine. "Italian macho," she
called it.

David told himself to stay cool. The darkly handsome
Moore had a reputation as a straight arrow. David wasn't so
sure about the other comics. Some of those studs would fuck

a tree. And with her gorgeous new figure and face, Cindy was a perfect target of opportunity.

At night he wrestled his damp bedsheets, wondering what she was doing. He felt abandoned, alone on his empty childhood block again. It galled him to think that she'd used him to turn herself into a butterfly and then flown away. There was something fundamentally unfair about it.

As the Allied Bank building passed the fifty-floor level, he grew careless on the job. Several times he came close to walking the air. All he thought about was nighttime, when she would allow him to drive her to the club and make him wait outside. He fought back waves of jealousy. Men licked her body with their eyes. It had nothing to do with talent.

Late on a moist summer night he waited at the door while she finished speaking to admirers. He watched as she tilted her head, batted her lashes, tossed her chestnut hair at a good-looking young comic the way she'd once tossed it at him. He wondered if she could possibly be cheating.

After a while he asked, "Ready to go?" She ignored him. "Cindy?" he said, trying not to show his irritation. "Come on. Let's go."

She flashed a bare shoulder and said, "Can't you see we're talking?"

David was embarrassed. "Well, ya know, I been waiting here. What am I, your chauffeur?"

She yelled, "Don't tell me what to do!"

He yelled back that he was sick of waiting for her every goddamn night, and she said if that's the way he felt, then he could piss off. He asked who she thought she was, Carol Burnett? She said he was "an oppressive son of a bitch."

"Yeah," he bellowed "I'm an oppressive no-good fascist! That's why I spent all this fucking time with you over the last six months. I'm just a son of a bitch, aren't I?"

The onlookers edged away and the argument spilled into the parking lot. David tried to lower the level; he disliked public displays. "Okay, *okay!*" he said, talking fast. "I'm just a no-good bastard. That's great. Now just get in the car and I'll take you home."

She ran down the sidewalk. He laid rubber leaving the parking lot and caught her in the 2000 block of Persa.

"Cindy," he called out, "just get in the car and I'll take you home."

"Leave me alone!" She walked fast.

He felt like a fool. "Why don't you just stop it, Cindy?" he called.

She ran up to a house and yelled, "Help me. Help me!" The door opened and she disappeared inside.

He slid his four-inch Colt Diamondback from under the seat. He let the gun stick out the back pocket of his jeans so the folks inside would know he was serious. Then he entered.

A party was in progress, six or eight people in their twenties; he thought he recognized one or two from the Workshop. He saw Cindy trying to hide in a corner. "We're just having an argument," he said loudly. "I haven't laid a finger on her." He took a step forward. "You come on!" he said.

A scrawny young blonde intervened. "She doesn't have to fucking go if she fucking doesn't want to!"

Gee, he thought, listen to Miss Bitch. She has all these dudes to back her up. A male voice whispered, "Let him alone. Everybody sit down."

David tried to placate Miss Bitch. "You don't understand. This is between my girlfriend and me, ya know? I'm taking her home and that's all there is to it."

The woman yelped, "You're not fucking taking her outa here!"

"Yeah, I am," David said calmly. He grabbed Cindy's wrists. The other woman ripped his shirt down the middle.

"You fucking bitch!" he yelled. He tore her dress to her waist, exposing bra and panties. She came at him with her fingernails and he jabbed her sharply in the eyes. She moaned and staggered in little half-circles, then dropped to the floor crying.

He shoved Cindy into the car. "See what you've done now?" he said. "None of this woulda happened except for your bullshit, ya know? All I was trying to do was give you a ride home."

She was silent, so he went on. "You say you don't want me infringing on you anymore. Well, you don't have to worry about it, 'cause I'm never gonna see your ass again!"

In the morning he got a call from Pat Souther, pianist and bartender at Comix Annex. "West?" Souther said. "You scared the shit out of everybody. Do you know I had a gun in my room? I coulda shot you."

"Yeah," David said. He was in no mood for discussion. "That goes both ways."

24

"Dogs don't care," Steve Moore was saying onstage. He felt great. Even the waiters were laughing. "Dogs are like twenty-year-old college kids. They just want to hang out, get laid, throw up. You can't do status on a dog. You can't tell a dog, 'I'm rich and you're poor.' *They don't care!* You can't tell a dog, 'Look at this house. It cost twenty million. It's mine.' The dog says, 'Oh yeah?' and raises its leg. I mean . . . *they don't care!*"

The crowd clapped and whistled. It was one of those Saturday nights when everything meshed: timing, material, audience. The tables were full, the bench jammed, fifteen or twenty were standing. He thought, It should always be like this.

"I don't trust cats," he went on. "They collect their shit in a little box and then they cover it. If cats were people, they'd work for the IRS. Lemme tell ya—"

A female voice interrupted him. "He won't fuck me!" the woman called out. Moore stared through the stage lights. It was Cindy Ray, cupping her hands around her mouth. "Fuck me!" she shouted. *"I want a fuck!"*

Nervous laughter circled the room. My God, the comedian said to himself, they think she's part of my act. That crazy bitch. . . .

She shook her red fingernails at the stage. "He's my artistic director," she yelled. "I want to fuck him. *But he won't fuck me!*" She sounded like a female De Niro impression.

The artistic director cut his act short and retreated to the greenroom. She was already there with some others. "What the hell's the matter with you?" he yelled. "If you ever do that again, I'll throw you the hell out of here."

She didn't answer. Something in her eyes cooled him out. What was the point of yelling at a woman who was known as "Crazy Cindy"?

He turned to talk to Chris Mueller, a blond female folk singer. He'd barely said hello before Cindy jumped on his back and clawed at his crotch.

Chris Mueller peeled her off and shoved her against a wall. "Stop!" Chris said. "Don't do this to yourself. You're degrading yourself."

Afterward Moore agreed with his friends that the whole scene had been oddly asexual, a dance of robots. Ray had offered no resistance when they ushered her out. He tried to think of the appropriate word: cataleptic, catatonic, something similar. Of course, there was a shorter word for her condition.

Nuts.

A week later she showed up and heckled the performers. The manager, power lifter Jason Morrow, told her, "Quiet down or we're gonna throw you out."

She yelled, "You just wanna fuck me! That's the only reason you're doing this!"

Morrow and another man muscled her out the door, but she ran back inside screaming obscenities. Again they took her out, and this time she went for Morrow's face with her fingernails. Steve Moore arrived to help. It was like subduing a wildcat. "Stop now!" Morrow yelled, trying to protect his eyes. *"Goddamn it, back off!"*

She clawed three scarlet lines down his cheek before he pinned her arms. Then she kicked at his legs. "He just wants to *fuck* me!" she yelled. Morrow deposited her on the sidewalk and Moore told a waiter to call the cops.

25

Craig Casper was off-shift from his part-time job at La Carafe, taking the air in his friend Steve Epstein's car. They reached the Comedy Workshop just as a woman came out the front door on Jason Morrow's knee.

Epstein said, "That's Crazy Cindy. She's a real trip."

Casper felt sorry for the woman, whoever she was. He was a bartender, slender, dark-eyed, given to understated clothes like corduroy pants and soft brown shirts. At thirty his tortoise-shell glasses and innocent expression made people take him for younger. "Eppie," he said, "let's stop."

Epstein stepped on the gas. Casper insisted that they go back and see if the woman was hurt. They circled the block and saw her walking away from the club as a police car pulled up in front.

Casper opened the door and the woman climbed in. "Those son of a bitches kicked me out," she raged. *"Comics!* Scum of the earth. . . ."

She was alternately loud and calm. Eppie offered to drive her home, but she said that her throat hurt and she needed a drink. Casper was intrigued and took her to La Carafe. Seated under a wall hung with Victorian drawings and yellowed old newspaper ads, she talked nonstop. "I'm a comic," she said. *"Cindy Ray?"* She recited her name as though it were widely known. "Have you heard of me?"

Casper had to admit that he hadn't.

"I'm thinking of calling myself Gabriela. Isn't that pretty?"

Before he could answer, her voice dropped an octave. He strained to understand. "They won't let me perform," she said in a Janis Joplin growl. "They're trying to shut me out."

"Who?" he asked.

"Steve Moore. Jason. Your friend Eppie. They're after my body."

In a minute or two her voice returned to normal. After

her third drink she said, "I'm a singer, too, but I can't sing now because I hurt my throat. A vitamin pill got stuck and I tried to pull it out." She displayed long red fingernails. "I scratched the inside of my throat and the doctor told me not to talk till it gets better."

Casper asked, "Is that why your voice changes?"

"Changes?" She looked baffled. Something in her big hazel eyes told him to change the subject.

After more drinks she started to slip off the stool and Casper had to prop her up. He looked around. The dark little bar was populated by the customary collection of Urban Animals, businessmen and gawkers. A pretty blonde in black tights and kneepads skated down the narrow aisle between bar and tables, bounced into a middle-aged customer and sent him crashing to the floor, then continued into the ladies' room. Casper thought, Business as usual.

He took the inert Cindy to a friend's house, carried her inside and put her to bed. In the morning she began a harangue. "You took advantage of me! You creepy creepo fucker you! You're just like the rest!"

When he insisted that he never made passes at drunks, she called him a liar and demanded a ride home. Before they'd gone a few blocks, she smiled and said, "You like-a me, behbee? You like-a . . . Gabriela?"

"Yeah," he said. "I like you." In a strange way, he did. She was all weirdness, openness and scary vulnerability. He could imagine her name on a police report.

Her apartment wasn't far from the Comedy Workshop in an unadorned two-story building. When she opened her door, an early warning system buzzed in his head. This woman, he told himself, isn't just eccentric. The table and floor were littered with dishes. Cigarettes had been extinguished on the rug. A half-eaten sandwich looked as dry as sandpaper. The furniture was draped with clothes. Open pots of make-up lay in a general stink of perfume and rot.

"I own this building," she said.

I'm sure, Casper thought, but he refrained from comment. She pulled out sketches of Linda Ronstadt, Burt Reynolds, a self-portrait or two, and said she was thinking of giving up her performing career to work the lobby of the Hyatt Re-

gency as an artist. He could see that she was skilled enough.
That wasn't the question.

Two nights later he took her to dinner. She was dressed in
a sheath that gripped her hips and accented her bust. As he
led her into the restaurant he kept thinking, This is a dream,
a fantasy. She's too damn gorgeous!

He found it hard to relax. She kept assuring him that their
love would last forever. He thought, What love? We've just
met. She said, "I'll never hurt you. I'd give my own life to
protect you." He thought, What the hell's she talking
about . . . ?

Men sneaked glances at her and talked behind their
hands; waiters buzzed their table; the sommelier and musi-
cians chatted her up. She flirted, batted her long lashes, exchanged banter. Sometimes she seemed left over from the
twenties or thirties, a *femme fatale,* a flapper. He was sure
she was playing the role and enjoying it. She'd been right
about one thing. She was an entertainer.

After dinner she wanted to return to La Carafe to hear a
favorite Edith Piaf song on the vintage jukebox. Walking to
his car, they passed some street people sprawled at the curb.
"Hi!" she called out cheerfully. "Nice to see ya. How ya
doing?" She acted as though they were old friends. "Everything okay?" she asked. "Need any money?" Casper hurried
her away.

Drinkers stared as he led her into the old bar with its
guttering candles and shadows. She chugged a drink and
began dancing with another woman's date, then spun him
off to dance with another. Craig thought, This woman could
cause serious damage.

On the way to her apartment she chanted in a Holy Roller
style: "Mary washed Jesus' feet with her hair. Amen,
brother! Mary washed Our Savior's feet with her own
blessed hair. *Yeah!*"

As they turned onto the Southwest Freeway, she said,
"Oh, Craig, honey, let's go to the Hyatt so I can wash your
feet in the fountain."

He said he didn't think the hotel would approve.

"Why the hell not?"

"Cindy, it's two o'clock in the morning."

He sped by an off-ramp. "Goddamn it!" she yelled. *"We're going to the Hyatt!"*

"No, we're not," he said. "I'm taking you home. You've had too much to drink."

She grabbed the door handle. "Why can't I wash your feet?" she said. "Why? *Why?*"

"We'd be arrested."

"No we wouldn't! Jim McConn's a good friend of mine. Whenever I'm in a jam, I call him up and he takes care of me."

Craig thought, Jim McConn's been out for a long time. Kathy Whitmire's mayor now.

Cindy mumbled something, then sat straight up and said, "Let's go to the zoo! Oh, Craig, I have to swim with the seals. Mother and Daddy let me do it all the time. What a lovely night for a swim!"

He veered off the freeway at Shepherd, headed for her apartment. "Cindy," he said, "we're not going to the zoo."

When he stopped at a traffic light, she jumped out and ran between the darkened houses, carrying her high heels. He thought, That's the last I want to see of Cindy Ray or Gabriela or whoever the hell she thinks she is.

A day or two later she phoned to apologize. They met and talked for three hours, fueled by La Carafe's white wine. He listened in fascination as she told him that her mother was "an incredibly evil person," her three sisters were mean, her father cold and uncaring. She said her only nice relative was a paternal grandmother who liked to quote scripture and parroted, "You shall survive and overcome."

She spoke in a stentorian voice when she quoted the Bible, waiflike tones when she spoke of "our love," a guttural trampish voice when angry. She slipped in and out of Italian and French and southern accents. And when she discussed her mother, she sounded like an overplayed villain in a melodrama. Craig didn't know what to make of her.

After another date he realized that she lied constantly, inconsistently, brazenly, lied to her own advantage and for no advantage at all. But, he thought, how persuasive she sounds if you don't know she's lying. She seemed so open, so vulnerable. Every man needed someone to slay a dragon for.

She told how she'd been raped in present and past lives. She was the reincarnation of Helen of Troy, Cleopatra and Marilyn Monroe. Through thousands of years of history she'd been at center-stage, caused wars, hurt people. God had named her after the angel Gabriel. "Atsa some lovely name," she said. *"Capisce?"*

He asked discreetly if she'd ever seen a shrink. Oh, yes, she said, and an alchemist, too, and witches and goblins. They'd lived in her house when she was a child. She'd shown them to her little sister Jamie and scared the silly child witless.

He began to realize that underneath her model's looks this woman was a certifiable mental case. He wished there were some way to help her, maybe even get her committed, but he had no idea where to start. In pure self-defense he told her that he didn't want to see her again, but wished her the best.

She phoned him at home repeatedly, and when he moved and changed his number, she showed up at La Carafe, borrowing money for the cab fare each time. He asked her politely not to return. She was back the next night with sheaves of drawings. He steered her to the end of the bar and said, "Look, Cindy, I work here. You're embarrassing me."

She wouldn't stay away and there wasn't much he could do about it. La Carafe was about as public as a bar could be, a registered historical landmark with its own brass plaque. Every night it was jammed. Cindy glided up and down the narrow aisle trailing clouds of scent, introducing herself as the bartender's old lady, working the crowd. When she was drunk, she railed that the women's movement was a joke and females were meant to be subservient; any goddamn idiot could read it in the Bible. She hit on regulars and strangers, solicited drinks from eager studs, then pirouetted away to tantalize others. She was always ready to accuse someone of propositioning her. "How dare you!" she yelled. "Do I look like a whore? Me? *Gabriela?*" When a woman bumped against her, she shoved her away and said, "You dyke! You touched my breast!" It took a while to calm her down.

Casper was a tolerant man, but she was annihilating the old bar's ambiance. He refused to serve her, ignored her megaphonic demands, turned away when she bellowed, "I want a drink! *And I want it now!*" He never learned how things turned out. He quit.

26

Houston's fall arrived with its usual lack of definition. The same damp air that had been spinning out of the Gulf of Mexico all summer pushed stacks of clouds high above the city, raising the humidity and making everyone sweat. David West was inured to the steam-room climate of his hometown, but he began to long for a change—hailstorms would do, a hurricane, a *typhoon,* any old change.

He felt like an all-world loser. He hadn't seen Cindy for weeks. He paced his buckled floor and thought, Is that it? Is this gonna be another goddamn tragic romance? Of all the women he'd ever lost, Cindy needed him the most. He remembered how she'd looked at Crooker Center the day they'd met. She was helpless without him; didn't the dumb bitch know that? What was she doing with the terrific new persona that he'd created for her? *Didn't he have any goddamn rights?*

October dragged. He was so listless that he even avoided fights. The victimized females of Houston had one less hero. Chivalry required energy. He got up the strength to enroll in a few night courses, then dropped out.

Five or six weeks after she left his bed and board, she phoned to chat. Things weren't going well at the Annex. Jason the muscleman had propositioned her, she said, and thrown her out when she refused. Someone had lied about her at La Carafe and she'd been barred. No, she didn't want David to put in a good word: it wouldn't do any good with those jerks. Anyway, he wasn't to worry about her problems.

There were more phone calls, more shared reminiscences, and finally she agreed to meet for a drink on condition that he not ask to come to her apartment. At the bar she said, "You know, David, we're just friends now." She admitted that she'd been drinking too much lately.

A week later they met at the River Oaks Shopping Center and he poured on the unconditional positive regard. She threw a fit at an innocent remark and phoned later to apologize. "You know, David," she said in her little-girl voice, "you're my only friend." God, how he hoped it was true!

The next time they met she showed him a set of seminude photographs of herself with umbrellas and other props. He tried not to show his aggravation. "The photographer's a professional," she explained. "I told him I wanted to be an actress and he said all actresses did nudie shots." Later she told him that the "professional" had given her drinks and drugs. "He made a pass and I freaked out."

David thought, She looks calm enough in the pictures. She looks like she's having a fine old time.

He took a night job as a bartender at a place called the Alehouse and invited her for a beer. He knew it was better to play hard to get, but he loved her and missed her and once again she'd stopped calling.

She swilled beer almost as fast as he could pour. When he held back, she yelled, "Fill 'er up, barkeep!"

He leaned across the bar and whispered, "Cindy, it's my job here, ya know? I've already given you three."

She turned to smile at a young dude who'd been eyeing her down the bar. The two of them slid together. David held his temper till he heard the guy ask for her phone number and watched as she wrote it down. He walked around the bar and said, "Gimme the phone number."

The man said, "You gotta be kidding."

"I'm not kidding!" David was shaking. "Gimme the phone number!"

Cindy piped up in her baby voice, "What's wrong, David? I didn't do anything."

The words annoyed him more than ever. "Shut up!" he told her. He thought, What kind of sucker does she take me for?

The guy said, "It's that bad, huh?"

"Yeah," David said. "It's that bad. Now gimme the number."

The guy handed it over. Cindy walked out. David said to himself, Let the bitch go.

27

Cecelia wondered why Cindy had stopped calling. David hadn't mentioned her lately and Cecelia knew better than to ask. He hadn't knocked her off any more chairs, but once or twice he'd seemed on the verge.

At last Cindy phoned. She slurred her words as she apologized for not coming over. "I love you, Cecelia," she said. "But things are . . . hard."

"Hard?"

"The Mafia. They're after me."

Cecelia asked what she meant, but Cindy said she couldn't talk. She promised to visit as soon as the heat was off.

She showed up a week later and said she'd damaged her vocal cords. It turned out to be a tragic story, so revealing about the poor child, and it took Cecelia a while to coax it out. "I want to be a singer more than anything else," Cindy finally began. "I try to be like Barbra Streisand, but . . . I'll never make it. And I've been feeling down since David and I broke up."

Cecelia suppressed a gasp. David hadn't mentioned a breakup.

Cindy fell silent, then said, "I've been kinda hating myself. You know how that feels?"

"Rawther well," Cecelia said.

"And I—I . . . something came over me and I wanted to hurt myself and . . ." Her voice trailed off.

"Go on, child," Cecelia said, reaching for her hand.

Cindy shuddered. "I—I . . . reached down my throat . . . with my fingernails, and . . . ripped at myself."

"My Lord!"

"It got infected. The doctor was afraid I'd choke to death and I had to have an operation. He did it free. For a long time I couldn't eat. That's why I haven't been over lately."

Cecelia ordered her never to do a thing like that again. "Call first, or come by. Nothing's so bad that you and I can't talk it out."

Cindy said she was still depressed. She dreaded going to Memorial Drive for Christmas dinner in a few days. Her father would ignore her and the others would gang up on her. The holiday would be one long torture.

Cecelia tried to think the problem through. It was clear that those revolting Campbells looked down on Cindy for being childish. Well, she *was* childish at times, but no less charming for it, no less bright and quick. What the parents needed, Cecelia realized, was a revised image of their prize daughter as a resourceful adult. Cecelia had an idea.

They ran through the recipe, wrote it down, repeated it back and forth. The trick, Cecelia said, was to seal in the turkey's juices. Use plenty of butter, close *every* opening with butcher's twine. Make sure the skin is icy-cold before you brush the bird with melted butter. Sift on flour, salt and pepper so that it bakes to a golden crust. And for God's sake don't break off the crust when you turn the bird over! Thrust two giant forks through the breast and into the base of the wings and lift straight up, *straight up*, keeping the forks projected at right angles to the keel of the breast. *At right angles!* Did Cindy get that?

After eight or ten dry runs, the student chef seemed ready to impress her family with the meal of a lifetime.

Cindy reported after Christmas, "They ate like hogs, came back for seconds and thirds. The turkey was tender and moist and the stuffing was perfect. But they didn't say a word of thanks. Not one word." She sounded nearly in tears.

Cecelia thought, Those obscene Campbells. They're dirt.

28

"I met this guy at Rudyard's," the young woman known as "Tina" told a friend. "One blue eye and one brown. He'd tell me, 'You really shouldn't be involved with so-and-so, ya know?' He was *so* protective. He'd say, 'Is that dude hassling you? I'll bust his face!' He told me I shouldn't be buying my own drinks or parking my own car—men should be doing those things for me. Can you imagine?

"He'd get bent when I'd wave at a friend. We were talking in Rud's and a guy asked where the rest room was. David said, 'Excuse *me?* Do you have no manners?' He berated the shit out of the guy.

"I said, 'This is a pub, for Christ's sake! . . .'

"He'll walk up to a table and say, 'Hi! How ya doing?' A few seconds later you'll hear his voice: 'Well, somebody oughta blow the motherfucker away!' Maybe he's talking about the ayatollah, or maybe just somebody in the neighborhood. He'll go, 'We gotta kill that motherfucking Khaddafi!—oh, excuse me, I'd like you to meet a friend of mine.' After a polite introduction, he'll switch right back: 'Well, fuck that goddamn sand nigger. . . .'

"He talks about guns and war. I don't know if it's from a braggadocious nature or what. I think he sees himself as the ultimate SS officer who spoke four languages and collected works of art and he would protect all the frauleins and be the ultimate strong he-man. He talked about getting in a fight at a bar and wasting somebody, but it sounded like barroom bullshit, ya know? . . .

"Sex? Oh, sure, he wants it, but he's passive. The more I held back, the more he wanted to see me. I felt like I was being tested, to see whether I would or wouldn't. If I would, it was over. A clearcut impression, ya know?

"After a few dates I realized he isn't that interesting. Like he's been overseas but he's only taken a superficial look. He's traveled but he isn't well-traveled, ya know? He didn't bother to look at how other people lived. No interest in humanity. He talked about seeing three hundred people mangled in a train wreck in Morocco and how one of the other Marines kicked a head loose from a body. He told it like a soccer game. He talked about going to a black funeral in North Carolina and seeing the dead man's mistress jump in the coffin and freak the wife and kids. Now that's pretty tragic, isn't it? He acted like it was the funniest thing he ever saw. He doesn't approve of the brothers, but I don't think he approves of too many whites, either. No sympathy, no empathy.

"He pawed me a lot, but not lovingly. It was like he held on to me so I couldn't get away. He started dropping in without phoning—another test, ya know? I'd say, 'Hey, David, please call first,' and the next day he'd be at the door.

"He finally decided I couldn't function without him. He had to open the car door to let me out—if I opened it, it was like I slapped him in the face. He said I needed him for protection. I thought, He desperately needs somebody who needs his help, somebody who's in trouble. And if you're willing to play the part with him, he'll like give you anything you want. I couldn't relate to that, so I just faded away."

29

Women came and went, none a shadow of the one he'd lost. Tina had shown promise till she started acting like a sleazy bitch. Fuck her, David said to himself, *and* her independence. There were other short-term affairs: losers, dopers, airheads, opportunists. Not one gave a shit about courtliness or gentlemanliness. Not one was interested in old-fashioned romantic love. He was twenty-five years old, and all he could find was a bunch of sluts who lived from high to high. No respect for their bodies or their human potential. Look at what he'd done for Cindy. But he couldn't think about her. Until New Year's Day he hadn't even admitted to his mother she was gone.

He spent more time at Rud's, usually talking about vio-

lence. David was against it. Violence, he preached, was for
kids and psychos. He was put off by some of the macho
assholes at the bar. They seemed to think it was great to beat
up any old son of a bitch. Gays, for instance. That was cruel
and stupid. But stomping a genuine asshole—that felt good
because it *was* good.

Sometimes he fantasized himself in the role of plain-
clothes traffic cop. "Get outa that car, mister! Who the hell
taught you to drive? *Idiot!* Gimme your license! *Now park
that piece of shit and walk!*"

Trapped in freeway traffic, he imagined that he was driving a '57 Chevy with welded angle irons all around. He'd
ram one offender after another, then say: "Oh, sorry! Did
you want to change lanes? *Well, use your turn indicator,
penis-breath!*"

One night he was forced to slap a smart punk for mouth-
ing off, and a crone at the bar called him "a menace to
society."

"I am *not* a menace to society," David insisted. "I am a
menace to the menaces to society." Later he explained to his
friends, "Most people espouse a high degree of morality, but
they don't live by it. They see something wrong and they
say, 'This is wrong,' but then they look down at their feet
and shuffle around and don't do anything. Me, I'm always
putting my ass on the line. I *live* by my values."

When he arrived at Rud's a few days later, the regulars
were whispering about "the lads from Leeds," two pasty-
faced Brits sitting in the corner. As David looked, one wiped
foam from his mouth and mumbled, "Americans are pussies!"

David flashed on a night he and some Royal Marines had
cleaned out a sailors' bar on Gibraltar. Loudmouthed York-
shiremen held no fear for him. But he didn't want to be
called a "menace to society" again. He retreated to the back
room and shot a game of darts; he'd bought an expensive
new set with tungsten points, but his game still stank.

A friend staggered in and said, "Those sons of bitches hit
me with a barstool."

"What?" David said. He strode to the enemy table and
said, "I hear you been calling Americans pussies."

"It was on me lips, mate," one of them said.

David threw a sucker punch to the jaw. The guy popped back up and caught an uppercut that had every ounce of David's 160 pounds behind it. The other Brit waded in, but he was knocked flat by a lean figure in a gold skull-and-crossbones earring. The fight was over.

The new guy slapped palms and said, "I'm Wickie. Hey, that was good clean fun!" He wore an Urban Animals emblem on a cutoff black T-shirt that revealed several tattoos. With his curly black hair, dark blue eyes and thick eyebrows and eyelashes, he looked like a Jewish James Dean. David had seen him around, a cool dude, light on his feet, reputed to be a supercocksman and one of the best skaters in Houston. When the Animals convened at midnight on the empty downtown parking ramps, Wickie was always in the thick.

David bought beers and they rapped. Wickie Randolph Weinstein turned out to be twenty-three and a former Airborne Ranger who contemptuously referred to ground soldiers as "legs." David had heard that he used hard drugs, but he found the guy cool. "Where'd you learn to fight, man?" David asked.

"Me and five other white kids were integrated into an all-black school in Jersey. It was fight or die, man."

David was surprised. "That's *my* story," he said.

"Moved here when I was seven," Wickie went on. "My father's in oil. The other kids gave me a hard time 'cause I had a funny name. I kicked the shit outa one kid, hurt him bad. They took away my pointy-toed cowboy boots."

David noticed that Wickie was outdrinking him two to one and didn't seem to show it. "I got drunk on Passover wine when I was eight," Wickie explained. "When I was bar mitzvahed I sneaked back to the pulpit and drank the chalice. I just have a talent."

In the next few weeks the two new friends met frequently and discussed tactics and logistics, firearms and ammo, anything military. Wickie insisted that David "don't know dick about guns" and talked him into subscribing to several gun publications and *Soldier of Fortune*. "They run great stuff," Wickie advised him. "Last month they had a good article on how to kill with an ax."

Sometimes they met with other friends and talked half the night. It took David's mind off Cindy. He told about educating assholes with his fists and Wickie described his first hundred parachute jumps. David told how he'd manhandled some murderous Arabs in Morocco and Wickie told about shooting at peons in Panama as a mercenary. They outdid each other in jargon: the bathroom was the "head," the wall the "bulkhead," the floor the "deck." They watched war movies; David showed his expertise by pointing out which of the German ribbons were authentic. Wickie usually arrived drunk or high. His life seemed to consist of a little carpentry and a lot of dope, booze, guns and girls. David thought, He's a great guy but he's running awful fast.

Wickie showed up drunker than usual one night and fired David's .38. The bullet passed through a pair of Jordache jeans and shattered a dish in the kitchen cabinet. "Well, shit!" Wickie enthused. "This is a nice little piece!"

Indoor target practice became a tradition at 1409 Vermont. Wickie put a round through G. Gordon Liddy's picture. David snapped a broom handle at ten paces. The place reeked of gunpowder. One night the two marksmen leaned out the back window looking for targets. A rat popped from a dumpster and Wickie fired. The rat ran up a tree. Wickie fired again, then twice more. The rat climbed on. David grabbed the gun, led his target and squeezed. As the dead rat spun to earth, David barked, "Marine Corps!"

With Wickie as his companion, he found himself smoking more pot and drinking more booze, mostly Everclear, the straight grain alcohol with "more bang for the buck." They talked about joining a foreign army, hung around gun shops, attended the annual convention of the Houston Gun Collectors, so well attended that it was held at Astroworld. David would always love Cindy, but his new interests were helping to ease the pain.

30

Gwen Sampson was worried about her old darkroom pal. Cindy seemed down in the mouth lately, tired, spacier than usual. Where were the one-woman shows, the zany impressions, the mad-genius acts in the dark Little Theater off Gwen's living room? The Comix Annex hadn't been mentioned in weeks. Neither had David West. A few bold hints produced nothing but shrugs.

One sticky afternoon Cindy sat in the darkroom chugging Coors and talking about making money. She said she'd found a way to hustle old men without putting out. "How?" Gwen asked, bemused.

"I took an ad in the paper saying I'll do nude portraits. I've done a few dirty old men. They pay pretty good."

"You paint *them* in the nude?"

"Yeah. I need the money."

A male friend of the Sampson family dropped in and Gwen introduced him. He acted as though he'd just met the Playmate of the Year. Gwen thought, I've seen this happen before. What is it about Cindy that paralyzes men? Her weight was up and she was a study in disinterest, but when she used her little-girl voice to ask for a ride home, he stumbled all over himself saying, "Well, sure!"

Late that night the phone rang. "Gwen?" Cindy said excitedly. "We made it."

"Made what?"

"Love." She explained that the man had bought her a new blouse at Foley's and then insisted on payment.

"Well, uh . . . how was it?" Gwen asked.

"Hideous! He's the worst-looking naked man I've ever seen."

"Then why'd you do it, Cindy?"

"Well, you know, I felt like I owed him something."

Cindy seemed to view the incident good-naturedly. "His tink looks like a misshapen carrot," she said between giggles. "I think we'll call him Carrot Tink. His ass is missing

—it must've been amputated. His teeth look like corn." She stopped; Gwen imagined her laying down the phone to wipe her tears. She finished, "Maybe I'll come over tomorrow and we can relive the whole horror."

Gwen thought, It's nice to hear her laugh again.

The next day Gwen greeted her with a piece of cauliflower over one eye, a canned-corn label across her mouth, and a large carrot in her hand. Cindy broke up. Gwen thought, This is more like it. This is like the old days.

A few weeks later Cindy met another of Gwen's friends, a Viet vet and respectable family man who'd come to pick up some freelance work. Gwen introduced Cindy and returned to the darkroom to finish up a shot. When she came out, Cindy and the man were leaving.

A few days later Gwen accepted a collect call from Lubbock, five hundred miles northwest. "Oh, Gwen, it's just terrible," Cindy complained. "The sex isn't going well."

"The . . . sex?"

"He had to be here for a week, so I came along."

Gwen thought, Why not? You'd already known him for ten minutes. "Well, Cindy," she asked, "what's wrong?"

"He's small, ya know? But I'm doing exercises and I've got it so tight I could take on a midget."

Gwen managed not to comment. A few days later the man returned to his wife and Cindy went into a jealous rage. She pestered the poor guy at home till the phone company issued a cease-and-desist. She painted a rag doll to resemble his daughter, splattered red stains on it and put it in his mailbox. She told Gwen that she waited down the street for hours so she could see the expression on his face.

A few days later Gwen admired a couple of silk blouses lying on the floor of Cindy's apartment on Kingston. "Take 'em," Cindy said. "I've got plenty more."

Gwen thought, I wonder if Carrot Tink bought her this one. Cindy collected blouses like postage stamps, but she never seemed to wear them. Gwen rubbed her sculptor's hands across the soft silk and encountered price tags from Foley's: $65 and $115. She couldn't resist. At least two of Cindy's blouses would get some use.

By way of repayment Gwen returned three days later with a vanload of food. Cindy seemed tottery and said she'd been drinking. While Gwen put away the groceries and straightened up, Cindy guzzled Coors. "I don't know what the hell to do about Nanny Helen," she muttered after a while. "She's getting to be a pain."

Cindy's maternal grandmother, Helen Amaya, lived in the apartment across the hall. Gwen had met her once. She'd seemed like a nice old lady, painfully ill but brave about it.

"You know what Nanny does?" Cindy asked in her mean, raspy voice. "She goes out on her balcony and peeks in here when I'm with guys. She's a dirty old woman."

Gwen watched anxiously as Cindy popped another can. "Men knock on my door," she continued in the same growl, "and Nanny comes out in a negligee and tries to entice 'em."

Even for Cindy, Gwen thought, that sounds like a fairy story. She realized that her friend had been sounding more disturbed lately. Once it had seemed she had two personalities, but alcohol was bringing out more.

"I'm sick of her spying on me," Cindy went on. "I'm gonna get rid of her."

"How?" Gwen asked.

"I'm gonna kick her out. It's the first goddamn thing I'm gonna do when I get ownership."

Gwen wondered how she intended to get ownership when James Campbell had deeded the quadruplex to all four sisters. Well, she thought, poor Cindy hasn't been making much sense lately. That Coors sure has a loud mouth.

31

Cecelia West decided to find out why she hadn't been hearing from her good friend Cindy. She had a handy excuse for dropping in; she'd made some sketches of possible renovations to the Kingston fourplex and wanted Cindy to check them out. She smelled the room before the door opened.

The child was a sight. Her hips had broadened and her face was pale and puffy. A shedding dog and a bony cat stared through rheumy eyes as they grazed among their own deposits scattered on the rug along with wads of used Kleenexes and a Kotex pad.

"Honey," Cecelia said, "you've got to flush those down the toilet."

"You do?" Cindy said. "My mother just dropped them."

Cindy seemed ill at ease, and Cecelia wondered if it had anything to do with the men's boots propped against a suitcase in the corner. The poor child complained that her teeth were loose: "Sometimes my mouth fills with blood."

Cecelia didn't have to ask what she'd been eating; the floor was littered with junk-food wrappings. "Why, child," said the country doctor's granddaughter, "you've got scurvy!"

Cindy gnawed at her knuckle and said, "I'll be all right." Cecelia just wanted to cry.

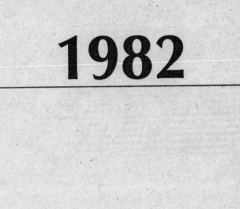

1982

32

1987

By the spring of 1982 David hadn't seen Cindy in several months. Every few weeks she called to chat or ask a favor, but she didn't invite him to her apartment and didn't encourage return calls. Once or twice a man answered and David hung up. Maybe it was a wrong number. He preferred not to know.

He no longer found it necessary to bay at the moon and toke on the analgesic herb available at the floating midnight bazaars on Westheimer. He told himself, David West is going to survive Cindy Ray after all.

He embarked on a new program of self-improvement and opened it with a lecture to himself: "Goddamn it, David, when you went into boot camp you were pudgy, but you used your will power and worked out and changed yourself. Goddamn it, man, do it again!"

Cindy called to ask a favor. Strictly as an act of kindness she said, she'd taken in two bums in their forties. It had worked out for a night or two, but they'd been in her apartment for two months now and refused to leave. "Oh, David," she cried in her tiny voice. "I'm a prisoner in my own home." She said they were armed.

David grinned and thought, She's got the street smarts of a retarded nun. Who else would give two middle-aged squatters a flop and expect them to behave?

He began to organize Operation Eviction. He tried recruiting Wickie, but he wasn't around. He went downstairs and separated his good tenant Jim Daggett from the pet wolves that he raised. Armed with a pistol and a shotgun, the two friends drove to Cindy's apartment in David's Capri.

He felt bad when he saw his old love. Her face had gone soft and her weight was up—maybe 150, he guessed. She was still pretty, but a far cry from the wonder woman he'd seen at Christmas. He thought, How sad, but . . . it's not my prob.

The squatters were out for the evening. David threw their gear in the hall. A while later a male voice yelled through the door, "What's the deal?"

David and Daggett crouched behind the door as Cindy yelled in a coarse voice, "The deal is you're gone, ya know?" There was no argument.

Two days later David dropped in to see if the deadbeats had returned. No, Cindy said, and she owed it all to him. The place smelled better, thanks to Cecelia. She'd made another visit on her trike and helped clean up. The little apartment smelled of Lysol and perfume. He wondered how long it would last.

Cindy seemed friendly, but she refused to discuss the evictees or any other men in her life. That, she said, was *her* business. Of course David was always welcome to drop in. *More* than welcome.

She blinked her hazel eyes and kissed him good night. It felt like old times. He hadn't realized how much he missed her.

33

Cindy Ray's older sister, Betty Hinds, was worried about their mother. Betty lived in Austin, 150 miles west of Houston, but she called her parents every week. In their most recent talks, Virginia Campbell had sounded upset, anxious. Betty wondered why.

At thirty, the second-oldest Campbell daughter had a B.S. in zoology from the University of Texas and a scientist's curiosity. With her wide-set brown eyes and heart-shaped face, she radiated the sweet naïveté of a yellowed old photograph, but the look was an illusion. Betty had always been considered the strongest and most determined of the four sisters. She went right to work diagnosing this latest problem.

She suspected a Cindy connection; there usually was.

Betty couldn't remember a time when her mother and father hadn't lived for their children, Cindy included, but their love and kindness hadn't always been reciprocated. Back when all four daughters had lived at home, their parents had taken them everywhere: five trips to Disneyland in as many years; frequent visits to Houston's Hermann Park Zoo (Cindy loved the seals) and the Astrodome and Astroworld and the Johnson Space Center; weekend trips to Lake Livingston, the Alamo, Six Flags Over Texas, Galveston Bay, Padre Island—the wonders of the world as viewed from Houston.

Now that they were grown, oldest sister Michelle and next-oldest Betty phoned home every week, and so did the baby, Jamie, checking in from Knoxville, where she had decided to study broadcasting. The fourth sister, Cindy, seldom called except to ask for money or help. Nor did she hesitate to phone Betty or Michelle long-distance collect. Neither complained. Cindy had been a joint reclamation project for twenty years.

After a little sleuthing around, the persistent Betty began to sniff out the family's latest problem. Cindy was causing trouble between Mother and Daddy again. They'd tolerated her egocentricities since childhood, but James had finally put his foot down. He still loved Cindy, he told his wife, but he felt she'd become a parasite and it was partially their own fault for indulging her. One night he snapped, "Cindy's driving me crazy!" and stormed out of the house. After a few hours he returned and swore he would never talk to his daughter again.

Her mother still slipped Cindy money, Betty learned, but Daddy stayed true to his decision. At the office he would ignore the daughter who'd always bragged that she was his pet. The treatment was harsh, but Betty and the other sisters talked the matter over and decided she'd brought it on herself.

When Jamie came home from Knoxville for spring break, she confided to Betty that their mother had told her, "Jamie, stay away from Cindy and David West. Promise me! They want to ruin you."

Betty wasn't surprised to find that Mother didn't want to discuss the remark. "It's just something that slipped out," she explained. "But I'll tell you this, Betty. If the house fell on us and we all died, Cindy wouldn't care one bit." She admitted that she was afraid of her own daughter. "I can't tell you the details. I won't tell one of my children how bad another one is. For a long time I just thought she had problems, and it almost led to a divorce between your father and me. He saw what she was like long before I did."

Betty thought about West. Could he really be a threat to Jamie, or had Mother been imagining things? Betty had had strange feelings about Cindy's old boyfriend ever since December. She'd been standing next to the family Christmas tree looking out the picture window toward Memorial Drive. A car pulled in; Cindy emerged and trudged up the tree-shrouded driveway. The driver appeared as a faint outline, his face turned toward the house in the dying afternoon light. Betty knew that there'd been trouble and West wasn't allowed inside. For several minutes he stared in her direction, and she could feel his envy and hatred. God, she thought, that guy could be dangerous. Then she admonished herself: Betty, you're acting like a child! Cindy's brought home plenty of creepy guys, and we're still alive, aren't we?

That whole holiday season had seemed different. It started with mounds of gifts for Cindy's two little boys. Her parents were raising them as their own; the boys called them "Mother" and "Daddy." Cindy didn't seem to mind and hardly saw them anymore.

Betty remembered Cindy's delectable Christmas turkey. What a surprise! She could still hear Daddy's robust voice: "Cindy, honey, when I was a little fella, I thought the best turkey dinners came from Cross Plains, Texas. But this takes the gold ribbon. Now please, honey—don't say anythang about this in Cross Plains!" Cindy seemed to enjoy being the cynosure. It wasn't her usual role.

Betty also recalled how relieved they'd all been when her mother had gone to the hospital and learned that the lump on her breast was benign. Daddy was so happy that he bought her a new Cadillac and promised a trip to the Alps. They planned to leave in May.

As the date approached, Betty was pleased to see that her mother seemed to be taking a more realistic approach toward Cindy. She still provided small handouts—"If I didn't, she'd starve"—but she turned down the incessant demands for designer jeans, for Italian silk blouses to go with the unworn ones in her closet, for more shopping trips to the Galleria.

Betty knew that Virginia had also warned Cindy that certain tenants in the Kingston fourplex were complaining about the way she lived. Tidy up, Mother warned, or face the consequences. And she'd resumed her pressure on Cindy to make something of herself, starting by looking for work.

Betty thought, At last they're treating her like an independent adult. Let's see if she can handle it.

34

Attorney J. Robert Harris was happy that his friends James and Virginia Campbell would be traveling to Europe with him and his wife. Harris, Campbell and several other solo practitioners shared a wing of the downtown Houston Bar Center, an unstylish old lump in the shadow of dazzling towers of silver and onyx and teal thrown up by the moguls of oil.

Harris knew Campbell as a clever man, *sui generis,* who used a down-home persona to beat the slickers at their own games. No one called him James or Jim; around the unglamorous law office he was plain "Campbell." He strolled the courthouse corridors in a white Panama hat and rumpled pants that usually clashed with his coat. His friend Jim Brannon once said, "Campbell, are you going in front of a jury dressed like that? Come on! Can't you look like if they're gonna award you money, you'll at least know how to spend it?"

Bob Harris, an affable man whose half-glasses and gray brush moustache made him resemble a retired British major, knew that it never bothered a Houston jury if your shirttail hung out or your cowboy boots were worn. Might even help, especially if you had Campbell's gift for making everybody feel sorry for your client. The country-boy lawyer took old-dog cases and milked every dime. He called himself a "sore-back lawyer" and told a friend, "Y'all can have your big glamorous cases. All I ask is a Nigra with a sore back."

Embittered insurance lawyers referred to Campbell and a close colleague as "Snake and Slime," but Bob Harris considered the names sour grapes. Campbell ran off skeins of modest victories and never broke a sweat. He shunned law libraries and refused to spend weekends preparing for Monday openings. "Gimme the file, hon," the other lawyers would hear him say on his way out the door. An hour or two later he would return to the office puffing a victory cigar.

One day Harris ran into him in a courthouse corridor and asked, "What kind of case are you trying today, Campbell?"

"I don't know," the tall lawyer said as he ambled along. "I haven't looked at the file yet."

Just thinking about his antics brought a grin to Harris's face. At night lawyers sat around the Inns of Court Club exchanging tales of Campbell. At a deposition the opposing lawyer backed into the hall to illustrate a point about distance, and Campbell locked him out. "Goddamn it, Campbell!" the irate man yelled. "I'm gonna get your case dismissed!" After a few minutes the flustered man was allowed to return.

"Don't know what you're het up about, son," Campbell said. "We got a lotta questions answered while you were gone."

In court an angry lawyer complained, "Your Honor, let the record reflect that Mr. Campbell has just wadded up Plaintiff's Exhibit Number Two and thrown it in the trash can."

"I don't know what he's talking about," Campbell said as he waved the exhibit. "Here's Plaintiff's Two." He'd discarded a blank page.

Opponents who took James Campbell for a buffoon found themselves cut off at the knees. His rusticity hid the fact that he'd earned his first university degree at an age when most students were still in high school. He took his law practice seriously enough to study psychology on the side. As a young lawyer he'd hung around the Alley Theatre to sharpen his acting skills.

He was the only occupant of the suite who drastically limited his own practice. He wouldn't touch multimillion-dollar product liability cases where there might be three opposition lawyers and twenty depositions to take and a half-dozen expert witnesses. He routinely "fired" difficult clients. He seemed to know exactly how big a caseload it took to maintain a relaxed life on Memorial Drive, send his girls to college, take care of his two young "sons" and secure his old age. He didn't party, seldom drank, never entertained, and went straight home from work. The only signs that he was a millionaire were his Cadillac and his house. Fred Lewis, a colleague down the hall, was bemused by the Campbells' mom-and-pop office: "On a scale of one to ten, where ten would be a corporation office with statuary from Florence and one would be a mobile home, Campbell's office is a two." The place was a study in polyester and Naugahyde. The rug looked like a reject from a beach house. The plant was plastic.

Bob Harris regarded his friend Campbell as the best trickster and dissimulator he'd ever known—wry, sly, and totally unpredictable. He enjoyed challenging his friends with brain twisters as hard to grasp as the ribbon of smoke from his mangled cigar. "Here's a new one," he would say, drawing the others around the receptionist's desk. "I got it out of the *New York Times,* solved it in eleven minutes. Let's see how long y'all take. A man's uncle marries his former wife's second cousin. . . ." Then he would heckle the other lawyers as they tried to figure it out.

Or he would stroll into the office and say, "Y'all listen up now. If a boy and a half ate a duck and a half in an hour and a half—*got it so far?*—what's the capital of North Dakota?"

His only exercise seemed to be golf. He thought it a great joke to improve his lie, cheat on his score, nudge enemy

balls into the rough. He jiggled his keys when opponents
leaned over to putt. If he lost a ball, he would drop another
and yell, "Found it!" His partners figured his antics were
worth eight strokes a game.

The lawyers in the suite didn't know Virginia Campbell as
well as they knew James, although they saw her at her desk
every day. She was a dark-haired Wisconsin woman of fifty-
five whom Campbell had met and married when they were
in college in Los Angeles. Her head barely came to her husband's chin.

To Bob and Sue Harris, Virginia came across as a hard
worker with a sense of humor to match her husband's. She
had a big smile and the deepest blue eyes and a friendly face
that she'd tried to improve with plastic surgery. Scoliosis
and twenty years of typing had tipped her forward, but few
noticed. She liked to wear baubles, none expensive. Like
Campbell she seemed mainly interested in her grandsons—
took them to movies, stuffed them with Big Macs and Ken-
tucky Fried Chicken. Both Campbells were in hog heaven
with the only "sons" they'd ever had.

Virginia ran the office, typed briefs at high speed, directed
traffic, arranged her husband's calendar, mailed the bills and
solved puzzles with her right hand while holding the phone
with her left. She told Sue Harris that James didn't want her
to work, "but I just have to. I can't stand being cooped up at
home." Her efficiency enabled Campbell to disappear now
and then for golf.

Over the years the Harrises had met all four Campbell
daughters. Cynthia seemed to be the only problem. She was
viewed by the other lawyers as *non compos mentis*. She ignored their friendly greetings and rushed away as though
threatened. Recently Campbell had run her out of his office
and told Bob Harris that he'd cut her off financially—"she's
been bleeding us white." A few weeks later he bought a .38
and visited a pistol range to sharpen up his eye. He kept the
weapon under his pillow till he found young Matthew spinning the cylinder. Then he bought a shotgun.

These days, Harris noticed, Cindy waited till her father

was away to visit the office. Sometimes she sat outside for hours. Once or twice mother and daughter had words; Virginia was always the one who backed down.

Well, Harris said to himself, it'll do them good to get away to Europe for a while. Campbell can forget his weird daughter and his sore-back cases and relax for a few weeks in the Alps. We always have a hell of a time with the Campbells.

35

"Look," David told Cindy on the phone, "what do you want Mom and me to do? We can't be with you all the time. Why don't you just get your shit together?"

She'd been calling at all hours to tell him her troubles. The unexpected attention was unnerving. His wounds were barely healed and he didn't want more. He felt like asking, *What about your pals at the Comix Annex? Where are they now that you need them?*

Knowing he was taking a risk, he dropped in to buoy her up. He tried out his benign old therapies—provided focused attention, complimented her, bestowed unconditional positive regard. She seemed to melt. "David," she said, "you were right about the guys at the Workshop. They were just chasing my ass. Oh, David, you were right about so many things. . . ."

When she finished her *mea culpa* he said, "Cindy, look at you. You've started falling apart again. You're gaining weight, you look like shit. Why can't you get a job and take care of yourself?" She stuck out her heavy lower lip. "You look like when we first met," he went on. "Dirty clothes, greasy hair, chain-smoking. Your posture's terrible. Your whole bearing's different. Look how your hands shake! What's happened to you?"

"I couldn't support myself," she said. "I had to go to my parents. And they . . . they started all over again."

"You mean . . . your father?"

"Yes."

He couldn't believe it. "Your mom, too?"

"Yes."

He didn't know what to say. Would they ever let her up? She said, "They're doing it to me again. Mother and Daddy. My sisters. Nanny Helen. The same old things. . . ."

It didn't make sense. Her mother and father lived way out on Memorial. Her two older sisters lived in Austin, and Jamie was in Knoxville. The grandmother lived in the Kingston apartments, but she was old and infirm. What "same old things" could the family be doing to Cindy? He reminded himself that she'd always had a touch of paranoia. Maybe she was just feeling sorry for herself. She'd always had a touch of that, too.

He steered her off the subject of her family. It was always such a bummer.

A few nights later she knocked on his door. "Cindy!" he said, blinking his bicolored eyes. "Hey, come in!"

She settled at his feet and began complaining about the "head trip" her family was doing on her. She talked fast, her hazel eyes flaring with anger. "Nanny Helen's helping them. She goes through my stuff. She sneaks in and turns on the water. She made it overflow into the apartment downstairs and they had to repaint." Her shoulders shook. "Nanny comes in and turns on the gas and the lights. She calls mother and says, 'Cindy did it!' And Mother and Daddy say, 'Cindy, you're screwing up again!' "

David thought, It all sounds like Looney Tunes, but if you're a crazy person in a crazy family, then Looney Tunes is the norm. He wondered why the Campbells would try to *Gaslight* her. He remembered the movie and the eerie attacks on Ingrid Bergman's sanity: candles relighting themselves, faucets turning on, noises in the night. Cindy was close enough to the edge already.

She returned to his house a few nights later, had a few drinks and slept over for the first time in ages. It was better than the old days. She acted like his slave, and when she allowed him to enter her body, she didn't call him Daddy.

But afterward she seemed agitated. "David," she said, "I have to tell you something."

"What?"

"It's . . . Daddy. He's, uh, coming on to me again."

He thought, Oh, shit. I can't handle this. It's too goddamn revolting. It's fucking *torture*.

"Cindy," he said, "I'd rawther just sleep. Okay?"

She returned to the subject in the morning. "No more," he begged her.

A few days later he arrived home to find her sitting next to a scattering of butts on his stairs. Her bare feet were tucked under her body, her hair was a mess, and she wore no make-up. Everything about her said defeat; she reminded him of the Cindy he'd met at Crooker Center a year and a half ago. He could tell she was back for good. It made him glad and sad.

As he helped her up the wooden stairs, she began another monologue in a tiny voice. She told him how right he'd been about the other men, the health program, the diet, looking for a job, accepting responsibility. She also told him that her father was still bothering her.

David drove to Kingston for her things. As the days went by, she kept griping about her parents. It wasn't only her father, she told him. Her mother was abusive, too, worse than ever.

He thought, Maybe I should just sit her down and say, Cindy, let's get your story straight. Exactly what is your father doing to you? Is it sex again? *Tell me what's happening!* But he couldn't stand another description of James Campbell thrusting himself into his own daughter, and—far worse—Cindy thrusting back.

He brooded. He thought, That goddamn family, they'll never leave her alone. They'll be messing with her head as long as they're alive, making her crazy. And that father. He's, he's . . .

He couldn't find words. The man wasn't good enough to be called a snake. Snakes didn't fuck their daughters.

36

Betty Campbell Hinds had a husband and child to look after and a job as a state biologist in Austin, but on the weekend before her parents were scheduled to leave for Europe, she dropped everything and sped to Houston on a premonition of horror. At the end of the three-hour drive, she wondered what had made her so apprehensive. Mother seemed preoccupied, but that was only natural on the eve of a trip. Daddy was playing golf. Betty felt foolish but happy. It was always so nice to see them.

Betty asked for the latest in the continuing saga of Cindy. Was she still living like a hermit and giving Nanny Helen fits? A troubled look crossed her mother's face. Or was it fright? She said, "I don't want to talk about it." She'd been saying that for months, but this time she seemed emphatic.

Betty decided that nothing had changed. Or ever would. She herself had a word for her younger sister. The word was "evil."

That night she slept in her childhood room, then kissed her parents good-by on Sunday and drove back home between double carpets of bluebonnets. She still felt anxious, but she knew it was irrational. Still, she wished mother hadn't mentioned the dream about a blond man coming into their bedroom and killing them.

37

David and Cindy sat in the weak breeze from one of his rackety air conditioners. The May temperature stood at ninety-one degrees. In the heat his rotting house smelled like three feet deep in a dumpster.

Cindy lowered her can of Pearl to light another cigarette. The flare of the match illuminated her face. God, he thought, she was so beautiful six months ago. She lifted herself from the floor and sank onto the couch next to him, mumbling about "Mother and Daddy." He thought, Oh, Christ, not again.

"David," she said, "remember you said if anybody did something bad like that to you, you'd, uh . . . kill 'em?"

Sure he remembered. It was just talk, though, and a long time back. He nodded.

"Well," she said. "I think you're right. We should."

He thought, Of course I'm right. People like them don't deserve to live.

She said, "It's the only way I'll ever be free." When he didn't respond, she said, "David, you know they deserve it. Think about what they've done to me." She was talking fast now. "Will you . . . will you do it?"

He turned and looked. Her lips were tight, straight. He thought, Holy shit, she's serious. "Whoa!" he said. "I wasn't volunteering. I just said that if somebody was doing that to me, I'd kill 'em."

"But David—"

"If you killed 'em, I sure as hell wouldn't blame you."

She walked to the window and looked out. "I couldn't do that," she said.

"Yes you could."

She looked over her shoulder at him. "I wouldn't know how."

David thought, Well, *I* sure as hell know how. He'd studied killing in military school and the Marine Corps, read articles about it in *Soldier of Fortune*, discussed the subject with Wickie and others at Rud's. All his life he'd been Captain Justice, an expert on dealing with assholes. But . . . a cold-blooded killing?

He stood up. "I'll tell *you* how to do it," he said, "but I wouldn't think of doing it myself. You get a gun that's not traceable. You pick a time and place where there's no witnesses. You getcha an alibi. You make damn sure you don't leave any fucking evidence. You wear gloves. And if there's any possibility of being seen, you wear a disguise. . . ."

She asked a few questions. After a while he began to realize that the tone of their conversation was veering from the hypothetical toward the real. She was concentrating, puffing rapidly on her cigarette. Her beer was turning flat.

"You're right, David," she said. "That's how we can do it."

He said to himself, Hey, skip the *we* shit! She was right on one count, though. Her father deserved execution.

"I didn't say I'd do it," he told her. "That's a big trip, ya know?"

She grabbed his arm and he felt her nails dig into the skin. "Think about it," she said. "Look at me. *Look at me!*" Her eyes glittered. "It's happening again! Think what they're doing to me."

He halfway listened as she grew more excited. He'd concluded long ago that her story was essentially true. She wasn't the one who'd planted the first information about incest; in fact, she'd shied from the subject. If it had been solely up to her, he would never have learned what her father was doing to her. Cecelia had made the awful diagnosis and Cindy had only confirmed it under pressure.

When she finally wound down, he said, "Well, frankly, I can see killing him, ya know? I got no problems with that at all. But . . . your mother?" He was thinking that Mrs. Campbell was kind of a freaky bitch, but just because somebody locks you in the closet, you don't kill 'em.

Cindy said, "Well, think of everything she's done to me. She'd say, 'Silence is golden,' and slap me. She wanted me to drown. She's part of the whole damn thing, always fucking with me, coming at me. She'd never let me alone even if he was gone."

He said he needed time to think about it.

After several days he still couldn't decide. The mother was the problem. She was a slimeball, all right, but did she deserve to be killed?

Cindy told him, "Listen, I'm liable to inherit some money, maybe three or four million dollars. You can have half." She said they had to kill her mother to keep her from inheriting the whole estate.

David thought, I'm not a fucking hit man. "If I do it," he snapped, "it'll be for the principle, not for the money." She stared hard as though she wanted an answer. He said, "Gimme a few more days."

Slowly he worked his way through her proposal, examining each aspect the way his father studied chess. He started with the fundamental fact that he and Cindy were bound to each other forever. Otherwise, why would she have returned and offered herself all over again? She was still reluctant about letting him penetrate, but it happened occasionally. Her eyes would glaze over and she'd switch to a foreign accent or talk like a little girl, and then she'd be willing, even eager. That was the trip her father laid on her. He wondered if she would ever change. Sure she would. They were working on it.

Well, then, he told himself, if we're committed to each other, then her pain and shame are mine. Every human being has a right to live a normal existence. If I'm really a moral person, if I've got the strength of my convictions, I'll secure that fundamental right for her. There's no excuse not to, especially since I'm not doing it for the money. Besides, it feels . . . right.

He thought, She's turning back into a chain-smoking beer-sucking wreck. Her parents dragged her down before and they're dragging her down now. Her words repeated in his mind, *They're doing it again.* He thought, Sick, sick, *sick.* . . .

He could forgive Cindy. She'd only reacted to pressure. That fucking creepo had rammed it to her when she was too small to fight him off. It was worse than beating a newborn. How could a twelve-year-old girl hold off a full-grown man who kicked down doors? No, it wasn't Cindy's fault. Campbell could use his money and power and legal tricks to get away with his crimes, and not a goddamn thing could be done about it. How unjust!

But there were practical problems. Did he have the balls? The stomach? Brave men fainted at the sight of blood. He cast his thoughts back to the train wreck in Morocco, the body parts strewn all over the desert, the disemboweled children. He hadn't even thrown up. He thought about the car accident he'd seen near Camp Lejeune. The driver's nose was gone; his teeth were embedded in reddish pulp; his tongue looked as though he'd licked a chain saw. The man tried to speak through a bubble of blood and dirt and hair. David had pulled him away from the burning car and sat with him till the ambulance arrived.

Now he said to himself, I've stood up to blood and gore. I can handle death. But can I *inflict* it? He decided he needed some guidance.

38

Wickie Randolph Weinstein gunned his motorcycle into the backyard and slalomed to a stop. "Hey, Dave!" he yelled.

"Ya know, Wickie," Dave said when the engine noise died, "you'd be all right if you didn't dress so fucking weird." Wickie thought, Weird? How can a guy with different-colored eyes tell me I look weird?

Wickie's curly dark hair was in a Mohawk. He wore tight jeans with an ammo belt, a pair of jump boots in a high gleam, and one golden earring. He was bare above the waist. "Why're you dressed like that, man?" Dave asked.

"I'm making a fucking statement, I guess. Who knows?"

"You remind me of one of those low-life sleazebuckets."

Wickie grinned and said, "Well, fuck you, too!"

Dave grabbed his arm. "C'mon, let's take a walk. I gotta ask you something." Wickie parked his bike and they strolled toward Rud's. "You know those assholes I've been telling you about?"

"Which assholes?" There were quite a few of them in Dave's life.

Dave said, "Didn't I tell you about a coupla people that're giving me a hard time? The, uh, man and woman?"

Wickie tried to remember. Yeah, Dave had been griping about some rich punks who pissed him off. Hadn't mentioned their names—or maybe he had. Each day Wickie was becoming hazier about details. There were big outs in his memory bank and he was beginning to realize he had to cut down on booze and dope. Maybe next week . . .

"You ever killed anyone?" Dave was asking.

"No."

"Well, would you?"

In the context of some of their other dialogues, the question wasn't surprising. They frequently sat at Rudyard's till closing discussing the best ways to destroy a square block of downtown Houston or Boston or New York. "Yes," he answered without hesitation, "I would." He thought for a second. "But it would depend. If I was in combat, no problem."

"Have you ever, ya know, shot at anyone?"

"Yeah. Lotsa people."

"Ever hit any?"

"Some." It wasn't exactly true. Once he'd been burned on a Buick and shot up the guy's house, but nobody was home. And he'd been arrested for discharging a firearm in the city limits, but Houstonians did that all the time.

Dave asked, "When?"

"Just. . . . growing up."

"But you didn't kill anybody?"

"No, Dave," Wickie answered patiently. "I didn't kill anybody."

They walked past Rud's toward noisy Westheimer Road.

"Where're we going, man?" Wickie asked above the traffic noise.

"No place. I just want to talk. Listen, man, would you assassinate somebody for money?"

"Well, I don't know. It would depend on how I felt about it."

Dave went on about moral issues. What if the victims deserved to die? What if they were criminals themselves, hideous monsters, deformed vermin who destroyed lives?

"If I was doing it for money," Wickie answered, "I guess the money would motivate me and I wouldn't care what they were like. But no way I could kill anybody just for money."

"Neither could I, ya know?" Dave said quickly. "There'd have to be a hell of a lot better reason than that."

After a while Dave said he didn't think he would have a problem killing dope dealers, especially the ones who sold to kids. He wasn't crazy about blacks, either; he'd been fighting them since childhood. Rapists had it coming, he said. So did child abusers. "If you had to assassinate somebody," he asked, "how would you do it?"

Wickie thought, He's sure hipped on this subject. "Well, let's see," he said. "First, wear a mask. Take a forty-five and lots of loaded magazines for backup. Have no contact whatsoever with the person—no touching, nothing. Just, ya know, hit and run. Shoot him twice in the chest and once in the head to make sure." He'd learned about *coups de grace* in NATO war games as an Airborne Ranger.

"How about the getaway?"

"Don't leave a thing behind. Destroy your shoes and clothes so the fibers can't be traced. Strip completely. If you use a car, vacuum it. Cut the gun into little pieces and throw each piece in a different area. Preferably in water."

They doubled back toward Dave's house on Vermont and began discussing specific weapons. Wickie had owned Uzis and MC-10s, but Dave seemed interested in something smaller. He asked, "You got a pistol you want to sell?"

Wickie said, "Yeah. A Colt forty-five."

Dave rubbed his chin. "I hate that fucking nineteen-eleven. We had 'em in the Marines. To me they're just big clunky things that rattle and jam. I'd, ya know, hate to trust my life to one."

"You don't know dick about guns, Dave," Wickie said. "This is a Combat Commander. It's shorter than the nineteen-eleven. It's got a satin nickel finish like textured silver. Rubber grips, combat sights—"

Dave interrupted. "The last time I handled a forty-five, we were fam-firing on a range in Morocco. Somebody threw up cans and I hit very few, ya know? I'll bet you couldn't hit the inside of the Astrodome with your fucking Combat Commander."

"I had it customized and rebored, accurized. It makes patterns like a target pistol."

"What's it worth?"

"Five hundred."

Dave said, "Well, I'll tell ya. I need a gun, but I don't want a forty-five. Uh, how many rounds does it hold?"

"One in the chamber, six in the magazine. I'd use silver-tips."

"Silvertips?" The look on Dave's face showed he'd never heard of them.

"Sorta like those Devastators that Hinckley used. It's a hollowpoint with a soft blob in the middle, covered all over with silver. It splatters and explodes. *Destructo!* There's no ballistics."

Back at the house, Wickie remounted his bike. "A forty-five seems like overkill," Dave was saying. "All the pros use twenty-twos. You don't need a hog-ass weapon for this kind of job."

"Maybe not," Wickie said as he kicked at the starter. "But it's sure as shit certain."

39

"Have you thought about it?" Cindy asked him again. "About . . . my idea?"

David almost laughed. He hadn't thought about anything else. "Don't pressure me," he said.

His conscience still held him back. The voice droned in his brain: David, this isn't right. You can't just go out there and kill these people, ya know . . . ?

Sweltering on his black couch, he gave himself a pep talk. You've fully justified this thing intellectually. The Campbells don't have the intrinsic value of a roach. The authorities can't punish them because the old man has too much power. So what's left? Execution, of course. It's like *Death Wish.* The killer had to step outside the law to prevent greater injustices. The result was *right.*

He told himself, Cindy's mother isn't so bad, but does she deserve to inherit all that money? Fuck no! She's always treated Cindy like shit. If we eliminate them, we won't just be righting wrong or taking revenge—we'll be saving a good life by eliminating two rotten ones. It's pruning apples.

He felt himself edging her way. He decided that the voice

in his head wasn't conscience; it was fear. And fear was weakness. In military school and the Marines he'd been taught that brave men felt fear but overcame it. He said to himself, Cindy's at the mercy of monsters and it's my duty to help her. He couldn't call himself a man if he abandoned a person he loved more than he loved himself. He'd put so much into her. She was more than an extension of his ego. She was *him.*

He asked himself, Why be afraid of getting caught? That's the coward speaking. Quit confusing conscience with fear.

He was facing his bookcase when he heard the familiar sound of bare feet slapping the wood floor. It was evening and hot as hell. "David," she said, "have you decided?" Her voice was low, soft.

He said, "Tell me again what he did."

He felt her breasts against his back. "Daddy came up behind me," she murmured in his ear. "My hair fell over my shoulders. He pulled it back and stroked it. He put his hands on my shoulders and told me I'm pretty. . . ."

He couldn't see her, but her voice was hypnotic. "He stroked my breast. I was aroused, confused. He told me, 'It's okay, it's okay. You're a good girl. You're Daddy's little girl. It's okay 'cause it's Daddy.' Then he . . . put me on the bed."

David compressed his lips. The twice-told tale angered him even more this time. She whispered: "Think how many times he did that to me. And my mother—she's still after me. She'll never leave me alone, bitching at me, embarrassing me in front of my sisters, giving them things and not giving me things."

He turned around. Her eyes looked black in the shadows. He thought, Knowing what I know, seeing the pain and sickness in those eyes, what choice do I have?

"Okay," he said. "I'll do it."

He drove her to the house on Memorial with instructions to check the lights and unlock a ground-floor window. She would sleep over and he would pick her up in the morning. At 6 P.M. on Tuesday, June 8, he dropped her off at the head

of the driveway. Her parents were due back from Europe the
next night.

A few hours later she phoned him from the big house and
mentioned that the maid had seen her fooling with the windows. "But don't worry about it, David," she said. "It's
okay."

He wondered why the *pinche puta* had been snooping
around. It wasn't the best start for the perfect crime.

40

Maria Cruz Bravo Gonzales wracked her brain trying to
make sense of Cindy's strange visit. Like so many things
about the problem child, it came under the phrase *poco loco*.

The maid was fifty-eight, a dour, adobe-colored woman
whose album bulged with photos accumulated since she'd
come to live with the Campbells in September 1977. When
friends asked how she remembered the exact date, she explained, "I never thought I would come to such a home."
She was intensely superstitious and as devoted to the two
little boys as Señor and Señora Campbell.

She wished she felt the same about the boys' natural
mother. Year after year Maria had watched in mute disapproval as Cindy extracted cash, clothes, food, *todo,* from her
mother. The maid had only a little *inglés,* but it wasn't hard
to understand the bitter words that passed between the elder
Campbells about Cindy, or the loud harangues when daughter attacked Mother with everything but her fists. Lately
Mr. James had stopped talking to Cindy altogether. Maria
admired him for that.

A few months back Mrs. Virginia had told her that Cindy
was returning home for good, and Maria cried as she explained that she would have to leave. The *señor* said he
would leave, too. The next day Mrs. Virginia said, "My
husband and you mean more to me, Maria. Cindy's my
daughter, but she's trouble." Maria had never heard her talk
like that. And Cindy hadn't moved in after all.

Now the maid thought about the evil one's visit the day before. Maria had peeked out and seen her walking along the overgrown driveway with shoes in hand. Cindy stepped into the flower bed and began trying the first-floor windows. After failing with several, she opened the window to the boys' room. *Por qué?*

Maria ran outside. "Cindy, don't do that!" she called in Spanish. "I'll let you in."

Cindy appeared annoyed. "It's okay," she said. "It's *okay, Maria!*"

The maid followed the delinquent into the house. Cindy bedded down on the sofa in the den. She left on Wednesday with two bags of groceries and household goods. Maria checked and found the window of the boys' room unlocked. She locked it and made a mental note to check the windows every day. She wondered if she should tell the Campbells about their daughter's odd behavior when they got home. No, she decided. It wasn't that odd for Cindy.

She almost forgot the incident in her joy late that night. *Dios mío,* she said to herself, they're back! Every day since the *señor* and *señora* had left, Maria had lit candles in her apartment above the detached garage. Every night she'd asked the Virgin to cleanse the wayward Cindy's heart and bring peace to Mrs. Virginia after so much torment.

The *señora* looked drawn, haggard. Maria wondered if Cindy had met the plane.

Two mornings later, on Friday, June 11, the maid tried not to listen as Cindy berated her mother in a loud voice. Mrs. Virginia had always been *tímida,* slow to stand up for herself, but Maria couldn't imagine why she put up with such treatment. She seemed in mortal fear—but of what? Her own flesh and blood? Better to show firmness, better to order Cindy away till she learned courtesy, or send her to the priest to learn respect. But of course Maria would never give such advice unless asked.

Late Friday afternoon Mrs. Virginia took her aside and said in Tex-Mex: "Tomorrow's payday, Maria, but no *dinero* for you till next week, 'cause it's *mucho necesario* that I take

Cindy downtown to the stores tomorrow. Cindy is very mean. *Mucha problema* for me." She seemed upset.

Maria thought, *Mamacita,* I would give up all my paydays to save you from your child. . . .

Overnight Friday and into the early hours of Saturday morning, Maria listened to her favorite Spanish-language station and said her beads. She couldn't stop thinking about Cindy. The *señora* had continued giving her handouts behind Mr. James's back, but no amount seemed enough. Cindy sneaked into the house and loaded up on towels, clothes, groceries, liquor, beer, cigarettes. Last Christmas she'd stolen a blouse from one of her sisters. The *señora* tearfully banned her from the house, but after a few days Mrs. Virginia told Maria, *"Por favor,* let her in. Whatever you do, don't anger her!"

And then the *señora* had said, "Please, Maria, don't leave me alone with her. I'm very frightened of her."

Madre mía, Maria thought, what is going on here? Daughters do not harm their mothers.

At dawn on Saturday, two and a half days after the Campbells' return from Europe, Maria climbed down the outer steps of her apartment to begin another working day. She'd hardly slept for worrying. As she started to enter the back door of the house, she saw Matthew's face pressed to the glass. He was about to celebrate his seventh birthday. Maria loved the brightly inquisitive dark-haired boy with the wild streak of humor like his grandfather. No one took care of the two *niños* the way Maria did. Hadn't she made Mrs. Virginia drive all over town to find the right herbs for Michael when he had pneumonia? And hadn't he recovered *muy pronto?*

She saw that her baby had been crying and comforted him in Spanish. Both boys spent most of their time with her and were bilingual. *"Qué tal?"* Maria asked.

Matthew hugged her and whimpered. She stroked his soft hair. *"Dile a María!"* she instructed him. *"Qué pasa, bebé?"*

"Oh, Maria, lots of problems," he blubbered. "Cindy fought with Mom yesterday. A lot! Cindy says . . . she'll kill Mom with a gun."

He cried so hard that Maria was afraid he would wake the others. He told her that Cindy had shown up last night and demanded a ride to her apartment. His mom had asked him to come along. Maria thought, It's been that way for months. The *señora* won't allow herself to be alone with Cindy. "Cindy said many bad things," the child went on.

Maria felt his body tremble. "Cindy says things she shouldn't," she said, patting his eyes with her skirt. Once it had felt strange to call the boys' mother "Cindy" and the grandparents "Mother" and "Daddy," but now it seemed natural. Maria said, "You mustn't believe a word Cindy says."

An hour later Mrs. Virginia came downstairs and announced she was taking Cindy shopping. Her darkly luminous blue eyes, the most beautiful Maria had ever seen, were laced with red. Her mouth twitched, and her hands fluttered in front of her face. She acted like someone who has given herself over to fear, someone who has lost hope. Maria tried not to cry.

Mother and daughter returned from the shopping trip that afternoon, and Cindy showed off two new silk *blusas*. Maria thought, How she loves them. Why would someone who lives in T-shirts and jeans want so many expensive blouses? It was a mystery.

41

It didn't take long for James Campbell to resume his favorite pastime. On the weekend after his return from Europe, he played eighteen holes in a foursome of lawyers, chewing on the stump of a cigar till his old friend Jim Brannon said, "Campbell, that's the most obscene-looking thing I've ever seen in a human mouth."

On the fifteenth fairway, Brannon watched as Campbell nudged his ball out of the rough with the edge of his shoe. On the next hole he lost a twenty-dollar bet and claimed that he had only ten in his wallet. "That's okay, Jim," the winner said, "you can owe me."

"That's against the rule," Campbell said as Brannon tried to keep a straight face.

"What rule?" Campbell's competitor asked.

"You never heard of the Virginia rule?"

"What's the Virginia rule?"

"I can only lose as much money as my wife put in my pocket." Brannon thought, I've never known a guy who can play the dumb rube like Campbell.

The opponent suggested that the debt could be settled tomorrow.

Campbell's expressive brown eyes showed horror. "Oh, no!" he said. "That would violate our statute of limitations."

Overnight Brannon had a disturbing dream. James and Virginia Campbell died. Then they were all together in his car and someone was trying to run them down. Virginia ran up to him yelling, "Help, Jim!"

"Hey," Brannon called back, "I need help myself!" He was glad when he woke up.

The next morning he walked down the hall to Campbell's office. The nightmare had been so vivid that it gave him chills.

"Wait, Jim!" Campbell said after Brannon had started recounting the dream. "I want Virginia to hear this."

Husband and wife questioned him closely. To Brannon their serious demeanor seemed as odd as the dream.

A few days later a salesman friend named Ed Benson picked up an uncharacteristically glum James Campbell. "Hey," Benson said as they headed toward the golf course, "if you don't get your mind on the game, you're not even gonna be able to hit the ball."

Campbell played poorly and made no jokes.

42

Jamie was baffled. Whenever there was a break in her school schedule, Mother and Daddy always sent her an airplane ticket to come home. But now it was summertime and they'd told her to stay in Knoxville. It didn't make sense. She had no job, she wasn't attending summer school, and she wanted to go home and hear about their trip to Europe. And of course she missed them.

"Don't worry, honey," her mother consoled her over the phone. "We'll come up to see you in a few weeks. We'll bring the boys."

"But Mother," Jamie implored, "why can't I come home?"

Virginia talked on and on and never really answered the question. She sounded nervous and afraid.

To her youngest daughter, Virginia Campbell hadn't seemed herself since before the spring break in March. Jamie had gone home then and found her sad and upset. For the first time she'd seemed dependent on cup after cup of coffee. It wasn't like Mother at all.

Jamie had called home three or four times a week since then. Sometimes Daddy picked up the extension phone and barked like a dog, his silly way of letting her know he was there. Virginia's mood seemed unchanged.

On Thursday, June 17, eight days after the return from Europe, Jamie talked to her parents again. When she put down the phone, she realized that they just plain didn't want her around this summer. She wished she knew why.

43

David considered himself a good Marine. Once he'd made his decision, there was nothing to do but move forward. It would be a cold kill, emotionless, carefully planned. He told Cindy that the only question now was how to do the job right—"quickly, painlessly, quietly, simply, effectively." He said, "We've already made the value judgments. Now it's a matter of mechanics."

Cindy asked what he wanted her to do.

"You're going with me," he told her. It was only fair; they were her parents and this was her deal. Besides, he needed a second pair of eyes and ears and someone to alibi him later. Of course when you took a partner you took the partner's liabilities. Cindy could get them both killed.

Once again the acolyte sat at his feet. "You're gonna be fucking scared," he lectured her, "but you've got to suspend your fear. You'll feel a tight thing in your chest, ya know? You'll have to hold it in and suppress it."

He tried to remember his B. F. Skinner. "You consider yourself an actor, right?" he asked her.

She nodded, her hazel eyes open wide.

"Well, then, act!" he said, "Act cold, cool, calm. If you act that way, you *are* that way." She dragged on her cigarette till the ember glowed. "Being scared has to be overcome," he went on. "You can do it, Cindy. You can do anything!" Good old unconditional positive regard.

He taught her basic hand signals. "Use 'em!" he snapped. "We can't say one fucking word inside. Too many people know our voices." He taught her how to breathe silently, a technique he'd learned hunting deer. He would take an hour to cover a hundred yards, then stand stock-still till his respiration slowed and his body turned to stone. It was like being a jungle Marine in *Guadalcanal.* You didn't shift an ounce of your weight. If you had enough patience, the enemy came to you.

"Try it," he instructed her. She wobbled across the room

like a calf. "Distribute your weight," he said. "Walk heel to toe, heel to toe. If you step on something, you can feel it and pull back. And make sure to *listen!* Stop breathing when you listen. You can hear a lot more that way, ya know?"

They went over the house plans. She showed him where her parents slept in the front bedroom upstairs, so he taught her how to climb steps without making noise. "Stick by the wall. That's where the main support is. If you walk in the middle or out at the end, you'll creak sure as shit. Put your foot down slowly, evenly. *There!* Now try again."

They tiptoed up and down his staircase till she had it right. He expected her to gripe, but she didn't. It proved what he'd always known: Cindy could be as competent as anyone.

They spent an evening shaping alibis. "No way we won't be questioned," he advised her. "Don't be too cool. Act upset, scared. Remember, your mother and father have just been killed. The cops won't expect you to be calm about it. Look for their tricks. Like they'll separate us and they'll say, 'You might as well confess. We know the whole story. We got this and we got that. David already told us.' Or 'So-and-so saw you.' *Bullshit!* Don't give up a thing. Make 'em prove it."

"Won't the police just *know* we did it?" she asked. "And, like, make things hard for us?"

"They may suspect us," he said. "They may *know* it's us. But they'll never be able to prove it, because there'll be no evidence. And they won't be able to shake our alibis. So fuck 'em, ya know?"

She came up with the idea of weaving in a few discrepancies so their stories wouldn't sound too pat. She would tell the cops that they'd gone to a bar but she wasn't sure which one, only that it was a bar they didn't frequent. Oh, yes, she would say, now I remember. Then she would get the name a little wrong—the "Pink Pussycat" instead of the "Pink Poodle." David thought it was a master stroke.

She asked him where he'd learned so much about murder. "On TV," he explained. "See, my mom criticizes TV constantly. She'll say, 'Real people wouldn't act like that.' She's always punching holes in plots. I watched with her, and I learned that you just get an idea, punch holes in it, then keep refining and improving till there's no place left to punch, ya know? I've been doing it for years."

He remembered something crucial. "What about Rufus?" he asked her. Rufus was her daddy's pet, a big floppy klutzhound with a heart of gold.

"Rufus? No problem."

"No problem? Well, shit, Cindy, he always runs up with that silly bark. Roo-roo-roo-roo-roo. He'll wake up the whole fucking neighborhood. We won't be able to get near the place."

"Don't worry about Rufus. He's disappeared."

Late one night he asked, "What'll this do to your sons?"

"They're mostly attached to Maria," Cindy said. "She's more of a parent than Mother and Daddy."

"You don't think they'll be upset?"

"They'll get over it."

He wrestled with the problem of getting away without being identified. "The boys might wake up and see us," he told Cindy. "That damn maid might be wandering around. I don't want to kill half a dozen people. I'm no mass murderer, ya know."

He decided they had to be covered from head to foot. The former Marine supply clerk went to a shop called Skate Escape and bought a white hockey goalie's mask, like the ones worn by the Urban Animals for jousting, and spray-painted it black. In his closet he found a dark ski mask for Cindy and two hooded field jackets that were big enough to disguise their shapes. He dragged out matching pairs of combat boots in his size eight.

"They're too big," Cindy complained.

"I'll give you extra socks," he said. "You weigh as much as a man. If they do forensics on the footprints, they'll think it was two men."

In a bin at a hardware store he found translucent rubber gloves, rough-stamped so there were no lefts or rights. He tried one on and flexed his fingers. They would do fine.

He hunted up Wickie. "You still got that forty-five?"

"Yeah."

"Would you sell it?"

"Well, sure. What do you want it for?"

"Uh . . . an operation. You don't wanna know, Wickie. Maybe I'm gonna kill somebody."

"I don't care," Wickie said. "If you want the gun, fine."

"But I'm not buying any gun till I test it," David said. "I still don't trust automatics."

They drove to Shooter's Cove in a thunderstorm, inching through the pools that always collected at Houston's storm drains and wiped out brakes. He'd complained to Cindy that morning, "It's been raining like a son of a bitch ever since the first of June. We don't want a storm when we go inside. There's enough variables as it is. We don't want to get there at three in the morning and find somebody looking out the window at the lightning."

On the range he put a box of bullets through the Combat Commander and was pleased that it didn't jam. He reloaded and squeezed off a clip as fast as he could pull the trigger—*pop! pop! pop! pop . . . !* The action was smooth. He checked the target and found tight groups. "Well, goddamn!" he said. "That's impressive."

They made the deal on the spot—five hundred for the Colt, the extra clips and a box of silvertips. Guaranteed to kill anything up to a mastodon, Wickie promised.

Wickie invested $239 in a new .357 Ruger. He told David, "I wouldn't want to go unarmed in Houston."

On Thursday, June 17, after a week of training and preparation, David woke Cindy with his decision. "We're ready," he said. "We're a team. We go tomorrow night."

"What time?"

"I figure about three-thirty. The late movie'll be over by then. So will the talk shows. They'll be asleep."

She looked cool. He hoped she stayed that way.

44

Ordinarily Maria would have enjoyed the shopping trip on the next evening Friday, June 18, but the *señora* was so nervous and jumpy. Maybe it had to do with the calls.

For the last four days the phone had rung each morning between seven and seven-thirty. Mrs. Virginia seemed to expect each call. Twice she'd taken them downstairs and twice in her bedroom. The conversations were short. This morning Maria had heard her say, "Okay, honey. *Poquito tiempo.*" Maria wondered, Why is she asking for a little time? And why such a placating voice? She was sure that Cindy was on the other end and the subject was money. That was always a good guess.

Mrs. Virginia, Matthew and Maria walked slowly past the stores at Memorial City. The *señora's* heart didn't seem to be in it. She'd never been comfortable around shopkeepers. If they made a mistake on her bill, she wouldn't argue. It was her nature not to make trouble.

Tonight the *muchacho* wanted everything in the mall. It was like leading a hungry pup. At Foley's the *señora* bought him a porcelain cow and told Maria to pick something out for herself. "I have lots of money," she said. That was part of the problem; she'd always been too generous. Cindy had been handed too much, and she'd never had to work.

In a cafeteria Mrs. Virginia lit a cigarette, stubbed it out and lit another, then bought a Coke and let it sit while she poured herself a cup of coffee. *Virgen mía,* Maria thought, what is going on? She felt jumpy herself.

They got home around nine. The *señor* and eight-year-old Michael had just returned from a shopping trip of their own, and Mr. James was watching TV in the den. It had been close to ninety degrees all day with high humidity, and Mrs. Virginia suggested that Maria stay overnight in the air-conditioned house. "It's too hot in your apartment," she said.

Two or three times Maria started to turn back from the bottom of the wooden staircase that led up to her garage apartment, but then she called out in mixed Spanish and English, "That's okay, *señora*. Maybe another day. I'm going to mend my clothes."

She didn't want to intrude. Every Friday night the boys dragged their bedding into the adults' bedroom and watched a cassette movie, then slept at the foot of the big bed. It was already nine-thirty; Mr. James would start the tape any minute. Matthew liked Snoopy best and Michael preferred monster films, but the whole family's favorite was Star Trek. Maria thought about her loved ones. After all the tension around the house lately, it was nice that they could spend a night together in peace.

45

At 10 P.M. David drove Cindy to the house on Memorial to make one last check on the unlocked window. She went inside on a pretext while he waited in the car. He noticed that the bluish mercury-vapor security light wasn't working. That was a nice break.

Cindy returned in a few minutes and told him that her mother had come halfway down the stairs to hand her the ten dollars she'd requested.

"Did you see anybody else?" he asked.

"No."

She said she'd checked the entry window on her way out and found it locked. David thought, That meddling *pinche puta!* "Did you unlock it again?" he asked.

"Yeah."

"Anybody see you?"

"No."

He sighed. On track so far.

They drove to the Galleria. One of the theaters was showing *E.T.*, but the line was too long. They stopped at the Parlor, a little bar on Fairview, and he showed the bartendress how to mix a few exotic drinks so she'd be sure to remember his face. Then they shot darts at Rudyard's till the 2 A.M. closing. He thought, Six or eight different friends can alibi us so far. Still on track.

46

An hour before midnight Maria looked out her window and saw Mr. James drive off in the Cadillac. The bedroom showing of *Star Trek* must be over. She hoped the boys were sleeping okay. Sometimes they got too excited when they stayed overnight in the adults' bedroom.

The *señor* returned in about ten minutes. Cigarettes, Maria deduced. The *mercado* was only a mile or so away.

She put out her light at eleven-thirty but couldn't sleep. She kept seeing the lines on Mrs. Virginia's face, the untouched drinks and half-smoked cigarettes. *Pobre señora!* She hadn't been herself for weeks.

Soon after midnight the maid noticed a glow from the house. The light was on in the master bedroom. Somebody must be reading. Maybe Matthew had had another nightmare. She rolled over in her warm bed and told herself not to worry.

She was bothered by dreams. Someone was being killed. She waved her hands in front of her face to shut out the siren and lights.

She sat up. Not a sound came from Memorial Drive or anywhere else. *Qué absurdo,* she thought. A breeze barely moved the leaves in the thick stand of trees. She was afraid to get up and turn on the light.

47

David had expected to suffer last-minute doubts, but they
didn't come. He'd made the right decision. Cindy's painful
childhood would soon be over. She'd be free of her tormen-
tors—the two worst, anyway. The sisters would still be
around, but at least they weren't in Houston. He thought,
Goddamn, she'll inherit *millions!* That's poetic justice.

He thought back on all the planning and prep. He'd kept
discovering one last glitch, one last hole to punch. Cindy
was a fifth wheel. She knew nothing about guns and killing,
and her disorderly mind didn't lend itself to planning. If she
freaked, James Campbell could blow them both away.

He was shaken by the idea. Cindy said he'd been keeping
a shotgun by his bed. David thought, I might as well face it;
this could be my last hour on earth. He had no one to pray
to.

He tried to regain control. Only fools borrowed fear in
advance. But every time he thought of crawling through the
dark window and climbing the twisting stairs to the second
floor, his small hands shook.

He looked out on Vermont Street. For once no sissies did-
dled each other under the oaks. The weather was holding—
warm and humid, no thunderstorms or rain. There'd been a
sprinkle earlier, barely enough to measure. The forecast had
said "slightly cloudy," which in a Houston summer could
mean just about anything.

At 2:30 A.M. he cleaned, oiled and dry-fired the Combat
Commander for the last time. He slid a magazine in and
heard the reassuring click. The ejecting mechanism worked
smoothly. He explained to Cindy that it was ejectors and
extractors that caused automatics to jam; revolvers were
simpler. She looked like she didn't give a shit.

He ran her through a last-minute drill and added a few
reminders. "Don't talk inside. I don't want anybody to hear
a female voice. After we get inside, we'll stand still for a
while till our eyes get accustomed to the dark, and we'll

listen to see if anybody's moving. Then we'll move a few feet at a time, stop, and listen again. It's just a matter of, ya know—shoot 'em and get the fuck out."

At 3 A.M. he held a final inspection. The men's field jacket concealed her shape. It was O.D. green with expandable pockets, Velcro flaps and a hood in a pouch in the back. His old combat boots laced halfway to her knees. She wore two pairs of sweat socks. With her hair tucked behind her ski mask, she looked like a short, round man.

He pulled on his rubber gloves, then ordered her to hold out her hands. He thought, Goddamn, she'll puncture the ends with those fucking nails and then she'll leave prints. But she'll never let me trim them. She thinks long nails are hot shit.

He worked the latex over her fingers. "They're plenty tight," he told her. "Don't try to make 'em tighter."

He thought about stuffing his personal .38 in his belt for backup, but decided it would be one item too many. He had two extra magazines for the .45 in case he needed more firepower. He could ram them in place in seconds.

He wiped down the Combat Commander, slid it into his shoulder holster and said, "Okay, this is it, ya know." He took a deep breath. "You're sure about this?"

Cindy nodded.

Neither spoke as they pulled away from the house. Everything had been said. Cindy didn't seem frightened. A little wired, maybe. He felt plenty nervous himself.

Off to their left in the darkness, Buffalo Bayou looked as dark as axle grease as he steered out Memorial Drive toward the western edge of the big flat city. He'd timed the run: about ten minutes. He was still driving the hog-ass gold Coupe de Ville that his friends at Jerry's Automotive were letting him use while they built a new 302 V-8 engine for his Capri. The rear license plate was smeared with mud, a trick he'd learned from TV.

Out past the heavily traveled West Loop, Memorial Drive turned into a two-lane country road with thickly landscaped properties on both sides. He slowed at a narrow street just east of the Campbells' and flicked off his headlights. The night was even darker than he'd anticipated—no moon, no

light from neighboring houses. He turned into the side street
and eased the Cadillac onto the shoulder.

The loudest noise came from insects—crickets, he
guessed. Across the road the house seemed to float on the
blackness like a barge, a great dense hulk set back from the
road. He pictured the Campbells sleeping in their bedroom
at the top of the stairs, the boys dead to the world downstairs, the *pinche puta* snoring in her detached apartment in
back. Cindy had sketched the layout and he knew it cold.
They hadn't even brought a flashlight.

He looked at his watch: 3:20. They were right on schedule. No cars were in sight. Cindy adjusted her woolen mask
while he did his own. The goalie's mask had a plastic pad in
the back and four adjustable straps. He'd set the lengths at
the house, but it took some fiddling to get them right. He
didn't want the opaque part sliding over his eyes at the
wrong time. The mask smelled of solvent and made him
sweat. He wished he could take it off.

He reached into his shoulder holster and stroked the .45
lightly. The safety was on. He still didn't trust .45s, even the
"accurized" models.

He motioned to Cindy to get out of the car with him. The
warm moist air seemed to have weight. The insects had
turned quiet. He wondered why. Was someone approaching
on foot? A security guard? He cocked an ear and picked up
a stirring, an unaccustomed pressure or turbulence. He
couldn't figure it out. He stopped breathing and realized he
was hearing the unaccustomed absence of sound. At three
o'clock in the morning his own neighborhood hummed like
a turbine.

He grabbed Cindy's hand and led her across the road to
the driveway. Anyone who saw them now would rush to the
nearest phone and call the police. In places like Memorial
there were private patrols up the kazoo.

At the head of the driveway a steel gate barred their way.
He wondered if the Campbells suspected something. Had
Cindy run her mouth? He thought, If the gate's locked, we
might as well pack it in. We'll never get over that fence
wearing all this heavy shit.

A chain had been wrapped around the latch. He undid it

link by link so it wouldn't clank. He thought, If a car comes by now, our ass is grass. The chain fell away. He checked his thin gloves for damage. They looked intact.

Branches scratched at his jacket as they walked toward the rear of the house. A limb scraped his mask and the sound jarred his ears. The driveway was littered; as far as he could tell, it was never swept or raked and the trees never pruned. He tried to feel the paving with his feet, heel to toe, trying not to snap a twig. Indian lore. Something else his mother had taught him.

He spotted the steel water tank behind the house, faintly backlighted by stars. The garage lay in shadow, the security light still out. He wondered, Are we walking into a trap? Is Campbell watching from inside?

Cindy stepped into a bed of ferns bordering the rear wall and he followed. He tried not to snag his gloves on the thin wire of the screen and realized that he should have brought spares.

The screen lifted out, but the window stuck. He looked at Cindy and she nodded emphatically—this was the window to the den, the one she'd unlocked. He tugged harder and it popped loose. He raised it an inch at a time. Once or twice the metal scraped and made him gulp.

He brushed off the rubber soles of their boots to keep from tracking dirt or sticks. He checked his watch again. It was H-hour: 3:30. He stuck his head inside and came up against the back of a sofa. He shoved it away, then boosted Cindy and followed her in.

They crouched side by side listening for movement and adjusting to the darkness. He heard thumps and realized they were coming from his chest. His throat was parched. He kept imagining the lights coming on and a shotgun opening up at point-blank range.

He tried to channel his fear into alertness. He told himself, You're the point man; if you show indecision, Cindy bursts like a bubble. He reminded himself that heroes felt fear. You just picked up one foot and put it in front of the other, like . . . that! If you acted brave, you *were* brave: B. F. Skinner. He thought, David, you're fine. *You're not afraid.*

But he was.

Crossing the living room, he unholstered the .45 and eased off the safety. His shirt was soaked under the jacket.

He followed Cindy up the stairs. She did a good job of keeping toward the wall. Every step had been choreographed, but in the doing it seemed strange and new. At the landing halfway up, they paused and listened again. The house was silent. They climbed the last few steps to the upstairs hallway.

A night light cast a thin yellow wash on the walls. Three or four doors were shut to left and right. He listened for breathing and heard nothing. He wondered, Are the Campbells out? Impossible. Earlier, Cindy had seen her mother in nightclothes.

Cindy stopped at the first door on the right and opened it slowly. He stepped in behind her. In the faint light he saw a queen-sized bed broadside to him, the headboard to his right. The Campbells lay atop the covers, Virginia on the near side. He heard faint breathing.

Cindy's hand slid to the wall switch. He squared into his combat stance, both hands on the gun. "Hit it!" he whispered.

The room jumped into focus. Everything seemed twice its size. Cindy rushed out the door as he took two steps to the foot of the bed to improve his angle. He almost tripped over some blankets.

James Campbell rolled on his right side. The first slug seemed to hit him in the neck. Goddamn, David thought, that's *loud!*

He aimed at the woman's head. She moved as he fired and he thought he'd hit her in the upper arm. He told himself, Come on, man! You need clean head shots. Concentrate on your aiming points!

His third round pierced the man's eye. The fourth caught the woman in the head. His ears hurt. He never imagined that a handgun could make such a noise in a room. It was like standing inside a thunderclap.

He stepped up to the bed and fired a round into each of their chests. Ten or twelve seconds had elapsed since he'd entered the room. Where was Cindy?

He ran down the stairs and out the front door to the lawn. He was twenty or thirty feet into the bushes when he stopped. *Where the fuck was Cindy?* He must have passed her in the dark.

He retraced his steps and found her on her hands and knees inside the living-room door. She was clawing at the rug.

He said, "What . . . ?"

He couldn't make out her reply. Her voice was distorted through her ski mask and his eardrums still rang from the shots.

She stood up and said, "I dropped the glove!"

He grabbed her by the arm. "C'mon," he said. *"C'mon!"*

"I dropped the glove!"

"Fuck the glove!" Any second now, the boys would come running out of their downstairs bedroom. They couldn't have slept through those shots. The whole goddamn neighborhood must be awake.

"The glove!" she repeated. *"The glove!"*

"Fuck the glove! Let's go!"

He urged her out the door. As they stumbled across the lawn, he babbled under his breath: "Oh, God, this bitch is crazier than I thought. She deliberately dropped a glove! She wants to get caught! Oh, shit, it's Twilight Zone. . . ."

They were still in their masks, clomping across the road, when headlights approached from the east. "Quick!" he said. They hurried across and crouched behind a bush.

The car sped past. They ran to the Cadillac. He reached in the right pocket of his jeans for the keys. They weren't there. He dug deeper. They had to be there; he *always* kept his keys in his jeans.

He decided that he'd dropped them. "Where the fuck are the keys?" he asked out loud. He heard a jingle. They were in the field jacket.

He drove to the first curve with the headlights off, then snapped them on. He said, "What the fuck do you mean, you dropped the glove?"

Cindy huddled in the corner. "It just came off," she said. *"It just came off!"* He mocked her in a falsetto voice.

"How do you drop a tight-fitting rubber glove? Whattaya mean, it just came off?"

"I just . . . dropped it."

"Bullshit!"

"David—"

"Fuck you!"

As they drove under the West Loop, she kept repeating, "The glove. Oh, the glove!"

He thought, Forensic technicians can turn gloves inside out and lift prints. They can analyze the moisture. Men's sweat has a stronger smell than women's—hormones or something. He thought, If the cops find out the glove was worn by a woman, we're dead meat. . . .

He turned off Memorial at Shepherd and hit the Allen Parkway. Driving along, they shucked off incriminating parts of their clothing. Cindy was still whimpering as he turned at the Jewish Cemetery. "Why don't you just shut up, ya know?" he told her. "You're fucking up my concentration." He thought, It's my own fault. What made me think I could depend on her?

He killed the lights and coasted down a narrow dirt road toward the bayou. The Caddie slid noiselessly into a stand of trees. They parked and carried their loads in the dark. He was familiar with the area from his runs with Tiger and Max. The place was so remote that his pit bulls couldn't find other pets to kill.

He led Cindy to a narrow point of land. He stuffed the .45, the nylon shoulder holster, the two extra magazines, Cindy's ski mask and the three remaining gloves into the pockets of the field jackets. He rolled the two jackets together, tied them with the sleeves, and pitched the package out into the water. He figured the bottom was murky and the depth at least six or eight feet. Sometimes the bayou was as stagnant as a millpond, but in midsummer it flowed strong from rains.

"Gimme your boots," he said as he yanked off his own. He pitched both pairs far out in the dark water.

"Can't the cops trace the boots to you?" Cindy asked in a frightened little voice.

"No markings," he snapped. He didn't feel like talking.

"But they could match our footprints right here."

"Well, big whoopee shit!" He was still enraged at her. "So what? I mean, whose prints are they? I mean, the FBI doesn't have a file of footprints, for Christ's sake!"

She acted as thought she didn't get it. He realized that her grasp on reality was much weaker than he'd imagined. The thought was worrisome.

They ran up the slope to the car. He still had to jettison the plastic hockey mask; it wouldn't sink. He'd stowed it on the back seat next to his skates. If they were stopped by cops, he figured they could claim they were Urban Animals; 4 A.M. was prime time to them. He drove to a big trash container behind an apartment complex on Dunlavy and buried the mask deep.

Cindy kept caterwauling as they drove. "Cindy," he said, "don't worry about the goddamn glove." Anything to shut her up.

48

Maria wasn't sure if she heard or dreamed the sound. It had been a long hot night, the kind that wore you out. She thought, Maybe it was a blowout or some *lunático* throwing a firecracker. She'd been dozing off, but now she was wide awake.

She stared out her window into darkness. The security light was out again. She would mention it to the *señor*.

A reedy voice sang faintly of the *esperanza* in his *corazón*. Loneliness made Maria keep the radio on as she slept. There were 800,000 Mexicans in Houston and plenty of Spanish-language stations, some local and some beamed up from border towns like Matamoros and Nuevo Laredo. They played too much modern music, even rock, but sooner or later the trembling voices sang of the images of her childhood: the white *paloma*, handsome *caballeros, mi vida, mi amor*. . . . Every night the same words returned her to the dusty plazas of her childhood.

She slumped back and listened. The announcers always rolled their *r*'s like schoolteachers. She liked the station because it piped in the news from Ciudad México.

She couldn't sleep. Her open windows only seemed to let in more thick, hot air. She heard a gong and an announcer saying that it was 3:40 A.M.

Outside something slammed. It sounded like the door to the kitchen. Footsteps pounded up her stairs and someone banged on her door as she pulled the sheet to her neck.

"Mia, Mia," the voice yelled, "Oh, Maria, *abre la puerta!*" It was one of the boys. He was yanking at her screen, crying, almost screaming. "Open the door, Maria. *Please!*"

As she jumped from bed, she heard Michael shout, "Maria, Maria! My parents are dead! *Muerto, muerto, muerto!* They just killed them!"

She opened the door and the boys jammed against each other to get inside. Michael was babbling. Little Matthew grabbed her nightgown. *"Por favor, Maria,"* he said, "call the hospital. Call an ambulance. *Please!* My parents are dead!"

Maria thought, *Madre mía,* they've had the same nightmare!

"Wait," she said. She hugged Matthew and stroked Michael's red hair. "You had bad dreams. Wait!"

Matthew said, "No! My parents are dead!"

Maria mixed sugar water and made them drink. Years ago it had calmed other babies. She saw that both boys had wet their pants.

"Mira, Maria," Michael said. "I was sleeping when they turned on the light." He said there were two killers, but he didn't see any faces because it was dark on that side of the bed. Maria frowned. Mrs. Virginia's bedlamp hadn't worked in several days. She thought, This dream is getting too real.

Michael said he'd burrowed into his sleeping bag when the man at the door pointed a gun at papa. "Time passed," the child went on in Spanish, "and when I saw that no one was there, I got up first to see papa. Then I told Matthew, 'Wake up! My dad has lots of blue on his chest.' "

Then Matthew had taken a look. "No, no, Michael,"

Matthew had said. "No, Papa doesn't have blue. It's blood. My dad is dead. *He's dead!*"

Michael said he looked again and saw that his mother's face was stained red and his father was covered with blood. Maria thought, How lucky that the boys came to me after such a dream. They might have run out in the street and been run over.

"Come in the house and see for yourself," Michael begged her.

"No," she insisted. "You've had a nightmare."

Michael told her to call the police. Matthew slid off her lap and yanked at her hand. "Let's go!" he begged her.

Maria told herself to be strong for the boys and not frighten them.

"The police!" Michael repeated. "I'll call the police."

"No!" Maria said. It would make *la policía* angry to drive out here for a dream. She tried to decide what to do. Maybe James Campbell's older brother could help sort things out. "Call your uncle!" she said. She wished she could make the call herself, but J. W. O. Campbell's Spanish was about as bad as her English. She told the child to hurry.

Michael said he didn't know his uncle's phone number, but Matthew was good with numbers and had it in his head. The little boy was so upset that he spoke Spanish into the telephone. "Don't cry, *mi amor,*" Maria told him as she gently took the phone from his hands. "Don't cry. Let Michael talk to uncle in English."

The older brother took the phone. "Hurry!" she heard him say. "Come to the house! My parents are dead. There's blood all over their faces!"

Maria grabbed the phone. "Hurry, Mister J.W. !" she said, and added in Spanish, "We will wait for you in the apartment." She hoped he understood.

By now the boys were wailing. She looked into their faces and wished she knew how to console them. If she could, she would take out her heart and hand it to her babies.

Waiting for the uncle's arrival, she tiptoed down the wooden staircase and called softly to the second-floor window of the house. "Señora Virginia? Señor James?" There was no answer. She called louder. She thought, If they wake up and don't see the boys on the floor, they'll worry. She yelled in Spanish, "The children are in the apartment!"

The house stood silent.

J. W. O. Campbell and his wife Brucene arrived in fifteen or twenty minutes. They weren't frequent visitors, and J.W. told Maria that he'd overshot the driveway and had to double back. He said that he'd found the front security gate and front door open. Maria exclaimed, *"Dios mío!"*

J.W. listened to the boys' story and then dialed the police. He explained that he hadn't called them from his house because he'd thought it might be a false alarm.

The five of them huddled together in Maria's stuffy apartment. Maria was just as pleased that J.W. showed no inclination to go into the house. It wouldn't be wise. He'd had heart problems.

But then she thought, What if my loved ones are still alive? What if they're in pain? *Señora* Brucene said she would like to check, but she was too afraid. Maria said she was afraid, too. Maybe they could support each other.

The kitchen door was unlocked. The house was like a tomb. The two women held hands and tiptoed up the stairs.

Maria saw that the door to the master bedroom was open. Señora Brucene peeked inside, then turned and said, *"Sí,* Maria."

Maria whispered, *"Muertos?"*

The other woman nodded.

Maria peeked through stubby fingers. She saw blood and ran down the stairs behind Mrs. Brucene.

On the way out she noticed that the sofa in the den had been moved and the window was open. She remembered that Cindy had tried to open that window a few days earlier. Maybe it was a coincidence.

An ambulance braked to a stop behind Señor J.W.'s red and white Cadillac. Two men in uniform instructed everyone to stay out of the house; the killer might still be inside. Maria embraced her boys. The Mexican announcer said it was 4:13.

49

Detective Sergeant Michael St. John, four inches over six feet tall and built in the general shape of a night stick, was nose-deep in a textbook on contract law when the phone broke the early morning silence. It was the shift lieutenant assigning him and his partner to an "ooh-and-ah," the most urgent of Houston homicide's informal classifications. The young detective looked at the clock. It was 4:35 A.M.

All killings in River Oaks or Memorial were considered ooh-and-ahs. There were five or six hundred murders a year in the "Golden Buckle on the Sun Belt," but not always enough ooh-and-ahs to keep things interesting on the grave-yard watch from 10 P.M. to 6 A.M. As scene detectives, St. John and his senior partner Carl Kent were responsible for collecting evidence, overseeing the transfer of bodies, inter-rogating witnesses and, with luck, taking confessions. They seldom followed through on a case. That was the day shift's job.

Friday nights were usually good for a couple of barroom or family murders, but this night had been quiet. St. John was a college-educated redhead, working on a law degree in his off-hours, and he'd welcomed the chance to study.

"You do the pokin'," Carl Kent said in his pleasant North Houston accent as they headed out of the parking lot. "I'll do the talkin'." As usual, the older man was smoking one of his six-inch cigars. Sometimes he used a new one to measure distances on a corpse, rotating it down the body. Kent was in his forties, built like a shot-putter. He spoke sleepy but worked fast. St. John felt lucky to be working with him.

They reached the house at 4:55. The rookie detective studied the "scene" side of the five-by-eight-inch homicide card and told himself not to miss a single item on the list. Even though he'd scored high on the sergeant's test and won early promotion, St. John was still something of a trainee. He had the feeling this would be the biggest case of his life.

A uniformed officer met the detectives behind the house. "Two," he said. "Upstairs."

Kent spoke just above a whisper, "Where's the shooter?"

"I dunno. Two little boys were in the room, but they got out."

"Where're they now?"

"Up in back." He motioned toward a detached garage.

The homicide detectives stepped into the house. The rooms were large and the décor plain. The furniture looked rented. One old television set sat atop another in the large living room. A heavy-footed patrolman came down the stairs and said, "We were worried about a locked bedroom across the hall. But it's empty. The maid had a key."

A paramedic pointed out a surgical glove on the rug near the open front door. An odd thing to leave behind, St. John noted. Those gloves don't just fall off.

He blanched at the sight of the bodies. My God, he thought, I've been on the force for six years: why am I reacting like this? He'd just come off a string of family-fight murders, drunken murders, barroom murders, Saturday night specials, and mutilated bodies were nothing new to him. But this was his first cold execution. He thought, Why, these are respectable folks, lying on top of their covers on a hot summer night. Innocent victims asleep in their beds. That's what's so scary about it. There's no way to defend against something like this. It could happen to me.

The woman lay on her left side facing the bedroom door. Her freckled arms were bare, her knees curled up, her nightgown bunched around her waist. She was naked from the waist down. He couldn't help thinking it was an unusual way for an older woman to dress in the presence of children.

Blood had spattered on the headboard and made a fan-shaped pattern on curtains three or four feet behind. There were flecks on the ceiling. The woman's pink pillow was stained maroon. The freckles on her arms turned out to be blood. There appeared to be a graze wound on her shoulder, an entry wound on the right side of her face, and another by her right breast. She wore big rings and a gold watch.

The man was big, a two-hundred-pounder. He lay on his back in a pinkish-lavender T-shirt and blue boxer shorts. He wore an expensive watch. His left arm was crabbed across his chest, as though he'd tensed. His right eye was dark brown and opened wide; the left eye had been shot out.

St. John thought, He must have seen what was coming. There were bullet holes at the base of the left jaw near the ear and in the cheek along the jawline; he couldn't be sure whether they were entrance or exit wounds. Bubbles of blood trailed from his mouth. There was a wound in his left side and a larger one on the right.

St. John looked around the room. A double-barreled shotgun leaned against a dresser. He thought, Too bad he didn't get to use it. A wallet looked undisturbed on the dresser. There were a few oil paintings, a vase with limp flowers, a lampshade still covered by tattered strips of clear plastic, a gun case containing rifles, and a TV across from the bed with a VCR on top. He peeped at the cassette. Someone had watched *Star Trek.*

Except for the VCR, the setting was early Holiday Inn. Books were stacked a foot high on the man's bedside table, along with an empty mug. St. John figured he must have had a nightcap before turning out the light. He peeped at some of the titles and realized that the man was a lawyer. Well, he thought, this is one of the occupational hazards. You work a little too close to the horns and get blown away. Maybe by your own client. . . .

Something gleamed on the floor. Three or four hulls had collected between the bed and the wall. He found another on one of the sleeping bags. That placed the shooter at the foot of the bed, since most automatics ejected to the right. A .45 silvertip slug lay on the pillow next to the dead man's head. Only professionals used silvertips. Someone had planned to leave no survivors.

Two light-brown sleeping bags lay crumpled together at the foot of the bed. St. John wondered why the perpetrator hadn't killed the boys. He took a shooting stance between the foot of the bed and the doorway. The perp must have overlooked them. He thought, Thank God for small favors. This hit man was a hell of a shot.

He went downstairs to take notes on the entry room. Off to one side he heard his partner reporting to headquarters in his Houston drawl: ". . . They was asleep in bay-ed. . . . He'd had a night cay-up, a highbowl or sumpin'. . . ."

The den was as plain as the master bedroom. A pair of TVs were stacked in front of an old sofa that had been shoved away from an open window. That made five sets, all of them old. The place was a TV graveyard. A side table held an empty Michelob bottle, a newspaper and a pair of eyeglasses. It looked as though someone had watched TV before going to bed.

He stepped through the kitchen door and found himself behind the house. The ambulance was just pulling away, its dome light staining the leaves. A window screen was propped against the side of the house in a bed of ferns. The window had been shoved up from the bottom. He made a note to ask the lab men to cast the soil for footprints.

He heard a sound and spotted a blocky Aztec face approaching. The woman wore black-rimmed glasses. Her thick dark hair was tied in a bun.

St. John thought, I'll be glad when I pass the bar exam.

50

To Detective Sergeant Carl Kent, the murder scene was beginning to look a little too much like a bus depot. The ambulance had come and gone, but a crime-scene unit had pulled in and so had a couple of extra squad cars. Any minute now the brass would begin arriving on their sirens. When it came to ooh-and-ahs, they were like kids.

Kent preferred solo work. Under his breath he muttered his all-purpose expletive, "Shoot!" He was capable of using standard police scatology but refused to take the Lord's name in vain. If a stone killer refused to join him on his knees to ask Jesus for forgiveness, Kent would say, "Well, *shoot*, man!" At such times his fellow detectives gave this 240-pound ex-Marine a wide berth.

Kent wanted to develop a suspect before the day shift took over and the case slipped away. There was one possibility already: J. W. O. Campbell. With his thinning, greased, graying hair right out of a forties movie, the dead man's brother looked like a traveling card-shark, one of those guys who played Hold-'em for more money than Kent made in a lifetime. Campbell acted quiet and withdrawn, bordering on furtive, and he'd already made a couple of wrong moves.

First off, Kent wondered, why had it taken him an hour to call the police? Why hadn't he phoned right away from his own house? And when he arrived, why did he refuse to go in the murder room and send his wife instead? *Because he already knew what was in there?* Then he stands out in the driveway till the ambulance arrives, escorts the crew into the house, and turns around and walks out, leaving them to find their own way.

And that wasn't the whole book on the man the others called "J.W." One of the uniformed cops said something about him stepping on or near the surgical glove in the living room, and then acting as though it was an accident. Why, that glove was the only tangible clue in the whole deal! Kent thought, An accident? Shoot!

He conducted an impromptu interview with the suspect in the kitchen, a large room with shiny plastic off-white walls, faded burgundy panels, and paint flaking from a vent. J.W. had a weathered look, a large nose and a soft voice. He said he was the older brother, a lawyer himself, and often shared cases with James. He seemed disoriented, said he had no idea who might have committed the crime unless it was a disgruntled client. That wasn't much help.

"What about the boys?" Kent asked. "Did they see anything?"

"They said they didn't," J.W. answered. It didn't compute. Those kids had been in the room when it went down.

Kent found the boys padding around in their underpants in the apartment above the garage. A five-foot Mexican woman dogged their footsteps. She shook her head when he asked, *"Habla inglés?"*

The redheaded kid seemed more excited than sad. A smaller boy bawled in the corner. When Kent approached him, the older boy abruptly switched moods and began to cry. "What's your name, son?" the detective asked.

"Michael."

Kent spoke softly. "Well, listen, Mike, I'm a police officer, heah? I'm trying to find out what happened to your daddy and mama."

The boy dragged his hand across his nose and said, "I have a right to remain silent."

Kent thought, Your folks were just murdered and you talk about your rights? Why, shoot, that's unnatural! The kid held his ground.

At the foot of the stairs the senior detective ran into his partner, busily measuring something. "Listen to this, Mike," he said. "That damn J.W. done schooled the fuckin' kids before we got out here. I feel sure he did."

"Maybe he thought they did it," St. John said. "Maybe he's covering up for them."

They decided to work the kids together. When they returned to the maid's apartment, the older brother was saying, "There was blood all over!" The smaller boy spoke in Spanish and then switched to lightly accented English. Neither boy offered useful information. Maybe they'd seen nothing, Kent decided. Or maybe they were being cute. When he bore down, the older boy repeated, "I don't have to talk to you."

"No," Kent said, "but it sure would be a help."

The kid said he would think about it.

Kent turned to the maid. He wasn't fluent in Spanish, but every Houston detective knew a few hundred words. She said she had no idea who'd killed her loved ones. Kent asked if there were any *problemas* in the family.

The maid said, "Only the *hija* Cindy."

"*Hija?*" Kent asked.

"*Sí!*" the maid answered. "*Hija.* Daughter. Cindy." Kent made a note of the name.

51

David had preselected their alibi party, a semipunk affair featuring the Bounders and attended by fifty or sixty young people, several of whom he knew. There were hard-core rockers with razor blades gleaming from lacquered black hair, bikers smelling of engine grease, yuppies in grays and browns, dopers chippying on coke and pot, and good ol' boy rockabilly fans like him—devotees of Elvis, Buddy Holly, Bill Haley, Chubby Checker, any fifties music that was uncomplicated and loud. Most of the rockabilly folks wore ducktails, leather jackets and square-toed boots with chains.

The party was breaking up, but David and Cindy talked to enough friends to establish their presence. No one would remember exactly when they arrived or left. Cindy seemed to have her shit together again. He thought, Those drama courses sure weren't wasted.

They mingled with departing guests and wound up at Perky's restaurant at Kirby and Richmond talking to a couple of the Bounders, another useful alibi point. They stayed for an hour or so, picking at their food, till the place was nearly empty.

On the way back home Cindy resumed her dying-swan number. "David," she said, "we've got to find the glove. They'll get fingerprints."

He'd already decided that the danger wasn't as great as they'd imagined. "Cindy," he said, "remember how sweaty our hands were? There's gonna be nothing in there but a big smear." He wished he could be sure.

At home they worked at remembering whom they'd seen, so the names would come to mind when they were questioned. They took baths to wash away fibers, gunpowder residues, driveway dust, anything that might place them at the death scene. They watched TV for a while, but he was still too nervous to concentrate. Around 6 A.M. he noticed that Cindy was breathing hard. He fell asleep.

52

Sergeant Mike St. John walked the perimeter and marked fresh tire tracks for casting. Even at daybreak, it was soppy work. The temperature had dipped into the seventies, but the air was drenched. It was a typical night in June. The weather hadn't changed much in a month and wouldn't till October, except to get hotter.

A crime-scene unit arrived and began videotaping room by room. The young detective was impressed. But of course these were no ordinary murders. A well-to-do lawyer, a wife with a gold watch, diamond ring, gold ring, gold ear studs, and two gold necklaces around her neck when she was blown away in her bed—all the ingredients of an ooh-and-ah.

He conducted spot interviews with neighbors, passers-by, the newspaper delivery boy. He watched as Carl Kent took another crack at J. W. O. Campbell and the kids. A Spanish-speaking detective arrived to interrogate the maid and heard more detail about a daughter named Cindy. There'd been loud arguments lately with the mother. She had a boyfriend named David who was *muy malo* and had slapped one of the boys. The interviewer asked where this Cindy lived. The maid came up with an address on Kingston.

"Let's go," Kent told his junior partner.

They knocked and an old woman stepped from the apartment across the hall. "Police officers," St. John told her, showing his ID. "We'd like to take a look inside."

"You can't," the woman said, rubbing sleep from her eyes. "My granddaughter's not home."

Kent pushed and the door swung open. The woman cried, "You can't go in there!"

St. John entered to loud music. The stereo and lights were on. The old woman made a few more comments outside the door. Kent said, "Look for anything that'll tie in Miss Cindy —receipts for the gun, ammo, any damn thang."

It was a cramped one-bedroom apartment. On the kitchen table to the left, mold grew from opened cans. Battalions of roaches ran for cover. The young detective tried to remember if his tetanus shots were current. "Carl!" he called out. "Don't touch anything!"

They found pencil sketches of a young woman with lovely Asian eyes and a shy smile. Two or three were tasteful nudes, and the others could have been hung in a church auditorium. Kent pulled out another and said, "Looky here."

It showed the same woman sitting on a floor, legs akimbo, knees pulled up. She appeared to be masturbating with her hand or an object.

"And looky *here!*" Kent said. "She musta held a mirror around her knees, aimed it at her crotch, and sketched what she seen."

St. John took a look. A vagina was in the foreground of the drawing, backed by plump breasts and that same Mona Lisa face. In the middle of the vagina were tiny silhouettes of a naked man and woman embracing. Kent said, "You can see the mentality of this ol' gal."

The door opened and the grandmother hobbled in. Kent told her why they were there, and the news seemed to hit her hard. "Virginia's my daughter," she said as she rubbed her hands down her face. St. John thought, This is always the toughest part.

The woman gave her name as Mrs. Helen Amaya. She said she'd last seen Cindy at eight-thirty the night before. The granddaughter had left a phone number, 522-6089, and said she would be reachable there in an emergency. The detectives thanked her, washed their hands and left.

The phone number produced a sleepy-sounding man who loudly convinced St. John that he'd never heard of Cindy Ray and why was some miserable asshole waking him up the first thing Saturday morning? Obviously the woman had left her grandmom a phony number.

53

David awoke Saturday morning at nine and remembered that he and Cindy had a breakfast date at his mother's. Cecelia greeted them warmly; she'd always seemed pleased to see them together and David knew why. She flat out wanted them married. "Where do you think you'll ever find another Cindy?" she asked him once. "Why, she's an angel!" With a few reservations, David agreed.

His father didn't appear for breakfast. David thought, He's probably in his rabbit warren reading a book. You can't even see him behind the stacks. After we leave, he'll come in and make those pukey butter-poached eggs that he likes and then he'll read *Emma* for the fifty-first time or listen to Louis Armstrong while Mom tiptoes around all day.

David couldn't eat. He'd been monitoring the radio and hadn't heard a word about the Campbells. He thought, What the hell do I have to *do?* When he realized that sleeplessness was making him a little irrational, he called himself to order. His own unreason could set off Cindy's, and that could be disastrous.

After breakfast she insisted on stopping at her apartment for a few minutes. David thought, Some day she's gonna get home and find everything gone. She never locked her door because she lost her keys so often.

Cecelia came along for the ride. Cindy told the two Wests to wait in the car. A few minutes later she ran out and said, "Somebody's been here!"

David went up. Garbage was strewn on the floor and some of the cabinets were open. He told himself, This is nuts. It had to be the cops. He wondered how they'd picked up the trail so fast. *From that fucking glove?* Or had somebody snitched them off? Wickie was the only one who knew anything, and he was getting closer and closer to burnout these days. He was capable of anything.

At the second-floor landing, David recognized Cindy's grandmom. She looked as though she'd been crying. "The

police were here," the old woman said. David had never
liked her. She'd invited him in for tea one day and he'd seen
her breasts through her gown. He could never respect her
after that.

"The . . . police?" Cindy asked.

"I've got something to tell you, Cindy," Mrs. Amaya said.
"Honey, I've got to tell you."

David thought, Well, *tell* her, for Christ's sake! He still
felt testy. "I've got bad news for you," the old bag droned.
"Cindy, your mommy and daddy were . . . killed by burglars."

Burglars? David liked that.

Cindy went limp. The blood seemed to drain from her
face. She threw out her arms in a crucifixion pose. "Oh, my
God," she moaned. *"Nooooooo!"*

David thought, Natalie Wood couldn't play it better. She
wailed like a Moslem atop a minaret. Tears slid from her
eyes in twin black streaks. Her shoulders bucked and
heaved. "Oh, David," she said breathlessly. "It can't be. Not
. . . Mother and Daddy."

Grandmom and granddaughter embraced. Mrs. Amaya
sniffed, patted Cindy a few times and pulled away. Cindy
slumped to the floor and covered her face, breathing like a
distance runner. The old woman's narrowed eyes made
David wonder what she was thinking.

He dialed the police emergency number and reported the
break-in for the record. He drove his mother home and then
took Cindy to the nearest One's A Meal. *Killed by burglars.*
Things were looking up. This time he ate.

In the afternoon he drove Cindy to J.W.O. Campbell's
house for a meeting of the survivors. She looked shocked
and shattered, but she told her sisters that she wanted to
share their time of grief.

54

Dr. Eduardo Bellas of the Harris County medical examiner's office spent Sunday afternoon autopsying the bodies. Virginia Haefner Campbell, he dictated into his tape recorder, was a well-nourished and well-developed white female measuring 5 feet 4½ inches and weighing 131 pounds. Her black-brown hair was 4½ inches in length, her ears pierced, her fingernails and toenails painted red, her teeth natural. Her heart weighed .67 pound, her lungs 1.71, her liver 3.54, her spleen .14, her kidneys .66. There were six ounces of partially digested material in her stomach, including multiple fragments of vegetables, plus traces of salicylates in her urine and nicotine in both blood and urine. The victim had come to her death as a result of "gunshot wounds (2) of the head (face) and gunshot wound of the chest through and through." She had also suffered a through-and-through wound and a grazing wound of the right upper arm, probably from one of the bullets that caused her death.

The assistant medical examiner found James Hiram Campbell to be a well-nourished, well-developed white male who measured 6 feet 4 inches and weighed 201 pounds. He was dressed in blue shorts and a pink short-sleeved shirt and was wearing a white-metal wrist watch. His black hair measured 4 inches in length at the top of the head. His right eye was brown; "the left eye was collapsed with a gunshot wound of entrance in the internal angle of the eye." His nose was freshly fractured. His teeth were natural and in good condition. He had not been circumcised. His heart weighed .92 pounds, his lungs 2.01, his liver 4.16, his spleen .44, his kidneys .68. "The stomach contained 3 ounces of a light brown fluid with nearly digested particles, some of them identified as vegetables." There was a trace of nicotine in his blood and urine. The victim had come to his death as a result of "gunshot wounds (2) of the head and gunshot wound of the abdomen into chest."

Except for a slight curvature of Virginia Campbell's spine, both victims had been normal and healthy at the time of death.

55

Late Saturday afternoon Betty Campbell Hinds and her husband left the rendezvous at Uncle J.W.'s and drove to the old home on Memorial. It seemed to Betty that Richard's grief had already transposed into anger. He was an intense young computer programmer with the reddish face of a Scots Guard and a stiff crop of bronze hair. Nobody called him Dick.

The Hindses found the family house unlocked and dark. It was a surprise. At the least they'd expected a police guard.

The other survivors wandered in, first Maria, then the oldest and youngest sisters, Michelle and Jamie. Michelle poked inside her mother's beige purse. "There's nothing in here," she called out. "No money. No keys." Betty thought, Mother always carried a blue key chain with a silver letter C. Where is it?

Maria said that the *señora* had had much money at the mall the night before. "She showed it to me." Betty checked the purse and found only an empty rust-colored wallet and a checkbook.

They looked around the house and couldn't find the keys. Daddy's attaché case was also missing. He was scheduled to try an out-of-town case Monday morning, and he usually stashed cash in the case when he traveled.

How ugly, Betty thought. For a few hundred dollars Mother and Daddy are dead.

Someone had to clean up the bedroom, but Betty couldn't bring herself to volunteer. Michelle and Jamie also hung back. After a while Richard and Maria carried rags and a bucket upstairs. They returned in an hour with the bloody curtains and bedding and a bullet casing that the police had somehow overlooked. Betty started to ask what the room looked like, but a look at Richard's pale face told her not to ask. A shaken Maria disappeared into the laundry room. Betty thought, Thank God for both of them.

No one had seen Cindy since her brief afternoon appearance at Uncle J.W.'s. The other three sisters sat up late talking. After midnight, they bedded down in their childhood home.

Betty thought, Less than twenty-four hours ago Mother and Daddy were alive. She clung to Richard and tried to sleep.

56

Detective Sergeants Gilbert Schultz and Paul Motard caught the case about thirty hours after the first cries of *"Muertos!"* The scene men had worked around the clock, but normal procedure called for day teams to take over ongoing investigations. Carl Kent and Michael St. John would remain on the case in secondary roles.

Gil Schultz was a former steelworker, an ex-Marine and a streetwise investigator who frequently handled special assignments for the chief. In his early forties, he fought weight, neither drank nor smoked, and spoke in a soft, compressed voice that seemed to leak out the edges of his mouth. He was heavyset, with sandy brown hair worn modishly over his ears, a small hawk-nose, and pale eyes which his detractors described as "piggy." He bought his polyester doubleknits at J. C. Penney's and joked that they were from "Jacques Pen-yay's." He was cynical, stubborn, sardonic and liked to poke good-hearted fun at blacks, Orientals, females, homosexuals, politicians and himself. "I run my house," he said. "I run the vacuum cleaner. I run the dishwasher. . . ."

His partner's background was books and scholarship. Paul Motard, son of a college professor and grandson of a Canadian Mountie, was in his late twenties and so shy that it was almost a handicap. But he'd been a virtuoso homicide investigator since scoring second highest on the detective test at twenty-four.

He hadn't taken to Schultz when they'd first paired off a few months before the Campbell murders. "Gil messes with people's heads," he told his wife. Before long he'd revised his opinion. "You gotta learn not to take Gil seriously. He manipulates, he tries to get a rise. He'll take some semipsycho into an interrogation room screaming and fighting. Fifteen minutes later he sends for the confession form."

Now it was Sunday morning, June 20, 1982, and the partners were en route to the scene of the crime. So far, the forensics stank. There were no fingerprints on the casings, none in the murder room, and not even a smudged palm print on the opened window or the ledge. The rubber glove was on its way to the FBI lab for laser-testing, but it was the type that seldom produced prints. And anyway, both detectives knew that fingerprints were overrated. You didn't solve one case in a hundred with prints. You solved cases with your mouth—and other people's.

The nightshift detectives had already looked at a couple of suspects: Cynthia Ray and her boyfriend David West. They appeared fairly straight—college types, good backgrounds. Ray had no priors; West had taken a misdemeanor fall for pot on the West Coast. He was an ex-Marine corporal, Good Conduct Medal, marksmanship medals, honorable discharge, nothing to suggest criminal tendencies. One of the other cops knew his parents and said they were old-time Texans who went back to an ambassador to Mexico and a bunch of judges and doctors. He said the father was an electronics genius who designed transformers and the mother had been an actress. It didn't sound promising.

The homicide team met J. W. O. Campbell and came away with the same impression as their predecessors. He seemed to be cooperating but didn't reveal anything they didn't know. They made a note to run at him again.

They interviewed three of the sisters and learned that some of James Campbell's clients paid him with TV sets and other merchandise. Motard thought, There're at least five old TVs in this house and I'll bet every damn one's hot.

Maybe one of Campbell's clients came back to settle a score. It made for a long list of suspects.

One of the sisters mentioned the dogs. "What dogs?" Schultz asked.

"Mother and Daddy had two dogs," Betty Hinds answered. "I took one to the Humane Society last month."

"Where's the other?"

"Rufus?" Jamie Lee answered. "He wandered off." Schultz made a note.

The sisters said they had no idea who'd killed their parents or who might have borne a grudge, but they all seemed nervous about the absent sister. "Could Cynthia have been involved?" Motard asked quietly.

Jamie yelped, "Cindy?" Her hand flew to her face. "No way!"

"Well," Schultz put in, "who else might have wanted them dead?"

"I don't know," said the tall young sister with the straight chestnut hair and the slightly vague manner. "But it certainly wasn't Cindy. She was dependent on Mother and Daddy."

"Where's she now?" Motard asked. "I thought she was gonna help us out."

"She'll be along," someone said.

Schultz wondered what made Jamie so certain that Cynthia was clean. Years ago he'd read a little abnormal psychology. A phenomenon called "denial" was common in close-knit families. He hoped he wasn't encountering it.

Late in the afternoon an old Cadillac turned into the driveway, and a bearded man got out with a good-looking woman. "It's them," said Betty Hinds.

Both looked hung over. West shook hands and trotted off to the den as though he were familiar with the house. Cynthia said she'd be glad to answer questions, but first she needed coffee.

The group assembled in the kitchen. Schultz wished the others would butt out, but he didn't make a point of it. Onlookers didn't help interrogations. The best setting was a small room with no windows, not a kitchen with folks standing around. The way you did it, you sat real close and stared at their eyes and watched every movement. After a while you began saying things like, "Ma'am, I'm afraid you're not being truthful. I can tell because your eyes are starting to water. You're not looking at me. Your voice is quivering." You just kept hammering in a quiet way. It worked.

Motard slipped out the back door while Schultz began questioning Cynthia in a soft voice. She said that she'd lived at the Kingston address for a year, that she'd known West for two years and had stayed with him last night. Her cup rattled in its saucer as she told how West drove her around a lot, most recently in the loaner Cadillac parked in the driveway. She said she was unemployed. She'd divorced Michael Ray five or six years ago. The last she'd heard, he was in Philadelphia. No, she didn't think her exhusband would have any reason to kill her parents.

Goddamn, Schultz thought, if I could get this audience out of here, Cindy and I could do some business. "Is it true," he asked, "that your parents were trying to adopt your sons?"

"No," she said firmly. "I never heard anything like that."

"Cynthia, when's the last time you saw your mother and father?"

"Friday night around ten." He noticed that her hands were shaking less. "I got ten dollars from my mother. David drove me here." She stubbed out her cigarette. "I don't know how to drive."

Motard walked through the kitchen door and whispered that he had the license number and description of the Cadillac. Schultz asked Cindy, "Will you be available to come down and give us elimination statements and fingerprints?"

"I'll do all I can," the woman said calmly. "I can't imagine who would do something like this to Mother and Daddy."

Schultz wasn't satisfied but withheld judgment. A lot of detectives jumped to early conclusions that bit them in the ass later. As a young officer he'd made that mistake a time or two. For now, Cynthia Ray would be just another suspect.

As for West, there was even less to go on. He watched TV

in the den as though bored. That's not a natural reaction, Schultz decided. His girlfriend's daddy and mom were murdered in this house last night. We'll wait a few days and see if Mr. David DuVal West stays as bored as he seems.

On the way downtown Motard asked, "Well, Gilbert, is it them?"

"They might be good for it," Schultz said as he navigated the undercover sedan in the heavy Sunday traffic. "But it looks a little too professional."

"She seems too klutzy to me," Motard said. "Can't drive, can't earn a living. It's hard to imagine her walking into a bedroom and shooting people." He was thinking, Women don't use forty-fives. They like cute little handfuls, twenty-twos, twenty-fives.

"West might be dirty," Schultz said. "He's a cold-looking little bastard. What's the matter with his eyes?"

"One's blue and one's brown."

"What's that mean?"

"Nothing."

They stopped at the medical examiner's office and collected the evidence from Dr. Bellas's autopsy. "Hey, look!" Motard said as he picked up a clear plastic bag. "That's a silvertip. No wonder there's no ballistics."

Schultz frowned and thought, What kind of triggerman is this? He takes the trouble to use silvertips so they'll self-destruct, but he uses an automatic that leaves hulls with extractor and ejector markings. That was why most professional hit men preferred revolvers; the hulls stayed with the weapon. He decided they must be dealing with a very unprofessional professional. In a way it was a relief.

57

On the way back to Vermont Street, David bought the *Post* and the *Chronicle*. "Hey," he said when he opened them in his living room, "we made the headlines!"

He read aloud from the *Chronicle:* " 'The Campbells' bodies were found at about 3:55 A.M. in the master bedroom of the home after their ten-year-old grandson who was spending the night heard noises, police said.' " He stopped. "They must mean Michael," he said. He thought, Well, they got the kid's age wrong, but at least they didn't make the same mistake as "Crimestoppers." The TV show had shown an artist's rendering of a man in a ski mask firing a pistol while a kid cowered at his feet. Some shit.

He held up the *Post*'s page-one story so Cindy could see the headline: LAWYER, WIFE SLAIN IN HOME. "It says they were shot as they slept in their Memorial-area home," he said, " 'with their two grandsons asleep on the floor near their bed.' What the fuck does *that* mean?"

"Oh, my God, David," she said, "didn't you feel something under your feet?"

"Yeah," he said. "I thought it was bedding."

He read on: " 'Kent said the maid, who police refused to identify, told him the children were allowed to sleep in their grandparents' room each Friday night.' "

He asked Cindy if she'd known about the arrangement. "I guess so," she said.

He flared up. "You *guess* so? Why the fuck didn't you tell me?"

She said she was sorry. She didn't seem concerned. Goddamn, he said to himself, what a partner I picked!

He read on: " 'Kent said the boys were awakened by the shooting and covered their heads with the sleeping bags. They did not emerge from the bags until the noise stopped. . . . He apparently did not see the children, or maybe he just did not want to kill any children. But he was in there long enough to kill those people and scare those little kids," Kent said. "The children did not see the assailant," he said.' "

David thought, Maybe they saw me and maybe they didn't. The cops might be lying to protect them. They did things like that on "Hill Street Blues" and "Kojak." He remembered seeing the boys Saturday at J.W.'s house. They were unusually quiet. Maybe they'd been coached.

The *Post* story described the killings as "an apparent execution" and quoted a detective as saying, "Someone appar-

ently had a grudge against them and killed them or had
them killed. . . . The person apparently knew precisely
how to get where he wanted in the house and do what he
wanted. . . ." That was a little too close to the truth. He
wondered, What happened to the burglary theory?

He almost laughed at some quotes from the Campbells'
friends. "Listen to this," he told Cindy. " 'He was just a
regular guy. He was a very good lawyer and very well liked,
had no bad habits. His wife was lovely. There was just no
reason.' Some shit, huh?"

Cindy nodded. He read aloud, " 'Virginia never had a
cross word for anybody. . . .' "

Cindy laughed. He continued: " 'They both were very
dedicated to each other. They were just a fun-loving family.' " Yeah, he thought, except for a little incest.

Cindy handed back the *Chronicle*. There was no mention
of children in the room. David wondered if the *Post* might
have made a mistake. Or been taken in by the cops. It
wouldn't be the first time.

He thought, Those kids are time bombs. We'll have to do
something.

58

Schultz was on the phone when Paul Motard walked into
the office Monday morning. The junior man poured black
coffee and sat.

Schultz's office was Schultz. A placard bore his name and
rank. A picture of a kitten desperately clinging to a rope
bore the caption LORD HELP ME HANG IN THERE. In a place
of honor was a photograph of a barren thirty-acre plot that
Schultz had bought in the hill country, intending to convert
it to a retirement paradise in about four years.

It was morning, but the air already smelled of kippers.
Schultz had been having trouble with his diet and was ballooning toward his upper limit of 250, at which point,

Motard reflected, he'll begin starving himself back down to 195 and the office'll stop smelling like kippers.

When Schultz hung up, Motard said, "I've been thinking about the boys."

"Me too," Schultz said.

The funeral was set for 1 P.M. the next day, and one of the sisters had mentioned that Michael and Matthew wouldn't be attending. The two detectives decided to do some volunteer babysitting.

This third day after the murders went slowly. Michelle Campbell phoned to say that a few years ago Cindy had considered killing their father and told Jamie about it. Motard told her to send Jamie down to make a statement, but the oldest sister said, "Jamie's not ready. She's still trying to disbelieve that Cindy did it."

A brass hat from the chief's office dropped by and mentioned that the Campbell case was one ooh-and-ah that better by God be solved P.D.Q.

A private security guard reported that the Campbells' automatic backyard light had been jiggered so that it wouldn't go on automatically at night.

A man named Carson "Ed" Watson called to say that he'd seen a white male standing by a red and white car outside the Campbell house at around 3:45 or 4 A.M. on Saturday. Motard and Schultz figured he'd seen J. W. O. Campbell and his Cadillac.

The two detectives interviewed the brother and came away realizing that he was probably clean—a little salty, maybe, but that was just his way. J.W. said he would do anything to catch the killer. The rumor that he'd deliberately stepped on the surgical glove turned out to be false; no one could figure out how it started. The rubber glove was still being lasered at the FBI lab in Washington.

J.W. volunteered the names of a couple of disgruntled clients; one had filed a complaint with the bar association. But J.W. said that his brother hadn't made many enemies. A few years back he'd been crosswise with a respected Houston lawyer named Donald Thiel, but it was mostly loud words and heavy breathing. Thiel had met Cindy Ray and blurted out, "Oh, you're Dirty Jim's daughter!" James

Campbell had blown up when his daughter recounted the story, but peace had been restored.

"What about the will?" Schultz asked. It would be interesting to see how the estate was parceled out.

"A 1962 document leaves everything to Virginia," J.W. said. "That's all we found." Other important papers were missing: insurance policies, deeds, contracts, stocks, notes—documents needed to assess the estate.

The detectives visited James Campbell's old friend and traveling companion, J. Robert Harris, in the Houston Bar Center building. Harris said he was probate attorney for the estate and guessed it was worth at least $390,000. No, he hadn't found a current will; it was probably hidden away. "It'll turn up," he said.

Motard asked, "Did Mr. Campbell talk about cutting Cynthia out?"

"Never."

"Did he talk about adopting the boys?"

"Not in front of me."

Schultz asked Harris who might have done the killings. "No idea," the friendly lawyer answered. "Nobody could've hated the Campbells that much. They were a likable couple."

The lawyer refilled his pipe and offered a tidbit of information. "A couple of months ago Campbell bought a pistol and went out to a range. Seemed strange at the time. He'd never mentioned guns before that."

"Why'd he do that?" Motard asked.

"Dunno. We had an office break-in sometime back. One night he chased an intruder out of his house. It was probably one or the other."

Motard wondered, Did Campbell know in advance that somebody was gunning for him? Did Virginia? That would explain the shotgun in the room. He said, "We heard he gambled. Did he pay up?"

"Oh, yes," Harris said, puffing on his big pipe. "He made a little game out of cheating at golf, but he was an honest man. My wife and I used to go to Vegas with the two of them. He'd make five-hundred-dollar bets and almost always come out ahead. He didn't run tabs."

Descending in the creaky elevator, the detectives agreed that lawyers seldom died without leaving an up-to-date will. Motard said he'd noted a placard on the receptionist's desk: "Have you made your will yet?"

They checked building security and confirmed the break-in. No one had reported any documents missing. "Where's that leave us?" Motard wondered aloud as they headed back to headquarters.

Schultz sighed and said, "Nowhere."

59

That night, Cindy Ray's old friend and art teacher Gwen Sampson answered her phone on Tonawanda Drive. "Hi," a man said. "How ya doing?"

Gwen recognized the voice of a former student who'd kept in touch. "Oh, hi," she said.

"How'd she do it?" he asked.

"How'd who do what?"

"Cindy Ray. Her parents were killed."

Gwen blinked. "Are you *sure?*"

"Do they live on Memorial? Is their name Campbell?"

"Why . . . yes!"

"Well, it's them." He read a passage from the Sunday paper.

Gwen had to offer her sympathies to Cindy. Her darkroom was out of business, and the two women hadn't seen much of each other since Cindy started waltzing away with her male visitors. But they were still friends.

She called and asked how she was holding up. Cindy said, "As well as can be expected." She seemed thankful for the call. They agreed to meet for lunch.

60

"I think it's best if I go with you to the funeral," David told Cindy. "They're not my family, so I don't have to pull my hair out. I'll just act respectful and ask if there's anything I can do. Remember, act sad and uptight. Don't overdo."

Cindy looked up at him from the floor. She looked jumpy.

"Cry a little," he instructed her. "But don't wake up the dead."

On the way to his mother's house, he warned, "We can expect the police to be there. That's the standard thing. They'll be checking everybody." Cindy said she'd be careful.

Cecelia gave her a big hug. "I'm *so* sorry, baby," she said and patted her on the back. Cindy looked properly bereaved. His mom said, "You don't have to feel bad about not having funeral clothes. I've got everything you need."

She produced a complete outfit, even to a pair of black shoes that David hadn't seen in years. Cindy left her jeans and T-shirt to be picked up later, and they headed for the house on Memorial.

61

At noon, Betty Hinds's quiet husband Richard stood alone in the dusty front room of the Campbell house, waiting for the members of the funeral. No one had been sleeping well in the murder house. Not only were they all in mourning, but they were worried about the assassin's return. Hinds had admired the elder Campbells and keenly felt their loss, but at the moment most of his sympathy was for his wife. Betty was devastated. Lying alongside him, she'd awakened him nightly with wrenching gulps and sobs.

It seemed to the computer programmer that the best way to help out was to find the murderer. Until these killings he hadn't considered himself a vengeful man, but he seethed with indignation over the thought that someone, for whatever misguided or stupid or insane reasons, had violated this house and executed its owners in their beds, had destroyed the flesh of his wife's flesh, the blood relatives of their dear baby, Amelia. He couldn't imagine a crime more foul.

He suspected West and Cindy; she'd always been a disruptive force. If you plotted the family behavior on a graph, the line would be steady except for a jagged spike here and there. The spikes would be Cindy—running away five or six times, getting married three or four times, dumping babies on her parents, complaining that the family was persecuting her, stirring up trouble between her parents, accusing and griping and carping. . . . He stopped. The list was unending.

He kept reminding himself to be fair. Right now Cindy was the people's choice for killer, simply because killers were usually square pegs and so was she. Was the parallel reasonable? Did parricide extrapolate from a lifetime of troublemaking? He wasn't sure and he kept his peace. There was enough trauma already.

Betty, Michelle and Jamie were upstairs dressing when Hinds answered the first knock on the front door. It was the thickset detective with the pursed lips and the tall one who looked like Dennis Weaver in *McCloud*. They were dressed in dark suits. "We'll stay here and keep an eye on things while you go to the services," the younger one said in a solemn voice. Hinds didn't object when they retired to the family room.

A few minutes later he admitted Cindy and her boyfriend. It occurred to him that this was the second straight time they'd come to the front door instead of using the well-worn entrance in the rear. They seemed to be going out of their way to show an unfamiliarity with the house. But that was silly; Cindy had grown up here; she couldn't distance herself from this place or this family. It seemed suspicious.

Cindy wore a black dress and West a blue suit that looked retrieved from storage. She excused herself to join her sisters upstairs and Hinds escorted West back to the family room. The detectives smiled as they entered.

Cindy's pal started talking immediately—fast, jerky, mal-apropos. There was a rehearsed stiffness to him as he fin-gered his beard, crossed and uncrossed his legs and babbled about the heat. In fact it wasn't any hotter than usual for a June day in Houston, and there were more relevant subjects on the table. Hinds decided that his first speculations stood up.

62

Schultz didn't feel optimistic. The redheaded kid and his little brother had been jabbering, chasing each other, acting like colts on oats. They'd walked right up to West with no sign of fear. Schultz wondered, If he was the shooter, wouldn't they have reacted?

"Hey, whatta you guys like to do?" he asked on the patio behind the house. He loved children, enjoyed "messin' with 'em," as he put it. He'd cracked a few cases that way.

Michael, the eight-year-old, answered, "I don't know if I can talk to you. I gotta call my uncle. He's an attorney."

Schultz thought, I done heard enough legal bullshit. "Come over here, pardner," he said. "Me and Sergeant Motard, we don't bite."

The boys hung back.

Motard said, "Come on, guys. Let's go for a ride." He gestured toward the police cruiser.

Seven-year-old Matthew edged alongside his big brother. "No, thanks," he said warily.

"It's got a radio," Schultz said.

"A siren," Motard said.

The boys stayed put. Out of the corner of his eye Schultz saw the funeral procession passing in front of the house and nudged his partner. He thought, They must be on their way to Memorial Oaks. It was a solemn scene, the hearse and the gray stretch limos moving slowly past the big old house where the Campbells had tried to do the right thing by these boys.

After a while the kids began dragging out their toys. They had it all, from miniature cars to Turbo bikes to robots that talked and took orders. Schultz thought, They got more electronic equipment than our goddamn intelligence unit. They were typical Memorial kids. Where he grew up, boys played with rocks, fists and clubs, followed by knives and zip guns. "How about a game?" he said.

Michael said, "Pac-Man?"

"Great!" Schultz said. "I'm the champ of Texas and Louisiana."

The boys steered them to a game room in the garage. "Hey," Motard said, "what else y'all got in here?"

"We got Donkey Kong," the smaller boy said. "Grand Prix racing. We got. . . . whatever." He's a cute little guy, Schultz said to himself. Dark hair, dark eyes, a hint of a frijole accent. That's the way it was in these rich neighborhoods. Wetbacks did the child-raising.

The boys won big. Schultz restored his confidence by beating Motard at a game while Matthew screamed advice. It was a slow process, but they were becoming friends. He looked at his watch. One hour gone, not much more to go.

The boys insisted on shooting pool. They weren't strong enough to use English or draw, and Schultz had to throw a game or two. Where he'd grown up, men earned their livings narrowly missing shots.

The kids wanted to shoot arrows. It was getting tiring. "We'd like to," Schultz said, "but it's against regulations."

"Why?"

"Uh, we're only allowed to shoot guns."

The boys fell quiet. Schultz knew how to use silence as an interrogation tool, and let it thicken. After a while Matthew said, "Did you know that Cindy's really my mother?" He gave the impression that he'd only recently found out.

"I didn't know that," Schultz said. Slowly he began to steer the talk to the murders. "What'd y'all see?" he asked after more sparring.

"It was awful," Michael said.

Matthew piped up, "We saw the man's arm. It had a tattoo."

"Yeah," Michael said. "It was dripping blood."

The killer, both boys agreed, had fangs and bad breath and stood seven feet high. He threatened to come back and kill the whole Memorial Drive. Schultz said to himself, Go ahead, kids. Get the horseshit out of your system.

When they slacked off, he smiled and said, "You guys are jivin' me, right?" Sheepish grins responded. "Now c'mon," he said. "We need y'all's help. You want us to catch the bad guys, don'tcha? Tell us what you really saw."

Michael said he'd been awakened by the light going on. "I thought my father was gonna read a book. I heard four or five booms. I closed my eyes tight and covered my ears." He said he'd peeped over the top of the bed when the booms stopped. Both parents' faces were red.

"Michael woke me up," Matthew said, "and I asked him if the red was dark or light."

"Why'd you ask that?" Motard put in.

"I don't know. I was sleepy. I stood up and looked and then I ran out the door screaming."

"We ran to Maria's," Michael said.

Schultz asked, "Did you see the bad guy?"

Both boys frowned and shook their heads, but they didn't seem too sure.

Schultz caught his partner's eye. Paul's look said he agreed: they were spinning their wheels. Maybe later. Now it was time to go after adults.

63

At the funeral, Robert Harris's handsome gray-haired wife walked up to Cindy and said, "Hello. I'm Sue Harris. I've always wanted to meet you." She squeezed Cindy tight. Cindy's body stiffened. Sue stepped back. It was embarrassing.

Betty Hinds sat next to Cindy and thought, She looks real nice in her black dress. When Betty started crying, so did

Cindy. It was almost as though she'd been cued. Betty hoped the tears were real and her sister was innocent.

Jamie felt too stressed to cry. She glanced at Cindy and her boyfriend and got the impression they weren't upset at all. Cindy looked as though the funeral were a minor ordeal.

All through the services, Maria stared hard at Cindy. It seemed to her that underneath the put-on facial expressions the *delincuente* daughter was laughing.

David was glad that Cindy didn't overdo her reaction. She was a hell of an actress and he was proud of her.

In a way, he was sorry the caskets were closed. He would have liked to check his marksmanship. He figured he'd shot about a B+.

When the morbid deal was over, Cindy dug her nails into his arm. "David! J.W. says we all have to go to headquarters."

"What for?"

"Something about fingerprints and formal statements."

"No big deal," he said. He patted her back, trying to calm her.

"Come along!" she insisted. He could feel the tension in her body through his mother's black dress. God, he thought, is this the same cool bitch that just won the Academy Award?

"No, go on," he said. "They didn't ask me, ya know?" She gave him an imploring look. "Just *go!*" he snapped.

He watched her rejoin the sisters. As their limo drove away, he thought, I can't let her think I'm abandoning her. She's scared shitless. I'll just drive on down there myself. It'll look like I've got nothing to hide.

64

Schultz and Motard watched as J. W. O. Campbell and the sisters were processed at headquarters. "We surely do apologize," Schultz said as the forlorn family gathered in the ugly old building just north of the downtown. "This is strictly for exclusionary purposes."

The detectives had intended to polygraph J.W. but changed their minds after they got to know him better. He'd once earned his living catching bail jumpers. The old bounty hunter had a lawman's eye and was fuming to catch his younger brother's killer. From now on he would be considered an ally.

Jamie, Betty and Michelle looked worn and abused in the bleached Polaroid prints. No suspicion had attached to any of them, since Betty and Michelle were at their homes in Austin the night of the killings and Jamie was in Knoxville. Cynthia's snapshot turned out better. With her narrow new nose she was almost beautiful.

When the boyfriend showed up, Motard took him aside and said, "Say, Dave, as long as you're here, why don't you give us a little statement?" He motioned West to a seat and deliberately fumbled for a sheet of paper. "This is what we call a confession form," the detective said, staring hard with his dark Gallic eyes. "You'll see that it has the Miranda warning across the top." He read the warning aloud.

West's weird eyes narrowed. "Confession form?" he said.

"Don't worry," Motard said as he rolled the pale blue paper into the typewriter. "It's because we never know where these interviews are gonna lead. If somebody confesses, we don't have to yank the form out and start over."

Motard pecked away as West talked. He told how he and Cindy had rapped with Rudyard's bartender and a guy named Rick Murray till 2 A.M. the night of the killings. "About what?" Motard asked.

"Dogs. Beer. Then we went to my place."

"What'd you do there?" Motard asked.

There was another pause. "We, uh . . . we made love. But don't put that in. Just say we went home for a while."

Motard obliged. It was West's statement; eventually he would have to approve and sign it.

West said, "We woke up around three-thirty and went to a party in a one-story wooden house."

"See anybody?"

"A guy named Paul. A guy named . . . Riley, I think." The party was breaking up, he said, and they went to breakfast. Around 9 or 10 A.M. they dropped by Cindy's apartment and found trash on her floor. That was about it, West said. He wished he could remember more because he'd sure like to help. Poor Cindy, this was so hard on her. Hard on all of them. If anything occurred to him, he'd be happy to call.

Motard handed over a card with his office and home phone numbers. "Thanks," West said. Motard thought he came off as semicool.

Schultz worked Cynthia slow and easy. It was like a first training session with a fractious mare. She kept lighting cigarettes while others smoldered in the ashtray. Typing was hard on Schultz's stubby index fingers and he hated smoke with an ex-smoker's passion, but otherwise he was in his element in the windowless chamber. He'd once told Motard: "I used to argue with murderers, bawl them out. Now I talk nice. 'Hey, you hungry? Can I get you a candy bar or sumpin'?' A few sessions later they're telling me where they hid the ax."

Cindy started to cry when she read the passage on the top of the confession form. He reminded himself to be charitable; she'd just laid away her parents.

He stared intently as she fluttered her hankie and spoke in the voice of a choking child. As usual he committed the bare minimum to paper: "I last saw my parents around ten P.M. Friday night. David brought me over. He lives with me. Mother gave me ten dollars. I thanked her and told her I loved her. She asked if I wanted to see the boys. I was in a hurry and left. David and I went to a movie, 'E.T.' It was sold out."

Schultz didn't push. Cynthia Ray wasn't going anywhere. The next time they met, she'd remember how easy it had been to talk to a nice old guy named Schultz.

65

For years Betty Hinds had been accustomed to her sister Cindy's curious lapses of taste, but she was still surprised by the latest one. It was Wednesday, June 23, the day after the funeral, the fifth day after the killings, and the sisters were gathered in the family dining room to discuss the estate. Cindy showed up in a tight T-shirt with a logo across her breasts: DOUBLE TROUBLE. Betty despaired.

As administrator, Uncle J.W. planned to put the furniture and other main assets in storage for the time being, but he'd suggested that the daughters might want to select a few items of remembrance. Betty asked for the piano. Michelle picked out a favorite Oriental rug. A tearful Jamie said she didn't want anything. Maria hovered solicitously around the group, and when Michelle asked her if she wouldn't like a memento—a watch, a ring—the Mexican woman turned a grief-stricken face and said, "No! From your mother, *nada.*" Betty turned to Cindy, who'd arrived with her boyfriend West in a blue truck. "What would you like? Is there anything of sentimental value?"

Cindy and West exchanged glances before the hesitant answer: "Oh, well, I . . . don't know. I guess the VCR and the TV are the most salable."

Betty watched silently as they also selected an exercise bicycle, the well-stocked liquor cabinet and several other mementos. West carted each item to the truck in the driveway. In the kitchen he asked, "Can I have this French-English dictionary? I'd really love to go to Paris."

Betty glanced at him. He was holding a book her parents had bought years ago on a trip to Europe. She walked away.

Uncle J.W.O. Campbell reported that he still hadn't found a current will. Michelle came up with an updated list of current bank accounts and insurance policies provided by her mother. It was incomplete, but it was better than nothing. She reported that the estate appeared to include $150,000 in cash, a $150,000 double-indemnity insurance policy, fifty waterfront acres at Toledo Bend, fifty near Hempstead, several smaller lots and the fourplex on Kingston. The family home was worth $450,000.

Cindy asked, "What's the total?"

"Maybe a million and a half. Until we get more appraisals, I can't be definite."

Cindy looked annoyed. "A million and a half?" she repeated. Betty thought, She's never worked a day in her life and has no idea what a dollar means. She probably thinks Mother and Daddy were billionaires. I wonder if she'll make trouble later.

Michelle mentioned that Houston real-estate values were on the rise and if they could hold on to the undivided properties for a year or two, they would realize substantially larger shares. "We have to squeeze out every penny," she said. She was thirty-three and sensible, a Master of Fine Arts who taught photography at a private Catholic college in Austin. "We have others to support besides ourselves."

Betty nodded. She'd already agreed on Michelle's approach. So had Jamie. The three sisters turned toward the fourth. Betty thought, If this isn't a metaphor for our family history! We're smiling at her and she's glaring at us. "Cindy?" Michelle said. "How do you feel about waiting awhile?"

Cindy said, "I think you have a nerve telling me how you're gonna spend *my* money."

"We have to take care of Nanny Helen," the oldest sister said calmly. Michelle was the family head now, and she didn't seem reticent about it. "We have to provide for your boys, Cindy. I'm talking hundreds of thousands of dollars."

Cindy grabbed West by the arm. "Let's go," she said.

Michelle was usually even-tempered and pleasant, but she yelled after them, "If you don't want our help, then why don't you raise them yourself?"

The door slammed. The gears ground loudly as the blue truck backed out. Betty checked the kitchen table for the *Anglais-Français* dictionary. It was gone.

66

When Paul Motard arrived home the next evening, there was a message to call Homicide. He and Schultz had spent the day poring through stacks of forensic reports and ballistics and Xeroxes of Cynthia's drawings provided by various relatives. There were pictures of eyes and noses, nude studies, human figures with breasts and long hair on top and male genitalia below. The collection was like one big ink-blot text and they wished they could interpret it.

Motard called in and the duty man told him that Michelle Campbell had reported a problem at the house. "What kind of problem?" Motard asked.

"She wouldn't say. But she sounded scared."

Motard dialed the house. He'd hardly identified himself when Michelle shrieked, "Cindy's got the boys! They dragged the boys away."

"Wait a minute," Motard said. *"Who* dragged 'em away?" He thought the killer had returned.

"Cindy and West. Please, Sergeant, you've got to do something. Michael, he, he . . . clung to the doorframe. He clawed the walls. They grabbed him by the legs and pulled him out. He was screaming!"

Motard advised her to take a few deep breaths. "How'd Matthew take it?"

"He just looked . . . shocked." She paused. "Don't you see what this means?"

"I, uh—"

"Michael saw them kill Mother and Daddy! That's why they took him, why he's so scared. He knows what they'll do to him. *Don't you see?"*

Motard said he'd be right out.

67

Michael had turned docile on the way home, but as soon as they got inside David's house, Matthew picked up where his older brother had left off. To David his shrieking sounded like fingernails on a blackboard. He tried to shame the boy into shutting up by imitating him in a whiny Donald Duck voice: "I wanna be with Maria. *Neena nànna neener.* When are we gonna see Maria? *Whaagggh! Whaaagggh! Whaagggh . . . !*"

Cindy comforted her younger son, but he just cried louder. David knew what was going on. They were used to a mansion and a Mexican maid and grandparents who bought them enough toys to stock the Depelchin orphanage. They hated his house and everything about it. Well, he couldn't blame them. They were only seven and eight. He just wished they'd shut up.

But Michael wouldn't stop making ugly faces and Matthew wouldn't stop crying. David told them, "I'm not real crazy about this dump either, ya know? We're only gonna be here till we can get you set up better."

Matthew yelled for Maria. Cindy told him, "Not right now. Maybe later."

David took her aside and said, "You might as well shoot straight. They're not gonna see Maria again." Cindy said she wanted to wait a few days before breaking the news. He thought, she always puts things off. I love her, but she's about the most incompetent woman I've ever known.

It took a while to get Michael talking about the killings, but then he seemed eager. "Boy, you shoulda seen it! There was blood all over the place. It was real wild!"

Listen to him, David said to himself. It's strictly adventure. No sense of loss or grief. What a little monster! It's like, Fuck 'em, they're dead. He turned to Matthew and asked, "What'd *you* see?" The younger boy was still gulping and bawling, but he told his story. The two versions

matched, and David was convinced they'd seen nothing. He
was relieved. Not that he'd ever meant them any harm.

"Boys," he said, "I gotta tell you the truth. Your grandparents are dead and Maria doesn't have a job. So she's
gonna have to get her another job and you're not gonna see
her anymore."

"Not . . . ever?" Michael asked.

"Nope."

Matthew ran screaming into the bedroom. David hoped
the neighbors didn't hear.

68

At seven-five that night, the two detectives headed for the
house on Memorial in Schultz's 1979 green Chrysler four-
door. To the southeast, lightning flicked at Hobby Airport
and the Johnson Space Center. Goddamn, Schultz thought,
that last one hit close to Gilley's. "We're in for it, pardner,"
he said. It was one of those summer storms that suck up
moisture in the Gulf and dump it on Corpus and Galveston
and poor old Houston.

Motard glanced up. "Look at that green," he said. In
South Texas a blue-black sky was bad news and a gray-black
sky was worse, but the killer storms began with a menacing
hint of green.

Midway on Memorial Drive the rain fell so hard that
drivers gave up and pulled onto the shoulder to wait. Pine
trees shook like wet dogs. West of the Loop, muddy water
surged from storm drains and flooded the two-lane asphalt.
Schultz slowed to keep from drowning the brakes, and they
didn't reach the Campbell driveway till seven-forty.

Motard got out and opened the gate. In the stroboscopic
light of the storm, the blocky old house looked more like a
mausoleum than ever. Branches whipped the car as they
inched along the driveway. He grabbed his notebook and
ran for the back door. Schultz beat him. Motard wondered,
How'd he do that?

As they entered, all three sisters seemed to be talking at once. The most frequent word was "kidnap."

"Hold it," Schultz said. "It's not kidnapping to take your own sons."

"But the boys didn't want to go with her," Jamie said. "They *dragged* 'em out."

"Maybe you should call Child Welfare," Motard said. "You might have a child-abuse case." He hoped they would follow through. Then he and Schultz would have an excuse to jack at Cynthia and West again.

The lights guttered like candles as Betty described the karate exhibition West had put on for the kids just before leaving—"to show us how macho he is, I guess. Like 'Don't fool with me, I'm a tough Marine.' "

A wall lit up and then blackened as she asked why they didn't just arrest Cindy and West and interrogate the hell out of them. "We can't," Motard said. "We don't have the evidence."

"But we know it's them!" Michelle put in. "It couldn't be anybody else."

"We'll be back at 'em," Schultz said. "If they're guilty, we'll break 'em sooner or later."

"Not Cindy," Betty said. "She's a cold fish."

While Betty made coffee, the detectives studied the living room. Rain drove against the picture window. A creaky sound spun Schultz around; it was holly leaves rubbing the panes. The pendants on a chandelier tinkled as though in a light breeze, and then the place went black.

Someone screamed. "Paul?" he said.

"Right here," Motard said.

Michelle lit candles. Paul looked a little green. He was staring at a painting above the TV, a round vase of flowers on a small canvas, about two by three feet. A small signature said, "Virginia." Something drew Schultz closer.

The picture seemed to be pulsing, in and out, in and out. Schultz thought, Holy shit, the goddamn thing's alive.

He watched for several seconds, then went upstairs to compose himself. He'd never been bothered by murder scenes, but this one disturbed him. It felt as though leftover

violence still hung in the air. It also felt as though someone
were in the bedroom with him. He hurried downstairs.

Driving back to town, both detectives were quiet. They
were halfway to headquarters when Motard said, "Gil?"
"Yeah?"
"Did you see what that painting was doing?"
Schultz said, "I don't want to hear about it."

69

At two o'clock in the morning, Matthew ran screaming into
their bedroom and said he was scared. David thought, Goddamn, there goes our privacy! Cindy hadn't felt like sex
since the killings. Now the place would be a nunnery.

Lying in bed, he tried to figure out what to do with the
boys. He'd always wanted a son to play with and teach, but
he hadn't planned on a couple of wild animals.

Cindy was no help. She lacked spine; that's why she'd
dumped the kids on her parents in the first place. He told
her, "Cindy, you're gonna have to be the authority figure,
'cause I don't have the right, ya know?" But she wound up
yelling and losing control and begging him to take over.
"Okay," he said, "but I'm gonna do it my way."

He tried to remember his psychology courses. The trick
was to combine positive reinforcement and a touch of pun-
ishment: the carrot-and-stick routine. "People hate it when I
say this," he told Cindy, "but human nature and pit bull
nature aren't that different."

Little Matthew refused to eat, play or talk. "Poor little
me," he sobbed. *"Poor little me!"* He would cry himself into
exhaustion, uttering little whaaaggghs and whimpers, then
take a nap and start all over again. Once David shook him
and yelled, "Look, ya know, *stop it!*" A hand clamped over
the mouth only made things worse.

"It's a weapon he's using against us," David explained to
Cindy. "He's not hurting all that much, ya know, because

little kids don't have that much capacity to feel for someone else. They're all wrapped up in themselves. He's a selfish little kid. He's not sad. He's mad at the situation, not the death of his grandparents. He's thinking, How can the world be so mean to me? It's all a buncha bullshit, ya know?"

He tried a session of man-to-man, the kind of talk he'd longed for as a child. "Listen, Matthew," he said, "who the hell do you think you are? I realize you love Maria, but you gotta face facts. Look, your brother's not crying. He's got enough snap to realize this is reality, ya know?"

The kid blinked big reddened eyes. "You're not gonna be here any longer than you have to be, ya know?" David went on. "But you're making yourself obnoxious and it's not fair to us." He thought, Look at him. He's freaked! Nobody's ever talked straight to him before. "We realize you want Maria, but there's nothing can be done about that. And frankly, the world's not run on what you want. You're just gonna have to face up to that. Nobody wants to be around somebody that's whining like a baby all the time. You know damn good and well that you're not really crying, ya know? You're just making noise."

The kid didn't respond. "We'll try to do some good things together," David said. "But not if you keep making an ass outa yourself."

That night he took the boys to a Chinese restaurant. They complained that the food was stringy and goopy. Maybe my tastes are too exotic for them, he said to himself, but they need to eat something besides tacos and Pepsi.

At Tokyo Gardens the second night, Matthew whimpered all through the meal and neither kid would taste the sushi. "They're a coupla hicks," he fumed to Cindy. "That's one thing I can't stand. When it comes to food, they're fucking rednecks."

After dinner he took them to see *Firefox*. Michael liked the part where Clint Eastwood stole a Russian plane, but Matthew fell asleep. Back home, he yelled all night for Maria.

David thought, This has gone on for two days and the little bastard's louder than ever. Maybe I'm doing something wrong. He looked through one of his old psychology textbooks but couldn't concentrate. He realized that he needed assistance from an expert on child-raising. No prob, he said to himself. I know one of the best.

70

Cecelia pedaled painfully on her Schwinn. The Monopoly board protruded from the basket. Summer heat and humidity activated her arthritis and made the three-wheeler feel like a truck. But this was an emergency.

She was sorry David was having trouble with the boys, but glad for an excuse to see Cindy. It would be the first time since the murders almost two weeks back. She thought, The poor woman must still be in shock. She always idolized her father.

At Waugh Drive, Cecelia brought a speeding car to a halt with her upraised palm. She thought how much she still missed her own father, dead all these years. She saw him in brush strokes: gleaming tanned shoulders, muscles like rocks, black hair shining red in the sun, brilliant tiger-eyes, jet-black brows and a double-row of dark eyelashes like Tyrone Power's. He'd worked as a Western Union telegrapher till his death from a heart attack while fishing in Galveston Bay. In our family, Cecelia thought, everything begins and ends with the water.

She had her own idea about the deaths of the Campbells, but as usual no one was interested. Her theory grew out of a well-remembered conversation with Cindy several months back:

"Every year," Cindy had said, "my mother and daddy go to Las Vegas."

"Well, if you like it and can afford it," Cecelia had said, "I suppose that's all right."

"But my daddy's so smart! He always wins."

"*Always?* How often does he go?"

"Sometimes three times a year. He takes my mother. She wins, too."

Cecelia had thought, Hoo-hoo-hoo, that's a payoff if I ever heard of one. James Campbell works for the Mafia.

Somehow he'd overreached and they'd killed him. Plain as the nose on your face. She wondered why the authorities hadn't caught on. Of course she hadn't spoken to them and didn't intend to. The Campbell deaths weren't the worst disasters in the history of the world.

She heard the screaming child before she saw him. It was a hot afternoon, and the sound poured from David's open windows: "Help! They're hurting me! *They're killing me!*"

Before she could park her trike, the accusations had turned to shrieks. "Help. Save me! They've kidnapped me! Help! *They're killing me!*"

She hobbled up the warped wooden stairs carrying the Monopoly game. My God, she thought, David won't have a shred of reputation left.

Pedaling home three hours later, Cecelia felt warmed by her triumph. She couldn't wait to recount her adventure to DuVal. "When I went in," she told him, "Cindy looked ready to explode. David was so exasperated he was just trying to keep from wringing Matthew's neck. That boy knew *exactly* what he was doing. He'd worked himself up. 'I wanna go home! I wanna go back to my daddy!' He never mentioned Mrs. Campbell. He yelled, 'These are awful people! They're killing me! *Aaaaaaaaagh!*'

"I let him scream and then I screamed louder than he did. He blinked. I said, 'Now didn't that sound rawther silly?'

"His mouth kinda dropped open. I said, 'Look, your screaming isn't helping things one bit. No one here is trying to harm you. There's no way anybody can put things back the way they were. You're just gonna have to make the best of it.'

"I talked to him like that for a couple minutes. Then his crying ran down. I gave him a Kleenex and he blew his nose.

"I got out the game and in about three minutes he was learning Monopoly. I made two deliberately wrong moves and he beat me. He crowed 'Oh, boy!' and wanted to play again. I played at random to give him an edge, and I beat him.

"After two hours he wanted to play again, but David had to take them out to eat. I got the impression they were very bright boys. Michael was adapting, chattering like a little monkey. But Matthew didn't know how to adjust to a situation that was scaring the heck out of him. I settled him down. It just took a little patience."

71

Later that night David phoned his mother with a success story of his own:

"I took 'em to the Black-eyed Pea for dinner. Michael said he wanted a chicken fried steak. I said, 'Are you sure you can eat it all?'

"He said, 'Oh, yeah.' He eats the skin, leaves the meat, and starts on the potatoes. I'm saying, 'Look, eat five more bites of meat, and from now on we'll be real careful not to order too much.'

"He just said, 'Naw. I'm full.' *Ya know?*

"I says, 'Now listen, you're not gonna sit there and tell *me* no. You're gonna eat those five bites or we can go outside and I'll give you one hard swat for every bite.'

"He said, 'Well, I'm not gonna be able to eat 'em.'

"Outside I said, 'You're not gonna bulldoze me.' I gave him five good ass busters. Then I said 'Listen, when you dry your eyes, come back in. I'm sorry it came to this, but you chose your fate. Now don't go running off, because in the first place we'll probably find ya, and in the second place there's nowhere you can go, and in the third it's liable to be really dangerous, and in the fourth your mama and I really care about you.' I figured I had to make that gesture of trust and respect.

"I went back inside. I was really nervous. Two or three minutes later he came back in. That's it, Mom. No prob."

The next day Matthew screamed so hard that passers-by stopped on the sidewalk to listen. Michael pumped a little iron but mostly sat around moping. "Can I go out and play?" he asked.

"Not in this neighborhood," David said.

He thought, It's not really their fault. They're used to wide-open spaces and a game room and they're stuck in the city. There's nothing for kids to do in a dump like this. They're bored, that's all.

"Cindy?" he said. "Now that you've got your boys, what're you gonna do about 'em? I mean, do you want to raise 'em here? Do you think that's right?"

He left her with the problem while he walked Max. When he and the pit bull returned, he heard, "They're killing me! Help! *They kidnapped me!*" He thought, It sounds like the goddamn Texas chainsaw murders.

Cindy's face was cadmium red. She explained in angry gasps that her sister Betty had dropped in while Michelle and Jamie waited outside in the car. Betty had fed Matthew a big line of bullshit. "She put her arms around him and promised to come back tomorrow. He ate it up!"

David thought, *That's it!* If the weird sisters are gonna start coming around, then fuck it. Somebody else can raise the kids. "Grab their stuff," he said, "and put it in the car."

"Where're we going?" Cindy asked.

"The Depelchin Home."

72

"J.W. says the little one has a coupla bruises on his shoulder and neck," Schultz told his partner as they sped toward the Campbell house. "Like finger marks. But at least they're safe."

As a former steel mill laborer, Schultz could handle heat, but this was one day when he was grateful that the City of Houston had blessed him with an air-conditioned car. The temperature was fixing to break a hundred before noon. Reddish streaks of lightning flashed between bone-white cumulus clouds surging up from the Gulf.

"Maybe that's why the home rejected 'em," Motard said. "I don't think they accept damaged goods."

Schultz said it was more because of the high-handed way Cindy and West had acted. "Driving up and announcing she had a coupla kids to drop off, for Christ's sake! Like dogies in a chute! For all the Depelchins knew, those boys coulda been kidnapped. Michelle said Cindy called from the home and asked what to do next. Michelle told her, 'Take 'em to J.W.'s and we'll do the rest.' West couldn't drive 'em there fast enough."

Matthew and Michael seemed to take to the detectives this time, especially after a drive in the park and a visit to James Coney Island for hot dogs, but they were reluctant to talk about their experiences with David West. "Just tell us one thing, guys," Schultz asked. "Did David and Cindy want to know what you saw the night of the killings?"

"Yep," Michael said.

Schultz thought, That's what it was all about. Cindy never intended to raise those boys herself. That sidewinder, she just wanted to see what they knew. Paul and I could've saved her a lot of trouble.

The detectives decided to check out the house on Vermont. Heat rose in waves from the concrete parking pad. Schultz and his "Jacques Pen-yay" polyester suit stuck tightly together.

West trotted past with a mean-looking dog and refused to stop for an interview. Cindy came down the stairs with her hands on her hips, looking heavier in her jeans and T-shirt. Schultz asked, "Could we just step inside? We'd like to ask you a few questions."

"No," she said.

Motard said, "Why don't we sit in our car and we'll turn on the air conditioning?"

"I have *nothing* to say to you," Cindy snapped. She sounded like a boss telling off a worker. "Talk to my attorney. I want *nothing* to do with you." She turned and headed up the inner steps. *"That's it!"* she shouted. The door slammed shut.

73

Wickie ran into his friend coming out of Rud's. He hadn't seen Dave since they'd gone to Shooter's Cove to try out the accurized .45. Wickie had just done some sinsemilla and walked merrily along. He had a ready answer to Dave's friendly, "Hey, whatcha been doin', man?"

"Mostly drinkin', smokin' and fuckin'."

"Cool," Dave said.

"How you feeling, man?" Wickie asked.

"I been having cop trouble," Dave said, and he was off on one of his long stories. Wickie thought, If you ask Dave how to get to Alabama Street, he tells you the history of the Confederacy. "Those cops were stupid and weaselly at the same time," he was raving. "They said, 'Well, why don't you just sit in the back of our car and talk to us?' I thought, Man, gimme a break! Sit in the back of a car with no door handles and no locks? Sure, said the spider to the fly. I said, 'No, thanks.'"

Wickie agreed it was a bummer. He wished he knew what Dave was talking about.

They reached Dave's house and climbed the stairs. A good-looking chick with nice tits and a nose job was trying to turn herself into a ball on his living-room floor. She looked at Wickie and asked in a wistful voice, "David, who is that? Is he gonna hit me?"

Dave answered soothingly, "No, Cindy. He's not gonna hit you."

Dave's friend Pete was there, and for a while the three men talked guns. Cindy sat on the floor and mumbled, "I'm gonna do a ballet tonight."

Wickie said, "What one?"

She looked up and said, "I don't remember."

Every few minutes she glanced at the three men in a sweet, coy way, drawing her shoulders in, all innocent. She kept asking, "David, can I sit on the couch?" "David, can I go to the bathroom?" "David, can I . . . ?"

"Yes, Cindy," he would say. "It's okay, Cindy. It'll be all right."

Wickie thought, Is this for real? Outside, he asked Dave, "What's with the chick?"

"Oh, she's my ol' lady. We been together a coupla years, off and on." He told how she'd been brought up in the Memorial section, abused as a child, all kinds of bullshit. She claimed that she'd been reincarnated several times. He also said he wouldn't mind getting rid of her, but he couldn't.

"Why not?" Wickie asked.

"I just can't, ya know?"

Wickie asked what happened to the hockey mask. It had seemed an odd purchase a few weeks ago, since nerdy Dave had about as much chance of jousting with the Urban Animals as Nancy Reagan.

"I, uh . . . wore it," Dave answered.

He saw that Dave didn't want to talk about it. He started to ask about the forty-five, but something told him to shut up. He had a fuzzy remembrance that Dave had said something a month or two ago about killing somebody, but he'd thought at the time that Dave was too damn disorganized, too flaky and weird to follow through on anything that heavy. Now he thought, Holy shit, you don't suppose . . . ?

Forget it, Wickie told himself. You've heard too much already.

74

Later on David wasn't sure how it happened or even how long Cindy had stayed under his roof. Maybe a week, maybe two. He went over it in his mind obsessively, but he really didn't understand. All he knew was that after the killings they spent too much time in their own heads, coping, instead of working things out together. He kept expecting her to improve now that her parents were dead, but she didn't.

He told himself, You went out and made this ultimate

commitment to her, and just look at her! She won't try to get a job, won't go to school, won't exercise, won't clean the place. Won't even clean herself, for Christ's sake! She's starting to drag me down with her. My God, look what we accomplished together. For what? She's a fucking amoeba. She'll never change. Every few days she threw a fit about dropping the glove. He told her, "It's *weeks* afterward, Cindy. Forget it!"

"Oh, David," she said. "What made me do it?"

He thought, That's the big question.

She retreated into her hurt fawn role. He took her to a party and she wound up in a back room, crouched behind a clothes hamper. She spent most of her time chain-smoking and popping brews and ordering food. When he hinted about sex she explained that she was too uptight or tired.

David sipped ale and smoked a little pot and went on long walks with Max while he tried to think things through. At a time when they both should be on top, when their personal and financial worries were just about over, she was still acting like a lame. He thought, Back when she was falling apart, she came to me and said, "They're doing it to me again." Well, she's *still* falling apart. *Who's doing it to her now?* Nobody! So why the shit did we do what we did?

"Where's your pride?" he asked her. "You're getting fat!" He repeated his old warning that she depended too much on others, especially him. "I've got problems of my own to work out," he told her. "I gotta get my own head straight."

She said she agreed. The next day she was gone.

75

Craig Casper hadn't thought much about Cindy Ray since spring, when she'd made a pest of herself at La Carafe. He'd lent her a few dollars, mostly for cab fare, and didn't mind losing it if she would just stay away. And now she was phoning him at home.

He listened politely. She apologized for not calling sooner, said she'd been in St. Louis all summer studying art. While she'd been gone, her parents had been murdered by the Mafia. She was a millionairess now, except that her uncle was trying to steal her money. She'd hired a lawyer to fight back, and she intended to get every goddamn penny.

He jollied her along and said about six times, "Well, it's been nice talking to you." Finally she hung up.

He didn't know what to believe. She sounded so positive and straightforward, but she'd been just as convincing three months ago as Blanche DuBois.

A few days later he noticed an item in the paper about a legal fight over the Campbell estate involving daughter Cynthia Campbell Ray and other family members. He thought, So it wasn't entirely a fantasy. Looking back, he realized that she saw everything that way: part real, part unreal. He hoped he never had to deal with her again.

76

Wickie couldn't figure out what was happening to Dave. His house had always been a disaster area, but at least he'd worked on it, made a few improvements, kept it clean. Now he just lived there. You never used to see him without Max, but lately he'd been leaving the pit bull home. He stopped lifting weights and running, sucked up brew and smoked a lot of pot. The old Dave read magazines, went to school, had loud opinions. The new Dave was a putz.

One night as they were getting wasted at Rud's, Wickie said, "Hey, man, what'd you do with my pistol?"

Dave seemed surprised. "Well," he said, "I, uh . . . used it."

"Whattaya mean?"

Dave leaned closer on the barstool. "I killed those people with it."

"What people?"

"The ones we were talking about. They were bugging me."

Wickie tried to remember who'd been bugging him. He said, "Did you *really?*"

"Yeah. I wore the hockey mask painted black."

"What'd you do with the gun?"

Dave waved a cautionary finger. "Threw it in the bayou."

Wickie was astounded. "You . . . cut it up?"

"No. I just threw it in there. By now it's under ten feet of silt and mud."

Wickie thought, This is fucking unreal. Why didn't I hear about this before? These days he didn't see a newspaper unless he skated past a rack. He took another look at Dave and thought, This nebbish actually killed people? It was too hard to believe.

77

Gwen Funk Sampson took her bereaved old friend to a cheer-up lunch. They'd hardly sat down before Cindy started talking in a thick accent: "Gabriela gon' get even wit' whoever killa my *paaaa*-pa. Gabriela, she's-a one mean Italiana." Gwen thought, It's like the old days in my dark-room. Next she'll be talking about Carrot Tink and her vagi-nal exercises.

The Anna Magnani impression continued into dessert. "It's a vendett'," Cindy said in a voice that carried through the restaurant. "Gabriela getta the sumbeetch 'atsa killa my *paaaa*-pa."

On the way back to Cindy's apartment on Kingston, she finally dropped the accent and spoke in a rush of words that Gwen found almost as disturbing. She complained about the pace of the probate process and "those vultures, my sisters." She said, "My Uncle J.W.'s in cahoots with them. They're trying to cheat me out of my share." In the same breath she talked about a rich lover who'd promised to fly her to Wash-ington. She said she was going to call on President Reagan because "I want to see the killer put away." Gwen breathed easier after letting her out.

The next day Cindy phoned and told her to forget everything she'd said. "It was just a big act," she confessed. "I was having fun with the Italian part." Gwen thought, She's out in left field somewhere. I'm just not sure how far.

A few weeks later Cindy called again. "He's cut me off," she said angrily. "Nasty old bastard! He won't give me any more pills."

"Who?" Gwen asked.

"My doctor." She said that he'd been giving her sleeping pills and Valium in return for an occasional feel.

"So why'd he cut you off?" Gwen asked. "Did you cut *him* off?"

"He said I was mixing pills and alcohol and he didn't want to be responsible. I said, 'How about my parents and all? I can't sleep.' He said I'd get over it. Oh, Gwen, what now?"

Gwen decided that a final act of mercy was in order and gave her the name of her own physician. Cindy called back the next day to say thanks. But a week or so later she was anguished again. Gwen's doctor had refused a refill. "Why?" Gwen asked.

"He said that the help I needed couldn't be found in pills."

Gwen thought, He's right, of course. And this is the perfect time for me to bow out.

78

Schultz and Motard plugged along in the late-summer heat. The Campbell sisters had returned to Austin and Knoxville, but they called almost daily with tips and ideas. Jamie finally confirmed what Michelle had mentioned earlier, that Cindy had once talked about killing her father. It was interesting, but not the hard evidence that they needed to bring an official charge.

There was a flurry of activity when Michelle phoned to

say that the maternal grandmother had reported seeing Virginia Campbell's missing brown wallet and black coin purse in Cindy's apartment. Nanny Helen had also spotted James Campbell's black attaché case in the trash outside Cindy's door. Michelle reminded Motard to treat Mrs. Amaya gently. She was in her seventies, rendered an invalid by deep radiation therapy. And she lived in mortal fear of Cindy.

Motard arrived to collect the evidence and found Cindy's apartment littered as usual. Mold sprouted from the rug. There were black marks on the bathroom wall; it looked as though someone had squirted ink.

Mrs. Amaya opened her granddaughter's closet for the detective, then reacted with surprise. Everything had been rearranged: the wallet and coin purse were gone. Her bony hands shook as she told Motard that Cindy had been discarding Virginia Campbell's gifts, including expensive silk blouses. The outgoing trash had become so enriched lately that street people waited in front of the house. "There was a nice black briefcase that looked like my son-in-law's," the old woman said. "A man grabbed it. I'm sorry." So was Motard. He'd gone to the Kingston apartment expecting to crack the case.

79

Dean Thomas Samuels* considered himself an expert on sushi and sashimi, raw delights like the mahogany-red *maguro,* the wriggling live-shrimp *odori,* the dangerous blowfish *fugu,* Kobe beef fattened on beer, fish eggs the color of bloodied gold, creamy cross sections of octopus and eel, dainty white strips of mullet and trout. At Houston prices, the twenty-three-year-old stagehand could down a hundred dollars' worth without a burp, conversing knowledgeably with the waitress and writing his name in lacy Japanese ideograms.

* Pseudonym

Such tastes could be hard on cash flow, especially in the long Houston summers when most of the theaters were dark and there wasn't much work for a skilled artisan who could untangle the complex pulley system at the Alley or build a new set for *Death of a Salesman*. Samuels was sharp and quick, short, 140 pounds in his tool belt, with close-set dark eyes, curly brown hair, and pale skin menaced by zits. His brightness was appealing, and he was usually able to solve his summertime financial problems by moving in with a female. This, of course, brought its own hassles and strains, which was why he was happy that he'd met David DuVal West at the Rud. "Why, shit, man, I got a whole goddamn house," West had said. "You can live free while you help me fix it up."

In the subtropical heat, the stagehand moved into the lower part of the house on Vermont and soon wished he hadn't. "It's like living in an Egyptian tomb," he told a friend. "You wake up at night and you want to yell, 'Ramses, bring me an urn of water.' I've seen cockroaches down there big enough to have names, wear clothes and ride bikes."

For two weeks he hacked away at improving his habitat, but no one could Sheetrock twelve-foot ceilings alone. "Look, David," he said one night, "I can't fulfill my end of the bargain if you don't help. It's hard living down here, Dave. I mean, it's not the Hotel Meridien."

As usual, West seemed preoccupied. "Okay, Dean," he said. "Then move upstairs with me till I have some time. It's a lot nicer."

Samuels learned that West maintained an open house for young people. Peter was the son of a foreign diplomat and a devotee of muscle-cars, exotic women and stroke mags like *Gallery* and *Genesis*. Wickie floated in and out on his own personal clouds. Robin lived in a back room and kept to himself. Sometimes the place seemed like an armed camp. West owned two pistols and several knives, but his pride was a Ruger Mini-14 that he'd modified by adding a folding combat stock and taping banana clips butt-to-butt for quick reloading, leading Dean to ask himself, What enemy threatens our Montrose shores? There was also a big stock of hollow-point ammunition.

Samuels found his host a fascinating study. West recounted his winning brawls, smoked a lot of pot and bragged about a big hash deal he'd brought off in the Marines. "Man," he told Dean, "when I was in Morocco I did things that I *never* want to think about."

He raved about American womanhood and praised his dear mother. In a place of honor on his bookshelf he kept a glossy snapshot of a handsome woman and often stared at the picture for minutes at a time. He took a lot of late-night calls and acted depressed or irritated afterward.

Early one evening Dean answered the phone and heard a female ask, "Is David there?"

"No, I'm sorry," he said. "He's not."

"Well, I'm his friend and I'm really sick. I need some soup. I can't get out and I don't have any food in the house."

Dean said to himself, *Sexy!* He patiently recited the standard show-biz remedy for sickness on the road: "Make a pot of tea. Add a shot of Scotch, some peppermint and honey. Drink it, get under the covers, and sweat."

"But I don't have any tea!" She sounded panicky. He didn't understand; being out of tea wasn't life-threatening. The woman sounded so alluring that he promised to bring a pot over. "Where do you live?" he asked.

She gave him an address on Kingston and told him to knock at apartment 4, upstairs. "Don't go to three," she warned him. "That's my grandmother across the hall."

The stagehand had always tried to be honest, so while he dressed he admitted to himself that his immediate goals were to do a suffering human a favor, make a friend, and get into her pants.

The door opened and he said hello to the woman in David's picture. She apologized for looking so disheveled and explained that she'd been in bed. She wore jeans and a blouse, no shoes, no jewelry, heavy eye make-up. He thought, Nose by Modigliani, eyes by Sophia Loren, fingernails by the Dragon Lady. She was overweight but carried it well. She introduced herself as "Cynthia Gabriela Ray" and beckoned him in.

He stepped through an L-shaped entrance area and into a mess. Open paint tubes had dribbled on puke-green carpeting. The sink was crammed with half-eaten cans of moldy beans, okra and corn. One corner was piled knee-high with Burger King and Popeyes chicken boxes and other Styrofoam products. He took a seat, smiled, and said to himself, This girl is out of her fucking gourd.

She showed him around like a proud owner. In the claustrophobic bedroom a forlorn kitten looked up and meowed; the hardwood floor was its litter box and a pile of silk blouses its litter. He leaned over and saw that urine had eaten through a blouse with a two-hundred-dollar price tag. "You've got a problem here," he said.

Cynthia Gabriela Ray shrugged.

He felt sorry for her. "Look," he said, "I'll clean this place for you."

She shrugged again.

They talked while he worked. It soon became clear that she was rolling in money. She mumbled that her uncle gave her five hundred dollars every week. Dean remembered a favorite precept: money can't buy happiness, but it can rent it for a while.

She told him that her parents had been murdered. "We could drive out to the house and climb the fence," she offered. "I'll show you where it happened."

"Listen, baby," he said, "trespassing at a murder scene is the last thing we wanna get fucking nailed for."

She said she stood to inherit about a million dollars; the estate was worth three or four million, but she had to split with three sisters.

"You'll never see a whole mil," he explained patiently. "There'll be all kinds of taxes and other bullshit. You'll lose at least half."

She seemed surprised at the news and he wondered why no one had told her before. Didn't she have a lawyer? Didn't her sisters confide in her? She said her murdered father had traveled a lot. "My poor departed daddy was a very kind, gentle man busy with his career." A stepmother named Vir-

ginia had come on the scene after her real mother died when
Cynthia Gabriela was three or four. The stepmother brought
three cruel daughters of her own into the family. They
locked Cindy in a closet and kept her there for days, making
her do vile things. She told her horror stories in a flat mono-
tone, sounding neither angry nor annoyed.

It was after midnight when the stagehand started to make
his move. He figured she would succumb after enough grop-
ing and grabbing, but she didn't. She admitted that her first
sexual experience had been rape and she'd enjoyed it. But
tonight she didn't want sex in any form.

He dragged his 140 tired pounds home at 3 A.M. He
couldn't sleep. He had a lot of planning to do.

80

David was glad that Cindy was communicating again, but
he wished she'd try a different rap. She phoned three or four
times a week, usually late at night, talking like a computer in
a loop—all emotion, no control or balance. He still loved
her, but he was tired of hearing the same old line about the
earth and all the planets being against her.

Sometimes he cut her short. One night he hung up. She
called back and whined, "Oh, David, what have I ever done
to be treated like this?"

"Cindy," he said, "you haven't done anything. It's just
that you keep running off at the mouth about mindless driv-
eling bullshit, ya know?" He told her that she needed help
and attention—but not his. "I already struck out, Cindy.
I'm sorry."

He gave her a ribby Irish setter that had been hit by a car
and saved by his old boss, Ron Westphal. She left it alone in
the apartment for days at a time. After David's mom told
her she was being cruel, she gave it away.

He continued in his role as chauffeur, driving her to the
doctor, the grocer and her downtown lawyer's office; he figured it was better than losing all contact. He made repairs

on her apartment, installed a locking bar across her door,
bought her a .22-caliber Saturday night special and gave her
a Gerber combat knife that Wickie had traded him. After
he'd turned her place into a fortress, the midnight phone
conversations shortened, then stopped. At first he was relieved to get more sleep, but after a few empty nights he
realized that he missed her silly chatter. He decided he was
into another of his famous no-win situations; she angered
him when she called and also when she didn't. It was his
lifelong pattern with women.

81

Dean Samuels's morality encompassed accepting shelter
from women, but not without giving something in return. It
seemed to him that the deal he struck with Cindy Ray was
fair, especially in light of the fact that she was about to
inherit a bundle. He would move in with her, do some sorely
needed remodeling, find her a good lawyer, show her how to
bank, teach her to drive and turn her into a self-sufficient
woman. In return, she would buy him a road case, a large
wheeled wooden cabinet with drawers—lockable, durable,
with steel corners and steel edges and every tool for every
need. A road case would enable him to work rock concerts
and other big-buck shows. He knew where he could find a
nice one for $15,000.

"Fine," Cindy said. "Great. I'm gonna be rich. I don't
care how much it costs." Dean thought, She's like a thirsty
millionaire who'll pay a hundred grand for a glass of water.
He was also thinking, If it's not me, it'll be somebody else.
At least I'll treat her right.

It took him four days to finish cleaning up her apartment;
then he quietly moved out of West's place and into hers. He
bought shelf paper, wire, light bulbs, linoleum runners, a
shower curtain, towels and other household items. He tore
out the ruined carpeting, replaced the fixtures, scrubbed the
kitchen sink and the bathroom, carried armloads of clothes

to the dry cleaner. Five of her fifteen silk blouses were ruined; urine had dissolved the fabric. The dry cleaner said he would try to save the others.

The more Dean learned about his hostess, the more perplexed he was that she wasn't living out her years in a rubber room. She was helpless in the simplest business dealings. He was stupefied by the maneuvers she went through to collect her weekly advance from the estate. Having spent all her money on Cokes and candy at Kojac's market on Shepherd, she would don jeans and T-shirt, sometimes remembering to put on shoes, and phone for a taxi. The driver would take her to the lawyer's office and wait while she went inside and borrowed the fare. Then the lawyer would have to walk her to the bank to identify her; she had no ID. After cashing the check, she would take another cab home and immediately phone Colonel Sanders.

Dean escorted her to the Texas Commerce Bank to open a checking account, but when they were filling out the application, he realized she couldn't handle the arithmetic. He compromised by starting a savings account in her name, and she was issued her first photo ID.

Driving lessons were out; she bridled when he discussed the subject. Sometimes she asked him to run her over to Cecelia West's house so she could borrow twenty or thirty dollars. She called West's mother "an earthbound saint" but despised David. She said she'd lived with him for three chaste months till he broke down her door and "had his way." After the attack she'd moved away. Dean was a little surprised that wimpy David had committed a rape, but he took her at her word.

She seemed ambivalent about the grandmother across the hall. In a childish voice she would say, "I've got to take care of Nanny Helen. Nanny needs me. I love her dearly." But a few minutes later she would yell, "I don't trust Nanny. She's on my sisters' side. She's out to screw me! Look out for Nanny Helen!"

Her favorite subjects proved to be the family cruelties and the fight over her inheritance. Dean thought, She's convincing, but she's wearing out my ears.

Every morning she splashed on cologne, but it didn't

mask her odor. Feminine hygiene was a mystery to her. He prided himself on knowing about trichomoniasis and candida and certain other female problems. "You need to take care of these things," he told her. "For a starter, let me suggest a bath."

After her body housekeeping improved, he began to find her more desirable physically. She ran around the apartment naked from the waist down, but always covered her breasts. When he came near she jerked away. One day he threatened to belt her and thought he detected a sexual flush. He suspected that she had an S-M complex. By treating her more forcefully, he scored about fifteen seconds of fellatio, but she refused an encore. He spent a lot of time in the shower.

He landed a stage job in September and started a string of eighteen-hour workdays. The apartment deteriorated. He came home one night to find the refrigerator empty. He said, "Didn't you tell me you were gonna buy food today?"

She replied in her little-girl voice, "I bought a hundred dollars' worth. But I don't know what I did with it. I . . . lost it."

"You stupid bitch," he said, shaking her by the shoulders. "Have you fucking lost your goddamn mind? *What's your problem?*"

He came home another night to find phonograph records scattered all over and fresh catshit on the rug. Cindy was on her hands and knees reading a record label. He put his boot against her ass and gave her a shove. "Clean this place up now!" he ordered.

The next night he arrived home to find David West waiting inside the door. "Pack your things," he said. "You're moving out right now."

Dean said, "The hell I am."

"The hell you're not," West said in a soft voice. "You beat her up."

The stagehand knew better than to deny the charge. With Cindy's paranoia, she'd probably convinced herself that he'd tried to murder her. He said, "Look, Dave, it's three o'clock in the morning and I'm exhausted. Let's talk about it in the morning."

"Get your fucking shit and move out," West said, shuffling toward him. Cindy peeped from behind his shoulder. David still hadn't raised his voice.

Dean said, "I didn't beat her up, and I'm moving out when I get the money she owes me for the work I've done. Two hundred and fifty bucks or I go to the police. That's just my materials, not even my labor."

Cindy said, "David, get the receipt for my dry cleaning."

Dean thought, Of all the fucking nerve, after what I've done for her. "You're not gonna get the goddamn receipt," he said. "I'll give it to you when I get my money and no sooner. I'll fucking take it to my grave with me."

Dave stepped closer. "You're giving it to her right now," he said.

"Fuck you," Dean said in his face. "Fuck your dog, and fuck the horse you rode in on."

Dave gave him a shove. Dean kicked back and caught him in the thigh. Then he felt himself breaking through the second-story window. He scrabbled for a handhold and looked straight down at twelve feet of air.

"David, don't!" Cindy screamed. *"David, stop!"*

Dean clung to the window frame. His body was half in and half out. West let go. Dean pulled himself in and brushed off the broken glass.

"I'm calling the cops," Cindy squealed.

"Fine," Dean said.

They waited in silence on opposite sides of the room. David held Cindy and patted her on the arm.

The cops said Dean had to go. He called a friend who owned a '63 Chrysler Newport. As they drove away he thought, She's the only chick I know with her own junkyard dog. . . .

The next morning he returned to pick up his things. Cindy smiled and said in her baby voice, "Stay with me, Dean. I'm sorry. It was all a big misunderstanding."

He made her sign a note for the $250. "You've got six months to pay," he said. "It's due in March." Then he left for good.

82

Cecelia West had never seen David so downcast and sullen. Maybe, she thought, it's because his inheritance is gone. He'd spent tens of thousands on bloodsucking roommates, wild parties, rounds of drinks for false friends, momentary convivialities, all on money that was supposed to be spent on his house. She asked him point-blank, "David, what's upsetting you?"

"Nothing," he said.

There was an edge to his voice, but she persisted. "Are you having problems with Cindy?"

"I said no!" he snapped.

As fall approached, his disposition grew worse. One night he yanked a post off her oaken staircase and smashed it. He'd been prone to momentary rages ever since falling off his trike and hitting his head at the age of three. She hadn't known how to help him then and still didn't.

DuVal remained behind his books. He'd never had much of his son's respect and forfeited that small amount while David was in Morocco. For eighteen months the Wests had boarded a brilliant high school boy named Ronald Henley, the most promising chess prospect in Texas. They'd put him up in David's room and the admiring DuVal had let him use the family car. As Cecelia interpreted the situation, Henley was the son that DuVal had always wanted. David was crushed. He'd never excelled at anything that mattered to his father. Poor David, Cecelia thought. He and his father are right out of Eugene O'Neill.

Cindy started phoning again, overwrought as usual, and Cecelia finally learned of the breakup. "How long ago did you leave?" Cecelia asked.

"Oh, weeks."

Cindy blamed David's high-handedness. Cecelia said softly, "I understand, I understand." Cecelia knew the mulish illogic of young love. These two were born for each

other, and yet they were stubbornly staying apart. Foolish
pride, Cecelia thought. But she wasn't going to push for
reconciliation. That way it wouldn't stick.

In early October Cindy phoned and said someone was
after her. "I need a hideout," she said in the gasping voice
that Cecelia had heard so often.

"You come right on over, honey," Cecelia said. "We've
been using David's room for storage, but I'll clean it out.
His couch makes into a queen-sized bed. The only two
things I ask in return is that you help me keep up this place
and keep your own room straight."

"Okay," Cindy said. She sounded relieved.

Cecelia hummed to herself as she went to work on the
upstairs bathroom. A few weeks earlier she'd started strip-
ping the cloth wallpaper; now she carefully stapled it back.
She fixed the broken light, scoured the rust stains from the
sink, and scrubbed sink, tub, toilet and floor till they
gleamed. She put out fresh towels and soap. She installed a
Louis XV card table, an easy chair and an ottoman in David's room. She thought, Cindy will *love* it. This will be the
home she's never had. Why, she might just stay on!

At dusk Cindy arrived by cab with sacks and bundles of
belongings. She paced the front room, mumbling that the
Mafia had killed her parents and Nanny Helen wouldn't
stop spying on her and there was poison in her food. Her
hair looked thin and patchy, she'd put on weight, and she
spoke in a peculiar slur as though her teeth were loose.

Cecelia thought, She's drunk. But why doesn't she smell
of alcohol? My God, I've got a walking nervous breakdown
on my hands! "Sit over here, honey," she said, pointing to
one of the three sofas.

Cindy yelled, "I want a drink!"

Cecelia mixed a highball and watched as it disappeared in
two or three gulps. Then Cindy grabbed a bottle of dark rum
and began bellowing in another new voice, this one at least
an octave below Melina Mercouri or Tallulah. Cecelia was
apprehensive, but she also had to marvel at the performance.
If this poor child ever harnesses her natural talents, she
thought, what a gift she'll be to the stage!

When the rum was gone Cindy drained a bottle of gin,

then managed a splash of Weller's before passing out on a couch. Cecelia covered her with a blanket and went to bed. She wasn't worried. The first step toward rehabilitation was a good night's sleep.

In the morning Cindy shook like a wet pup. Her lovely hazel eyes were laced with red. Cecelia made her an old New Orleans breakfast with plenty of chicory coffee, but she wouldn't touch a thing. "I'm going!" she yelled as she jumped up from the table.

"Going where?" Cecelia asked. "You just got here."

"I've got to go," she said in a strange flat voice. "I've got to go." Then she seemed to brighten and asked, "Is it all right if I use the telephone?"

"Of course," Cecelia said.

"I'm calling Gwen," she explained. She dropped the phone and bent to retrieve it. "She's my dearest girlfriend." Her long nails clacked against the dial holes. "Oh," she said, slamming down the phone, "I can't go to Gwen's. Her son keeps making passes at me. But . . . I've got to go." She waved Cecelia from the room. Cecelia thought, She wants to talk to her friend in private. Well, that's her right.

A pickup truck arrived and a polite man and a teen-aged boy carried out the bags. After Cindy had driven off with the strangers, Cecelia lit a Carlton menthol and thought, I worked so hard cleaning out her room, and she never went upstairs! Never saw it at all! It was so disappointing.

83

Gwen knew she'd made a mistake the second Cindy walked in. The poor thing's hair was coming out in clumps and there were black specks on her tongue. Dear God, Gwen thought, I've got two sons and a husband and I've invited the plague.

She also thought, Don will be *pissed* when he takes a good

look. He hadn't wanted Cindy to come in the first place. Gwen wondered how she'd let it happen.

It had started with a desperation phone call: "Gwen, I'm at Cecelia's house. She's, she's . . . being mean to me! I can't stand it here. I need a place to be safe from the Mafia. Gwen, I think they killed Mother and Daddy!"

"Didn't you tell me that Mrs. West loved you because you're bright and her son isn't?"

"She's changed, Gwen. She . . . hits me."

"Well, maybe you can come over here. Let me talk to Don. He won't be thrilled."

"I know the son of a bitch doesn't like me," Cindy said with surprising heat. "Tell him I'll bring my color TV. I don't want it anyway. It was in Mother and Daddy's room and it's got their brains on the screen."

Don and fourteen-year-old Jeffery had picked up Cindy at the house on Kipling and collected the TV from the apartment on Kingston. Now both TV and Cindy were ensconced in the Sampson home on shady Tonawanda Drive along with the five handmade dolls she'd always slept with. Gwen crossed her fingers and hoped the arrangement would work out. Don had despised Cindy since the days of the Darkroom Follies, but he seemed to be enjoying her TV.

In two days Cindy drank her way through the household liquor supply. Gwen complained to her mother, Billie Funk: "She's on a jag where she hangs right in your face and it's talk, talk, talk. At night I'll be trying to go to sleep and she'll be hanging over my side of the bed still talking in a drunken stupor. I've got her on one of the day beds in the den. She bothers John and Jeffery. She leaves clothes around, dirty dishes, bottles. She's driving us to the nut-hut."

Four days after Cindy moved in, Gwen came home from work to find the houseguest on the couch. "Don made a pass at me," she said.

"Aw, bullshit, Cindy," Gwen said. She thought, Jeez, man, this chick's hair's falling out, she's got black stuff on her tongue, and her mouth's full of blood from loose teeth. And my husband hit on her? *Come on!*

"Here's what he did," Cindy said drunkenly. "He touched his tink and said, 'Hey, I'm big. I'm *really* big, ya know?' "

Gwen thought, How utterly ridiculous. "I don't believe you," she said.

Cindy raised herself to a sitting position, then slid back on the bed and muttered, "He took off his pants and held it in his hand."

Gwen laughed. "Did he throw it over his shoulder?"

"You don't believe me," Cindy squealed. "You're just upset 'cause he did it. Well, he did!"

Gwen managed a Bronx cheer. She was thinking, Oh, God, who needs this?

When she told Don, he said, *"Whaaaat?"* and shook his head. Then he said, "I want her out."

Gwen came home from work the next day in time to hear Jeffery yell, "Help, *help!* Mom! Get in here!"

Just as she reached her son's bedroom door, she heard Cindy say in a sultry voice reminiscent of Mae West, "I don't want to be the next notch on your bed."

Jeff stood by his door looking scared. Cindy was stretched across the bed, her eyes rolled back, clutching a pillow. "Mom," her son pleaded, "get this weirdo out of here!"

Gwen grabbed the bloated body by the ankles and pulled her into the hall.

"You're my best friend, Gwen," Cindy purred at dinner that night. "I'm just so grateful to you for saving my life." Gwen thought, She knows exactly what's on my mind. She's always had that damn clairvoyance.

Cindy said, "I'm so lucky to have you." Then she sucked the dregs from a whiskey bottle left over from a Christmas party three years ago.

Gwen stayed up late, thinking. She didn't want a screaming scene in front of the kids. She thought, We've got to be out of the house when I break the news that she's gotta go. That way there'll be no physical stuff. Gradually she worked up a plan.

* * *

Cindy seemed restless when Gwen returned home from work. She'd run out of Valium the night before. "Cindy," Gwen said in her most convivial voice, "remember the fun we used to have on girls' night out?"

"Yeah!"

"Well, let's go have a Mexican dinner. My treat. We'll start at Pico's. Their margaritas make the hair stand up on your arm."

Cindy acted excited.

On the way in the family car, Cindy hardly spoke. Gwen thought, I wonder if she suspects that Don and Jeffery are already loading her stuff in the van? She decided that the Felix restaurant in University Village was a better choice for the final act of the drama. She asked for a table near the exit.

They ordered two Corona beers and the deluxe dinner. Midway through the meal Cindy began calling Gwen "Mommy." She said she'd always needed a mommy and Gwen was it. When the remark brought no reaction, Cindy dipped a nacho and switched to a pensive look. Look out, Gwen thought, something's coming.

"I was there, you know," she said in a hushed voice.

Gwen knew exactly where she meant. The subject of the killings had always been between them. "Oh, really?" she said.

"Yes."

"I sorta thought you were."

Cindy said she couldn't live another day with her secret. She said she had a boyfriend named Salino, a Vegas Mafioso whom she'd picked up at Birraporetti's restaurant. He'd stayed at her apartment for a few days and nicknamed her Gabriela.

Gwen thought, Hold it! You were calling yourself Gabriela two years ago.

"Salino felt sorry about the way Mother and Daddy treated me," Cindy hurried on. "He wanted to cure me. He said if they were eliminated I wouldn't have any more troubles and I'd have a lot of money. He said he was gonna kill my parents to make me well. 'I'm gonna make-a you well.

I'm gonna do-a thissa for you. . . . This issa for you, Ceendy.' "

Gwen knew what the Mafia did to people who knew too much. "Cindy," she said in a compressed voice, *"please!* Just shut up."

Cindy told how she'd gone to her parents' house with Salino when everyone was asleep. She said that he'd known the floor plan better than she did. My God, Gwen thought, she's doing the whole number. "Please, Cindy," she broke in. "I don't want to know. I want to go home to my family and live a normal life. *Don't do this to me!"*

Cindy said they wore bulky men's clothing, men's shoes and gloves, and covered their faces so her sons wouldn't recognize them. She said Salino had known that the boys would be in the bedroom but hadn't told her in advance. She leaned toward Gwen and said, "Do you think I would've done anything like that if I'd known my children were there?"

Gwen warned herself, Don't comment and maybe she'll shut up. Then your house and your family will be safe. . . .

Cindy said she'd panicked when she saw the boys. "This is how it happened," she said, looking straight at Gwen. "I stood beside him with my children on the floor. I didn't look when he shot Daddy. I didn't look when he shot Mother, but I felt her body go up and down."

"Oh, Cindy," Gwen blurted out, "how could you stand there while this was going on?"

"Salino held the gun to my head." Her hand shook as she touched her temple.

Jesus, Gwen thought, don't show everybody in the restaurant! She was too exasperated to hold her tongue. "Cindy," she said, "you're telling me he was shooting your parents and also holding the gun to your head? He can't point in both directions. Why didn't you holler, scream, run?"

"He woulda killed me, too." Tears flowed as she babbled about leaving a glove behind so the police would know she'd been there. Gwen thought she meant a textured glove or a mitten. It made no sense. Fingerprints off a glove? She eyed the exit.

"Cindy," she said, reaching across and touching her friend's arm, "let's stop, okay?"

"So now you know," Cindy said. "Salino and the Mafia are gonna kill me and that's why I need a place to hide."

"Fine, fine. Don't tell me any more."

The meal was nearly over, but Cindy ordered another Corona. Gwen thought, I can't let her get drunk. I've got to get her to her apartment without a scene. In the end she'll be hysterical, but I'm gonna go through with this if I have to carry her up the stairs.

As they left Felix's, Cindy said, "You're taking me home, aren't you?"

"Yes, I am."

"What about my stuff?"

"It's already there."

Cindy bawled. She said she didn't believe what was happening. They got into the car and Gwen said, "It won't do any good to cry, Cindy. I'm the ice lady tonight. I've gone as far as I can go."

It took ten minutes to get to the apartment. Cindy asked, "Where's my stuff?"

"Don and Jeff already brought it over."

Cindy wailed, "I don't believe you!"

"I'll go up with you. I'll show you."

They climbed the stairs to the second floor. Cindy's door was unlocked. She saw her things and slumped to the mattress on the floor. "I'm dead," she cried. "It's all over with. They're gonna get me for sure." She thrashed around.

Gwen steeled herself. No matter how much Cindy suffered, she couldn't drag her own family any deeper into someone else's personal nightmare. They could all wind up with the Campbells.

Cindy gripped her head with her hands and moaned. "I'm so afraid," she said. *"So* afraid. What should I do?"

"Call the police," Gwen said.

"The Mafia! They'll find me!"

"I'm very sorry for you, Cindy, but I have my own life to live. I can't do any more."

Cindy wailed, "I've lost the best friend I ever had!"

Gwen stood up. In her mind's eye she saw John and Jeff

gleaming with blood. She thought her heart would stop.
"Cindy," she said, "I've taken out a restraining order to
keep you from calling me or coming to my house." It wasn't
true, but she'd had enough. She walked down the steps to a
loud obbligato of sobs.

For the next week Gwen was convinced that the Mafia
was watching her. She jumped at every noise. As she walked
past windows, she thought, Ooh *bam!* I'm *gone!* She kept
the place dark and stopped breathing each time she turned
the key in the van. Her husband told her to take Cindy's
story to the police. She said, "Don, I'm as scared of them as
I am of the Mafia."

She thought of Cindy's uncle, J. W. O. Campbell. He was
a lawyer and knew the case. She told him the confession
story on the phone and was left with the impression that he
was bored.

She thought, That's all right with me. At least it's off my
chest and in God's hands. If God wants to carry it further,
fine, but I'm not doing another thing.

84

On Friday, October 15, four months after the murders, Paul
Motard found a note in his box at headquarters. The scribbled message said that J. W. O. Campbell had talked to a
woman who reported that Cindy Ray had confessed. Sure,
Motard thought, and I'm Renfrew of the Mounties.

At eleven the next morning the homicide team sat across
from a pretty blonde named Gwen Funk Sampson in an
insurance office on Merwin. She'd already warned them over
the phone that she didn't want to talk to the police. Schultz
opened the interview by pointing out that withholding evidence could land her in jail.

She sighed deeply, said she was thirty-four years old and
had known Cindy Ray for five years. She told a long story
about taking her under her roof and dumping her a week

ago. The detectives listened with mild interest—they'd been hearing weird tales about Cindy since the day after the killings, and one more wouldn't matter. No matter how many stories they heard, whether in secondhand confessions or suspicions or deductions or theories or ideas, they still couldn't go to the D.A. without hard evidence.

Their interest picked up at the news that Cindy had mentioned leaving a glove on the floor. Sampson seemed to notice. "So if there was a glove there," she asked, "then there's some credence to the story?"

The detectives played dumb. Nothing about the glove had appeared in the press. Maybe they were onto something worth taking to a grand jury, but they didn't want to tip their hands to this woman or anyone else. She might go back to Cindy; she might have been sent by Cindy. Stranger things had happened in murder cases.

On Monday morning they played the tape of the interview for an assistant D.A. He advised them to wire Sampson and send her back to Cindy Ray for more details.

The blond insurance woman seemed aghast at the idea. "The Mafia," she said. "I'm . . . afraid."

"There's no mob connection," Motard told her. "We think it was strictly Cindy and West."

Her pale face showed disbelief. The detectives were still trying to persuade her when the phone rang in the small insurance office. Sampson talked for a few minutes, then said, "That was my husband." It was the height of the Crunch of '82, when the peso was devalued and oil prices dropped and ten thousand Houston workers were being laid off a month. Don Sampson had just become the latest. Gwen didn't want to talk just now.

The next time Schultz and Motard visited, she seemed even more cool to the idea. She said that her marriage was headed for divorce, her sons were upset, and her mother had just been diagnosed positive for cancer. "My world's turned upside down," she said. "I really don't have time for you anymore. I'll stick by what I told you, but that's as far as I want to go."

Schultz took a last stab. "You've confirmed what we've

suspected about Cindy," he pleaded, "but there's not a
damn thing we can do without your cooperation." She
didn't react. "There's a murderess on the streets," Schultz
went on in the righteous voice that had convinced so many
culprits to confess.

"There's also a Mafia on the streets," the woman said,
"and they're involved in this case, whatever you guys say.
I'm not gonna endanger my family."

"But we'll protect you," Motard put in.

She laughed. "You'll protect me and my husband? My
sons? Twenty-four hours a day?"

"No," Motard admitted.

"Then I can't help you. It isn't that I don't want to. It's
that I can't."

The police computer disgorged nothing for "Salino,"
"Solino," "Celino," "Salina," or any close spelling. Mafia
experts said the name wasn't familiar. Schultz and Motard
realized they'd hit another dead end.

Then Mrs. J. W. O. Campbell called to say that young
Michael Ray had made new revelations about the murder
night to an Austin psychiatrist. The detectives arranged to
meet the child on a visit to Houston and repeated their old
itinerary—to the zoo, up and down elevators, to James Coney Island for hot dogs. The redheaded boy seemed coopera-
tive but provided nothing. "One of these days," Schultz said,
"we're gonna quit wastin' time with those kids."

"I'll sure miss the elevator rides," Motard said.

Schultz took a surprise phone call from Cindy Ray. She
said she'd just learned that her phone records had been sub-
poenaed.

"You can bug my damn toothbrush," she snapped.
"You'll never get anything on me." Schultz remarked to his
partner that they were dealing with one tough broad.

The Houston P.D. lacked the manpower for a full surveillance on its prime suspect, but the two detectives managed
spot checks. Fast-food delivery trucks came and went. Cindy
walked to the market and occasionally taxied downtown to
pick up advances against her inheritance. Once or twice she
drove off with West, but they didn't seem as tight as earlier.

She showed up barefooted in the lobby of the Hyatt Regency, offered to sketch one of the guests, and was asked to leave. Then she squirreled up in her apartment again.

A Pan-Am worker found a note in the bathroom at Intercontinental Airport saying that "Richard Duncan" had killed the Campbells. A few days after Schultz and Motard abandoned that blind trail, they drove fifty miles to Brenham to interview a Mexican prisoner who'd bragged to his cellmate about slitting the throats of a rich couple in Memorial. The detectives were chalking up so much overtime that they didn't dare claim it all. "You know what I miss most?" Motard said one day. "My wife's cooking." The young detective stayed skinny on M & M's and Diet Coke. Schultz had been forced to give up kippers; the aroma from his leftovers had brought homicide threats from homicide cops. Now he was getting by on Vienna sausages, dropping the empty cans in the wastebaskets of other divisions.

At last the trail became too faint to follow. Nothing new was turning up. West kept his nose clean. Cindy Ray sat tight and made no new mistakes. Her sisters, especially Betty Hinds, kept offering thoughts and ideas, usually along the lines that Cindy must be guilty because she'd said or done thus-and-so in the past. The detectives already had bulging files of thus-and-so's. They still weren't evidence.

Motard was writing out his latest overtime report when he overheard Captain Bobby Adams say, "Homicide's drawing two-thirds of the overtime in the whole department. The chief says it's gotta stop."

The young detective chucked his report into the wastebasket. He and his partner had been working twenty or thirty hours overtime a week for four months and putting in for half. He thought, What's the use? A few days later the two sergeants trooped into the lieutenant's office and Schultz slid a file on the desk. "Fuck it," he said. The Campbell investigation was shelved.

85

Gwen Sampson wasn't upset when Cindy phoned after six weeks of silence. Time had blunted Gwen's fears. The Mafia hadn't struck, and she'd missed her old friend's chatter and silliness. She told Cindy that she hadn't intended any harm by talking to the cops, that they'd pinned her in a corner. Cindy seemed willing to accept the explanation. The subject of the phony restraining order didn't come up. Gwen thought, She probably forgot all about it.

Their marathon conversations resumed. Both women were convinced that their phones were tapped. "Good morning, Sergeant Schultz," Cindy would start out. They giggled together about Motard's shyness and Schultz's attempts to be smooth. Cindy kept returning to the murders, but in code. "You know I was on the premises on that, uh . . . occasion," she said. "And *you* know who was with me."

"Yeah," Gwen said. "I . . . think so."

"It wasn't the S man."

"You mean it wasn't the salty guy from, uh"—she burst into song—"*Arrivaderci, Roma.*"

"He wasn't there."

"Oh?"

"It was . . . *oink, oink, oink. . . .*"

In a way, Gwen felt relieved that West and not Salino was the killer. Old Pigface might have called her a whore cow once or twice, but he was a minor threat compared to the Mafia. Besides, Cindy had said he was out of the picture now.

Gwen decided not to tip the cops to the new information. In one part of her mind she'd always thought that Cindy's parents had probably asked for what they got, at least if Cindy's stories were true. Let sleeping murders lie, Gwen told herself. We've had our problems, Cindy and I, but now we've got our friendship back.

86

David heard a singer croon a love song and thought he would puke. Love was a pain in the ass the second time around, and the third and the fourth and the fifth. Still—he thought he might be healing from the pain of Cindy's second departure. He'd been rehearsing this lovelorn act since high school.

She rattled him on the phone by mentioning that she missed her dead mother. He said, "Look, you better keep it straight in your mind, ya know? These were bad people. Don't go getting all mixed up and saying we shouldn't've done it."

In time, he realized that even though weird remarks popped from her mouth, she could be counted on to keep their secret. Her first and last mistake had been the glove, and that had been under combat conditions. The cops had no other physical evidence; careful planning had seen to that. Wickie might let something drop, but who would believe that dope fiend? Besides, Wickie didn't know the details. Half the barstool soldiers in Rud's talked about their kills, military and otherwise. It was an art form.

For a few doleful weeks he considered the possibility that Cindy had conned him into the killings, but he decided that she wasn't organized enough to run an intricate scam. He remembered the horror stories, the switches of voice, the tears. He thought of how she'd called him "Daddy" when they made love, shied from normal intercourse because he wasn't her father, avoided men and acted freaky about sex in general. He remembered every detail of her mistreatment as a child—the chains, the straps, the dismembered dolls. He saw her mother's smiling face as Cindy's five-year-old form slipped beneath the surface of the lake. Outrageous! He remembered the ramming incident—*Mama, mama. I didn't do it! Don't hit me!* How many childhood batterings had it taken to create hysterical regressions like that?

If it was all a scam, he told himself, she spent two years

laying the groundwork. That's a hell of a long time. But
Cindy's no master planner. Shit, she's lucky to remember
her house key.

Lying on his pull-out couch at night, he saw her father's
dark shadow pumping rhythmically till the soft little body
beneath him began to respond despite itself. Ah, he thought,
the shame, the shame.

No, he consoled himself, Cindy's story adds up. She
might lie about the little things, and God knows she gets
confused, but those dirty Campbells are where they belong.
We committed the perfect crime. We ought to get a medal.

1983–1984

87

Betty Campbell Hinds tried to settle back into a routine in Austin, taking care of her two-year-old Amelia and concentrating on her job. Holder of a B.S. in zoology, she worked for the U.S. Geological Survey, running tests for alkalinity, bacteria, pH level, and other factors on eleven streams and rivers. Every day she went out with her rubber boots and specimen jars and tried to see something other than her mother's or father's face in her field microscope. When she didn't see her parents, she saw Cindy.

Her husband insisted that Cindy's flip attitude about her parents was the ultimate proof of her guilt. Betty said, "She's always been uncaring, Richard. You can't convict her on that." There were times when she felt ashamed of her own suspicions. What kind of a scientist am I, she asked herself, letting my imagination take over like this? It wasn't Cindy who killed Mother and Daddy. It was an irate client. It was a maniac. It was . . .

Betty didn't sleep well.

Her sisters Michelle and Jamie confessed that they had the same misgivings about Cindy. Uncle J.W. advised them to reserve judgment. "She's your sister," the prudent uncle counseled.

All the family members were nervous about Cindy's life-long pattern of disappearing for months, sometimes years. Betty thought, Suppose the police turn up evidence and can't find her? She phoned Cindy often, analyzing every word and intonation for signs of guilt. "Well, Cindy," Betty asked her one day, "what do *you* think? Who killed Mother and Daddy?"

Cindy giggled. "I heard it was the Mafia," she answered, "and I heard someone say that I did it because I wanted the boys back." A peal of laughter came over the line and Betty forced a laugh in response.

After she hung up, she thought, How can anyone find humor in this? Mother and Daddy were murdered in bed.

They are never coming back. Damn it, Cindy, what's so funny?

The more she talked to Cindy, the more Betty realized that her computer-programmer husband was right. As a test she gave Cindy frequent opportunities to say that she loved Mother and Daddy and missed them, but Cindy refused to be drawn into elegiac statements. Her constant preoccupation was the estate, why it was taking so long to settle, how much cash she could expect, the niggardliness of her monthly advances. She bent every conversation back to herself. It was as though Mother and Daddy were statistics now, a couple of names on floppy disks in the basement of the cement-gray police building. Betty thought, She's always been the center of her own universe.

At a family council one night, Richard suggested a reward to move the case off dead center. The Hindses weren't rich; it took both their incomes to maintain a small house in an unstylish section of Austin. But they offered ten thousand dollars and figured they would pay in installments.

The only result was a squib in a newspaper. The AP and UPI weren't interested, and the TV and radio stations didn't return calls. The media had turned to other sensations. So had the police. Nobody cared. It was a dreary winter.

88

Cecelia wondered where Cindy had gone, but she didn't dare ask David. He'd made it known that he didn't want her name mentioned in his presence. Cecelia took her son seriously; she still suffered an occasional twinge from the time he'd sent her sprawling in the dining room.

Six or seven months had passed without a visit from Cindy, ever since the time she'd fled to her friend Gwen's. There'd been a hysterical phone call a week later, saying that Gwen had thrown her out after just two nights. Then— silence. Cecelia kept David's old room spotless just in case.

Cecelia missed the days when they'd done tarot cards to-

gether and talked about astrology and spooks and the theater. She had almost no old friends, and DuVal's reclusiveness prevented her from making new ones. When she hinted
that it might be nice to see a movie, he would drive her to
the theater, return home to read or watch educational TV,
then pick her up. Once or twice a year they attended a play,
usually one they'd already seen. "We're too much trouble for
him," David told his mother one day. "He doesn't want to
be bothered." Cecelia nodded.

In the spring of 1983, nearly a year after the murders, she
was thrilled to pick up the phone and hear Cindy's voice
apologizing for the long silence. A week later there was another call, and soon the phones were jangling again. One
night they talked so long that Cecelia's ear hurt. "I have
things to do, Cindy," she finally said. "I just can't stay on
the phone for two hours." But she was secretly pleased to be
found that interesting.

For a month or two Cindy seemed reluctant to resume her
visits to the house on Kipling, but she finally agreed to
come. Cecelia indulged in an occasional peek out the front
shutters as she waited. A taxi pulled up and a monstrous
form oozed from the back. Good heavens, Cecelia thought,
she must have done nothing but eat.

Just as the two old friends settled down in the amber-
tinted living room for a long talk, the front door banged
open and David's voice called out, "Hi, Mom."

Cindy ran upstairs. David whispered, "Who . . . ?"

"It's Cindy," Cecelia whispered back. "She's fat."

David chased after her. Cecelia thought, I wish he'd make
up his mind. Why, she's been anathema for months; now he
insists on looking her over when she least wants him to. She
heard faint voices. Then David came downstairs and left.

Cindy returned to the room wiping her eyes. "He doesn't
hate me for being fat!" she said excitedly. "All he said was
that I have to take it off. And I will, Cecelia. *I will!*"

The afternoon tea parties resumed, but Cecelia saw no
signs of weight loss. Cindy said she'd moved from Kingston
but didn't want to reveal her new address because the Mafia
was still on her case. "Don't worry about them," DuVal said

one afternoon in his dry voice. "If they were really after you, they'd have already found you."

Cindy usually left by cab, but occasionally she would ask DuVal to drop her off downtown so she could get a bus. "Doesn't it seem strange," he asked Cecelia, "that she never lets me drive her home?"

Of course it's strange, Cecelia thought, but we have to accept her strangeness to enjoy her friendship. It wouldn't do to push. The child pulled more disappearing acts than Harry Houdini. Without Cindy, she thought, who the hell would I talk to? The men in this family aren't worth a damn as conversationalists. David's always on the verge of losing his temper and DuVal acts like a boarder.

Cindy talked for hours about the skirmishing over the Campbell estate. She was having problems with lawyers. They all demanded payment, usually in promissory notes due after the settlement. Cecelia wondered what would be left when the cash was finally released.

"Cindy's still looking for the knight on the white horse," she told David when he dropped in for breakfast. "She actually said that one of her lawyers took the case because he loves her. She's fired three or four. I tell you, they're cleaning her out."

She also yammered about her uncle and sisters. She told a dramatic story about how J.W. had arrived at her father's office after the murders and looted his safe. Cecelia was willing to believe anything about the Campbells. "That uncle's such a louse," she told DuVal. "It makes my stomach turn that he's got control of those two little boys. *Such a louse!*"

Cindy vanished again, but this time for only a few months. When she returned she explained that a Mafioso named Salino had landed her a job as live-in housekeeper for an Italian restaurateur. "Where, honey?" Cecelia asked.

Cindy explained that she'd been forbidden to give out the name or address. Also, she said, she couldn't receive visitors or phone calls on the job.

Cecelia suspected that she was simply trying to wall off a part of her life. I'm sure there's a good reason, Cecelia said to herself. It's not my place to intrude.

Over tarot Cindy explained that Salino had introduced

her to a short, dark and handsome waiter who tenderly
called her "Ceendy." But the three-way friendship turned
out to be a scam. Salino wanted the waiter to marry her so
they could steal her share of the estate. A typical Mafia
trick! When she told the Italians that her inheritance was
worthless, they took a hike. "You made a good move there,"
Cecelia commented. "Nobody needs friends like that."

To herself she said, This child's life is like "The Young
and the Restless." I wonder why these things keep happening to her.

89

By the first anniversary of the murders Gwen Sampson's
friendship with Cindy seemed to be sputtering out. Once
they'd talked on the phone almost daily, but now it was
down to every month or so. Gwen found it hard to follow
her old playmate's stories. She said she'd found a new lover
named Talal, a handsome Arab who bought her pretty
things on his salary as a waiter. "You should see him,
Gwen," she burbled over the phone. "He's so *exciting*! He
took me to Foley's right after we met and socked me across
the face in front of the whole store! Of course I deserved it."

Gwen thought, Oh, God, more Sacher-Masoch. She'd
heard similar tales in the darkroom days. Cindy's husband
Moe had beaten her and so had her redneck husband and
her fruitcake husband and Pigface West and a couple of
others. Maybe she sent out the wrong signals. Gwen
thought, No wonder she broke up with Carrot Tink and all
those other guys. They probably refused to hit her!

One fall day Gwen was at work in the insurance agency
when her six-year-old son John phoned and talked so fast
she couldn't understand a word. "Baby," Gwen said,
"what's *wrong*?"

"Cindy was just here." He was crying.

"Are you *okay*?"

"Yes." He sniffed. "She grabbed me and held me. These

men drove up in a white van. They looked like Mexicans—
mustaches and stuff." He sniffed again. "Cindy wouldn't let
me go. I was scared. She kept saying, 'It's gonna be all
right.' "

"Well, baby, what in the world did she *want?*"

"The men ripped the TV out of the wall. Cindy told me,
'If you say anything to the cops, we'll come back and hurt
your mom.' Then they drove off."

Gwen thought, I always knew she was around the bend. I
just didn't know how far.

A few days later the phone rang at the Billie Funk Insurance Agency. Cindy asked, "Are you still speaking to me?"

"Yes," Gwen said, "but I'm not happy."

"Well, it was my set."

Gwen was disgusted. "Cindy," she said, "if you'd just
asked me, I'd've gladly given it back. All you had to do was
ask. But to come over and terrorize John—"

"I didn't terrorize him."

She decided to back off. There was no earthly point in
trying to make sense to someone from another galaxy.
"Look, Cindy, I can't talk right now," she said, and hung
up.

Just before Thanksgiving Cindy phoned again. "You're a
fucking whore cow!" she shouted. "David was right. You
know what Talal says about you? You're a thief! A goddamn
whore! You ripped off every goddamn thing I had!"

Gwen gently lowered the phone.

There was an eerie call a few weeks later. "I'm phoning all
the people I used to love," Cindy said in a low Bette Davis
voice. "I want to tell them hello and see if they're doing
well."

The call destroyed Gwen's evening. She thought, I could
deal with her insults better than I can deal with this. It was
time to change the phone number, and maybe a few other
things.

90

In the middle of the summer David tried to boost his morale by making a down payment on a used Trans Am. "Hey, Dad," he told DuVal, "you gotta see it, ya know? It's one of the original Trans Ams before they put the EPA bumpers on 'em—a 1970 with a 455 HO ram air engine. It's a collector's item!"

DuVal smiled pleasantly and said, "David, you know I don't know a thing about race cars."

Well, yeah, David thought, but couldn't you fake it a little?

He clipped an article about Sweden's new laser-controlled anti-aircraft guns and gave it to his dad. DuVal smiled again and said, "It's amazing the way you keep up with tactics and strategy and war. I went to West Point and I'm not nearly as interested as you." But he didn't seem displeased.

Father and son went to *Uncle Vanya* at the Alley, and afterward fell to talking about race. "I'm not a racist, Dad," David said, "but you gotta recognize the cultural differences between the races, ya know? The American low-class black person is one of the most obnoxious, sleazy, criminal, pushy, inconsiderate, belligerent, jive-ass, ignorant, intolerable assholes you'll ever meet—culturally, not biologically. But an intelligent black man, a guy like Sidney Poitier, is something else again. I don't have any prejudices against him."

DuVal said that was an interesting approach.

David didn't know why, but his old feelings about injustice came surging back. After months in the dumps, he was Captain Avenger again. He educated a few jerk-offs for mistreating women, a few more for driving errors. He beat a Rastafarian unmercifully for abusing a woman and almost got into a gunfight with a cook at a deer camp for putting corned beef in the burritos. Later he thought, I was ready to kill that son of a bitch. I've got to cool it. I'm a mellow guy.

He didn't hear from Cindy for a long time and was surprised to answer the phone and find her throwing a regular old shit-storm of a fit. "Oh, David," she said, "my lawyers aren't protecting me. J.W.'s lying about the estate. They're concealing assets. They're cheating me blind!"

He calmed her and learned that the final accounting had been put off again. The Campbells were forcing her to live on chickenshit advances that didn't begin to meet her needs. "David," she whined, "what can I do?"

He told her it was a lucky thing she'd called him; he'd been through the mill on inheritances. "Goddamn it, Cindy," he barked at her, "stand up for yourself!" He stood to collect half her inheritance for killing her parents, and when people cheated her, they cheated him. "As far as real estate goes, I know how to find it. I can go down to the goddamn tax assessor's office and look it up."

She asked him to go ahead.

A few days later he talked to his mother on the phone. "In one afternoon I found about fifteen pieces of property under the Campbell name," he said proudly. "It was real complicated—maps, tax stamps and all. The clerk helped me. Then I called Cindy and had her read off the list of properties in the latest accounting. Eight were unlisted! Jesus, Mom, if I can find 'em, why can't J.W.?"

Cecelia said, "David, that's obscene. They're trying to steal that child's rightful inheritance." He heard an angry snort at the other end of the line, then his mother's bitter voice, "Nothing would surprise me about those Campbells. *Nothing!*" Mother and son agreed on that.

91

Lyn Roebuck, sales rep for a Houston courier service, dropped into Rudyard's British Pub for a drink after work. Though fortyish, there was something about her of the drum majorette, energetic and vivacious. She was given to gold jewelry and heels up to here, but tonight she'd come straight from work and was dressed for business. So she was surprised when some idiot made turkey noises at her while her fiancé Paul Whitfield was over at the bar getting beers.

She turned and saw three young men seated at a table under a sign bearing the Urban Animals' slogan: SKATE OR DIE! One looked like a Mexican and the others like the white trash who hung out behind the Pik-N-Pak ice-house saloon across the street. What can you expect, she asked herself, from guys who live in an alley?

"*Gobble, gobble, gobble. . . .*"

Everyone at the bar turned to look. Lyn called out, "You're a dick!"

The remark brought an obscene gesture. Out of the corner of her eye she saw Paul stride toward the offender. He was an ex-Marine, an olive-complexioned, self-styled "pinkneck" ("That's a redneck who lives in the Montrose") with a thin face and a neatly cropped black goatee.

"If you wanna start some shit, buddy," he told the loudmouth, "start it with me."

Under her rose-colored aviator glasses, Lyn rolled her eyes. Nothing repelled her more than barroom machismo. "Drop it, Paul!" she said. She dragged him to a table with five or six of their friends.

One of the jerks wouldn't leave it alone. He was Mexican-looking, about five five, a strutting rooster whom the others called Martin. He snarled, "Hey, man, we gon' wait for you outside."

A reedy voice interrupted, "What's going on?"

Lyn turned to see Dave West. They'd met a while back. Lyn had been put off by his talk. He seemed to see the world as a collection of armed camps. He showed up once or twice with a greasy-haired woman who wore jeans, a loose T-shirt out at the waist and a big flannel shirt over the T-shirt.

The Mexican moved off as Dave pulled up a chair next to Lyn. "These punks won't leave us alone," she said. She glanced at the other table. The desperadoes were glaring. "I'm kinda worried about them," she said as Paul and his friends chatted. "They're waiting for us to leave."

"Well, it's just a buncha bullshit," Dave said. "I've seen those guys. They're dogshit."

He wandered off and returned in fifteen or twenty minutes. "They're still staring," Lyn said.

Dave took a look, then turned back. Lyn thought, He's got a cute smile. Take off the face fuzz and he'd look like a little kid. He watched for a few minutes, then said, "I'll be back."

When Dave returned, Lyn noticed that he'd exchanged his tight shirt for a loose one and his street shoes for sneakers. She told him, "We've got to walk home now and I'm kinda worried."

"I'll go with you," Dave said.

Two groups left: Lyn, Paul, Dave and a few male friends in front, the three punks eight or ten feet behind. They'd barely reached the sidewalk when Martin called Lyn a bitch, jerked at his crotch and yelled at Paul, "Hey, you in the green shirt. This is for you. Yeah, *you*, motherfucker!"

Dave rammed him into the entranceway to the Chinese market next door and kicked him in the balls. He turned to the one called "Lee" and slapped him hard. Martin staggered up and Dave slammed him back against the wall. The Mexican broke a beer bottle and waved it. Dave laughed and said, "I'm gonna kill ya now if you don't put that bottle down." To Lyn he seemed to be having a high old time.

Martin took one step forward, then veered off. The other two led him away. Dave called out, *"No cojones!"* He told Paul and Lyn, "You guys can walk on home."

Lyn thought, It was nice of him to defend my honor. But imagine going home and changing for a fight!

A few weeks later Paul brought Lyn a disquieting story: "Dave invited me to his house. He started talking about street trash, said they oughta be gotten rid of. He said rapists oughta have their balls cut. Stuff like that. Then he said, 'I've already had to kill a couple people.'

"I came back, 'Well, what happened? They broke in and you had to blow 'em away?'

"He said, 'Naw. They were just some trash. It had to be done.'

"I thought it might be a coupla guys in a bar fight. I just

kinda blew it off. We've heard so much bullshit from him and his friends."

Lyn thought, If Dave killed, why would he confess it to someone he hardly knows? She knew Paul would never go to the police. She didn't think she would either.

92

A few weeks after the second anniversary of the Campbell killings, David West sat in a Mexican restaurant with a thirty-five-year-old woman and tried to keep his temper. He'd dated her before, and their favorite topic of conversation was the no-good husband who beat her and screwed her over mentally. David was nearly drunk, and he found himself thinking, That motherfucker's gotta go.

But then, with the clarity that came from another swig of Belhaven, he instructed himself to butt out. He didn't want any more killing. It was too painful. He hadn't regretted dispensing with James Campbell, but lately he'd been wondering if Virginia deserved it. Cindy's talk about chains and beatings and being forced to eat shit—was it all true? *Half* true? He consoled himself with the thought that half would have been enough.

His date told him more angry stories about her sadistic husband. "Boy," she said, "I wish there was some way I could get that bastard."

"Yeah," he said. "Right on, ya know?" He was drunk.

"I'd like to lock him in a cellar and starve him to death, so I could go down every day and laugh at him."

David peered through the cigarette smoke. "Well, listen," he said shakily, "if this really bothers you this much, and, uh, you really wanna do something, just go out and, uh, ya know . . . kill him."

The woman frowned. "You can't do that," she said.

"Oh yes you can."

Later he figured it must have been the way he said it. She already knew the details of the Campbell case—they'd discussed it—and she studied him intently for several seconds. Then she whispered, "You didn't!"

He sipped his ale, wiped his lips and said, "Oh yes I did." By closing time he'd told her the details. She promised not to give him away.

93

By late fall Cecelia was seriously worried about Cindy. The war over the estate had destroyed the child's equanimity. She would snap at Cecelia, "Oh, that's not so!" or "You're not making sense!" The little flare-ups were new in their four-year relationship.

Cindy was still convinced that her share of the estate was worth millions, but the sisters had told her she'd be lucky to walk away with two hundred thousand dollars, most of which she'd already spent or promised to her lawyers. "It's my money!" Cindy would scream. "They're stealing my goddamn money!" Frequently she asked Cecelia for handouts, twenty or thirty dollars for groceries or toilet paper or other household needs. The poor thing seemed determined to play out her role of Blanche DuBois. *I have always depended upon the kindness of strangers.* Well, Cecelia thought, the final curtain can't be far off.

In November Cindy began having severe headaches. She told Cecelia that one of her husbands had fractured her skull years ago with a chair. She was suffering so much that Cecelia offered to pay for more tests.

In the hospital Cindy acted terrified of the machine and made the technician explain the procedure step by step. Her eyes were huge with fright as she clutched Cecelia's hand and said, "Oh, I don't think I can go through with it."

Cecelia said to herself, You've forgotten, Cindy, but you told me a long time ago that you've already had a brain scan. This is all an act. But . . . why?

The tests were negative.

94

Toward the end of 1984 Betty Hinds finally joined her husband and other sisters in the absolute certainty of Cindy's guilt. For Betty the final factor was Cindy's frenzied fight for her money. "Where does she get all that energy?" Betty asked Richard one night.

"She has nothing else to do," the computer programmer answered.

Through lawyers Cindy aggressively pursued her claim that she was being swindled. She inspected the vacant house on Memorial and had the locks changed. She hired appraisers to challenge the value of everything down to the doorknobs. She filed an ill-fated suit against J. W. O. Campbell, demanding that the court name her or her lawyer as coadministrator. She cursed her sisters on the phone and swore she'd see them in jail. "She hasn't spent much time mourning," Richard Hinds told his wife one night.

"Cindy doesn't mourn," Betty observed.

The two middle sisters began bickering by phone. Betty hated herself for it. The object of the phone contacts wasn't to vent anger; the object was to keep tabs on a murderess.

One day Betty phoned into a dead line. Cindy had moved and left no forwarding address. It was what they'd all feared. Where would she turn up this time? Oklahoma again? Colorado? *Brazil?* Under what name? Fat or thin? With what nose?

A week later she came in for her monthly advance, then dropped out of sight again, checking in occasionally by phone.

A settlement proposal was made: Cindy would get the Kingston fourplex, plus enough cash to bring the package to three hundred thousand dollars, less the money already advanced. It was substantially more than her rightful share, or so J.W. and the sisters contended, but anything was better than this unseemly brawl.

The negotiations stalled on a single point. Cindy demanded that the eviction of "Nanny Helen" be part of the deal. She told Betty on the phone, "I need to rent that apartment for extra income."

Betty was of two minds. Cindy had been acting paranoid about Nanny lately, claiming that she spied on her and tried to lure away her boyfriends. An apartment owned by a murderous granddaughter wasn't the ideal rest haven for a seventy-five-year-old woman whose bones were so wasted that she could hardly walk.

On the other hand, Virginia Campbell had promised her aging mother that the cozy little apartment was hers for life. Betty thought, This will break Nanny's heart. She asked Cindy for a ninety-day delay.

"No deal," Cindy snapped.

Richard Hinds's father had died earlier in the year, and when they were going through his papers they discovered that he'd made a discreet inquiry into the case via a former district attorney's lieutenant named P. M. Clinton. The private report concluded that Cindy was probably guilty. Confidential police sources had informed Clinton that the case was in cold storage and likely to stay there.

Betty and Richard had wanted to hire a detective agency for months, but held off out of respect for Gil Schultz and Paul Motard. After discovering the Clinton report, Richard said, "Listen, Betty, we'd better do something about Cindy or sometime when we're sixty or seventy we're gonna wonder why we didn't. Right now we don't even know where she is."

Betty sounded out Schultz. The homicide detective said, "You're not gonna hurt our feelings if you hire an agency. Sometimes these people can do things that we can't. Just be careful they don't screw you out of a buncha money."

Richard and Betty were so nervous about possible reprisals that they made their first calls to P. M. Clinton from a phone booth. It turned out that he was now working for Clyde A. Wilson, the most successful private eye in Texas. Wilson's agency came high—a thousand-dollar retainer and a fifty dollars an hour per agent.

Richard had expected the hourly rate to be no higher than

twenty-five dollars. Their inheritance might be held up for
years. But he told Betty he thought they should go ahead.
They used up their credit cards and applied for new ones.
Before long they'd spent twelve thousand dollars on the
hunt for Cindy. And hadn't found her.

95

Sometimes Wickie Weinstein wondered why he'd moved in
with Dave and Robin St. John and added his Airborne
Ranger gear to the décor. It didn't seem to improve the
place. The rats still thrived and the cockroaches partied all
night with the fleas that Dave introduced with his new semi-
Rottweiler Nana. Wickie thought, Home sweet home.

In his own fuzzy way he was concerned about Dave. The
black Trans Am had lifted his spirits, but not for long. His
life seemed to consist of pot, brew and TV. After he got
home from that stupid delivery-truck job, he didn't go out,
didn't take care of the place, didn't even seem interested in
his muscle car. Wickie thought, Dave needs an old lady. It's
been a while. . . .

The only time Dave showed a little snap was when war
broke out in the neighborhood. An ex-con named Virgil Lee
Johnson stole a set of mechanics' tools from Robin and
threatened to kill him if he snitched. Dave tried to cool the
situation by grabbing a handful of Johnson's shirt and telling him, "Get the fuck outa Dodge!"

A few nights later a .22 slug tore through the front wall of
Dave's house. In a discussion about the matter Virgil Lee
pulled a knife and Dave beat him senseless; then Wickie
reinforced the message by knocking him down with his
truck. The next day Johnson was back flipping the bird and
shouting threats. Wickie laid open his head with a pickax
handle. A half-hour later the goofy son of a bitch appeared
across the street from Rud's, head and face matted with
blood, yelling "Yah, yah, you motherfuckers!"

Dave and Wickie beat him up again and ran him off.

Word came back that Virgil Lee had recruited some of his Bandito friends and intended to assassinate Dave, Robin and Wickie, burn their house and piss on the ashes. Dave bought an 1100 Winchester shotgun from his friend Ron Westphal and sawed off the barrel to the legal minimum, seventeen and a half inches. Wickie contributed a rifle, another shotgun and two pistols. The home troops were ready.

After a few days on alert, Dave said he was bored. "Let's just fucking go over there and shoot Virgil Lee in the head," he told Wickie. "We'll put him in your truck and pour lye over him. That way he can't shoot at me or burn my house or wreck my car."

"No, Dave," Wickie said patiently.

"Yeah!" Dave said. His bicolored eyes gleamed. "Let's shoot that little bastard! Nobody's gonna miss him. They'll just think he went away."

"Dave, *no!*" Wickie thought, Doesn't he know the difference between defending yourself and murder?

Dave waited a few more days and then tipped police that a known thief, psycho and parole violator was hanging around the neighborhood. Virgil Lee was picked up and the war was over.

After the exhilaration of combat, Wickie returned to his pot, coke and alcohol and began dealing on the side. Occasionally one of his misfiring brain circuits would reconnect and he would remember that Dave had once confessed a murder. Or was it two? The details were hazy. The last they'd talked, Dave had tried to justify one of the killings by claiming that the victim had been terrorizing him. Wickie thought, Who knows? Who cares? Dave got away with it; that's all that mattered. It was no burden on Wickie's conscience.

Sometimes the phone rang in the house on Vermont and a squeaky voice asked, "Is David there?"

"Dave's out, baby," Wickie would say. He'd seen Cindy four or five times and every time she looked a couple of inches larger in circumference. She talked constantly: it didn't take a shrink to see that she was in bad shape. "I don't know where Dave is," Wickie would tell her. "You're gonna have to call back."

When he got the message, Dave would roll his eyes and say, "She's so fucking weird! She's so fucking *unstable!*" Then he would phone her. Wickie wanted to say, Dave, *Dave,* she's just a chick. But he knew better. No chick was "just a chick" to Dave.

96

Denise Moseley, a small-boned woman who looked more like a subteen fashion model than an agent of Clyde Wilson International Investigations Inc., followed Cynthia Ray's trail with the intensity of a wolverine. In her early thirties, Moseley was a career private detective with an exquisitely slender figure, a small upturned nose, ten perfectly manicured fingernails and a perfectionist's personality. She'd caught the case because her colleague P. M. Clinton had a full workload and didn't have time to handle the stream of telephonic advice from Betty Hinds and her sisters. Moseley had interviewed Richard and Betty in Austin when they'd first hired the agency. She realized that the struggling young couple couldn't afford many hours at fifty dollars per.

For a while the job looked hopeless. In boss Clyde Wilson's phrase, Cynthia Ray was "as hard to track as a piss-ant on a cue ball." The evil sister phoned Betty and J.W. but never left a return number. Whenever anyone asked for her address, she hung up. She'd never registered to vote, bought or sold or licensed a car, learned to drive or paid a traffic ticket, served on a jury or been arrested or opened a checking account. Except as a voice on the phone, she didn't seem to exist.

Denise read and reread the original file memo on the case, looking for ideas. According to the clients, Cindy had been married first to an alcoholic wife beater and then to an abusive semi-socialite; she'd lived common-law with a man named Moe who beat her; she'd dated the notorious David

West and a man from "up north" named "Dean Thomas Samuels." She had a diseased imagination and lied frequently, so some of the biographical information could be false. Under no circumstances was the agency to contact her uncle, J. W. O. Campbell, because "he may inadvertently let the word out and it will get back to Cynthia Ray."

The memo ended:

Cynthia had told our client in an unrelated conversation that "a Moslem does not feel that they will lose their soul if they kill a non-Moslem." Cynthia has been known to associate with men from the Middle East.

Denise wondered, Is Cynthia conspiring with a Moslem to kill someone else? If she would kill her own parents, who on earth wouldn't she kill?

The newest photograph of the subject was three years old and showed a woman with protruding, slightly Oriental eyes and a pretty face. Betty Hinds had advised that her sister ate compulsively when upset and she'd been highly agitated on her last phone call November 20. "How much heavier do you think she might be now?" Denise asked.

"Nothing would surprise me," Betty answered.

After three weeks of energetic skip tracing, Denise learned that a "Cindy Ray" had paid an electric bill for an apartment off the Gulf Freeway. The place turned out to be empty. The trail led to apartment 210 at 2801 Walnut Bend, where a woman named Ray had lived with a man believed to be Iranian or Syrian. The couple had been evicted owing several hundred dollars.

Denise interviewed a tenant who told her, "Their place stunk. We had to leave the windows open for two or three weeks after they left."

"Did they have dogs and stuff?"

"No. It was *them* that stunk!"

In mid-December Denise learned that a woman who matched Cynthia's description had been seen with a short swart man in an upstairs apartment at 5710 Glenmont, an ethnic neighborhood off Highway 59 near the suburb of Bellaire. The telephone, registered in the name Talal Makhlouf, had been disconnected for nonpayment. Other tenants said that the female was fat and didn't bathe. The man laundered his clothes in the building's washateria in his shorts.

Denise wondered, Is Talal Makhlouf the Moslem who could kill an infidel without losing his soul? Why would he tell Cynthia something like that? And why would she pass it on to Betty? It was time for a closer look.

Denise and her colleague P. M. Clinton knocked on the door of apartment 30. Clinton was thirty-four, a country-boy Texan with an open face, a gentle manner and muscles. Denise sheltered close to his six-foot frame as a male called from inside, "Who is it?"

"Margaret Denny," Denise answered. It was the first name that came to her.

"What do you want?" The man seemed to have an accent.

"We're here to buy the TV."

"What TV?"

"The one you advertised in the *Green Sheet.*"

"No TV for sale!" the man called out.

Denise nodded at P.M. In Texas it was considered hostile to talk through closed doors. The paranoid behavior fit personality profiles of Cynthia Ray and her paramour. Still, it would be helpful to see her face.

They walked down the stairs as a man with wavy black hair peered at them over the railing. Denise called up in an angry voice, "What's this about a TV? We drove all the way from Spring to buy your TV. And you tell me you don't know what we're talking about?"

A woman bellowed, "You don't have to tell her anything! *Just come in here!*"

Denise cupped her hands and shrieked, "Listen, lady, we drove a long way to see your damn TV! Why'd you advertise it, anyway? *I'm mad enough to spit!*"

The swarthy man spoke softly. "I'm sorry," he said. "You got the wrong apartment."

"Get your ass back in here!" The woman's voice was loud and coarse. "We don't need to talk to these people." Denise thought, She sounds a little nuts. That's Cynthia, all right.

The door slammed. They still hadn't seen her face, but they were sure.

On the drive to their office west of Houston, the two private investigators decided to begin a full surveillance. But first they needed to know a little about Cindy's potential accomplice, David DuVal West. Along with another colleague named Mike Manela, Moseley and Clinton visited 1409 Vermont with a realtor. The place was for sale, and they'd conned the agent into believing that they were investors.

They parked alongside a broken tree and walked past two skewed mailboxes to the landing of a decrepit staircase. A downstairs tenant with a single earring was making mobiles from cut crystal. Another man appeared to be brewing beer. A growl came from the back.

A quick study of the upstairs apartment revealed broken windows, camouflage netting, footlockers, clothes folded in a military manner, survival gear, cannabis detritus, a couple of .22 cartridges and some sleeping bags. A sawed-off shotgun was propped against a wall in front and a full-barreled model in back. An Urban Animals jacket hung in a closet. A weight set, "D.P. Gym Pac 1000," jutted from a wooden wall.

While Denise and Manela diverted the realtor, P.M. climbed in and out of the attic. Later he told his colleagues, "When I first went up there, I thought, This is it! I thought, Most killers discard the weapon, but this West is cocky enough to keep it for a souvenir. Well, it wasn't there. You could see daylight through holes in the roof, cobwebs, an inch of dust. Little animals were running around. I thought, Okay, P.M., let's go."

The "investors" returned with another realtor for a more thorough check. In a small box on the mantel an operative named Bill Elliott found a .45 silvertipped hollow-point bullet. The live cartridge bore no extractor or ejector markings, but the investigators were excited. "Goddamn, we got it!" P. M. Clinton said. "I knew that turkey would make a mistake."

97

It was getting close to Christmas, 1984, and Robin St. John slid his tortoise-shell goggles above his pale blue eyes and told a friend on the phone:

"I'm moving out. Dave's become apathetic about the place. He won't clean up or take out his trash. The windows are broken and it's cold. The electricity's been turned off for a month. He hasn't paid the water bill in a year. They came out and turned it off and he turned it back on, so they took out the pipes. He pawned his tape player and his camera. He just doesn't give a shit anymore. I've lost respect for him. . . .

"He has no room for new ideas. He thinks art should be done a certain way and all other art's shit. It doesn't matter if it's Picasso—it's shit if it isn't done his way. Same with music. If he doesn't like a band, he'll say, 'They should be shot and killed, ya know?' Or he'll see some guy and say, 'That dude's a junkie. Might as well just shoot him. . . .'

"He gets calls from this Cindy. You can tell by her voice that she's ready to snap. She's real strange. They both are. I'm getting out of here."

98

P. M. Clinton, former lieutenant with the Harris County district attorney's office, cast around for a way to smoke out the reclusive Cynthia Campbell Ray. With her aggravated paranoia, no one from the private detective agency stood a chance of getting next to her. He wondered about taking a run at David West. At least West was in sight. He drove a delivery truck, drank at Rudyard's Pub, walked his dogs and drove a big Trans Am that could be followed from a block away.

At brainstorming sessions Clinton and the other private investigators agreed that West was the key to reaching Cindy, but which of the P.I.'s could get next to West? Denise Moseley was the only other female available, and she'd been seen at his house. She'd also been seen by Cindy's boyfriend and maybe by Cindy herself. Her cover was blown.

P.M. was pondering the situation in his office when the agency's newest part-time employee appeared in the four-inch heels that she called her "FMPs"—fuck-me pumps. Kim Paris might dress like a show pony, Clinton said to himself, but she's not doing half bad around here. If she could only tell time, she might work into a first-rate agent. She never showed up less than a half-hour late, and sometimes not at all. It was a problem.

Even on the rare days when she wore her new Brooks Brothers suit, Paris seemed out of place in a business office. She had a thin waist and square shoulders and P.M. guessed she was about five eight. She had a deep tan (acquired, she'd told everyone, by sailing topless in the Gulf), a straight nose, gray eyes that she turned an unreal blue with tinted contacts, shag-cut dark hair and a hoarsely sexy voice. Months ago P.M. had sized her up as a street-wise manipulator who could sell sand to the Saudis, especially male Saudis. Proprietor Clyde Wilson, P.M.'s eccentric father-in-law, called her "Squirrelly" to her face but didn't seem to mind her lolling around his private sanctum. Stretched out on the sofa in her oversized sunglasses and personal cloud of smoke, she'd listened as the others discussed the undercover job, then piped up, "Let me do it! I've run around with people like West." They'd hooted the newcomer down.

"Hi, P.M.!" she said as she dropped into a chair and let her long legs dangle over the end. "How the hell are ya?" He thought, Sometimes she sounds like a schoolkid. She'd been seen coloring a Heckle and Jeckle comic book. But he knew she was bright underneath.

He took a second look. Well, hell, he said to himself, maybe we're playing things a little too safe. She's perfect for the job. What've we got to lose? The rest of us hotshots are turning up diddly-squat.

He just hoped she didn't get hurt.

99

This office has some of the top investigators in the world, and they're all prima donnas. All my investigators want to show the other'n up a little bit. But I tell 'em, "There's only one motherfucker around here that's indispensable and you're looking at that motherfucker."

—CLYDE A. WILSON

Kim Paris, daughter of a suburban St. Louis dentist, was getting discouraged with her part-time job at the detective agency. It paid twenty dollars an hour, less than she'd earned as a topless dancer, more than she'd made as an assistant pool hustler in the Montrose, but the assignments were becoming infrequent and the office politics were too painful. She told herself she would rather be sailing. She liked to paraphrase Mia Farrow as Daisy in *The Great Gatsby:* "I'd find it *paralyzingly* attractive to spend the rest of my life on a racing sloop. Nothing too big. Ten meters would be fine." All she needed was $250,000 for the boat.

At twenty-three Kimberly Ann Paris still hadn't found her niche. She'd been an air traffic controller in the Navy, but if she saw one more T-28 Trojan or T-44 Pegasus, she would scream. She'd done a little modeling, worked as an extra in *Raggedy Man* starring Sissy Spacek, tried waitressing and hustling, but nothing seemed as enjoyable as sailing in the Gulf. Back in Missouri her mother had kidded her, "If you were any lazier, you'd sink into a coma." But Kim didn't think of herself as lazy; she thought of herself as bored.

She knew about her reputation for tardiness and had to admit it was deserved. "But I'm constant," she liked to explain. "You *know* I'm gonna be late. If I say I'm gonna be there at seven, maybe I'll be there at seven-thirty. It's because I can't organize myself. I'm in my closet yelling, 'Where's my left shoe?' "

There'd been a few good times since her discharge from the Navy in 1983, but most of her Houston year had been a bummer. She'd been ogled, pinched, hassled by cops. She'd lived on Luckyburgers to stretch the budget for her drop-in family: her rebellious younger sister Michelle, her girlfriend Sami Smith, her scruffy bitch Miss Rock 'n' Roll Trash, and her stray cats, Toulouse and Lautrec. For a stretch of several months she'd lunched regularly with a seventyish oilman who slipped big bucks under her plate, sometimes as much as two thousand dollars. She'd awakened one morning hooked on cocaine, and kicked the habit cold-turkey while Sami anesthetized her with iced vodka. Broke again, she dated a private eye named Mike Manela, who handled maritime investigations in Galveston. "Mike," she told him, "let me know if you ever need any help."

Soon he did, and Kim lucked into a career that she found far better suited to her talents. She'd spent so much time deceiving her parents and other authority figures that it was easy to deceive others—or so she laughingly explained. She bought a Borsalino hat and posed in front of her mirror behind a smile and a curl of smoke. She couldn't decide which of Charlie's Angels she resembled the most.

She delighted in telling her friends how she and Manela exposed disability-insurance cheaters. "I drive up in front of the guy's house in my miniskirt and fuck-me pumps. I don't have a big chest so I play up my long legs. I put on extra lipstick, tease my hair up real wild, and look a little disheveled, which isn't difficult for me at six A.M. because my usual wake-up time is eleven.

"I let the air out of my tire in front of the guy's house. Then I knock on the door and say, 'Gee, can I use your phone?' At first they're a little wary. So I'll dial a pay phone number or my number at home. I'll pretend to ask how much a tow truck costs and say, 'But I only have ten dollars!'

"So the guy'll offer to change my tire—while Mike's filming from the van down the street. I swear some of these cheaters are so eager they'll do it without a jack! But a few will protest. 'My back's bad.' 'I'm on disability.' So then I say, 'Well, just show me how. I'll do all the work.' As long as I can get 'em out the door, they can't bear to watch me do it."

Her first solo assignment was on behalf of a Houston lawyer seeking evidence against a client's wife. Kim flew to the Esalen Institute in California, introduced herself as a recovering drug addict, and spent five days trying to get the woman to incriminate herself. The lawyer was impressed and wrote a glowing letter.

But Kim found few admirers among the women of the detective agency. "I'm an enigma to them," she complained. "I've never liked most girls. They're competitive, they're nasty, and men are more interesting. How many girls have big boats? While they're working, I'm putting my feet up on the desk and talking on the phone and making plans for sailing trips. Sometimes I have a beer for lunch. I lay back on Clyde's sofa and crack jokes with him. Clyde understands people like me."

Lately she'd even felt unappreciated by the irascible Clyde. Everyone in the office seemed preoccupied. A scandal had developed over something called the Hermann Hospital estates, and the Wilson agency was doing most of the detective work. She'd heard that there were millions of dollars at stake.

So she was pleased when her old boyfriend Mike Manela asked if she'd like to make a run at a guy named David West.

"Yeah!" she said. "Who do I report to?"

"Denise Moseley. She was against the idea, but she's accepted it. She didn't think we should put a female on a male. She's right. It can undermine the credibility of the whole case. You'll have to be careful."

For all her general light-heartedness, Kim took the assignment seriously. She'd had an abortion in the Navy and as a Catholic felt she'd committed murder and was probably damned. Murder was no joking matter.

With her roommate Sami Smith, she sped down the Gulf freeway to Galveston to reoutfit herself. She'd been briefed on West's tastes, and Col. Bubbie's Strand Surplus Senter catered to them all. She wiped out her bank balance with dummy bullets, a bandolier, an infantry jacket with hooks for grenades, several pairs of stone-washed jeans to show off her trim backside, a band jacket with braid and epaulettes and twitchy gold pendants across the top, and other flashy items. Everyone in the Montrose area had a gimmick; she tried to think up a name for hers. Yep, that was it: *survivalist punk.*

She parked in front of David West's house at 2 P.M. on Monday, December 17, 1984. Through her ultradark Figaro shades a mercury streetlight lit the depressing scene like a set at the Alley Theatre. She decided that 1409 Vermont was one edifice that hadn't been designed by Houston's favorite architect, Philip Johnson. Broken oaks and maples sent lacy shadows back and forth across a cracked concrete parking pad. A rusty transmission stood in grease-stained soil. In a downstairs window she saw a scraggy Christmas tree.

She wobbled up the uneven stairs in her new FMPs and knocked on the door. She was surprised that she felt no fear, only excitement. P. M. Clinton had warned that she might be in danger. "C-Y-A!" he'd boomed. It was an old Navy rule, too. But she'd never been good at covering her ass.

She intended to introduce herself as "Theresa Neel," Agatha Christie's pseudonym in the movie *Agatha.* After that she planned a free-style approach. She was sure she could handle David West without memorizing a bullshit story that would only sound rehearsed.

No one answered upstairs or down. A car was parked in front: she couldn't tell the model or year but made a note of the license. Then she drove home.

At 5:30 P.M. she dialed West's number from a pay phone down the street from his house. A male voice said he was expected in an hour or so. At 6:45 she knocked on the upstairs door and got no answer. She came back every hour till 11 P.M, when a downstairs tenant told her, "He hasn't been home." She gave up for the night.

The next morning she phoned in her report. Her case agent suggested that it might have been more professional to stay on stakeout till West came home instead of wandering off between watches. Thanks, Denise, Kim thought. I'll remember that.

The day turned unseasonably warm for December, with the afternoon temperature in the seventies. At 5 P.M., TAG-819 was still parked in front of the house, but no one was in the apartment. At 7 P.M. the downstairs occupant came out and said, "He'll be home any minute." He informed her that West was working as a deliveryman at A-1 Blue Print and got off at six.

She waited in the car. Rain fell in spurts. The Montrose's sexual underworld passed in parade: aging whores in backless heels and teen-age hookers in tight miniskirts, pimps with big combs in their hair, transvestites looking ladylike, gay duos and trios peeping in her car as they headed for the unending drag parties in their harlequin masks and satin jockstraps with tuxedo fronts. Kim recognized a few; when the sun came out, they had names like Marvin and Duane and Billy Bob and weren't much different from anyone else. The most pathetic were the transsexual whores who couldn't stand up to the streetlight. They crept along the gray clamshell sidewalks looking for johns, and sometimes got into bloody fights over money and territory.

By 1 A.M. she'd smoked a pack of Benson & Hedges menthols. She thought, Why didn't one of those *professionals* tell me to pack a lunch? The radio was repeating itself. She cranked up the blue Audi and headed home. It was her first experience with longterm solo stakeouts. She hoped Sami wasn't using the bathroom.

100

P. M. Clinton was trying to run the detective agency while his father-in-law Clyde Wilson rested up from his latest heart miseries. P.M. felt bad about the agency's recent billings to Betty and Richard Hinds. He picked up one of the daytime surveillance reports and read:

Dec. 17, 1984. No activity was observed at the apartment until 4:00 p.m., when the subject, Cynthia Ray, walked up to the apartment wearing a very loose fitting full blouse and slacks. At 4:10 p.m., the subject came downstairs from the apartment and walked into the interior of the complex in the direction of the mailbox. At 4:15 p.m., she returned to the apartment. . . . At 7:00 p.m., she and her roommate, Makhlouf, left the apartment walking to Glenmont Street where they were picked up in Yellow Cab No. 1116. At 7:12 p.m. the cab pulled into the Circus restaurant located at 6015 Westheimer. The subject and her roommate got out of the cab and went into the restaurant. . . .

The next day's report said:

At 9:40 a.m. Cynthia came out of the apartment, walked down the stairs, and went to the Stop-N-Go on Glenmont. At that time she used the telephone for approximately twelve minutes and then entered the store making a purchase. She returned to the apartment at 10:03 a.m. . . .

The next day's big event was a bus ride to her lawyer's office. An unknown male drove her home in a brown Datsun 280ZX. She walked to the Stop-N-Go, used the phone and made a purchase.

P.M. let the file slip to his desk. In a way he was glad that Denise was dealing with the clients instead of him. She'd already warned the Hindses that long surveillances weren't always cost-efficient: it took a minimum of two people, sometimes four, and a ten-hour day or longer. At fifty dollars per head per hour, it sometimes came to two thousand dollars a day. But the Hindses kept paying up and pleading, "Just one more day." Denise told P.M. that she'd never met a client as obsessed with catching a murderer as Betty Hinds. And her husband Richard and sister Michelle backed her up.

Well, shee-it, P.M. drawled to himself, we're wasting those good people's money sitting on West's empty house

and clocking Cynthia Ray to and from the market. He
didn't mind high billings; Clyde A. Wilson International Investigations Inc. was known as the most expensive detective
agency in town. But both P.M. and the proprietor felt uncomfortable taking money without results. As Wilson's son-
in-law, P.M. had more than an average interest in its sol-
vency and reputation.

He ordered the Cindy Ray surveillance discontinued.
"Maybe we'll pick it up again later," he told Moseley. As for
Paris, he figured he'd give her one more night, maybe two,
and then tell her to bag it. West was probably away for the
holidays. Thirty months had passed since someone had
pumped six dumdums almost a half-inch thick into the flesh
of James and Virginia Campbell. The investigation would
keep a few more days.

101

On Wednesday, December 19, Kim Paris phoned A-1 Blue
Print before noon and confirmed that David West was out
on the job.

She spent the rest of the day preparing herself. She applied green lipstick, carmine blusher, wide lines of kohl under her big eyes and along the inside of her lower lids. She
darkened her eyebrows, added false lashes, spiked her
frosted hair and brought it forward. She put on tight black
satin pants, a black jacket with satin lapels, a man's tight-
fitting muscle-shirt and a pair of black and silver earrings
that dangled to her chest. She tied three bandanas around
her neck and a fourth around the instep of her spike-heeled
suede boot. Then she looked in the mirror and said, "Aw
right!" She stowed a joint in her purse for emergencies.
Lighting up was something a Houston narc would never do.

At 6 P.M. she was on station with an order of crawfish
she'd picked up at a takeout joint. She'd just started on the
sweet meat when a man matching West's description ambled
into sight and climbed the inside staircase. She wiped her

fingers on a clump of grass, dried her face with her sleeves and stumbled across the street in her spiked heels.

The man answered and she shoved inside. He had blond curly hair, glasses, nice teeth and clear skin, but he was shorter than David West was supposed to be. "Charlie?" she asked.

"No," the guy said. "My name's Robin."

"Is Charlie here?"

"Nobody named Charlie lives here."

She looked upset. "Are you *sure?* Is this 1409 Vermont?"

"Yep."

"I can't believe this!" she said as she kicked the wall. "I came all the way out here from North Houston. Do you know a Charlie?" She lowered her voice confidentially. "I'm supposed to pick up some . . . stuff."

Robin said he didn't know Charlie. She segued into her old insurance-fraud technique. "Well, can I use a phone? I must've just written it down wrong. I hate to drive all the way back. Let me call my sister and see if she knows."

He ushered her across the room. She could feel his eyes. She dialed a dead number and told Robin, "The line's busy. Can I wait a few minutes and try calling back?"

"Sure."

She took a chance and offered him the joint. He fired up and passed it back. "No, no," she said. "I'm, uh . . . driving." She'd gone through a marijuana phase in high school, but now the stuff made her sick.

They talked. Kim said her name was Theresa Neel and she lived with her sister. Robin said he was in the process of moving out; he'd just dropped in to get his mail.

She glanced around. No guns were in sight, nor did she see the survivalist gear that P.M. and the others had mentioned. Robin said, "Well, listen, I'm meeting my friend Dave West at the Park Lane. Uh, wanna come along?"

She remembered the Park Lane as a straight bar popular with yuppies, journalists and just about everyone but gays. She wouldn't have cared if it had been the raunchiest S-M chain-and-leather slam-dancing joint in town. "I'd love to," she said.

* * *

She hoped it wasn't the power of suggestion, but her first impression of David West was that he was eerie. His sandy hair fell over his ears and was cut longer in back, obviously the work of a stylist. He wore a modification of her least favorite kind of facial hair: the Fu Manchu. He swaggered as he walked, chest stuck out, arms a little behind him as though muscle-bound.

Closer up she saw that there was something wrong with his eyes. One of his pinkies was missing. He wore tight jeans, motorcycle boots and a Harley-Davidson T-shirt pulled tight across his pecs. His muscles were big enough to show that he worked out. A collection of keys jingled on his belt. When he rolled up a sleeve, she saw a tattooed eagle high on his arm. It wasn't the Harley version to match his shirt but a heraldic eagle with a crown, talons and outstretched wings.

She went to the ladies' room and dutifully sketched it in her notebook. So far, she thought, I'm not impressed.

102

After the introductions David took Robin aside and said, "Hey, man, where'd you find *her?*"

"She showed up on the doorstep looking for a guy named Charlie."

Whoo-*eee,* David thought. He was a little wrecked. "Well," he said, "uh, ya know . . . gifts from Allah."

The two friends flanked Allah's gift on a soft leatherette bench facing out from an unlit corner. David wished the wildly colored abstract painting behind them didn't look so much like a vagina. Dominoes, chess and backgammon pieces were available, but no one was playing. A sign noted PROFANITY IS THE LINGUISTIC TOOL OF THE INARTICU-LATE. David thought, Says which motherfucker? It felt good to be semidrunk and sitting next to a new chick, espe-cially after driving that goddamn delivery truck all day.

Theresa's eyes were so blue they almost made him blink.

Her silly outfit didn't keep her from having a fresh wild look; he could imagine her on the cover of *Seventeen* or *Cosmopolitan*. The only thing he didn't like was the way she lit one long filter after another. "Well, uh, where ya from, Theresa?" he asked, fanning the smoke away.

"St. Louis," she answered. "I was in the Navy down here."

He thought, Navy, huh? He'd heard a lot about military chicks, especially big rangy ones like her. But she sure didn't come on butch.

He asked, "Where were you stationed?"

"Corpus Christi Naval Air Station."

"What'd you do?"

"Air traffic control."

David thought, Something in common! "I was trained in ATC in the Marine Corps," he said.

She scrooched closer as they discussed their military careers. She stared at him as though every syllable was important. Before long she was half turned away from Robin. It was a new experience for David; most women turned from him. He caught a signal from his old roommate to assemble in the men's room.

"Hey, man," Robin said, "she's on a date with me and you just move in!"

"Man, I didn't move in," David said. "She just seems taken with me."

Back at the table, his artist's eye noted her bone structure, her make-up, the way she'd run a line of mascara under her eyes. She had an Anglo-German face on a large frame, but it seemed proportional. He thought she was the prettiest woman he'd seen since Cindy at her best.

He told her he hadn't been to Nam. "I'm a lover, not a fighter," he lied. She giggled, repeated his words, and laughed louder. He felt her side touching his. It was warm all up and down.

When she went to the ladies' room again, Robin said, "Fuck it. I'm leaving."

"Are you pissed off, man?" David asked.

"Me?" Robin exclaimed. *"No!"*

David thought, He's my friend. Theresa just dropped out

of the night. Which is more important, a new woman or an old friend? "Look, man," he said. *"I'll* leave. Fine, ya know?"

"I gotta leave anyway," Robin said. "It's okay, Dave. It just . . . Well, it's like I'm talking to someone and they turn around and I'm out of the conversation. To me, that's rude."

"Right on, pardner."

Robin stood up. "It's okay, Dave," he said. "No big deal." They were both pretty drunk. David thought, We'll laugh about this tomorrow.

Theresa came back and said she'd seen a great graffito. "If you love someone, set him free. If he comes back, he's yours. If he doesn't, hunt him down and kill him!"

"Heav-*ee*," David said, and they lightly touched foreheads. They talked some more about the military. He couldn't believe how interesting she was—flip and outspoken, brash, funny, quick on the uptake. She had a staccato laugh that made people stare. Her Navy career sounded like *Mister Roberts.* She told how she'd driven the admiral's car wearing a bikini and jumped from one predicament to another. She told how a Marine had yelled across a crowded mess hall, "Come over here and sit on my face!" and she'd yelled back, "It'd be the first time I ever fell asleep sitting up!" Goddamn, that was . . . quick!

She used profanity that would have turned him off most women, but he recognized that she was just reflecting her Navy experience. He thought, There aren't many females who can talk like that and still sound feminine, but damn, Theresa brings it off!

After a while he got a chance to lay a little American and European history on her, but he'd had so many drinks he screwed up dates and places. She didn't seem to mind. He told her that he worked out, ate health food, didn't smoke or use hard drugs, loved his pit bull Max and his new hound Nana, and admired the work of the Stray Cats, the Fabulous Thunderbirds and the immortal Elvis. She raised her drink and said, "Elvis *lives!*" He drank to that.

At one-thirty they walked out through the fake pillars to her car. On the rear of her dark blue '74 Audi Fox he no-

ticed a Family Motors emblem. He'd bought his Trans Am
at the same place. He didn't believe all the karma and kis-
met bullshit his mother and Cindy laid down, but it was
amazing what he had in common with this chick.

He didn't usually try to score the first night, or even the
second or third, but he was drunk and she'd been so pliant
that he decided to try. In her heels she was taller by three or
four inches and he felt foolish trying to pull her face to his.
She backed away and got in her car.

He thought, Well, that's a pretty clear-cut statement.
Some guy probably tried to jump her bones right away, and
what the hell, she doesn't know me and she's just being a
good girl. He respected her for that. "Hey," he said as she
turned the key, "do I get to see you again?"

"Tomorrow night?" she said in that sultry voice.

"Where can I call you?"

She didn't answer. As the Audi squealed away, he said
under his breath, "Goddamn, David DuVal West done died
and gone to heaven."

The next night she showed up with a long-haired dude
named Alan. David shook hands and thought, Who the fuck
invited you? Alan looked and sounded like some kind of
heavy metal suburban 1980s pseudo-hippie. David thought,
Does she think she needs a duenna? Does she think I'm
gonna rape her in a dark corner or something? *Shee-it!*

He listened politely as she explained that Alan was the
younger brother of her sister's husband Buddy, and Buddy
kind of tyrannized their household and wouldn't let Theresa
out of the house without an escort—or some such shit. She
talked fast: he wondered if she was on speed. She was wearing a military trench coat with a tank-top T-shirt underneath and high spike heels and she looked real good and
sleazy. David, he said to himself, you will score for sure
tonight!

After a while she asked, "What're you gonna be when you
grow up?"

He didn't want her to think he was satisfied with driving a
delivery truck, so he explained that he was marking time till
he opened a straight bar in the Montrose. It wasn't entirely

untrue; a friend named Lane had approached him about turning his house into a saloon.

"Where ya gonna get the money?" Theresa asked.

"Well, one guy's made me an offer, plus I've got other possibilities." He was thinking of the money Cindy had promised him.

"Oh," Theresa said, "I bet it's the old rich girlfriend story."

Christ, he thought, she reads minds. "Well, it's like that," he said. "Her parents died and she's liable to inherit some money and she's thinking of possibly going in with me in a bar."

"How'd they die?" Theresa asked.

"A car accident," he said. It was the second time he'd told that same lie. Weeks earlier he'd taken Cindy to a lawyer for another opinion on the inheritance fight, and they'd used the car-wreck story so their motives wouldn't be questioned.

Theresa seemed fascinated by the information, but he felt squirmy and shifted his ground. He thought, Man, this car-wreck bullshit could come back to haunt me. The least number of lies is best.

They had so many drinks that he found it hard to control the conversation. They talked more about Cindy, but later he wasn't sure exactly what he'd said. She'd seemed so interested that he just went on and on. He made a big impression on the gift from Allah—he was convinced of that. She promised to meet him again the next night.

103

Kim came away impressed. She couldn't imagine why she'd had such negative feelings a couple of nights before. West seemed perfectly open—no games, no hidden agenda. He was bright and polite and couldn't have murdered a duck, let alone two innocent people in their beds. He salted his speech with words like "shit" and "fuck," but all young people talked that way these days. She tried to echo his language so he wouldn't be put off.

She wondered why he said the Campbells died in a car wreck. Why play down the murders? Wasn't it human nature to say something newsy like, "It was horrible! They were shot in bed." Maybe the subject was still too painful.

She told herself that it was possible he had incriminating knowledge. Maybe Cindy had confessed to him, or maybe he'd lent her a gun or something. He couldn't have been directly involved. Not with that little-boy smile and easy manner.

She hated writing reports, but it was part of the job. She tried to remember his rap about Cynthia. A lot of drinks had gone down, and somewhere in the fuzzier part of the evening he'd said something about Cindy's relatives' screwing her out of her inheritance. It took a while, but she finally assembled her recollections and wrote them in her lovely flowing hand:

David referred to himself as Cindy's Svengali. When he met her, she couldn't even look people in the eye, hiding behind her bangs. He encouraged her to improve her appearance and was her friend, confidant, and evidently her lover, although I don't know that they were ever a big boyfriend/girlfriend item. . . .

He said there were some awful things she had involved him in "that came between them." He refused to talk about it further. The impression I got that evening was that she depends on him a great deal for self-confidence. She has a very low self-esteem. He did make mention that since they had quit seeing each other, she has gone downhill real fast. She's gotten fat, she's paranoid, she doesn't have any friends. She's really freaking out. He described Cindy's present condition as "sick." He said he wouldn't even be seen with her.

She's living like a recluse according to David and is paranoid. David said she's been unstable since he's known her and attributes this to her upbringing. She was the family scape goat, the least favorite as he puts it.

They met again the next night at the Park Lane, with her power-pop composer friend Alan still flying cover. West had made noises about phoning her at home and meeting her family, and she decided to head him off before he became suspicious. "You know, David," she reminded him, "I live with my sister Sami and my brother-in-law Buddy. He just moved here from Corpus and he used to have a drug problem."

David asked, "What's Buddy do?"

"I don't know," she said. "We just always seem to have money. Sometimes we, uh, have to leave town, when there's . . . heat."

David nodded understandingly. "Buddy made a pass at me right after him and my sister got married," she went on. "He's a domineering son of a bitch. I was so pissed off about it that we had words. But deep down Buddy wants at me."

She glanced sideways through her cigarette smoke. West seemed concerned. "David," she said, improvising as she spoke, "I'll introduce you to my family. But until I get to know you better, they think I need to be watched. They don't even like me being out. I may have to lie sometimes to come out and see ya, because they're so fucking afraid I'm gonna get in trouble again." She hinted that she'd had a drug problem.

"And I don't want guys calling the house right off the bat," she went on, "because first of all my sister'll think I'm getting in trouble again with a buncha goddamn strangers calling, and second of all—this is really sick and I don't expect you to understand it—but Buddy beats the shit outa my sister, and if you called me, he'd just take it out on her. So . . . please don't."

"No prob," he said, patting her arm.

He was so agreeable, so eager to please. She recalled a few contradictions in her stories and how she'd pressed the subject of Cindy too hard the night before, but he didn't seem to be keeping score. There he sat, bedazzlement showing in his bicolored eyes. Maybe he was a loser, but he wasn't nasty or vicious.

God, she thought, what a way I've found to make a living. She was glad she wasn't really running at him but at Cindy;

it made her feel less of a professional fink. So far she'd logged fifteen hours at twenty dollars per, plus twenty-six dollars in expenses, mostly for sitting around bars doing two of her favorite things: rapping and drinking vodka. The private eye biz was looking up.

104

David was excited when Theresa phoned him at work the next day. "Somebody gave me tickets for the Teddy Boys!" he told her. They were a rockabilly group, a lot like the Stray Cats, and they were playing that night at Numbers, or "#'s," as it was sometimes spelled.

Theresa didn't sound enthusiastic. She'd rolled her Audi Fox and was upset about it. David offered to pick her up for the concert, but she said Alan would drive her. "Alan?" he said. "Shit, Theresa, I'd rawther we just went alone." He was getting tired of the chaperone. If Alan came, he'd have to shell out for another ticket, and his $150-a-week salary was already stretched to the limit.

"I'm sorry, David," Theresa said in the sweetest voice. "It's the only way I can get out of the house."

He figured this was no time to be chintzy, so he took them to Renu's, a Thai restaurant in the Montrose, and showed off his knowledge of exotic food. Theresa smiled warmly at him while her bodyguard downed two portions of swimming angel. The only discordant note was her smoking; the aromatic Thai dishes didn't blend well with contaminants. The bill came to forty dollars and he paid with a pained smile.

Under the high ceilings at #'s he was surprised to learn that his Theresa wasn't much of a dancer. She pumped up and down and seemed to have trouble with the beat. He had the feeling she would rather drink. He steered her back to the bar and went to the men's room.

When he came out, she was deep in conversation with a black guy. He looked like the kid who'd stolen David's lunch every day after he'd been transferred into a black junior high. This stud was putting on a friendly act and Theresa was going for it. He'd noticed before that she had a blatant flirting technique, flashing her eyes like Marilyn Monroe, not subtle at all. She whispered in David's ear, "Let me go talk to him and I'll be back in a little bit." The friends disappeared into the shadows.

David thought, What gives? Is it a dope deal? She says she just moved here a while ago; where'd she know this guy from? And why is her friend Alan letting her go off with some fucking black guy?

He seethed at the bar for twenty minutes. Alan tried to make small talk, but David was locked in his own head. Goddamn it, he said to himself, I'm not a racist, but when your date runs off with a black guy it kinda pisses you off.

The couple returned hand in hand, smiling at some shared secret. David looked for signs that she'd been shooting up or snorting, but she looked normal. He tried to be civil as she took a place at the bar, but when she draped her arm across the black dude's shoulders David snapped, *"You!* Hit the fucking road, buddy!"

The black flared his nostrils and said, "You wanna go outside?"

"Let's go," David said.

Theresa stepped in front of him. "Oh, David, David, don't beat him up! Don't hurt him!"

"You wanna be with him?" he said angrily. "Then fucking be with him! That's fine with me."

"Oh, David," she pleaded, "it's just a misunderstanding. You and I were having such a good time and I'm feeling real close to you. Don't destroy it now. . . ."

He could see that the other guy was having second thoughts. "Hey, look, man," he told David, "I didn't mean anything."

David told himself, You don't want to come across as some kill-crazy, belligerent redneck son of a bitch, ya know? He turned to Theresa and said, "Fuck this guy. I think I made my point." To the black he said, "Look, man, maybe I overreacted a little bit, but I was pissed off, ya know? As far as I'm concerned, she's with me, ya know?" He stuck his face closer and added one more "Ya *know?*" for emphasis.

The guy nodded. He ended up buying David a drink.

The next morning he realized that he'd diminished himself in Theresa's eyes. She was due to fly north to spend the holidays with relatives and he had to make amends fast. He drove his Trans Am to the flea market and paid $40 for a strapless harem outfit made in Pakistan. He thought, Jesus, that would go for $140 at the Galleria. He felt the material, black gauze shot through with metallic gold threads. The harem pants cinched at the waist and ankles. He could imagine her modeling it for him. He took it to a gift-wrapping service and had it done up in candy cane red and white paper with a white bow. Then he sat around waiting for her call. He wished he could phone her, but she'd refused to give him her number.

It came late in the afternoon. She said she was about to leave for the airport. "Fuck, no!" he yelped. "No, Theresa, no, no, *no!* Listen, I was out doing my regular Christmas shoplifting—I mean shopping"—he laughed to show it was a joke—"and I saw something at the Galleria and I thought, It's you. It's *you!* Meet me at Rudyard's, okay?"

She said she could spare a few minutes.

He waited for her among Rud's typical holiday crowd: the guys in leather, the Animals on skates, the Brits with their spiked hair, the slam-dancers in the back room, the dart throwers and gin guzzlers and ass patters. She rushed to his table an hour late, hair flying, the top buttons undone on her shirt. "Oh, David," she said, "I hate to pick up a gift and run, but . . . I've got to catch the plane."

He gave her the box and walked her to the gold Jetta diesel she said she'd borrowed from her sister Sami. He leaned in and pecked her on the cheek. "Merry Christmas, Theresa," he said.

"Merry Christmas, David." She ripped open the package and held the suit against her body. "How . . . lovely!" she said. She seemed moved.

He said, "That's gonna look even better on you than I

thought. It would look really nice with your black boots. Maybe I should get you a gold belt to go with it."

"No" she said. "No, no, that's okay, really. Please . . . don't spend another penny." Then she was gone.

He couldn't stop thinking about her. She wasn't a knock-out, but she was pretty and statuesque, with style to spare and all the intangibles. A sexy voice. A nice clean smell. Bright intelligent eyes. He'd solved the mystery of their cobalt color by staring at them so hard that she'd finally confessed to wearing contacts—and then it developed that her real eye color was smoky blue-gray. Gorgeous!

He told himself, She's so different. The way she brings her own chaperone. The way she gets right into my space when we sit or walk. Her conversation. Her background as an ATC—a tough job he hadn't been able to hack in the Marine Corps. Her knowledge of history and politics and stuff. And the sensitive aspect to her, the vulnerable aspect. God, he thought, how has this happened? She thinks the world of me. *She* selected *me!*

He knew he was infatuated with her, but he didn't even want to think the other word—all it brought was misery. He thought, she's a little street-worn, a little brassy and foul-mouthed, but that's just her cover. Underneath she's genuine wife material—a good breeder, big, strong, healthy. She laughs at my jokes! What more could a guy ask?

It was going to be a long holiday.

1985

105

On Wednesday, January 2, Mr. and Mrs. Richard Hinds waited anxiously by their phone in Austin. Cindy's final settlement check was due to be paid in J. W. O. Campbell's office in Houston. Betty wasn't sure of the exact amount, but it would come to about twenty-five thousand dollars after all the advances were taken out. Her biggest fear was that Cindy would collect the money and disappear. Then it wouldn't matter if they got the goods on her. All the money they'd paid Clyde Wilson's detectives would be wasted—over twenty thousand dollars in credit-card debt so far.

They'd made a hurried call to the agency and asked that a team be assigned to watch Cindy after the money changed hands. Early in the afternoon the detectives called to report that they'd missed the subject at J.W.'s office and were now sitting on the apartment house on Kingston. They said Cynthia wasn't in sight and the place was dark. My God, Betty thought, she got away.

Waiting for word, she tried to put together the latest puzzle pieces. Nanny Helen had been keeping a discreet watch on her troublesome granddaughter, now living with a small chow dog in the apartment directly below. Cindy had married her Arab, Talal Makhlouf, but mysteriously moved back into the Kingston building alone after a few months of marriage. Since then she'd busied herself abusing the other tenants and reminding Nanny that she was a squatter.

One day Makhlouf had stood under a tree in front of the building while Cindy rained curses on him. When he refused to leave, she called the police and had him removed.

Later the scorned husband had phoned Betty: "Please to tell Ceendy that I leave message for her on St. Thomas bulletin board."

"I have no way of reaching her," Betty said. They'd been out of touch for months. "Why don't you just call her lawyer?"

"Okeh."

And that, thought Betty, is the latest on my weird sister. But I hope not the end. Because she killed Mother and Daddy and *she's not gonna get away with it*!

Later in the evening the P.I.'s reported that Cynthia had arrived at her apartment by Yellow Cab at 6:05 P.M. The lights had gone out at nine.

106

Kim phoned David on Friday, January 4, the day she returned to Houston from her Christmas visit north. He sounded relieved to hear her voice. That night she pinked and punked her hair with vegetable dye and borrowed her roommate Sami's gold Jetta to meet him at the Park Lane.

It took an hour to get him started on Cindy. He explained what had attracted him in the beginning: her penchant for being abused and his own history of protecting women. After his fifth ale he opened up. Kim reported later:

He said that Cindy had a "disabling sense of inadequacy." . . . He kept stressing that she was a sick person, unstable, unhealthy, weak, and that he pitied her. He said her family was "a bunch of loonies" and that her father had repeatedly raped her from early teens until his death because she was the best-looking in the family. And her oldest son was fathered by her father. . . .

Telling about it, David's personality would change. His face would contort and he would mock other voices. He would get so into it. He would make his face ugly, twisting it around. "They're ugly, ugly, horrible people!" he said. "It's horrible, the most horrible thing I've ever seen. It makes you sick."

He said he used to try to protect Cindy from her family, and that's why they didn't want him around. He attributed his breakup with Cindy to her not appreciating him. They just stopped getting along.

He said that the Campbells' deaths in an automobile accident were "the best thing that ever happened to her."

The next night she squeezed out another reference to "something in the past" that had strained his relationship with Cindy. He said he felt sorry for her; she was deteriorating and her suicide wouldn't surprise him. Kim wondered how that remark squared with his claim that her parents' deaths had been good for her.

Then he made another strange statement; he said that Cindy was still so dependent on him that he could get just about anything he wanted from her. Kim wondered how she could be dependent on him if they weren't seeing each other. Were they broken up or not?

At times he seemed to be reliving Cindy's shame. She felt pity for him. He seemed to identify so completely with other people's suffering. She thought, Empathy. It's a nice quality.

After midnight he started talking about his childhood. He seemed to remember every humiliation and slight since the birth trauma: the time his mother made him sing in the chorale in plaid shorts, the month he'd gone to school in flap-soled shoes tied with a string, the friction in his house, his mom's impossibly high standards and his dad's disinterest, the slum schools full of marauding blacks, the military-academy bully who'd broken his nose with a sucker punch. "I daydreamed all the time, ya know?" he said. "I was insecure. I couldn't get along. You know how mean kids can be if you're little and weak? They were fucking with me, picking on me, and I didn't know how to deal with it."

The picture eluded her; he seemed so masculine in his muscle shirt and jeans and shit-kicker boots and bulging key ring on his thick leather belt. "I would think you'd be the last kid they'd pick on," she said.

"I was a nerd," he whined. "I was the know-it-all kid with the skinny little neck who doesn't play sports. A total misfit. I knew about Julius Caesar and Shakespeare, but I couldn't pitch a baseball or throw a pass. I'd never been exposed to sport. My dad's an intellectual. He always said sport is for cretins. There weren't any other kids on my block—where I lived, young married couples would have a baby and then move to the suburbs. Both my parents worked. For a long time I was a latch-key kid. TV was all I had."

He gulped down the rest of his drink as Kim thought, It isn't so much what he says—everyone can recite a garbage list from childhood—but the way he says it. The anger, the intensity! As he spoke, he mocked the cast of characters, stuck out his lower lip, curled his cheek into a leer, babbled like Mortimer Snerd to achieve the utmost in ridicule. She'd begun to like him a lot, but this number was making her uncomfortable. "The other boys got on me about religion," he went on before she could change the subject. "You know how *that* is."

"Got on you how?"

"My dad taught me evolution. I tried to explain it to the fucking rednecks at school and they'd say, 'Well, maybe *you're* descended from monkeys, but we ain't.' I'd try to explain: 'Hey, that's not what I said. I said lower life forms were probably something *like* the monkey, ya know?' Then they'd twist it around, Call me monkey man and slap the crap outa me. It kept up till I opened up a kid's lip with a big plastic ring I got from a gumball machine. Pratt the Brat never said shit to me again. I thought, Hey, that felt great: *Hey, that works!*" David smiled. He seemed himself again.

Kim looked at her watch. It was almost one, but he showed no signs of slowing down. "I discovered the boob tube after I failed the fourth grade," he said. "I watched Flash Gordon films on Cadet Don's show. I liked 'The Man from U.N.C.L.E.,' but 'Star Trek' was the best. I watched it twice a day, five days a week. I got every sound down."

He puffed out his cheeks. "The phasers!" he said, and made a rich warble. Then he did the *tooo-ee* of the photon torpedoes, the clicks of the communicators, the low whistle of the transporters. She wondered how many hours had gone into the creation of such perfection.

He switched back to words. "When I was ten, I saw Errol Flynn in Robin Hood. I said, I want to be just like him. Then I learned about the Prussian officer corps. What strength! What power! So I wanted to be a soldier. It was the closest thing to being a Robin Hood or a knight in our society. I wanted to be"—his voice dropped—"something special."

"Like your father," she said.

"No! Like a *real* hero. I thought of myself as Captain Justice, Captain Avenger, something between Don Quixote and Charles Bronson in *Death Wish*. Even as a kid, I knew there were a lot of people getting away with murder. I decided not to let 'em."

As he spoke, his cheek muscles flexed and unflexed and his voice rose and fell. "My dad wasn't anything like that. He just. . . . sat around. Never grew, never changed. He's got this narrow little set of things he likes—old-time jazz, Sidney Bechet, Eddie Condon, Jack Teagarden. He likes Shaw's plays, Henry James, Fielding, Jane Austen, George Eliot, Samuel Johnson, Shakespeare. Let's see . . . uh, he likes the Greeks: Aristophanes, Sophocles, Euripides. Oh, yeah, he likes articles on chess and electronics. That's about it, ya know? I mean, he's honorable, respectable, intelligent, decent—a great guy! He went to the Point, class of 'forty-one, but he doesn't even have his yearbook. In World War Two he ramrodded allied supplies from Iran to the Russian front, and he doesn't even have his medals, his uniforms. He lives in the past. But not his own."

Kim thought, How freaky! He's almost never mentioned his father, and now it comes spewing out all at once.

"A coupla times," he went on, "I challenged my father. 'C'mon,' I said. 'Fight me now!' He was above that kind of thing, and I respect and understand that now. But back when I was a child I thought, If he was a real man he wouldn't take this shit from his own son. I kinda lost respect for him." He stopped to grit his teeth. Then he chopped at the table with the edge of his hand and said, "He shoulda beat my ass!"

She offered her cheek at the car, but he spun her gently and kissed her lips. "Let me go, David!" she said as she pulled away. "Hard kissing makes me nervous."

He insisted on knowing why, and she told him that two huge black men had thrown her into their car and repeatedly raped her a few months back.

He seemed stricken by the news. He said he wasn't like

other men; he'd understood sexual assault ever since he'd sat at his mother's feet and heard her talk about the subject. "I'll never bother you, Theresa," he said. "I just wanted to kiss you good night. But . . . I understand." He smiled shyly. "It won't happen again."

She thought, Oh, God, he's so vulnerable. All that talk about Captain Justice and Charles Bronson and yet he looks like a grown-up poster boy. She knew about difficult childhoods. It was amazing how often he seemed to be talking about hers when he was talking about his own. There was rapport, all right, surprising resonance. Falling in love was out, but she'd certainly fallen in like.

107

Richard Hinds wondered what adventures lay ahead as he aimed the rented truck east out of Austin. He looked in the mirror and saw Michelle's car following. His rented truck would bring back Nanny Helen's belongings and Michelle's car would bring back Nanny. His wife Betty was sitting this one out. She was so angry with Cindy that she wasn't sure she'd be able to control her own temper.

For three straight weekends the Hindses had intended to rescue Helen Amaya from her Kingston apartment and her murderous granddaughter, but each time something had intervened. Twice there'd been snowstorms in the hill country, producing slippery games of bumper cars. The third time sleet had knocked down the phone lines to Houston and they couldn't get word to Nanny that they were coming. Now she was ready and waiting.

Three hours out of Austin, the rescue caravan approached Houston on Interstate 10. It was shirt-sleeve weather and Richard realized that nothing was going to head off this last meeting with his crazy sister-in-law. Even when she'd been at her worst, she'd always been polite to him, hung her head, spoke sweetly. But with Cindy, you never knew what to expect.

As planned, he picked up three laborers at J. W. O. Campbell's and drove to the apartment ahead of Michelle and her friend. No one stirred in the green old Kingston neighborhood; the loudest noise was the coo of a dove. He saw that Cindy had tacked sheets over her front windows and sealed off the cracks. A dog barked from inside.

As he backed the mid-sized truck toward the front door, he grazed a juniper. The door flew open and a voice screamed, "Don't you respect other people's property?"

At first Richard didn't recognize his sister-in-law. He hadn't seen her since the funeral two and a half years before, and it looked as though she'd doubled in size. Her eyes were set in gray-white folds. She wore a clownish pair of blue pants and a blue-green shirt out at the waist.

"Be careful what you do around here!" she yelled in a screechy voice. Windows slammed open in adjoining houses. Richard was a private man and he felt a flush on his face and neck.

Cindy waddled up the stairs and stationed herself outside Nanny's second-floor apartment, arms folded across her big chest. "Don't take the refrigerator!" she warned.

"It's Nanny's," Richard explained.

A few minutes later Cindy said, "Don't take the light fixtures!" Richard ignored the sarcasm.

"Don't take the phone!" she yelled, and grumbled under her breath as Richard assured her it was also Nanny's. When an end table scraped the staircase wall, she bent over and stared at the black mark. Three hours passed with infinite slowness under her gaze.

At last the rented truck was loaded and a tearful Nanny started down the stairs toward Cindy, stationed at the bottom. The crippled old woman managed a few steps and stopped for breath.

Out on the sidewalk, Michelle announced, "I'm going to go up and help her."

"You're not coming in here!" Cindy cried. "This is my place and you're trespassing." To Richard she sounded more proud than angry. She seemed to be saying, *At last I've got something of my own. Now you'll listen to* me!

Michelle started up the stairs and Cindy slammed her

against the wall. The sisters grappled as Richard rushed past
and carried the terrified grandmother to the sidewalk. In her
gauzy hat and best Sunday clothes, she felt as light as a
child.

The sisters rolled around cursing each other. "Michelle,"
Richard ordered, "let go of Cindy's hair! Cindy, let go of
Michelle's throat!"

At last they disengaged. Blood flowed on Michelle's face.
Richard made a mental note that she would need shots.

"Okay!" Cindy snapped. "Only Richard can go upstairs.
Nobody else!"

He picked up the last few items in the barren rooms. As
he walked out the front door, Cindy said softly, "Bye, Richard."

"Okay, see ya later," he said. He just wanted to get away.

108

David answered the knock and was surprised to see Theresa
on his landing. He'd intended to invite her as soon as he
could fix his place up; this unannounced visit was embarrassing.

As she walked in, he saw her take a hard look at his sign:
FORGET THE DOG. BEWARE OF OWNER. He wondered if she
approved. He was overly conscious of the military magazines lying around—*Soldier of Fortune, Eagle, Combat
Arms.* He'd always believed it was a citizen's obligation to
keep abreast of military hardware, but of course somebody
like Theresa might interpret his interest as proof that he was
a gun nut like Wickie.

He was relieved when she said that she was thinking
about buying a pistol. As he guided her to his old black sofa,
she asked, "What kind should I get?"

He held a match for her cigarette and said, "A small-
caliber revolver. They don't jam, you can depend on 'em,
you don't have to worry about safeties or having a round in

the chamber. You just pull 'em out and fucking fire, ya know? And they're not gonna buck on ya."

He mixed some Everclear and orange juice, all he had in the house, but she didn't seem to mind. The only difference between Everclear and the best imported vodka was about ten dollars a bottle. She said she'd just finished reading Barbara Tuchman's *A Distant Mirror* and was having nightmares about it. "Everybody was screwed back then," she said, "whether you were a serf or a nobleman or a knight or what. It was plagues and wars and pestilence and guys storming each other's castles and raping each other's wives and cutting 'em to pieces."

David nodded. He'd studied medieval cruelty.

"Last night," she went on, "I dreamed I was plummeting from the skies and boom! I landed in a field and a voice as big as the sky called out, 'Theresa, you are now in fifteenth century Europe.' I went, 'No I wanna go home! Anything but that!' "

He thought, Damn, she's like my mom. She pulls you right into the story with her. She has a way of throwing her head back and laughing at herself. She uses subtle little gestures and movements. He thought, Usually I do the talking, but I could listen to Theresa all night.

The discussion turned to Camelot and Guinevere and his all-time hero Robin Hood, but just when he started to get rolling she jumped up and said it was time to go. She said, "I don't want to piss Buddy off by staying out too late."

He looked at his watch. They'd been together for two and a half hours. He walked her to the car and kissed her on the cheek. As he climbed back up his stairs, he thought of all the nights to come.

109

As she drove home, Kim thought, what a dump! The rooms smelled like old socks. The bathroom was a total turnoff: no shower, a short tub with claw feet, pipes sticking out of the wooden wall, a bare light bulb hanging over a rusty sink. She couldn't imagine how Cindy had been able to live in the place. There wasn't even a make-up table.

It was odd, she thought, how the house didn't measure up to its owner. He was a class act, bright, warm, even endearing. She remembered how he'd flopped to the rug to talk baby talk to his hound Nana. At home Kim did the same with Miss Rock 'n' Roll Trash. He spoke proudly of the pit bulls he'd owned, but mostly of the one that had recently run off. "He drinks Löwenbräu Dark," he said warmly, as though reminiscing about a favorite human being. "He's a connoisseur."

He'd talked about finding her a replacement car, said he didn't like the idea of her borrowing Buddy's. He said she needed freedom. The suggestion was: freedom to be with *him*.

The morning after her visit to his house, she made a rare appearance at her office. As she passed the reception desk, she thought, Penny looks tired this morning. She wondered if the receptionist had been out with the same creep again. She'd been dating a mutual acquaintance whom Kim had once told, "If your dick's as big as your ego, I'll go out with you." Before he could reply, she'd pointed to his massive belt buckle and added, "I bet you wear that to compensate for something very small underneath."

Now she thought, Penny's a great girl, she deserves better. "Did you have a hard night?" she asked.

Penny nodded.

Kim said, "Well, I have something that'll pick you right up." She had a few Placidyls in her purse. "Now's the time to buy," she joked. "We're having a two-for-one sale. This week only." Penny turned back to her work and Kim walked off. It was one of those silly remarks that constantly flew from her mouth and meant nothing.

Before long her sessions with David West fell into a pattern. They met every few nights at bars like the Park Lane or Rud's and sometimes at his house. She enjoyed dressing for the occasions, but she couldn't bring herself to wear his

Christmas gift. She'd tried it on and Sami couldn't stop laughing. When David asked if she'd worn it yet, she said, "Oh, well, uh . . . *yes!* I wore it to dinner with Buddy and Sami and it's at the cleaners' and everybody complimented me on it and asked where I got such a lovely outfit and I told 'em a very special friend bought it for me." He seemed pleased.

She set about aligning the facts of her life as "Theresa" close to those of her life as Kim so she wouldn't get caught in unnecessary lies. Little by little she added to the story of the explosive Buddy and her poor battered sister Sami. Whenever Kim wanted to go home, she grabbed her purse and yelped, "I can't be out late or Buddy'll kill me!"

David kept wanting to go to her house and meet them— "I'm sure they'll like me, Theresa. Then I can take you out whenever I want."

"In my own time," she said. "I know what I'm doing."

She lived about ten minutes from 1409 Vermont but convinced him it was farther. She made every contact and set every date. To complete her control she refused to drive in his black Trans Am with the mag wheels and the fins and the booming engine. Most of the time it was in the shop anyway.

His idea of a terrific date was to sit in a bar and talk for five or six hours, lubricating his vocal cords with ale and an occasional straight shot. He was hipped on geopolitics and the abuses of power. Despite her Catholicism, he constantly attacked organized religion and the pope. "He's keeping a fourth of the world in misery. It's the one thing Marx was right about: religion partitions everybody off. Religion slaughtered thousands of people in the Crusades and it's still slaughtering people, ya know?"

It seemed to Kim that in between his flat statements and harsh opinions he showed little original thought. He admitted that he'd picked up much of his knowledge from his parents. She said that was something else they had in common. She thought, He's coming on a little superficial. But still . . . nice.

For a long time he shied away from the subject of Cindy. Kim was patient. If friends approached their table, he glared

them off. He liked to back her into the corner and stare at
her with his dichromatic eyes. Sometimes she heard him
grinding his teeth. "What's the *matter* with you?" she asked
one night.

He answered, "You are *so* beautiful."

"Knock it off, man," she said. "You give me the heebie-
jeebs."

He tried to pass it off as a joke. "You have good bone
structure," he said, rolling his *r*'s in his wild-and-crazy-guys
imitation from "Saturday Night Live." "Dot's good! Mek
strrrong bebbies!"

He treated her like an innocent virgin, a china doll, even
though she kept coarsening her language to match his. She
told Sami, "He doesn't even try to put his hand up my
shirt!" Sami observed that such behavior was rare in the
Montrose.

To keep him at arm's length, Kim told him, "I like you a
lot, David, but I've had too many relationships that I
jumped into too quickly. I'm at that stage of life where I
want to settle down and have a secure, lasting, stable relationship. But for that to happen, we have to be friends first,
a communion of souls." She thought, I'm so convincing, I
almost believe it myself!

Sometimes she enhanced her appeal by staying away for
two or three days. He seemed relieved when she phoned—
"Shit, I thought you didn't like me anymore. I thought
you'd *never* fucking call."

"Oh, David," she would say in her best Princess Di impression. "Don't be a goose."

In her private moments she realized that she wasn't giving
Betty and Richard Hinds much for their money, but it
didn't seem to matter. The other Wilson agents were sub-
merged in the Hermann Hospital case. Every time she visited the office it was harder to get attention. When she
phoned in, she was told to call back. When she called back,
the lines were busy. She had pressing questions; she wasn't
an experienced investigator and knew her limitations better
than anyone.

Every day she yearned for advice from the older heads.
She asked herself, Am I doing it right? What should I try

next? *Am I screwing up?* The curmudgeonly boss, Clyde Wilson, was either out with heart problems or talking on two phones. Gone were the days when she lolled on his couch blowing smoke rings.

Her reports became sketchy; it didn't seem to matter. They picked up ink blots and coffee spots on the corner of Denise Moseley's desk. Kim had turned in dozens of hours at twenty dollars per and hundreds of dollars in incidental expenses. The Wilson agency ran on the honor system, and no one questioned her claims. It made for a tidy income, but she kept hoping for something more. She could just imagine. . . .

David leads her to Cindy. . . .

The two women become friends, confidantes, and then . . .

PRIVATE EYE NAILS HEIRESS. MODERN MATA HARI SOLVES MURDER.

She would mail the clippings to her mother. When Kim had mentioned her new career during the Christmas holiday, her mother had joked, "Right, and I'm Cleopatra and your dad's Superman."

She began to feel she was doing something terribly wrong. David had clammed up about Cindy and her reports began to show it. "No new developments . . ." "No new information was gained. . . ." Any day now she'd be taken off the case.

She pressed. "David," she said, "I have a funny feeling about you. I think you're hiding something from me."

He smiled tolerantly. "Hiding what?"

"I don't know. Just . . . something."

"Theresa, I'd never hide anything from you."

She said, "It's not important. I just wish you wouldn't hide things from me, because it goes against everything I want."

One night she arrived at his house to find him lifting weights and smoking marijuana. She almost laughed; he'd always looked down his nose at her cigarette habit, but he seemed to think pot was therapeutic. She decided that the moment was propitious. "Hey," she said, "let's go visit Cynthia."

He sucked in some smoke and ignored her. She said, "Your poor friend. I feel sorry for her."

"She's sick," he said as he held in the smoke. "She's . . . out of my life. I don't wanna be . . . around her." He exhaled hard. "She's a walking infection."

For the next several dates Kim settled for tidbits. At Rud's he said that the incident that had come between him and Cindy was "very bad," something that he wasn't proud of and wouldn't discuss with Theresa in a million years "because you'd be afraid of me." But he insisted that his own actions had been justifiable.

He told her that Cindy visited his mother Cecelia occasionally to borrow food and money, but he appeared to have lost contact otherwise. Weeks after Cindy had collected her share of the estate, he was still talking about opening a bar "when she gets her settlement." It wasn't a good sign. If he couldn't lead her to Cindy, all her time had been wasted.

He cooked a rabbit stew in the Turkish style and served it by candlelight. "Did you like it?" he asked. "Was it tender enough? I made it just for you." His need for approval was almost childlike.

After dinner he took out a handbook and began showing her the difference between the bagatelle urp-urp machine gun and the Chrashneekoff rifle, or so the names sounded to Kim. When he came to a page depicting .45-caliber pistols, she asked innocently, "Did you ever have one of those?"

"No," he said. "I had a thirty-eight."

He ran on about guns till she thought she was going to fall asleep. She'd already noticed that he lacked an awareness of when he was being a bore. As he droned on, she thought about taking him to a pistol shooting gallery so she could pick up one of his ejected shells for comparison tests. But when she dropped a few hints, he explained that he'd sold his pistols to make mortgage payments. "Well, then," she said, "maybe you could borrow a forty-five. I've heard so much about them. I'd really like to try one."

He said he would look around. She had a vague hope that

he would borrow the murder weapon from Cindy—maybe she'd kept it as a souvenir. Sometimes long shots paid off.

He disappeared into the other room and came back with a shotgun. He sighted on her face and said, "How'd you like to be looking down the barrel of this bad boy?"

She jumped up and yelled, "Goddamn it, David, that's not funny! Don't ever point a gun at me again."

A few minutes later, as though to allay her anxiety, he picked up a copy of *Soldier of Fortune* and said, "I've matured. I don't believe all this garbage."

At home later, she wondered if he'd given her a subtle warning. The shotgun scene was certainly out of character. She decided to reinforce her cover story by introducing him to a member of her "family." Sami agreed to cooperate.

"So you're Theresa's sister," David said when they met at the Park Lane.

They got to talking, and Sami said that Buddy had been especially brutal to her lately and she didn't know what to do about it. "He's under a lot of pressure," she explained.

"Well, look," David said, "I can have that taken care of for you." Kim and Sami exchanged glances. "That's no problem at all."

Sami said, "Well, uh, let's wait and see."

Kim brought her roommate along on a few more dates and regretted it. Sami was a petite extrovert from Mamou, Louisiana, and she became garrulous when she drank. One night she called Kim by her real name.

David stopped in mid-sentence. " 'Kim'?"

Kim thought, I'm dead . . .

"Well, yeah!" Sami blared. "Her name is Kimberly Theresa, and sometimes I call her Kim."

"Oh?"

"She didn't like the name Kimberly so we called her Theresa." Kim had never heard Sami talk so fast. "But since I'm her baby sister, I've always called her Kim. It's, uh, hard for me to switch over." Sami stood up abruptly. "I hope y'all'll excuse me. I'm fixin' to shoot a game of darts." Oh shit, Kim thought, listen to that Cajun accent. He'll know we're not sisters for sure.

David smiled and went on talking. Kim watched him closely. Neither the blue eye nor the brown showed suspicion.

When Sami returned, he was describing Garibaldi's role in the unification of Italy. The "sisters" repaired to the ladies' room. "Keep your voice down," Kim whispered. "I think he's right outside in the hall."

"Listening?" Sami said.

Kim nodded.

Sami mused, "Is he playing us while we're playing him?"

Kim remembered the shotgun and shuddered.

On the way home in the gold Jetta, Sami said, "He did it."

"He . . . what?"

"Killed 'em."

Kim disagreed. "I think he knows about it, but no way he did it."

"He killed 'em," Sami repeated. She sounded so positive. "He gives me a sense of fear. There's a look in his eyes or something. I mean, basically he's just a li'l ol' blond boy. But he has angry eyes."

Kim thought, Sami's always had telepathic powers. How can she be so wrong?

Sami said, "The bartender asked me what I did for a living and I told him I was a private investigator. He said, 'Are you kidding? What're you doing here?' I said, 'There's a murderer here!' "

"What did he say?"

"He seemed bored. He said, 'No shit.' "

On Kim's next visit to the office, Penny the receptionist asked, "You remember what we were talking about?"

"What do you mean?" Kim asked.

"About the drugs. Like downers, Quaaludes, Placidyl, whatever you can get."

Kim thought, She sounds serious, but I was just kidding the other day. "I'll see what I can do," she said. It was the simplest way to end a silly conversation.

110

Cecelia was happy to hear her son's voice on the phone. Lately he'd been dropping in to borrow money, but it had been a long time since he'd taken her anywhere.

"Mom," he said over the phone, "I think I've found the right woman. Her name's Theresa. I've been seeing her a lot. Mom, I get along better with her than any girl I've ever met."

Cecelia felt a pang. He was her only son, and he'd loved before and been hurt so badly. For a time she'd doubted that he would ever get over Cindy, but apparently he had.

"How serious is this, David?" she asked.

"I'm gonna marry her, Mom."

She got out some old pictures. He'd been such a lovely child—warm, outgoing. She'd had one transparency mounted in a plastic viewer. She held it up to the Sears, Roebuck lamp in the living room and saw that the teachers had combed his hair on the wrong side that day. They probably didn't want his front cowlick to stick up. There were glints in his eyes and a separation in his front teeth. He was smiling; his dimples stood out.

She thought, So this little man's found his woman? She wondered what the woman looked like and how they'd become so thick without her knowing about it. She really didn't think he was the marrying kind. His home life certainly hadn't been any inspiration—the thirty years' war. In her mind's eye she saw him toddling toward the door and greeting his father, "Daddy, daddy!"

She saw DuVal draw back. "When I first come home," he told his three-year-old, "don't rush at me. You're rushing at me!"

Cecelia remembered the scene all too vividly. She'd taken her husband aside and said, "DuVal, you're the only man in Houston that would react that way to his little son." DuVal never fended the boy off after that, although he didn't show much emotion, either. Cecelia thought she knew why. In

1946 Captain DuVal West's first wife had left him and taken their only child. He was crushed when the daughter turned against him. She was nearly forty now, married, living in Houston with children of her own (DuVal's grandchildren, Cecelia reminded herself, and he doesn't even know how many!). Neither father nor daughter would recognize the other if they passed on the street.

Night after night Cecelia guessed at her husband's thoughts as he puffed away in his living-room chair, adding new layers to the amber tint on her paintings and walls. All his tastes and interests seemed to date to his days as a married young signal corps officer. He was a fine moral gentleman, but he was impervious to anything new, including emotions and hurts. Cecelia understood DuVal. And she understood their son. She only wished she could draw these last two male Wests together; the family tree would die with them. But it was much too late.

No, she said to herself, my David still isn't ready to marry. The years hadn't changed him much, either. He'd lost his childhood radiance as soon as he'd seen the dreary lives being lived around him. A psychologist had tested the sweet little boy at age eight and reported that he was seething with anxiety and hostility. Cecelia thought, He still is.

111

With her friend Lou Bocz, Kim took pains working out the script of her next dramatic production. David had been pressing to meet the tyrant "Buddy." Tonight they would all have dinner at the house on Vermont.

Bocz was an artist who etched glass, a good guy of about forty, with a darkly handsome face and rumbly voice that made him perfect for the role of a Mafioso. They'd met when Kim was dancing topless.

"Lou," she told him as they drove toward David's house, "you've got to make this guy scared to death of you. Intimidate him! Don't let him like you and don't let him think you like him, because if you do, then you're no longer the threatening person that I can rely on as an excuse. Remember, you're *Buddy*. You're a paranoid homicidal Vietnam vet with Mafia connections. Sami's my other prop. Make sure to mistreat us both."

Midway through dinner, Kim said to herself, This is kinda sad. David was sugaring up to "Buddy," lighting his cigarettes, waiting on him. Lou glowered at the Moroccan curry and little Sami turned up her Cajun nose. "This lamb tastes like something you throw together in the jungle to survive," she confided when David was in the kitchen. Kim told her to shut up or she'd be wearing it.

After dinner David escorted his guests into the living room and opened a fresh bottle of wine. He put on a Stray Cats record and said he had plenty of other music, including some vintage Elvis. He'd tarted the place up a little, but it still looked like the waiting room of an abandoned railroad. A small candle seemed to provide the only heat.

David had hardly started his latest lecture on politics when Lou said softly, "I don't have time for all this bullshit."

David started on another subject and this time Lou let him prattle for a while before dumping on him. Kim thought, Lou's *perfect!* If she didn't know him as a kindly man with the soul and sensibilities of an artist, she'd have run for a cop.

David turned to Vietnam and jungle warfare. "Kid," Lou murmured, "why are you wasting time explaining Vietnam?" Kim thought, He's the Godfather!

Lou spent the last painful hour of the evening alternately contradicting and patronizing the host. At 11 P.M. he ordered his women, "Get your coats!" Before Kim could stand up, he was gone.

Sami followed, but Kim stayed to comfort David for a minute or two. She thought, I'm the most important woman in his life and all he wants is to be accepted by my family. He must feel *terrible*.

He was smiling. "How'd I do? Did he like me? Do you think I made a good impression? Do you think he'll let me see you now?"

Kim thought, Didn't he *notice?* My God, nobody's that imperceptive!

Sami called up the stairs, "Buddy's ready!"

Kim ran down and slid into the back seat of the Jetta. She couldn't stop giggling; the whole evening had been such a trip.

Lou drove them to La Carafe for a nightcap. Kim said, "I think he fell for it."

"Yeah," Lou said. "But . . . he's not the triggerman."

Sami piped up: "Yes he is!"

Kim said she didn't think so. But all three agreed that he was involved.

Mike Manela phoned and warned her that the anti-Paris pressure was getting heavy in the Wilson office. "From whom?" Kim asked.

"Guess."

"For what?" she said. Mike didn't answer, but she'd picked up a couple of hints that certain parties were tired of working hard in the field while she sat around bars making twenty dollars an hour and expenses. One of the male agents had gone so far as to claim that she was filing phony expense reports.

"I'm disgusted," Kim told Mike. "No one's helping me. I've done every single goddamn thing on my own. I'm not even certain it's gonna work, and if it doesn't work, they're gonna say it's my fault. And I'll be fired."

"I dunno, Kim," Manela said. "Just do the best you can." She thought, Gee, thanks, Mike, for that great advice.

112

Wickie Weinstein wondered what the hell was happening to his friend and roommate Dave. "Hey, man," he said to their mutual friend John Lee as they shared some sinsemilla, "what is Dave doing with this Theresa? The minute he goes to the restroom, she flirts with other guys. She even hit on me. What the fuck gives, John?"

Lee had known West since childhood, and he said it was the same old story: Dave had fallen in love as only Dave could. "Shit, man," he said, "I saw him on his knees to her one night. At the Park Lane. Drunk."

Wickie knew that Dave was hipped on the tall blue-eyed Aryan type; maybe that explained it. Dave had been kicked out of military school for smoking pot, but not before picking up a lot of Nazi-type crap from the other little fascists. He talked about impure blood and the way the Jews brought the plague on Europe and all the other anti-Semitic bullshit. He made a sketch of an Orthodox Jew in a yarmulke looking out his window at a tornado and captioned it, "Oy, oy, dey never told me about dese in New Joisey."

"Hey, Dave," Wickie said when he found it on the table, "what's this shit? This stereotype shit doesn't go, man."

"That isn't you," Dave said.

"It isn't me? Well, I'm Jewish. I'm from New Jersey. Why isn't it me?"

Dave had jived his way out of it.

Wickie took another hit of John Lee's great pot and said, "He keeps telling me how neat Theresa is. Says the sister's bisexual. He's thinking about two on one. He actually wants to marry into an incestuous family!"

They agreed that something wasn't quite right about Theresa—her punk look and military outfits, her great vocabulary and diction, the way she drove Dave around and paid the checks, the way she'd latched onto a loser even though she could obviously do better. They figured she must be a loser herself, but why didn't she look like one? She was a mystery to everyone but Dave.

113

David wasn't in a good mood. The Trans Am had a flat and he didn't have a spare. He and Nana had been living on vegetables and rice. His unpaid tabs festooned the Montrose bars and he had visions of being kneecapped by collectors. The night before, he'd had dinner and drinks with Theresa at the Bavarian Gardens, and when she paid the check, he felt like a denutted bull. He was glad that they were meeting tonight at the Park Lane, where the bartendress let him pay his tab in installments.

He walked all the way to the bar on West Alabama. It had rained hard, but the clouds were driving toward the Gulf on a cold west wind. He arrived a half-hour late and Theresa wasn't there. She consistently ran an hour behind the rest of the world and seemed to think it was cute as hell.

He was nursing another free coffee when she burst in the door looking flushed. "Oh, David," she said, "I'm sorry. My sister took me to Caligula and it was an *amazing* experience." David wondered why two sisters would go to a topless bar.

"Sami was flirting with the dancers and putting money in their G-strings," Kim went on, staring intently at his face. "It was a real shocking eyeopener to me."

He had the feeling that she was trying to get a reading on his attitude about dykes. He'd picked up early that she ran subtle little tests. He remembered how she'd grilled him about Cindy, kept insisting that they visit her and try to help. What she'd really wanted was to scope out her competition.

"You know what was weird about Caligula?" Kim said as she lit one cigarette from another. "I have to admit I was kinda jealous when Sami got turned on by the titty dancers."

"Okay," David said. "I pick up on that." But he still wasn't sure what she meant, or even if she meant anything at all. He'd wondered about Theresa before, her being so big and rangy and ex-Navy. Was she hinting that she had lez tendencies? Well, shit, baby, he thought, don't expect to shock me. I've lived in the Montrose all my life.

Lately he'd become frustrated about the pecks on the cheek, the tightly compressed lips, the last-minute sprints to the car to get home to Buddy. He relieved his horniness by visits to a few old dependables, but he wished he could bring it all together with Theresa—his physical and emotional needs, his need to love and be loved, his need for a sweet, docile woman.

He'd been spending a lot of time analyzing his own feelings. Maybe, he told himself, you're trying too hard to fall in love. Maybe you're making a big romance out of air. You've done it before. There isn't much real romance around these days, so you kinda fake it. He thought, It's kinda like a con game on yourself, ya know?

Finding a wife was a serious business and Theresa met the job description—witty, intelligent and, above all, devoted to him. She wasn't Jane Seymour, but she wasn't Lassie either. He wore her on his arm like a Rolex, felt enhanced by her long body and her classy face. He liked the way she matched him drink for drink and joke for joke, and the way she was beginning to say what he'd always wanted to hear: "David, I feel closer to you than anybody ever in my life. . . ." "We're getting there. . . ." "I think I want you, David. . . ."

Now sitting across from her at the Park Lane, he thought, So she has some bisexual tendencies. Who cares as long as she likes me? What are you waiting for, David? The Virgin Mary? You've rehabilitated women before. You could Pygmalion the hell out of Theresa; there's so much to start with.

He turned and saw sister Sami prancing into the bar on the arm of a dude with styled gray hair. Sami introduced him and explained that he was a next-door neighbor who gave her shelter after Buddy beat her up. Sami said they'd forgotten their money and David told them to put their drinks on his tab.

The older guy sat down and immediately asked David how he'd managed to get himself involved in so much paramilitary bullshit. David thought, What paramilitary bullshit? Does he think I'm Wickie? The guy confided, "I used to be a pilot for Air America."

David knew that Air America was a CIA cover. "I used to be in the Marines in North Africa," he said.

"Say, have you ever made any contacts with mercenaries?"

"No," David answered.

"Maybe you'd be interested in getting hooked up?"

David wondered where this was leading. He doubted that the CIA did its headhunting in the Park Lane. "Uh, I don't think so," he said. "From what I've heard about the CIA, everybody's expendable and they fuck up a lot, ya know?"

"Well, what about the NRA?" the old guy asked. "Have you considered joining that?"

"The National Rifle Association?"

"Yeah."

David thought, What a freaky rap! Is this guy recruiting for the CIA *and* the NRA? How about the NFL and the NBA? He thought, Where do Sami and Theresa find these dickheads?

Around 1 A.M. he got tired of the crazy conversation and asked Theresa if she was ready to go. He couldn't bear to look at his tab, but they'd been drinking for six hours and he'd be lucky if it was under eighty bucks. It would take him weeks to pay off.

Theresa drove him home in the gold Jetta. At his house she allowed him a small kiss, but when he tried to tilt her across his lap she said, "Oh, David, I wish I could, but Buddy'll take it out on Sami if I'm late."

"Yeah," he said. "I understand."

He climbed his stairs, fed Nana, smoked a joint, and pulled out his sofa. Goddamn, he thought, what do I have to do? Jump from the Texas Commerce Tower? Set myself on fire?

He fantasized a three-way with Theresa and Sami. As he drifted toward a cannabis sleep, he thought, That isn't what I want. A two-way with Theresa is all I ask. . . .

He met her the next night at Rud's, and she was back on her Cindy kick again. Christ, he thought, we gave up on that subject a month ago. Why won't she let it lay? He couldn't figure out her interest, unless it was that she found his old romances threatening. Maybe it was the lez business again. She kept hinting that she was telepathic and knew that he was holding something back. She warned that his secretiveness was a barrier to their romance. She couldn't pinpoint it, but he was hiding something "big." She said, "Whatever it is, I wouldn't hold it against you, David." He caught the clear implication that if he would just confess to a few heavy-duty sins, she would jump into his bed naked. It was something to think about.

Out on the street a few days later, he ran into Cindy. Oh, great, he thought, just what I need to clear my head! The large economy size! He figured her goal must be three hundred pounds, and she was damn near there.

He told her he was trying to get a relationship started, but he didn't mention Theresa's name. "She's pretty nice," he said. "An Anglo-Germanic Midwestern American girl, ya know? Kind of a big farm girl."

Cindy said she was having financial troubles, and he said he didn't feel that he had the right to give her advice. He said that he'd lost his innocence that night on Memorial Drive—"I can't be righteous and holier than thou like I coulda been before."

Cindy frowned. "Well," she said, "you're not gonna freak out and have a big conscience problem, are ya?"

He thought, I remember when I told her the same thing, a year ago, maybe two. Now she's afraid I'll tell Theresa. "No, no, no, no, *no!*" he assured her.

She said a mob leader named Salino had arrived at her apartment in a big black sedan. She was hiding him and his henchmen. He thought, Why the fuck would a bunch of Mafiosi hide out in *your* grubby-ass dump? "He's my protector," Cindy said. David thought, She never changes. She's still trying to make me jealous. . . .

One night toward the end of January, Theresa looked soulfully at him and said, "I could never trust you as long as we kept secrets from each other."

"I'm not!" he insisted. "Gimme a break, Theresa."

He thought, She's like challenging me to prove I love her. My real secret doesn't have a thing to do with her, but it's a constant weight and she's making it worse. He wondered if he should just go ahead and confess; it wouldn't be the first time. But Theresa wasn't Wickie or Lyn's friend Paul or the battered housewife he'd told at a bar. A confession might turn Theresa off completely. She wasn't a steady church-goer, but she was a believer and she had morals. She'd been proving both points week after week. He didn't dare risk losing her.

The quandary was on his mind the next few times they met, but all he could manage to say was, "Something's bothering me, Theresa."

When she asked what it was, he said he wasn't ready to talk. "Maybe later," he added. She still seemed willing to wait.

114

Parked in front of 1409 Vermont in Sami's car, Kim took a shot in the dark. "David," she ventured, "I had a dream about Cindy." She leaned across the seat and nuzzled his ear. "I know what you're hiding. I feel it has to do with Cynthia."

"No, no!" he said. "You're crazy. I don't know what you're talking about, Theresa." His trembling voice was pitched higher than ever. "It doesn't have *anything* to do with Cindy. And . . . I'm not hiding anything anyway."

She drummed her nails on the dash. "I didn't mean to freak you out, David. But I feel it strongly, and it bothers me. It *really* bothers me. You don't have to tell me, but I just want you to know that I know."

He leaned across the seat and put his head in her lap. "You're right," he said. She could feel his body quaking. He yelled, "You're right!"

He gave a deep sigh and began to cry. "It has to do with Cindy," he said. "You're absolutely right. But . . . I can't tell you."

She thought, Bull's-eye! But she also felt sorry for him. She'd never seen a grown man cry. She held him close. *"Sshhh,"* she said, rocking him gently. *"Sshhh.* It's *okay."*

"It's awful," he sobbed. "It's awful and I can't tell you. I can never tell anybody. This is my life we're talking about, Theresa. My life hangs in the balance." He went on and on between shudders. "It's horrible, its awful. She's awful, she's evil. I don't want her around me."

Kim lit a cigarette and inhaled to her toes. *"Ssshhh,"* she repeated. "That's okay, that's okay."

He cried off and on for twenty or thirty minutes. "Don't worry about it," she said as he got out of the car. "I'll talk to you soon."

She was quietly elated as she watched him disappear into the dark vault of his staircase. She thought, Goddamn, it paid off—the shucking and jiving, the stories and lies, the playacting and the scary moments. David knows plenty! He may even know who the triggerman is. And he knows all about Cindy. And he's gonna tell me *every last word.* . . .

The next morning she called to feel him out. He sounded surprised, grateful. He said that he'd been afraid she would dump him after last night. He said, "I feel much, much closer to you, Theresa."

She drove to the office in a good mood. "Listen," she told Denise Moseley, "David's ready to talk. I need a microcassette recorder. Can I borrow yours?"

Denise said she had to do some transcribing.

Bill Elliott said, "I'd lend you mine, but the last time I lent my recorder to somebody, they screwed it up."

After a few more turndowns, she barged into the boss's leathery sanctum. "Clyde," she said, "I think I'm gonna make some headway on this thing. Can I check out a recorder?"

The famous international gumshoe looked up from a stack of paperwork. His craggy face had thinned; he'd been fighting heart problems for months; a weaker man would

have been in the hospital, or the cemetery. He asked, "How
much did you make your last paycheck?"

"Uh, nine hundred dollars."

"Well, you can afford to buy one."

"But I can't, Clyde! I already spent it. Let me borrow one.
I'll put a deposit down in case I lose it."

One of his phones rang. He muttered, "Go ask Denise,"
and picked it up.

Okay, Kim thought as she left the office. I've gone this far
single-O. It's nothing new to me.

115

When P. M. Clinton got wind of the office plan to sting Kim
Paris, he was baffled. He'd grown accustomed to the accusations about her—that she was padding her hours, conning
the con artists, lying to her colleagues. But P.M. didn't see it
that way at all.

In his spare moments from the Hermann Hospital case,
he'd glanced at her reports, and he had the feeling that she
was doing a journeyman job—nothing showy, but steady
and promising. Undercover work took time and patience. If
anybody could turn David West, she could. But not if she
was thrown in the Harris County Jail.

P.M. sat back at his desk and tried to be honest with
himself. He didn't doubt that Kim might be a petty user—so
was at least one other top investigator he knew. It was also
possible that she'd sold a little. You had to be realistic in this
day and age.

But—pushing junk in the office?

Never. He would bet his job on it. It was too big a leap
from office oddball to dope peddler. But that was the allega-
tion. Penny had told Denise about certain conversations,
and Denise told Clyde, and the three of them had baited a
trap. If Kim followed through on the Placidyl deal and accepted cash in return, she would be arrested on the spot.

P.M. called in Moseley and asked, "What's the point of all this?"

"The point is we have to determine where Kim's loyalties lie," said the old hand. "She may be conning us, scamming us. We have to protect the reputation of this office." P.M. had to agree they were legitimate concerns.

He took a closer look at Kim's reports. Man, he thought, that West is some boozer. He read entries like "13 drinks @ $3.00, me 4, David 9"; "10 drinks @ $3.00, me 3, David 7"; "13 drinks @ $2.75 + tip, me 4, David 9"; "$40 beer"; "$30 drinks." He imagined the scene at the Park Lane or Rudyard's, Kim sipping slowly, trying to soften him up and stay sober herself. It was a subspecies of drink-hustling, but it was getting results. Her reports had changed from non-committal to tentative to promising. He smiled as he read, "The episode Saturday leaves no doubt in my mind as to his and Cynthia's involvement" and "I feel a confession is imminent."

He soul-searched through his lunch hour and then decided that he couldn't allow her to be busted. She'd been his personal choice as the decoy; if she turned out dirty, he would take the blame himself. So far, her hours had been billed to the clients at around four thousand dollars. Betty and Richard Hinds deserved a payoff. Then they could all attend to the Kim Paris problem, if there was one.

P.M. gave his father-in-law his personal view of the situation. He didn't want to challenge Clyde; the proprietor could be tough and unyielding once he'd set his mind. "Kim's doing the job I assigned her, Clyde," P.M. concluded. "I think she's onto him and he's ready to cop. She wouldn't say it if it wasn't so, 'cause she's having too good a time at the client's expense. What are y'all trying to do to her? If we're working on this together, why are you trying to put a dope case on our key operative?"

Clyde told him to handle the problem himself—"Quit pestering me with details!" As P.M. walked out of the office, he thought, The old man's had some tough times medically, but he didn't come to town with the first load of watermelons.

P.M. took Mike Manela aside and said, "Tell your friend

Kim that whatever she thought she was gonna do for Penny, *don't do it!*"

Manela reported back. "She said she was just kidding."

P.M. thought, Good enough. Now let's catch the rabbits.

116

Kim couldn't fathom David's new reticence. After the Saturday night sobbing scene, she'd expected a gush of revelations. She'd made it plainer than ever that there would be nothing between them as long as he didn't trust her with his secrets. His response was to ask her to live with him. She said, "David, you don't get it! When I'm around you, I feel . . . an uneasiness."

He peered through her smoke and told her how much he trusted her, but as soon as she mentioned Cindy or his secret, he turned stubborn. She tried to analyze his mental processes. Maybe he thought she was too delicate to hear the worst, or maybe, despite his pretty speeches, he still didn't feel that close to her. She tried to think up a way to forge a bond so tight that he would see them as one flesh, almost like an old married couple. She couldn't spend another six weeks squeezing out information by the drop.

Sex was out. The chemistry was nil. And besides, it would be unprofessional.

She decided to turn them into Bonnie and Clyde. There was nothing like shared danger to forge a bond. The plan unfolded before her eyes like a screenplay:

She tells David she's had a vivid dream that he's in danger. He laughs her off.

They meet at his house. As they walk out his front door, Mike Manela comes by in a truck and fires a shotgun at them. Blanks, of course.

They hit the dirt. She jumps up and says, "Let's get out of here!"

Later she drives the message home over a beer: "I'm

with you for a dime or a dozen, David. Whether people
try to kill you or not. . . ."

She thought, It's perfect! It'll convince him of my tough-
ness. It'll teach him to take my telepathic skills seriously.
And it'll create a tremendous closeness. Blooded together in
battle—*we're one!*

She phoned Bill Elliott at home and asked the former
HPD lieutenant, "What would the police do if you shot off a
blank gun in the city limits?"

"You might get a citation for noise disturbance."

She couldn't find Mike Manela, but she knew he wouldn't
mind firing the shots.

At 7 A.M. the next day she called David at home and
asked in a shaky voice, "Are you okay?"

"Well, yeah, sure," he said.

"Oh, thank God you answered the phone and you're
okay!" She tried to sound hysterical. "I had the most terrible
dream, David. I'm *so* upset. I had this dream that somebody
wants to hurt you. I don't know how to describe it, David.
Don't ask me to explain it 'cause I can't."

The words gushed out. "I can't read crystal balls, David,
and I can't read your palm, but I just feel so strongly about
it! Please . . . be careful driving to work. I care about you
and it'll make me feel better if you'll be careful. Tell me
you'll be careful."

"I'll be careful." He sounded pleased at the attention.

"David," she said, "who would want to hurt you?"

"Nobody I can think of."

"Well, just please, *please,* take care of yourself!"

At last she reached Manela. He told her that the idea was
crazy. He warned her not to mention her plan to Clyde or
P.M. "They'll think you flipped. You're already hanging by
a thread."

That night she had to call David again. "Thank God,"
she said, "I had another dream. You're out of danger now."

117

David thought, she calls me at seven o'clock in the morning, worries about me, dreams about me. *She loves me!* He thought, Just give us a few more days. . . .

A part of him wanted to tell her the whole story and ask for her absolution, but it was still too big a risk. She might dump him, might even go to the cops. Folks were funny about murder.

118

Sergeant J. C. Mosier, official spokesman for the Houston Police Department, thought it was a peculiar call, but then he was accustomed to peculiar calls from his old friend Clyde Wilson. Years ago the two had worked a killing together. Wilson had proved to be loud, opinionated, crotchety and the best damn private investigator J.C. had ever seen. Whenever a cop bad-mouthed Clyde Wilson—and many did—J.C. would say, "Don't put that country bumpkin down to me! If Clyde tells ya something, take it to the bank."

This morning Clyde wanted to know if J.C. was familiar with the Campbell case. Sure, Mosier said. "I was in homicide when it happened."

"Well, listen up, J.C.," Clyde said in the powerful voice he'd developed as a twenty-year-old first sergeant in World War II. "I've got this li'l gal who's a li'l investigator and she's gone out and become acquainted with this ol' boy who's the ex-boyfriend of the daughter. Got that?"

"Yes," J.C. said.

"They've got a li'l, uh, relationship going. Now I'm working on the Hermann Hospital scandal and I really don't have time to fuck with this, J.C., so lemme tell ya—the li'l gal's squirrelly as hell. You can't put a Baptist choir girl on something like this. She don't really know what she's doing, but I think she's getting some pretty good stuff. If you wouldn't mind, can I send her to you to set down and talk? And see if she's really doing anything worth a damn?"

"Clyde," J.C. said, "you know I'd do anything for you. Just send her down."

She showed up four days later, on the morning of Friday, February 8, bearing a file marked CAMPBELL MURDER CASE. She said her name was Kimberly Paris and she didn't look a bit squirrelly. J.C. had an eye for conservative clothes and her gray suit looked Brooks to him. She wore a little candy-striped blouse and a bow tie and purple eyeliner accenting the bluest eyes he'd ever seen off a movie screen. The only odd touch was the dark pink tint in her hair, but at least it wasn't purple.

Talk? She barely came up for air. In a blue norther of words, gestures and cute-ass remarks, she told him how *paralyzingly* pleased she was to talk to a real police officer, because no one at the agency wanted to listen and she'd worked her butt off cutting into this guy and now he was ready to cop to something big but nobody would lend her a tape recorder to take it down.

"J.C.," she said as though they were old friends, "I really don't know if David did it or not. At first I didn't believe it, but he's told me that he has a terrible secret that he can't tell me about."

It developed that one of her problems was that West was hot to trot. "J.C.," she said, leaning across his desk, "you gotta help me. I'm not gonna screw him! But he's pushing. I've been seeing him for five or six weeks and he's expecting some action."

She had some flaky ideas. She said she needed an under-cover cop to drive down Vermont Street and pop a couple of shotgun blanks just as she and West walked out the front door.

"Whoa there!" J.C. said blinking hard. "Nuh-nuh-nuh-*nuh!* What happens if we scare the pants off him and he hauls ass for Southern Rhodesia? Or what if one of our

patrol units drives by and there's a shootout. Or a neighbor
pulls a gun, or . . . any number of things. You folks in the
private-eye bidness, you can get away with some crazy stuff,
but not us."

She nodded. One thing J.C. liked about her: you didn't
have to tell her twice. He went on: "The main thing you got
going for you, Kim, is this guy wants to tell you about this
horrible thing that he's done. He's probably ashamed, but in
a way he'd like to tell somebody about it. Most killers do,
especially in a high-publicity case."

"He's ready," Kim acknowledged.

"Right! Well, what you need to do is you need to let him
know that you've done something terrible in your past."

"He thinks I'm living with a Mafia guy named Buddy
who beats up my sister."

"Well, good! Why don't you tell him you've seriously
thought of killing Buddy? Then you put him in the position
of knowing that you're the same type person that he is."

As he spoke, she scribbled in her notebook. He sized her
up as a good bullshit personality, a good actress, high IQ,
creative—and outlandish as hell. Flaky or not, she had the
potential to clear a very serious crime, provided everything
fell right. "C'mon," he said, getting to his feet. "We're going
to Homicide."

119

Kim thought, It feels great talking to a real cop. J.C. led her
through an open bull pen with teletypes clattering and
phones ringing and a couple of pots of coffee leaking steam.
Thick-waisted men with bulges in the sides of their polyester
suits leaned from their honeycomb dividers and looked at
her legs. A plaintive voice repeated on the intercom, "I need
a sergeant on line one. *I need a sergeant. . . .*"

Mosier led her into an enclosed office and introduced her
to a sergeant named Gilbert Schultz. At first glance Schultz

resembled one of her old mess cooks back at Corpus. He didn't show a glimmer of interest as she started on her story.

When she came to the part about firing shotgun blanks, Schultz reached for the confidential file she'd brought from the office. Clyde Wilson had ordered her not to show it around because it contained secret police reports that a private agency wasn't supposed to have, but she handed it over because Schultz was so intimidating. He glanced at the cover sheet and dropped it on his desk. A thin smile crossed his face as he said, "Did you sleep with this guy?"

"No."

"You never slept with this guy?"

"No."

"He's never been to your house?"

"No." She looked toward Mosier and he looked away.

Schultz asked, "He doesn't have your phone number?"

She tried to light a cigarette. Her lighter wouldn't work and there was an embarrassing silence till Mosier produced a flame. Apparently Schultz didn't smoke; he certainly didn't light. "No, he doesn't," she said at last.

"But you're so tight he's ready to confess to murder?"

"Right."

Schultz let out a low sigh. "I don't believe you. I can't believe he'd tell you anything if you haven't slept with him."

"I haven't!" She thought, What is this, "Mr. District Attorney"? Her mouth turned dry.

"We'll find out soon enough," Schultz said.

"You'll find out I'm telling the truth."

"Bullshit."

She flushed under her candy-striped blouse. "I did *not* sleep with him," she said. "I did *not* let him French-kiss me. I did *not* let him, uh, fool around."

"Bullshit," Schultz said.

She gave J.C. another pleading look, but his face was in his coffee. She felt like crying, but she didn't want to give them the satisfaction. She wondered what she'd done to upset Schultz. She thought maybe it was her pink hair. There were men like that.

". . . Tell ya something," Schultz was saying. "You're just the kinda flaky chick that Cindy went to acting school with. She's conniving and sneaky and smart enough to send someone like you in here to find out what we have on her. I won't have anything to say to you till I find out who you are."

Kim thought, Goddamn it, J.C., are you gonna sit there and let this jerk talk to me like this? *You* know who I am. Clyde told you! You know I'm legit.

Mosier was silent. She thought, Goddamn, this is dumb! She turned to Schultz and stammered, "You think I'm, I'm—"

"I'll come right out and tell ya," Schultz said softly. "I don't like ya. You're flaky, you're goofy." Kim couldn't believe that a stranger would talk to her like this.

"I don't like you either," she said.

"Leave the file," he said. "I'll check you out and get in touch."

At the door she turned and said, "When you check me out and find I'm who I say I am, be prepared for me to pull down my jeans, 'cause I'll expect you to kiss my ass."

"Yeah," Schultz said over his shoulder. "I'll do that."

All the way to the elevator J.C. was apologetic. "I don't understand," he said. "This case is gathering cobwebs, he's got nowhere to go, and here I bring him someone who maybe can clear it and he's rude to 'em. Gil's a good detective, Kim, but what he did was uncalled for."

Kim thought, Sure, J.C., but why tell me? Tell that pig back there. It was supposed to be her day of vindication, but she wished she'd stayed home.

120

Schultz picked up the phone as soon as the flake left. He and Motard were no longer partners and they'd shit-canned the Campbell case two years ago, but if it was revived, they would catch it all over again. "Paul," he said. "Listen to this." He outlined Paris's story and explained that she'd been hired by Betty Hinds. "She came up with ideas off the wall," he told his old partner. "That shotgun idea was the most ridiculous damn thang I ever heard of. I was thinking, Hey, this silly broad is trying to set me up. You know me, Paul. I'm not gonna be made a sucker or a fool of."

Motard said, "I know that, Gil."

"She came on too strong, batting her eyes, acting, playing a role, and I just wasn't buying none of it. I treated her like a suspect. She was trying to be cute, cuddly and feminine and all that bullshit, and I was just staring at her blankly and wouldn't react. I'm thinking, Where's this girl coming from? What is she? Who is she? I know I hurt her feelings."

Paul said she would probably be back. Gil said he certainly hoped Paul would be on duty that day.

Schultz stepped outside his office door and drew a cup of coffee. It was a quiet afternoon and he had private investigators on his mind. He didn't like them. Most of the ones he'd met thought their piss was Gatorade. They got away with all kinds of devious shit—wiretapping, taping, intimidation— whereas a cop could get his case thrown out of court if he wore the wrong aftershave.

On a whim he called Clyde Wilson direct. Wilson said that Kim Paris was just an old girl who hung around the office, used to date one of the agents, did a little undercover work. "I think she's just blowing smoke," he told Schultz. "She's a little dopehead, but I sent her to y'all because it's a murder case. I figured y'all'd want to hear about it."

Schultz said, "Okay. Thank ya." He thought, If her own boss doesn't think any more than that about her, what am I supposed to think? He decided to put her out of his mind.

121

The night after her painful meeting with Schultz, Kim met David at the historical shrine and saloon called La Carafe. Her battle plan was to convince him that she had an underworld mentality. Later she produced another handwritten report for the yellowing stack on the corner of Denise Moseley's desk:

> I met with David for 5 hrs. Saturday. It was *very* productive as far as reinforcing the trust between us. I talked about how I was wary of most people as they're untrustworthy, loyalty is difficult if not impossible to find in a relationship. I cited the example of Christine DeLorean and how she stood by her man when all the world was against him and how I admired her for this. I impressed upon him this is what I look for in a man "because you never know what could happen." We also talked about not being a snitch: "coming from the old school" meaning when we were young punks, running the streets—if one were to get busted for anything you could, *without a doubt,* count on him or her not to snitch you off. We concur, they just don't make kids like they used to! David told me he feels very very close to me in a psychic sense and knows he can trust me—we're "cut of the same cloth."

She left a few things out of the report because she wasn't sure the office would approve. On this cloudy February night it had seemed that every other word out of their mouths had been "fuck" or a variant. David even used it as an adverb, British style—"If you'd fucking pass the pitcher, mate, I'd fucking have a drink!"

When it was time to go, Kim had said, "Let's fucking get outa here. I'm goddamn getting sleepy."

Also missing from her report was her blatant admission that she was capable of committing serious crimes. "David," she'd said, snuggling close so she wouldn't be overheard, "if I go out and get busted for drugs, if I knock over a 7-Eleven store, I want to know that you'll stand behind me."

He'd seemed impressed. She thought, Drip, drip, drip. Each drip brings us closer. Now if I could just convince all the other drips involved. . . .

She intentionally ignored him for three days. On the chilly night of February 12 she picked him up at his house and drove him to La Carafe. He said he was afraid she was drifting away from him. "Maybe I am, David," she said. "You know why. We've talked about it so many times."

"You mean . . . I don't communicate?"

"You know what I mean."

She phoned Gil Schultz and begged him to return the Campbell murder file. "I'm in trouble at the office," she explained.

He told her she deserved it. "Giving me that report was very unprofessional," he said. "I could get Clyde Wilson in a lot of trouble with that stuff."

She decided to play dumb and helpless. "How?" she asked.

"*Nobody* gets police files. They're strictly confidential. How'd you get 'em, anyway?"

"Clyde has friends. Please, Sergeant, don't drop me in the grease and tell anybody you saw that police report."

He paused and said, "What police report?"

She thought, Thank you, God. . . .

They agreed to meet in the cafeteria of Foley's department store near Houston Intercontinental Airport. She put on her Brooks Brothers suit and a conservative pair of heels and depunked her pinkish hair as best she could. The prospect of a solo meeting with Schultz was unnerving. On the whole, she thought as she headed north on the freeway, I'd prefer another captain's mast.

He was sipping tea when she arrived. He explained that his father had died; he'd been on a week's funeral leave and that's why she hadn't heard from him. He handed over the file without comment. "I read the whole thing," he said with a forced smile. "At least I know you're real."

He seemed so mellow that she started baring her soul. She told him that West was ready to cop but her own people wouldn't help her. "I don't know where to turn," she said. She knew she was playing into his mind-set about female private investigators, but she didn't mind a little groveling. It was payoff time, and she might not be groveling long.

The chunky detective didn't change expression as she recited complaints about the office. "I know West is involved," she said. "He hasn't told me what he knows but I think I can get him to."

"Listen, kid," Schultz said, "if you got him, I'll work with ya hand over fist." She looked up, surprised. "I'm gonna tell ya, this case has been bothering me and I would *love* to clear it. If it's legal to tape him, we'll do it."

She thought, Now he's sounding like me! "But before I lay my ass on the line," he went on, "it'll be done legally, the way *I* say it's to be done. It'll be done so that it can be prosecuted in court by the Houston Police Department, not by Clyde Wilson."

Fair enough, she thought.

"This case is a real ball breaker," he said in a low voice. "We thought we had something when Cindy confessed to her girlfriend, but the girlfriend got scared off. Woman named Gwen Sampson. Said she had two kids and how the hell were we gonna protect 'em from the Mafia?"

He snorted as if Gwen Sampson were just another silly female. Kim thought, I know you, Gil Schultz! I was in the Navy with thousands like you. You put your worst feet forward, but you're not bad guys. You oughta be marked SPE-CIAL HANDLING.

He pulled out photographs of the murder house and sketched the layout on his napkin. He marked an **X** in the living room and said, "Right there's where I saw a painting come to life. And I saw Mrs. Campbell standing at the foot of the stairs in her white nightgown. My pardner saw her, too. Course, if you ever quote me, I'll deny it."

"Come on," she said. "Be serious. I might be a flake, but I'm not a fool."

He pushed back his chair and glanced at her backside. "You're putting on a little weight," he said. He smiled and said, "You'll be hearing from us."

That evening her old pal Mike Manela called with an astounding free offer. A Mexican client had offered his beach condo and racing sloop in Acapulco. How would Kim and Sami like a long weekend?

She thought, Bye-bye, David. Bye-bye, Schultz. Bye-bye,

Campbell murder case. She tucked her salt-water gear and deck shoes into a suitcase and headed for the airport. It was comforting to know that God was on the job.

122

David sat by his phone till midnight Friday and then made a frantic tour of the clubs, searching for her. On Saturday he monitored his phone till three in the morning, certain she would call. He couldn't imagine what had happened. They'd seen each other for six straight weekends, ever since her trip north at Christmas. Goddamn, he thought, I wonder if that fucking Buddy has hurt her. Or if she's wrecked another car. There was no way he could check; he still didn't have her address or phone number. He thought of calling the hospitals, but there were too damn many of them and they probably wouldn't tell him anyway. Ditto the cops. He would just bring heat on himself.

A frightening thought came to him. Maybe . . . she's dumped me. He tried to remember what they'd talked about the last night at La Carafe. He couldn't recall anything special. He'd quoted something from Nietzsche: "Anything that doesn't kill you helps you," some such shit. Had he rapped the Catholics again? She was always good-natured about that. He thought, Give me one more chance, baby, and I'll never fuck up again. . . .

By Monday he was ready to self-destruct. Family Motors had repossessed the Trans Am. Now he had neither money nor girlfriend nor car.

The phone rang early Tuesday. He picked it up listlessly. "Oh, David," she said in a drowsy voice, "I was out of town. I'm so sorry. I couldn't call you."

His breathing resumed. When he was sure that she wasn't pissed at him, he threw in a sop to his pride: "Goddamn, Theresa, I don't appreciate being treated that way, ya know? As close as we are and all. If I was going to leave town, I'd make damn sure I'd get in touch with you—"

"I couldn't!" she interrupted. "There wasn't time." He could tell she was revving up to her usual thousand words a minute. "All I know is Buddy came home and said we had to leave and don't ask any questions, we gotta go, and don't tell anybody where we're going. I missed you, David. I thought about you. A couple times I picked up the phone and was gonna call, but I really couldn't. You understand, I know."

He said he understood, and they talked for a long time. She told him, "I really care for you, David. I hope you know that."

He said he felt the same.

She came back to her favorite rap about crime and snitches and loyalty. That's all she'd talked about lately. "Ya know, David," she said, "the perfect crime is you do it by yourself and you don't tell anybody about it. Right?"

He said he guessed so.

She said, "My mind works just like yours."

They agreed to meet Wednesday night at his house. He jacked at himself, See, dickface? She was never in doubt.

123

Sergeant Gil Schultz discussed his feelings about the Campbell murder case with his main man in the Harris County district attorney's office, Terry Wilson, chief of the Major Offenders division, a heavyset charger who packed a .45. Whenever Schultz had a legal question, he went to Terry Wilson for a straight answer, minus all the ipso factos and habeas corpuses and other horseshit that only lawyers understood. Another nice thing about Wilson—he wasn't afraid to ride with the cops and get dirty.

Schultz had a list of questions about surreptitious taping. He'd taped a few jail inmates in his time, but that was strictly off the record. He doubted if secretly taped conversations were admissible in court. There were so damn many anticop laws these days; it was bound to be a penitentiary

offense to tape a poor misunderstood guy like David West or
his lovely girlfriend Cynthia.

He knew that other PDs wired up everybody but the
meter maids, but Houston cops had always made do with
less. In this tight-fisted community, all public agencies were
underfunded—schools, courts, hospitals, city offices, but
mostly police officers. It would be a miracle if they even had
the right kind of tape recorders.

"The young lady can't guarantee anything," Schultz told
the assistant D.A. "She just has this feeling." He tried to
present her case fairly, but he was afraid his face showed his
doubts.

He was surprised when the beefy prosecutor said, "You've
got a good idea there."

"You mean . . . taping?"

"Sure," Wilson said. "It's perfectly legal. But there's a
couple of practical matters you have to remember. The tape
isn't worth a damn if Paris does all the talking. She can't
lead him and entrap him and she can't beat him over the
head with a million questions. We don't want to hear from
Paris, we want to hear from West."

Schultz thought, Paris isn't the type you're not gonna
hear from. But he didn't bad-mouth her to the prosecutor.
This whole deal was shaky enough already.

They roughed out a plan. On Wednesday night, February
20, Paris and her concealed wire would call on David West.
It would probably be a waste of time, but that was the nature of police work. Once in a while you had to sing and
dance and take a chance.

124

Denise Moseley wasn't pleased about interrupting her bulging caseload to back up Kim Paris at a lunch with a couple
of homicide cops. But she was happy to be doing something
for Betty and Richard Hinds, no matter how unpromising it
looked. The petite investigator had developed an affection

for the Hindses and a deep respect for the way they'd backed
their suspicions with every dollar they could raise.

The two private investigators met the two detectives at a
downtown steakhouse. Denise preferred natural foods, certi-
fied contaminant-free, but she wasn't rigid about it. She
didn't know these particular officers, but she was prepared
to cooperate with them all the way. As she'd told Kim on
the way in, "City cops are underpaid, overworked, and un-
derpraised. There aren't enough hours in a lifetime to solve
the cases a Houston homicide detective gets in a year."

Sergeant Motard, the tall slender one, quietly picked at
his food. When he put in a word or two, it was usually on
point. The dominant mouth appeared to be Sergeant Gilbert
Schultz. The foursome had barely assembled before he
turned to Paris and said, "Ya know, Kim, you ladies got
something extra going for ya."

"What's that?" Paris asked.

"The power of the pussy."

Denise couldn't believe that a grown man would make a
remark like that or that Kim Paris would take it as a joke.
Oh, Kim, she thought, don't you realize you're being de-
meaned?

The formal agenda was short. Schultz told Kim that she
would carry a hidden transmitter and gave her instructions
on how to behave. He said, "You're gonna get a confession,
Kim. If you don't get it the first night, we'll go back out the
next night, and the next night, and the next night. Don't
worry." He winked broadly. "It could take a while."

Business dispensed with, the senior detective again
brought up "the power of the pussy"; apparently it was his
idea of the perfect rubric for the operation. He launched into
an obviously phony story about spotting Virginia
Campbell's ghost at the foot of her stairs. I believe you,
Denise wanted to say, because I saw Sam Houston the same
day, taking tickets at the Alamo. But she left the wisecracks
to Kim. The ordeal lasted an hour.

125

Kim was suffering a belated attack of the turistas, but she managed to be on time for the final strategy session at Clyde Wilson's suburban office, two hours before her 8 P.M. date with David. As she walked in, she heard Denise saying, "Clyde, I don't think I can deal effectively with Schultz and Motard. They use that phrase 'power of the pussy' and I think it's disgusting."

Kim thought, My god, she's still pissed! Denise should have been in the Navy; then she'd know what real chauvinists sound like. Kim remembered the supervisor who'd loudly proclaimed his doubts that her various hair colors matched. "Senior Chief," she'd responded just as loudly, "there's thousands of men on this station, and you'll be the last to know."

Clyde greeted Kim. "What's the matter, Squirrelly? You nervous?"

Kim said, "Mexico."

"Montezuma's revenge," one of the male agents explained. Kim didn't smile. David would expect her to drink tonight and she wasn't sure how her stomach would react. "Should we scrub the whole thing?" Clyde asked.

"No," Denise insisted. "Those cops are already negative enough. If Kim's sick tonight, they'll have something to say about it."

Clyde looked at Kim. "How about it, Squirrelly?"

"I'm okay," she said. She was surprised at her own coolness. And pleased.

The police contingent arrived at six-thirty. Schultz took Kim aside and reminded her to work West patiently. An electronic technician named Ron Knotts taped a transmitter smaller than a cigarette pack into her gray purse. On the first test it ran hot. Kim thought, My God, it'll melt the plastic and David'll smell it. Knotts told her not to worry. He handed her four small batteries and said, "Change these every two hours." He was a bright, twinkle-eyed guy and he gave her confidence.

When the expeditionary force formed up in the tree-shaded area in front of the office, Kim spotted a pair of cowboy boots under the rear of her borrowed Jetta. A tall, good-looking man wiggled out and introduced himself as Raymond White, the other police "tech."

"I put a tracking transmitter on your car," he said. It was a chilly night and his words made little white puffs. "That way we can follow you better."

She thought, This is too high-tech for me. "Do I have to change that battery, too?"

"Yeah," White said with a smile. "Every eight days." He tapped on the dash. "There's a back-up transmitter in here," he said. "It'll pick up anything you say in the car."

"How do I work it?"

"You just talk," Ron Knotts put in. "We'll be taping you from our van."

Kim thought, I hope they know what they're doing. I sure as hell don't.

The proprietor patted her on the shoulder and told her to watch her ass. "You'll be fine, Squirrelly," he said, sliding a finger along his pencil-thin mustache. "You can handle heat."

She thought, Heat? Heat is mixing three or four touch-and-go's off two runways, sequencing Trojans, T-44s, Corsairs, and A-4s with instrument traffic and transients, handling maybe two hundred ops an hour and keeping the warrant officer's hand off your knee. This isn't heat. This is fun. If only I felt a little better. . . .

The caravan moved out at seven-forty, Kim in Sami's Jetta, Schultz and Knotts in an unmarked police van, Motard and Ray White in an unmarked Camaro, and Denise and Mike Manela in the agency's van with the one-way windows. Kim stopped at a shopping center for a bottle of 190-proof Everclear, a six-pack of tonic and a bag of limes. Truth serum, she said to herself as she led the expedition east on Interstate 10. Too bad it isn't Pepto-Bismol.

For a change, she had a set plan. She and David would drink some Everclear tonics in honor of their first date in a week, then go out for an intimate dinner and return to the house for a nightcap. At the moment of maximum closeness, she intended to pry out his secret. On tape.

Just after 8 P.M. she turned into Vermont Street. She looked in her rearview mirror and saw that her support troops had peeled off. She thought, I won't see another cop till this is over. I hope they'll see me. She clomped up the wooden stairs.

126

David had spent the last hour pacing his floor and thinking, This is the pits! This is worse than the time I got busted for hash in Morocco, worse than breaking up with Cindy, worse than losing my dog. Goddamn, a Trans Am is *special*.

A few hours ago he'd gone to Family Motors on Buffalo Speedway, checked his repossessed car and discovered that the dirty bastards had changed the locks. The chief asshole told him he would have to bring the payments up to date and pay a five-hundred-dollar repo fee—in cash.

David had tried sweet reason. "Look, I only owe twelve hundred dollars and it's a five-thousand-dollar car. Can't we rewrite the paper or something?"

He'd lost the argument and stalked off the premises in a rage. And was still in one.

Theresa arrived with a sack of goodies. He was relieved to see her, especially after the mysterious absence. "Let's go out to dinner," she said.

"Baby, I'm busted."

"I'll pay," she said.

As he mixed drinks in the kitchen, he called out, "This has been the worst day of my life." He hadn't intended to start their reunion on a negative note, but he couldn't get his mind off his muscle-car. Soon he was striding back and forth and snarling, "I'm gonna kill that son of a bitch! Those kinda people don't belong in this world."

Theresa said, "Don't you think that's harsh?"

"No," he said. "They deserve to die."

"You'll calm down, David. You'll forget about it."

"I won't let myself forget about it! Every time I feel like I'm gonna blow it off, I'm gonna sit down and concentrate and work myself up to be as mad as I am now!"

She said there were other ways to get even—throw paint around the used-car lot, for example. "We'll do something," she said, "but we can't go killing 'em."

He said that vandalizing wasn't enough. "If· I don't end up killing 'em myself," he told her, "I'll hire a coupla niggers off the street and pay 'em five hundred dollars. No prob." The jerk-offs at Family Motors, he said, reminded him of Cindy's father, hard cases with no respect for other people's rights or feelings. "They're worse'n the fucking Catholic church."

He thought how much he hated the memory of James Campbell. "Goddamn," he told Theresa, "you wouldn't believe some of the things that happened in that family."

His guest picked up her purse and went into the bathroom. "David," her voice came through the door, "you have roaches on your toothpaste. Ugh! Goddamn!" He heard her whistling "London Bridge," then: "Goddamn, David, do you have an eyeliner pencil I can borrow?"

He thought, What does she think I am? "Yes, yes, it's right next to the mascara," he joked.

She said she'd found a dildo but no mascara.

"You got to plug it in to make it work," David said.

"The eyeliner or the dildo?"

After a few minutes she began singing, "I'm picking out a thermos for you, a very special thermos for you." He'd heard the lines on a comedy show. Steve Martin? "Saturday Night Live"? He wasn't sure. Hot damn, he thought, she's in a good mood, glad to be here. And just a few days ago I thought we were through.

She came out and sat next to him on the sofa. He went on about the Campbells, how James had always liked Cindy, how he'd wanted a son and namesake but had to settle for a daughter named Jamie, how the mother had always resented Cindy and treated her cruelly. Somehow it made him feel good to blow off steam. Theresa had always been a good audience.

"Listen," he said, "the mother was a hunchback, fucking, ya know, like Notre Dame. Big hump. I can't believe this fucking family. The father came from some jive-ass little horrible sleazy hick family in Tennessee . . . and because he was from the poverty environment, he was a real cutthroat and—you know, go right to the jugular—and he made a real good lawyer."

He repeated a version of Campbell family history he'd once heard from Cindy, that James had impregnated Virginia and been forced to marry her. "He made a real horribly disgusting fucking mistake, but back then you married somebody for something like that, ya know? I wouldn't marry a hunchback for anything. I'm not kidding!"

Theresa laughed. He held his hand up in the shape of a pistol and said, "I'd fire away. . . . Let's do the world a favor, ya know?"

"Kill her too, huh?" Theresa asked.

"Yeah. No! I'd kill *me.*"

They both laughed. Theresa said it was apparent that Cindy needed him and "there must be something that you could do to help a person like that."

"Ah, you'd think so," he said, shaking his head sadly.

She said, "I bet the best day of her life was when her parents were killed in that accident, man."

"Probably."

They sat side by side on his couch, Theresa with her legs tucked under her. She was smoking and drinking and peeking at the concert on TV. "Willie Nelson looks fucked with his hair cut, you know it?" she observed. "Look at these drunk motherfuckers at this concert."

It wasn't long before they were back on the subject of Cindy and her family. In a way it was comforting; he couldn't discuss the subject with anyone else except his mother. He told Theresa how innocent Cindy was, a good person, and how her father had exploited her innocence and left her with sexual problems.

"So she doesn't go to bed with anybody else?" Theresa asked. "She's not a sexual person?"

"She's . . ." He tried to figure how to put it. "She's . . . both. She's a fucking nymphomaniac and she feels guilty. . . . It's real weird. It's . . . it's total head-fuck all the time."

He wasn't sure if he'd ever mentioned that Cindy's older son was her father's, so he let her in on that little family secret and added, "It was just the most hateful back-stabbing weaselly fucked-up family I've ever seen in my fucking life." He said the maid raised the two boys, "and the maid is a stupid fucking ignorant *Catholic* maid."

"I don't like the italics you put there on Catholic," Theresa said. "But that's okay. We'll let it ride."

"Just teasing you anyway."

"I know you're teasing."

Willie Nelson launched into a song about a train as Theresa asked why Cindy didn't take care of her own sons. "Oh," he replied, "she wants them emotionally." He remembered all the phone calls on the subject. "She wants them . . . in fact, uh, a coupla times she'll call me up at fucking weird times at night, but I told her not to anymore."

He leaned over and lit her Benson & Hedges menthol. He thought, Oh, shit, she's caught me in a lie and I can see it on her face. He'd been telling her for two months that Cindy was totally out of his life.

When he tried to explain, she said, "I'm not angry." But he could tell she was.

"Listen," he said, "lemme tell ya. I lied and I didn't. I lied. . . ."

Theresa said, "I love you no matter what."

". . . I lied and I didn't, okay?"

"I love you no matter what," she repeated. "Do you understand? Huh? *David, do you understand that?*"

"Yes," he said. They kissed. Her mouth tasted warm and smoky, but she didn't let it last long. She never did. He thought, It's worth the wait.

"What I'm trying to tell you is this," he said, sliding to the edge of the couch. "When I first said it, I wasn't lying. I hadn't seen her or talked to her for months. . . . But I would hear these reports from my mom. Well, now she's moved about a mile from here and she's got this quadruplex and she's renting it out and she called me up to tell me how good she's doing. Well, it doesn't sound that fucking good to me."

Theresa asked, "She didn't get any money? She just got the place?"

"Oh, she got that and twenty-five grand . . . as a settlement to not sue her fucking uncle who was administrator of the estate, who bilked everybody out of a whole hunch of shit and fucked them all." He told how other lawyers had cheated Cindy, too, but "she's just all nonspine, she's just . . . her self-image is destroyed. She's just a worm, ya know? And I told her, I said, 'You better just get up off your ass and fucking have some balls 'cause ain't nobody else gonna do it for ya.' " He said that Cindy was bright, but that she suppressed her intelligence "because it alienates people and makes people feel insecure and all that shit."

He thought, Who started all this talk about Cindy? This is *our* night, David and Theresa. "Fuck it," he said. "It's too . . . I could go on and on and really, I don't want to talk about it. I spent fucking two years of my life trying to fucking psychoanalyze her and I've had two years of psychology and all this shit and I figured I could fucking help her out of it, ya know, and all she did was damn near drag me under to where I was about halfway going. . . . It's something I'm trying to shit-can."

"But you know that it bothers me."

"I know it bothers you. Somebody—"

"Not because she's a fucking threat."

He paused and said, "It's just because she's an enigma."

"No," she said. "It's not even that." She stared hard at him. "You know exactly what it is," she said. "But we'll talk about it later. . . ."

He took her by the forearms and told her that he wanted her physically, that he thought of it as giving, not taking. When it happened, he said, he wanted it to be reciprocal.

"I know," she said softly.

"I'm not demanding anything from you," he said gently. "If you don't want to give it . . . I don't want it. But it's fucking me up. It's a big thing to me. . . ." He said he had patience. He'd been saying that for weeks, both to himself and her. He wondered how much longer he would believe it.

Theresa said she loved him where it counted. "You know how tired I am of these add-water-and-stir relationships? They're fucked! And I'm trying to deal with you on . . . on something different." She began to sound angry. "If you don't understand, then you don't understand. That's fine. That's fucking fine."

He started to apologize, but she said something about going on her way.

David stammered, "Now, look . . . you . . . you. . . . *Look!* . . . What you're doing right now is—"

"I'm *not* being hostile," she said.

He accused her of reacting defensively, and she suggested that there had to be more to a relationship than sex; there had to be "a communion."

"But it's *there,*" he said. "It's there."

She said, "Well, you know everyone wants to, ya know, fuck. 'Let's fuck and then we'll get to know each other.' You roll over in the morning, and . . . we get to know each other." Of course, she said, the two of them weren't that way "because we've been seeing each other now for . . . what? Two months? And it's not that I don't care about you because I do very much, and I feel closer to you all the time."

He stiffened her drink with Everclear and lit her cigarette and said there was a big difference between having sex and kissing. But kissing seemed to repel her and "that makes me feel weird," he said. "It's not just repelling, it's like resentment." He told her it was a slap in the face when she'd pulled away from his kiss earlier. "It was like, 'What do you want to do, stick your tongue in my face?'"

She laughed. Wisps of smoke drifted up her face. "David," she said, "I don't do that."

He reminded her of the sweet kiss they'd shared the night Buddy had come over for dinner. "It was very sensual," he said, "and it was just for a second. That's what I wanted— just spontaneous, a showing of love." He raced on. "You know, I mean, it'll come, and when it'll come, it'll be the best."

"That's all I want," she said excitedly. "That's all I want! Perfection." She told him to drink up so they could go out and eat.

As they left, he noticed a little car parked in front of the apartment complex next door. Two men sat like statues. He thought, What're they doing there? It must be a faggot good-night. They still didn't move. He thought, Somebody's bronzed some fruits.

127

To Kim the evening was already a success. She couldn't wait to confront Gil Schultz. "Did you hear West bitching that I don't even kiss him right? How's that for the power of the pussy?" But . . . everything in time.

She laid rubber at the first turn and pushed the needle to forty-five. It was comforting to know that the Jetta was emitting a steady signal from the bug underneath. Wherever she went, the chase cars could find her in seconds.

As she turned into busy Westheimer Road, she edged her purse closer to David. He was complaining that he had to control his temper. She was thinking about some of the other things he'd already committed to tape. All that hostility about the Campbells, and she'd barely had to prompt him. And the rage about Family Motors. One phrase stuck in her mind: "I'll get a coupla niggers off the street and pay 'em five hundred bucks to kill 'em." She thought, Is that what he did for Cindy? Hire the hit man? No wonder he doesn't want to give it up.

She was nervous about what the tape might have recorded in his bathroom. Of course she'd had to take her purse and of course the goddamn transmitter was peeping out of one end and of *course* there was no way to turn it off. She'd taken a leaf from her mother's book and opened both faucets wide. An undercover agent with the Mexican quick-step had to improvise.

"For years I waited until I was just as big as he was,"

David was saying as she sped past a bus on the right, "just waiting for my dad. I told him off several times. I've got a bad temper. I can be real mellow, real nice, but it's like somebody gets to the point, like 'I'm going to fuck you over,' and all of a sudden it pushes me over. I just want to one hundred percent kill. *Yeah!* And when it's somebody like you, somebody that I care about, I would . . . I'll run out and beat the shit out of a tree and break a fucking kid." He paused as though he might have frightened her. "I mean, *you* don't have to worry."

As she lit a cigarette, she wondered about his choice of words. "Break a fucking kid"? It didn't make sense. She decided she must have misheard.

128

"Break a fucking kid. . . ." They were the last words Schultz and the technician Raymond White heard over their squawky monitor. Paris and West had climbed into her little yellow car and then—*gone!* Out of sight, out of range. Schultz thought, The race is on. I must've missed the green flag.

He wrestled with the steering wheel of the clumsy police van and bumped over the curb onto Waugh. White was supposed to be driving, but he was huddled in back fiddling with the tape recorders. Schultz thought, Goddamn, I've been a foot Marine, but this is my first shot at tank commander.

"They went left!" Raymond called out.

"My ass!" Schultz said as he spun the heavy wheel. "They took Montrose."

Paul Motard's deep voice came in from the Camaro chase car. "We lost 'em," Motard said. "You got 'em?"

Schultz unhooked the hand mike. "We ain't never had 'em," he answered. He was having trouble getting the van into third gear. "She took off too fast."

They rumbled along the back streets while White tried to pick up a signal.

"Anything?" Schultz asked.

"Nope."

"What's the range of that thing?"

"A few blocks."

"She musta thought we got a fucking Batmobile."

It's not my night, Schultz decided. The tape recorders had missed all the incriminating stuff about killing the guy at Family Motors; the reels hadn't started turning till Kim was in the bathroom. It was a failure of communication. At the meeting earlier Gil had heard one of the techs say that the batteries lasted two hours and had to be strictly conserved. "Not *our* batteries, Gil," Raymond White informed him after it was too late. *"Kim's* batteries. We got enough power in the van to tape all month."

"Well, why the hell weren't we taping from the start?"

"Because you didn't tell me to."

"Was it up to me?"

"That's what we agreed."

Strike one.

Strike two was hearing all the stuff about kissing. Gil had been relaxing in the van's big chair, barely listening to West's bullshit about trust and faith, when he thought he heard him say that Paris hadn't even given him a kiss. No, he told himself, the little scumbag didn't say that. "Well, whattaya know," Raymond White observed. "She swore she hasn't put out—and she hasn't." Schultz thought, There's something fishy. I wonder if Paris and West set this hoax up. . . .

Motard and Ron Knotts were having their own problems in the Camaro. The "cool car" had nearly twice as much horsepower as Kim's borrowed Jetta, but she'd already pulled out of sight two or three times. Her favorite technique was to apply a burst of speed through a yellow light, forcing Knotts to stop or run the red. She drove so erratically that it almost looked deliberate. "I don't get it," Motard said as he struggled with the direction finder. "I think she's in trouble."

"Yeah," Knotts said at the wheel. "Why else would she drive this way?"

They caught up as she was making an illegal left turn at one of the busiest intersections in Houston. Knotts was caught in traffic and had to wait. "Her signal's getting weak," Motard said as he watched the flickering red and green lights. "Oh, shit," he said. "We're gonna lose her ass." Then: "She's gone! Goddamn it, Ron, she knows we're trying to follow her. Maybe he's got a gun on her."

Every few minutes Schultz's voice came over the speaker asking for their location. As near as Motard could tell, his old partner trailed the action by at least a mile. Knotts said, "We might as well start crisscrossing." Motard nodded. It was beginning to look like a long night.

Fifteen minutes later they tracked the Jetta to Miyako, a Japanese restaurant west of the Galleria. The lovebirds sat at the counter in front of a display case of raw fish. They seemed relaxed.

Schultz and White pulled up alongside the Camaro in a parking lot across the busy six-lane street, and soon the private detectives arrived. They didn't have monitoring equipment of their own, and Schultz invited them inside the police van to hear the dialogue as it was being recorded. He didn't yield his easy chair to the Moseley woman. There's no honor among us old men, he admitted to himself. Her little butt's no better than mine, and mine's tired.

Gripes flew back and forth, jocular at first, but then more serious. Everyone was discouraged by the car chase. If Paris didn't know any better than to drive like a maniac when three different vehicles were trying to keep her in sight, there wasn't much chance she'd do anything else right. Even Kim's colleagues agreed that they were probably wasting their time.

129

The sushi tasted like cold liver wrapped in rice. The glass display case evoked Miss Rock 'n' Roll Trash on a spit. As Kim slid her purse closer to David, she thought, How long can I keep this up? The Everclear screwed up my stomach and the food's gonna finish me off.

David played the hip sophisticate enlightening a backward friend. She didn't tell him, but she'd already been introduced to raw fish and hated every bite.

"Take this," he said, offering up a spoonful of something gelatinous. "Pour the teriyaki sauce and a little bit of wasabi and you mix it in and what you have is a hot teriyaki sauce. And then you take it with your chopsticks. You know how to use chopsticks?"

She said yes.

"Okay, dip it in and that's one bite. One nice little flavored package."

"Yeah, yeah, sure," she said. "One nice little flavored package." With the green horseradish, it went down like a hot briquette.

He offered her salmon, squid, tuna and several kinds of fish with Japanese names. She chewed a piece of octopus for five minutes and then hid it under her rice. She forced down a few bites of seaweed-wrapped eel, pushed the rest aside and lit a cigarette.

"You don't like it?" he asked. He acted as though she was joking. "I thought you said you liked . . . oh, my God, you don't like it? *You don't like it?* I don't understand."

After a while it was time to change batteries. The ladies' room was too crowded. She gave David money to pay the check and said, "I'll go out and start the car."

She looked around the parking lot and saw no familiar faces. She wasn't worried. The cops could be miles away, watching electronically. She glanced across Westheimer at Caligula XXI; she'd danced topless there. The parking lot was always full.

She'd just snapped her purse shut when David jumped in. They were almost out of fuel, and she spurted in and out of several gas stations before finding one with diesel. As she pulled into darkened Vermont Street, she looked in the rearview mirror. No cars were in sight.

They climbed the stairs. She thought, If I didn't feel so shitty, this wouldn't be a bad setup. He's mellowed out on raw fish and alcohol. We'll cuddle on his couch and he'll spill his guts.

David opened the door to a blast of noise. Wickie Weinstein lay on an army blanket yelling into the phone. A big guy with wavy brown hair was singing off-key. Wickie dropped the phone and introduced his friend Fred. Both revelers looked as though they'd spent the evening in the company of Snow White. Fred had difficulty communicating. "And that's pissing me off," he announced, " 'cause I'm finding myself at this very moment as we speak, this point in time, this point in the fourth dimension, in this space in this time, finding myself doing that . . ."

Kim thought, Maybe they'll leave. Maybe they won't ruin my one big chance.

But they wouldn't leave and *wouldn't* leave. David seemed to be enjoying the show. They discussed his dog Nana, the Urban Animals, the latest Coca-Cola commercial, Wickie's Batman button, carpentry, drugs, gays, New Hampshire, Connecticut, Philadelphia, the A-bomb and a dozen other subjects, all at the rapid pace that she remembered from her own days as an addict. Fred admitted that he and his companion had "absofuckinglutely" done both coke and acid, and Wickie mentioned that they'd also visited bars. Kim imagined all the big ears listening down in the police cars. God, she thought, everybody will blame me. Especially Schultz. . . .

David brought out a studded black cowhide bracelet. "Happy birthday!" he said as he held it to the light like a jewel.

"All right!" she said. It wasn't her birthday, but who cared? "Why, thank you!"

"Happy birthday," he repeated. She could see that he was

a little wobbly. The fish eggs, probably. "Happy newness," he added. "That's it. *Happy newness!*"

She was touched by his gesture. He was a loser, dwarfed by events, but not really a bad guy. She let him slide the bracelet on her wrist and kiss her gently, then asked if the gift meant they were going steady.

"Hey, yeah!" he said. "You've got my colors on now, ya know?" He flashed the little-boy smile that made him seem so young. Ah, David, she thought, if you knew. . . .

Wickie passed a joint. She explained that she didn't smoke pot. When Fred insisted, she threw up her hands and joked, "Don't make me! Peer pressure, *peer pressure!*"

The partygoers didn't leave till after eleven. Kim decided to say good night. Neither the time nor the atmosphere was right. And her stomach still hurt like hell.

"I have to go," she said. She walked out the door and David followed her down the steps. "I probably won't see you for a while," she said, trying to soften him up for the next wiring session.

He grabbed her arms as she fished in her purse for the car keys. "Why?" he said. "Hey!" He sounded desperate.

She said coldly, "Thanks a lot."

"Well, talk to me!" he said.

She thought, The cops might give me another chance and they might not. "You want to talk?" she asked.

"Yeah."

She got into the Jetta and lowered her window. "Honest," she said, "I'll give you a call."

He started to protest. She said, "I care about you an awful lot, David, but I just really . . . I feel we've addressed it before and we have just like tonight, and you just fucking blow it all off . . . and it just doesn't matter."

He walked around and got in. As she slid the purse between them, she noticed that the downstairs Christmas tree was still lit up.

She used body language to show annoyance. He looked concerned. "I love you, David," she said, pretending to yield a little. "Come on, don't get all upset."

"All right," he said. "You're starting to sound real final. I mean, it's like, ya know, come on."

She said she would rather talk tomorrow. She was thinking, This is leading nowhere and the cops must be really pissed.

She decided to set a deadline. "If you're ready to be honest and put everything on the right track," she said, "then Friday I'm ready to make a commitment."

He said, "What do you mean, honest with you?"

"This is an all-or-nothing proposition. I'm ready." She thought, If he wants to interpret that as a proposition, fine. If he's involved in the killings, he'll be in jail before I have to pay off, and if he isn't in jail—well, I'll do some more shucking and jiving.

"I'm ready," David said emphatically. "I've *been* ready."

"It's an all-or-nothing proposition," she repeated.

"You got it all," he insisted.

"No I don't!" She stared out her window as though she couldn't stand the sight of him, then spoke in a tone of impatience: "I'll talk to you tomorrow. I have to go. I still love you, David. You think about love, and you think about commitment!"

He said that some things had to remain unsaid.

"Well, then, that's it," she said. "I'm not about . . . I'm not about—"

"No, I—"

"—to fucking trust you and you know—"

"Now listen! There's some things *you* got to give, too. It can't be all *your* way."

"Give?" She tried to sound dismayed by his choice of words. "You know I've given!"

"No, look—"

"I'm not going to argue with you. Why are you raising your voice at me?"

"All right. Listen, baby—"

"Why are you raising your voice?"

He started to stammer. "I'm just . . . I just resent that. I can't believe it. Listen."

"If I didn't know anything," she said, "it wouldn't make any difference. But the fact that I do and you admit to me—"

"Listen!"

"The fact that you admit to me that you're holding back. Maybe it's just something odd about me, but . . ." Her voice dropped wearily. "That's okay." She could see that she had him on the run. She accused him of being deceitful, then insisted again that she had to go.

"No you don't!" he said.

"David, I *have* to go."

"Now listen, we already started talking. So let's talk."

"For what?" she said. "Talk around in circles? Like we have been? We've been talking around in fucking goddamn circles for the last—how long?—a month? Do you think this is some tiny fucking thing that doesn't mean anything?"

"No!" he said.

"Okay," she said. "Don't raise your voice. I'm not screaming at you."

He told her that his ass was at stake. "I'm sorry," he said. As he spoke, a figure appeared in the darkness, walking slowly. It was a back-street transsexual. David didn't seem to notice. "Just like you said the other day," he said, "the perfect crime is doing something and nobody knowing about it and nobody seeing it."

"Yeah," she said sarcastically, "but I'm nobody, man."

"No!"

"I'm not just like anybody," she went on. "You're talking about fucking niggers and you're going, you're going to treat me like a nigger. But that's fine, because I'm not going to argue with you."

"No!" he exclaimed. "Bullshit!"

"I'm not going to argue with you!"

"I don't understand why you're taking it this way."

"How would *you* take it? It's turning into an argument, and I hate to argue. David, I love you. I don't—"

"Okay," he said, "I'm not going to argue with you. I hope maybe—"

"Don't treat me like a nigger or like some punk you pick up off the street to pay to do what you want them to do!" She sounded distraught again.

"What are you talking about?"

In the back of her mind she was still guessing that he'd hired the killer for Cindy, "a coupla niggers off the street" as he'd put it in his tirade about Family Motors. "You quoted me as the perfect crime, right?" she rushed on. "Do you think that I'm somebody that you have picked up off the street to pay to commit this crime for you?" She thought, I'm not making sense, but it's my attitude that counts.

"No, no!" he said, waving his hands. "Wait a minute! No, I don't understand what you're talking about at all. Frankly I've lost you somewhere."

"You just quoted me," she said quickly, trying to keep him off balance.

He said, "I quoted something that *you* said, which was that if someone was to commit a crime, the best way to go about it would be not to have anybody see it and not tell anybody about it. Right? And you're perceptive and you've realized something has gone on. . . ."

She thought, Something's gone on, huh, David? Tell Theresa, man! *Tell Theresa.* . . .

He said, "I could've sat there and stared in your goddamn face and said, 'No, I don't know what you're talking about.' But I can't lie to you. I don't *want* to lie to you. Everything I've said to you has been the fucking truth. But there's some things I just don't want to say because they don't matter to you and me and—"

"Yes!" she said.

"No they don't!" he yelled, then lowered his voice. "I'm sorry. This is where the trust comes in. I'm sorry, and maybe it's not in my favor . . . but believe me, give me a chance, I'll earn your trust. I know it's fucking weird. It's weird for me. And maybe you don't have to fuck with it. . . . I feel like rushing it, too, but goddamn it, what you're asking me is something that shouldn't be asked. It's not anything emotional, it's strictly legal. The need-to-know thing—you understand the idea of the concept of the need to know? You don't need to know this because it hasn't got anything to do with you and me. It's strictly mechanical. It's legal. It's got nothing to do with emotional."

"Yes it does!" she said excitedly. "Because you *have* talked to me! You talked to me goddamn last night! You talked to me about having fucking kids! You talked to me about how much you love me, about marriage!"

"That has nothing to do with this."

"Yes it does, because it's you and I—" She interrupted herself as if she were too overwrought to go on. "I . . . have to think."

"It's not—"

"*I have to think!* Would you just do me a favor?" She paused. "You say that it has nothing to do with me?"

"Nothing."

"And you have the unmitigated gall to sit here and tell me that you won't fucking tell me and at the same time you talked about marrying me, about loving me, about having kids and everything else?" She said that if he didn't trust her, "That's fine. It's not as if you have to bare your soul. It's not like you have to tell me of every indiscretion in your entire life. I don't expect you to sign an affidavit to everything you've done wrong, except this is fucking different because you know it bothers me, because you know I been thinking about it, because you know I have dreams about it, and you know it goddamn *bothers* me! It's like I told you ten minutes ago, if I didn't know a goddamn thing about it, it wouldn't fucking matter, *but it does goddamn matter!*"

He looked dismayed as she hammered away. "Because I do know about it," she raved. "We've talked about it, you've addressed it, and then you hold out on me and at the same goddamn time you talk about marrying me and having goddamn kids and I don't buy it and it makes me nervous. It just makes me fucking nervous and if you don't want to talk about it then we won't talk about it—*and we won't talk about another goddamn thing!*"

"Hold it!" he said, putting up his hands. "Hold it. *Hold it!*"

She spoke out the window. "Don't play games with me."

"All right. Lighten up."

"And now you got me screaming and I hate to scream."

He laid his head on her shoulder. She glanced at her purse and realized that she hadn't changed the batteries in the transmitter in two hours. There was no way to change them now.

"All right," he was saying. "Don't worry about it." He paused. "Give me a second."

She thought, To do what? Go for it, man! "David," she said softly, "I love you and this is driving me nuts."

"It's driving me fucking nuts," he said.

His voice fell away. "You know what the problem is. I'm a fucking lousy liar. That's the goddamn problem. I don't want to lie to you. Everything I've said to you is the goddamn truth."

"I know it is," she said, "but then you tell me half-truths and you tell me lies and I knew there was deceit there."

He reminded her of the lie he'd told about not being in touch with Cindy and insisted that he hadn't intended it as a lie because "I don't want her affecting you and me because she's nothing. She's just . . . a big fucking problem."

Kim thought, She's a problem, all right. She's involved you in two murders, and you're too stubborn to admit it. "I know she's nothing," she said with heat. "The problem is not Cynthia, it's *you*. I don't give a goddamn about your perfect crime. You know enough about goddamn me to know that I don't give a fuck about your perfect fucking crime. What I care about is you and me, and you're playing these fucked-up games and you don't want to talk about it and . . . we won't talk, we just won't talk! But all I know is that whatever this is, until it's cleared up, I won't handle it. I'm ready to make a commitment to you body and fucking soul and you're playing these fucked-up games with me, and that's fine." She paused and applied the clincher. *"You just won't ever see me again."*

He was silent, then reached across and touched her under the chin. "All right," he said. "Look at me."

She turned away. "I can't. I'm too upset."

"Hey, look at me." His voice was still low.

"What?"

"I killed both of her parents."

130

Paul Motard and Ron Knotts had been trying to stay awake in the "cool car" parked a block away. More than once during the long evening Knotts had growled under his breath, "Kim, just get outa there. It's not gonna happen."

When they heard the confession, both sat straight up. "He said it!" Knotts yelled.

"I can't believe it!" Motard said. The skinny detective recovered his composure long enough to look at his watch and write "12:12 A.M." in his notebook. Then he muttered, "Keep talking, West! Keep talking! Don't stop now!"

"Oh, man," Knotts said, "I can't believe it. This is great. You guys got him now."

"Not yet," Motard said. "We only semi-got him. We still need hard evidence." But he was smiling.

The two private operatives, Denise Moseley and Mike Manela, were sitting in the police van with Sergeant Gil Schultz and technician Raymond White in a parking lot a block and a half to the north. Just before the confession poured from the squawkbox, Schultz had leaned back in the van's easy chair and said, "Goddamn it, Kim, say goodnight to the asshole and let's go! We'll pick it up again tomorrow night."

When West confessed, Schultz said, "Son of a bitch! *What did he say?*"

Moseley's folding chair slipped into the door well and she grabbed Manela's shoulder to keep from falling. All four started whooping and hollering: "She did it!" "Goddamn, I didn't think she'd—" "She did it, *she did it!*"

Ray White said, *"Ssshhh!* He's still talking."

They huddled around the monitor. West was rationalizing the killings, describing his relationship with Cindy, telling how "everybody was preying on her" and driving her crazy. "I'm not stupid," the tinny voice went on with driving intensity. "I don't take shit at face value. This is over *years!* I knew that this horrible tale was real and it was driving her nuts and she had this overpowering self-destructive thing that had been beaten into her since she was a little kid. They hated her and she felt bad and unworthy and horrible and, ya know, there was no reason for it, because she was basically great, ya know?"

He said that he'd planted the original idea by telling Cindy that she ought to kill her parents and later she'd begged him to do it. "And she also offered me a lot of fucking money," he said. "And I said, 'Yeah,' and the thing was that I made her stand there with me when I did it, 'cause I wasn't gonna have her say, 'Well, you did it. I didn't have the belly for it.' I made her go in there with me and stand there right by the bed, and I shot each of them three times."

Kim began sounding as though she'd had it for the night, but West ran on. He told how the children had been asleep at the foot of the bed and how Cindy had run out the door before the shots were fired and how they'd originally entered through a window. When he was finished wringing out every detail, he said pleadingly, "There it is, blow by blow. Is that good enough for you? Do I trust you? You got my life in your hands now. Is that good enough? Is that what you want?"

In the van, White said, "The needle's in his arm." Everyone knew how Texas executed.

West's feathery voice resumed: "I don't feel like I've even compromised myself morally, frankly. They've just been executed is all. That's it. I didn't do anything wrong as far as I'm concerned."

They heard Kim say, "You be careful." It sounded as though she was saying good night.

West said, "You needed a commitment. You got your fucking commitment."

Kim said she needed time to think.

In the cramped van, Moseley thought, Is she gonna get out of there or are we gonna have to go get her? God, she's cool! I'd probably be yelling for the cops. I'd say, "Okay, guys, come get him! *You dirty rat, you did it!*"

Everyone heard Kim tell him to take a bath and "we'll meet tomorrow, okay?"

The response was a weak "I'm scared."

"Why?" Kim asked.

"I never said that to anybody."

They heard the scratchy noise that meant she was moving her purse. She repeated that she would call tomorrow. "Don't be afraid," she soothed him. "Go to bed. Rest easy and sleep real tight, David."

"Oh, well," he said, his voice fading, "back to reality. Bye-bye, sweetheart. See ya later."

"Bye," Kim said. Engine noise drowned the rest.

131

Kim thought about the phony hugs she'd given him, the times she'd mouthed "I love you." She'd never loved him, but she'd had a deep affection for . . . a murderer? She was shocked. At the instant of his confession she'd been so surprised that she'd almost said, "David, you let me down!" She remembered trying not to throw up.

As she turned into another dark street, she thought, I've gotta get some air. She was driving through an old neighborhood with wooden bungalows set behind trees and shrubs. She stopped the car and stumbled onto a narrow lawn. She remembered another awful thing about herself and covered her face with her hands. At the moment of the confession she'd thought, David, David, don't tell me! *The cops are listening!*

She fell to her hands and knees and tried to vomit in the coarse grass. She thought, Poor, poor David. If it were in my power, I'd let him off. She couldn't free her mind from his face and his voice, his last words. Bye-bye, sweetheart. . . . He'd never called her "sweetheart." She'd rested her chin on her hands and watched him walk backward toward his house, waving all the way up the stairs and smiling. Oh, David, she thought, what have I done to you? . . .

After a minute or two she sat back on her heels and tugged at her pink hair. She shut her eyes and remembered how he'd said, "I'm scared." At that instant two words had come to her mind: *lethal injection*. She'd told him to relax with a bath because she wanted him to sleep well on his last night at home.

She opened her eyes. The grass was damp, but it hadn't been raining. She looked up through the branches of a tree and couldn't find the moon. She asked God to make the evening begin again, give it a different ending.

A van pulled to the curb and Mike Manela jumped out and lifted her to her feet. Denise tried to whirl her around. "You did it," she yelled. *"Kim, you did it!"*

"David killed them," she said dazedly. "I don't believe it."

Michael gave her a squeeze. "You're a pro," he whispered in her ear. She started to cry.

Moseley seemed beside herself. "I knew you could do it! I *knew* it! And Schultz didn't believe you!" Kim thought, It's like our high school team just won the big game.

"Yeah," Kim said. "I did it." She couldn't stop whimpering.

Mike said the troops planned to assemble at his nearby house. Denise said, "I'll ride with Kim." As they drove off together, Denise kept saying, "You did it, you did it!"

"Yeah," Kim said. "Can you believe it? And those motherfuckers didn't think I could." She thought, And I mean *all* of you motherfuckers, not just the cops.

Denise said, "They just thought we were dumb women."

"Jerks," Kim mumbled.

She drove aimlessly, down Montrose to Richmond, then north again on Shepherd. She was in no hurry to reach Mike's house with make-up dripping off her chin. Out of the corner of her eye she saw a car whip a U-turn behind her, but thought nothing of it.

"Kim," Denise was saying, "I've never been more proud of anybody in my life. And I'm proud that you did it the first night, 'cause it showed we knew what we were doing."

"Yeah," Kim agreed, "and the cops didn't."

"Nerds," Denise said.

"Dorks."

Kim heard a light "beep" and turned her head. The police Camaro was running alongside with the technician driving and Motard waving. Oh, my God, she thought, my mike's still on. Well, there's no taking back what I said. Besides, it's mostly true.

They pulled up in front of Mike's and Motard gave her a bear hug. "Did you get everything on tape?" she asked.

"Enough," he said. "We missed a little on the front end. You did good. Except for your driving. You were going so fast a patrol unit came after us. I had to lean out the window and badge 'em. You had us mixed up with the Hill Street Blues."

She insisted she'd driven normally. No one had told her to keep it slow. She'd watched TV chases and thought a car with electronic equipment should be capable of tracking her anywhere. They both laughed and she wiped her eyes and started crying again.

Ron Knotts climbed from the "cool car" and told her, "Raymond and I were taping all day long on another job and we didn't get a thing. Thanks for making it all worthwhile. I've never heard a tape like it. West talked ninety percent of the time. That's what the prosecutor needs."

Inside the house Gil Schultz wore a big grin. "Well," he said, "you did it. And I never thought you would."

Kim felt too tired to mention the power of the pussy. She woke up the big boss with a phone call. "Clyde," she said, "he confessed."

"Who confessed?" the proprietor asked sleepily.

"David West."

He insisted on talking to one of the officers. Knotts spoke to him and then Motard.

"He wants us to arrest West tonight," Motard said after a long conversation.

"Well?" Kim asked.

"We've got work to do first." He told her to come to headquarters at 8 A.M.

"What for?" she asked.

"We've got more taping to do."

After a while she tuned the party out and drifted into a corner by herself. The vodka tasted bad after the eel and Everclear, and she didn't feel like celebrating anyway. Celebrating what? Outsmarting David? That poor guy?

Around one o'clock she excused herself and drove home.
Her roommate was waiting up and Kim showed her the
black cowhide bracelet. Sami said it was a nice engagement
gift.

Kim was too wired to sleep. She kept wondering how
she'd managed to misdiagnose David so thoroughly. If he'd
killed in cold blood, what were her other "normal" friends
holding back? If a nice guy like him could step across two
sleeping kids to commit murder, couldn't Clyde, Mike,
Schultz, Paul Motard, and . . . her own father? She'd
prided herself on knowing human nature. She told herself,
You don't know a goddamn thing.

132

David stared at the cracks in his ceiling. It had been a heavy
trip, laying all that shit on Theresa, but he wasn't sorry. He
thought, What if the worst happens and she tells somebody?
It's a silly worry, because she won't. I've told others and
they haven't said a word. Theresa and I love each other.
Why would she run to the cops?

And even if she did, he said to himself, it would be just
talk. He came from a long line of lawyers and knew about
hearsay. Besides, he consoled himself, I'd just deny everything. He felt secure.

He swallowed a yawn and wondered what she'd do next.
He thought, She can't say I haven't been honest with her,
and that's all she seemed to want. Now let's see if she's
gonna be honest with me.

133

At 9 A.M. Kim added up her fragments of sleep and figured they came to about an hour. She dialed A-1 Blue Print and caught David between deliveries. "How ya feeling?" she asked.

"Surprisingly, a lot better," he said. "I slept better last night than I have in a long, long time."

"Well, I'd like to see you again tonight."

"Really?" he said. He sounded relieved. "I was afraid you'd never want to see me again."

"Oh, David."

They agreed to meet at eight at the Park Lane. The cops would be pleased.

She sleepwalked through the rest of the morning while various Harris County functionaries escorted her in one door and out the other. She sat through strategy sessions and several playings of the confession. She waited for what seemed like hours while portions of the tape were played for the grand jury, then stumbled into the jury room to answer questions. ("Weren't you afraid, honey?" "Uh, I don't know. I guess so.") She was surprised to find that the jurors resembled ordinary parent figures; she'd expected them to look like Earl Warren and Eleanor Roosevelt. Assistant D.A. Terry Wilson, an oversized Texas Aggie who put her in mind of Deputy Dawg, seemed pleased that the jurors returned secret murder indictments against David and Cynthia. Kim said, "Oh, they did?" She was too damn groggy to follow the events.

All day long the battle plan was shaped and reshaped. She was surprised to find that the prosecutors still didn't feel that they had enough for convictions. They said they needed physical evidence, like the gun or the mask or the clothes, and more inculpatory information on Cynthia, ideally from her own mouth. Kim was told to crank West up again. "No way I'm going back in his house," she protested. "I've already looked down his shotgun."

"Kim's right," a voice said. "If anything goes wrong, we'd have to take him in the house, and that could mean a full-scale war. Let's do it all outside."

She turned and looked. It was Gil Schultz. She thought, Aren't we a pair?

The final plan seemed safe enough. She would meet David at the Park Lane and drive him to the Café Moustache, a glossy restaurant near the Galleria. They would sit in front of a big window where they could be observed by police teams in the parking lot. If she needed emergency help, she was to repeat a phrase from the night before: "Add water and stir." She was to rile David up by telling him that Cynthia had already received a twenty-five-thousand-dollar settlement and was obviously holding out on him. Then she was to demand an immediate showdown with Cynthia. If David refused, she was to drive him to the nearest convenience store, park, and run like hell.

"And do us one little bitty favor, will ya, Kim?" the usually taciturn Paul Motard added. "Make your right turns from the right lane and your left turns from the left. Don't use gas stations for shortcuts, and try to hold your speed under fifty. Okay?"

She said, "Did I mention I've been driving on a suspended license?" The lawmen groaned.

A few minutes later Schultz and Motard took her to a cubbyhole office and left her to herself. She wondered why. On the table she saw a stack of blown-up color pictures of the murder scene. She thought, They want me to look at them, but they're not supposed to offer.

She wished she hadn't peeked. Wild animals killed with more compassion. She hoped it was the end of her mixed emotions about David.

The crew rendezvoused at Mike Manela's house just before 8 P.M. Sami came along to serve as cosmetician and wardrobe mistress. On Kim's last night as "Theresa Neel" they'd selected her gear with care: a knee-length black linen pin-striped coat-dress, white muscle-shirt in a man's size, red tights, black spike boots with red bandannas over the heel and under the arch, a silver and black earring to her chest. Her sleeves and collar were up, her hair teased in a bouffant snarl—black at the roots, burgundy in the middle and pink at the ends. On her face she wore a half pound of make-up. What the hell, she thought, I might make TV.

Knotts and White phoned in to say they'd be an hour late. There was general grumbling about the cheap-ass Houston PD jeopardizing this murder investigation by working the poor techs to death on another case. Kim phoned the Park Lane to make her excuses to David. She knew his habits; by now he'd be half blitzed. It made him as tractable as her cats Toulouse and Lautrec. She recognized the bartendress's voice: "I know he's here somewhere, hon, 'cuz I just poured him a cup of coffee."

Kim thought, *Coffee?* David doesn't drink coffee before he drinks alcohol. Why the hell was he drinking coffee? Coffee makes you alert. Why the hell does he want to be alert? "How long's he been there?" she asked.

"I've poured him three or four cups."

Oh, Christ, Kim thought. *He knows.*

She called again in a few minutes. "Hi, hon!" David said. "How are ya?" He sounded upbeat, not at all like his usual mood after a day's work. "I'm really looking forward to seeing ya."

She said, "I'm gonna be a few minutes late."

"What else is new? Well, listen, I have to go home and feed Nana. Why don't you just meet me at the house?"

She thought of his shotgun. "No, no!" she yelped, and added a softer "No" so she wouldn't sound scared. "It'd be easier to meet at the bar."

"No, no, really!" he said. "I insist."

"No, David."

"Come *on,* Theresa." This stubbornness wasn't like him.

"David," she said, "I'm starving. If we get to your house, we'll have a drink, and I want to eat now." She tried to calm herself. "I don't feel so good from that sushi last night."

They argued a little more and he gave in. As she put down the phone, she began to shake. Why was he acting so different?

Gil Schultz asked, "What's wrong?"

"Nothing," she said. "I'm just real nervous." She

thought, It isn't only fear of David. There are so many people involved now—cops and prosecutors and the Campbells and all Clyde's people and so many others. It's gone way beyond just me and David. It's too damn heavy.

"Why're you nervous?" Schultz asked.

"Because David isn't acting like himself. He's never that insistent. I never have to ask for my way more than once." She realized that Schultz probably thought she'd turned gutless. She didn't care. Maybe it was fatigue or maybe it was the murder pictures, but something made her feel edgy.

"If you're afraid," Schultz said, "you don't have to do this."

"I'll do it," she said. "But don't get too far away from me. If you think there's anything wrong, *anything,* please move in."

He patted her on the shoulder. "Hey, flake," he said, "you're with *us.*" It was a comforting thought.

134

He'd had some money at the time of the killings, but he thought there was no limit to it. He has no foresight. He's very immature and as I've said from time to time, he's making real progress and some day he's gonna grow up.

—DUVAL WEST

When David saw Theresa walk through the door in that long-limbed stride of hers, he thought, Hey, just in time, man! One more cup and I'd burst. Payday was a week off and he had twenty dollars to his name. At the Park Lane coffee was free.

She was dressed like a punk-rock hey-look-at-me shitkicker from Flatonia, Texas, but that was just Theresa. This morning he'd told Wickie that he intended to marry her. Of course it would be nice to make love first, make sure all the parts went together. He told her she looked gorgeous and asked where she wanted to go for dinner.

"Café Moustache."

He thought, Jesus, why does she have to choose a pseudo-hippie, pseudo-continental bullshit jive yuppie joint where my twenty bucks won't buy shit? "Uh, listen, baby," he said, "I'd rawther go to a nice neat li'l restaurant where you get quality instead of a chance to sit around and say, 'Gee, aren't I cool.' "

"Don't worry," she said. "I've got some money. Buddy takes care of me."

She was being stubborn again. "Well, okay," he said.

They'd hardly walked through the restaurant door when she announced that she'd forgotten her wallet. He thought, What a ditz! Well, we're here now. My money'll buy a bottle of wine. Nana and I can eat veggies for another week. It's worth it. He'd already changed his sheets.

The maître d' led them to a horseshoe booth in front of a plate-glass window almost ceiling-high with a lovely view of a parking garage. He thought, How artsy-fartsy! A poster titled *Monet's Years at Giverny* hung next to what looked like a Degas print and the menu was in Franglais.

He glanced at the listings. Sorry, he reminded himself, no baked wheel of Brie with almonds tonight, no croque-monsieur, no "poor garçon croissant" and for *sure* no Dom Pérignon at $85 the copy.

"God," he said as they leaned against each other in the black leatherette booth, "that was the best night's sleep I've had in a long time." She was already enveloped in a cloud of smoke. "It was just so relaxed," he said. "Know what I'm saying?"

"Well, good," she said. "I'm glad you feel that way. I know that was hard for you."

"It was very hard."

"It was hard for *me*," she said, "and I didn't know if it was going to send you off on some trip. I didn't know if maybe it was something that should've been left because it would end up fucking our relationship altogether."

He said, "Actually it scared me. . . . A lot of fears, a lot of fears. It's given you power over me, and I don't like that at all."

She told him that the real power lay with Cynthia. He said, "Yeah."

They considered Fumet-Blanc but settled for a bottle of California chardonnay and a Seven-Up. He'd hardly taken a sip before Theresa was back on her favorite subject. Goddamn, he said to himself, can't she let up? For two months now it's been Cindy, Cindy, Cindy. Didn't I tell her enough last night? Why is she so obsessed with a woman she's never seen? This goddamn jealousy has gone far enough.

He reminded her that he and Cindy had never betrayed each other. Theresa said, "Right, and I wouldn't want to have three kids and another on the way and have her turn you around."

"And have me going to jail?" he said. "You mean 'turn me in'?"

"Yes." She said she'd chosen him after a lot of thinking. "You've fulfilled your commitments," she said. He thought, I sure as shit *have*. "And then this morning," she said, "I got up. . . ."

She paused. Oh, Christ, he thought, what's coming now? "To make a long story short," she said, "what would you say if I told you you couldn't trust Cindy?"

David thought, That one's real easy. "I wouldn't believe it. She's lied to me before, but it's always stupid little shit that doesn't matter anyway."

Theresa asked in a confidential tone, "Have you ever thought about checking up on her story?"

"I have," he said. "To a degree, as much as I could."

"You know what? She could tell us anything, and we wouldn't have known any better."

Once again he tried to steer her away from the subject, but she was so goddamn persistent! He said he wanted Cindy to be as small a part of his life as possible "because she's nothing but problems." He said he was thinking about ignoring his share of the money because it was incriminating. "I just want to wash my hands of the whole deal, ya know? You have enough problems by yourself, ya know, and, uh—"

Theresa interrupted. "She says that she hasn't gotten the money?"

"No, she hasn't. They're fucking her out of the house that she's got, and uh—"

"She lied."

"She's going to give me twenty-five thousand," he said.

"She lied to you. You can check it tomorrow. Go to probate court."

He thought, Theresa acts like she knows more about my business than I do. "Well," he said, "I don't know how you can check up on it, but I know she was living in total fucking poverty."

"Maybe so, but what I'm saying to you is why hasn't she told you she has her inheritance money?"

"Because she hasn't! The thing's been buried in fucking probate court for so fucking long it's ridiculous."

"But she's definitely lying!"

He wondered what made her so positive when she was obviously just guessing. "Why do you say that?" he asked. "Are you saying you feel it?"

"No. I know it. I don't feel it. I know it for a fact. I've *seen* it. You can go check tomorrow."

He didn't understand. "How do you know that's a fact?"

"It's a fact."

"You checked up, and you found out?"

"Yes," she said. "That's what I'm saying, David. I'm not going on intuitive impulses. I'm not going to go into something half-ass."

He took a hard look at her. She didn't seem to be kidding or running a game. He asked, "You've actually read some kind of documentation?"

"Yes. Cindy settled early. And she got her share."

He knew better. "She hasn't," he said. If she'd received one thin dime, he'd have heard about it from Cindy or his mom.

Theresa said, "She got her apartment deal and twenty-five thousand dollars cash. Now why is she—"

"She hasn't gotten the cash yet."

"I'm telling you she *has* . . . because I asked the people to explain it to me."

He thought, Holy shit! Who's she talked to? I just told her about it last night! He was baffled. He'd never mentioned the name Campbell. How the hell could she find out? "You ain't never asked names," he said.

"Buddy told me."

"Oh, my god," he said. He couldn't believe she was that stupid. Buddy with the mob connections? She'd told that fucking Mafioso? "You got him involved in this?"

She said she learned the last name from Buddy. David slid to the front edge of his seat and said, "You got to explain this to me. What happened? How did this come about?"

"I didn't bring Buddy into it."

He could feel his heartbeat. If she'd told Buddy his secret. . . . "I can't relax," he said, "until . . ." He had to calm down. "You got to explain this to me."

She said she'd learned the last name from a newspaper and then asked Buddy if he knew anything about the case.

He wanted to break her stupid face. How could anybody who looked like her and talked like her be so goddamn dumb! "Why did you ask *him?*" he asked, his voice rising again. "Every bit of information he gets is powerful. Information is powerful!" He was bobbing up and down in his seat. *"Don't you understand?"*

"It had nothing to do with you."

Fucking bitch! "It has *everything* to do with me," he said. He covered his eyes with his hand and moaned, "Oh, God." He told her he couldn't believe that she'd gone behind his back. "If you tell me something," he said, "I'm not gonna check up on it. It's none of my fucking business."

He told her she knew too much. "There's something we've got to get straight. I can't sit here and think that you're down there at the courthouse checking up on information and stockpiling a goddamn dossier on me, ya know?"

"Look," she said, raising her own voice, "gimme a break! I'm not stockpiling a dossier."

"You shouldn't have been around there."

"I have every right to see it, David."

"No you don't!"

She held out her cigarette to be lighted and he ignored it.

He looked up and saw the bartender staring. He lowered his voice, but he raised it again when she had the gall to tell him he was overreacting.

"Don't ever . . . listen, listen!" he sputtered. "Don't *ever.* . . ." She tried to talk and he kept right on. "Listen to me! Never, if you care anything about me at all, *never* check up. Don't talk to Buddy about *anything* concerning me. Now I'm serious!"

"I'm not going to blow anything!" she yelled back. "But I'm just taking steps for our security because I don't trust her and it's a good goddamn thing I did because I found out a lot."

He told her he couldn't stand nosy people checking on him. "The very idea gets my head. I *hate* it! I like privacy, okay?"

She insisted that Buddy was no problem. "He doesn't give a shit."

"I'll tell you one thing, and this is no danger to you, but before I get involved, before I go to fucking jail, I'll kill myself. All right?"

"Hey—"

"Bullshit! Before I get burned for something. . . . What do you think, I'm going to get put in there and get butt-fucked by fucking bodybuilders? Not me! I'm either scot-free or I'll check out." He meant every goddamn word.

135

Paul Motard was squirming. It was stuffy in the Camaro; the outside temperature was just under seventy but the humidity had hung around ninety percent all day. Ron Knotts had moved their "cool car" for better radio reception and they'd lost their direct view through the restaurant's plate-glass window. For fifteen straight minutes two angry voices had rasped from the audio monitor. Motard thought, Kim was supposed to piss him off a little, goad him into taking her to Cindy's, but nobody mentioned cardiac arrest. Any second now he was expecting her to yell, *"Add water and stir!"*

Knotts asked, "Do you think she's safe?"

"I hope so. She's tough, man."

More bickering poured from the squawk box and then Motard relaxed as Kim began sweet-talking the temperature down. Knotts observed that West might be a little easier to handle tonight—"He probably figures he can get mad or he can get laid, but not both."

Motard nodded. West had dropped the subject of Buddy and returned to Cynthia: "She's insane. I can prove it by twenty fucking people that have seen her do totally off-the-wall stupid shit." Then he shifted into a play-by-play of the murders.

Motard thought, Listen to the guy! Man, this is fricking fantastic! All the details that only the killer could know. He's really doing a number on himself. He let that fat hog get him into trouble and now he's letting this beautiful woman roll up his sleeve for the needle. It's almost funny.

136

Kim thought, It's strange how he can't make up his mind. One minute he says he doesn't want to talk about it and the next minute he's piling on the details. The cops can't complain.

"Look," he was saying, "how would you like to be making love to somebody and have her start calling me Daddy? It's just. . . . just that and a million other things. Makes me sick, ya know? I don't feel any remorse. All I did was administer justice. Really, I don't feel that I compromised my morals at all."

She was surprised. "Not to this day, you don't?"

"No. It may not have been the wisest thing to do, but I . . . it was *not* wrong. Look, it was clean, efficient, and painless."

They were almost head to head. She wanted to move away

but disciplined herself to smile and stay close. She was uneasy. A few minutes before, when he'd been railing about Buddy, she'd thought about using the code phrase. But now that he was talking about the actual killings, his tone had softened. Canned music poured from wall speakers; she hoped it wasn't drowning out their voices on the tape.

He showed her how he'd held the gun. He stood in a half-crouch, aimed his finger, and went, "Poong! Poong! Poong! . . ." The bartender glanced over again.

She gulped and said, "You went from one to the other?" A young couple strolled past. My God, she thought, doesn't he realize we're in public?

"Yep," he said. His eyes gleamed in the neon light and he flashed his childlike smile as he told how he and Cindy had crept into the house, walked up the stairs and opened the door silently. "I said, 'Hit the lights!' And she did, and the lights came on and I opened fire, and then I looked down and the kids were there."

"And you went, 'Oh, jeez.' "

"The first thing that ran through my mind was, Shit, they've got to be removed also, but then I thought, No, I got a mask and they don't know who the fuck I am and I don't want to kill kids."

When he finished describing the murders, he admitted that he sometimes felt bad about the fact that he'd killed " 'cause I've changed my entire opinion of myself."

She asked, "Have you ever killed anybody else?"

"No. That's what I was trying to say. I . . . I . . . I've changed my entire opinion. It's on my fucking hands." His voice turned pensive. "But I am a good person. That's the way I am, ya know?"

She was more afraid now than when he'd been shouting at her. She thought, He's talking too freely, too glibly. I'm not on the pedestal anymore, I'm a party to his guilt, and he's treating me accordingly. He's already said I have too much power over him. Now he's talking as though it doesn't matter what I know. I wonder if he plans to kill me.

She glanced out the window. The backlighting from the bar made it hard to see outside. No one was in sight.

She steered him around to the gun. The assistant D.A.

had emphasized that there might not be a prosecution without it. "That weapon doesn't exist," David said. "It's never been . . . I've never owned such a weapon."

"It's something that's gone?" she said. "I guess it doesn't matter." She was thinking, Gone *where?*

"Yeah," he said. "There can never be a case when it doesn't exist."

"Pitch it over a bridge, man," she said, trying to urge him on.

"It doesn't exist, period. It's just, it wasn't owned, ya know? And nobody ever found it."

She tried to sound light-hearted. "Did you melt it down and make yourself an earring?"

"No. It's buried under something. God knows how much water and everything else are on it. Can't be found. But even if it was, by now it'd be a big hunk of rust. You can't get no goddamn ballistics out of it, that's for sure."

She thought, What a change. Last night I was something you don't touch, don't hurt, don't even push a kiss on. Now I'm one of the gang. He talks to me the way he'd talk to a bank robber. The Bonnie and Clyde deal worked a little too well.

He splashed some wine in their glasses. Above the bar a three-foot orange sign said CAFÉ MOUSTACHE in script, and a neon band circled the bar lengthwise. His dichromatic eyes caught the light as he stared hard at her. "I lost my innocence, ya know?" he said. He sounded tired. "You know what I'm saying? Before, I always felt like . . . well, I didn't really believe in heaven, if there was a heaven. But I have never done anything that I was ashamed of. . . ."

She thought, That's the David I know. That's the David who doesn't gloat when he talks about murder. That's the David who knows he did wrong.

But then he began making a comedy skit out of his search for the getaway car keys. "Mister Cool, Calm, and Collected," he called himself. *"Where the fuck are the keys?"* The shots had been so loud, he said, he was sure someone would show up and grab him. *"Pow! Pow! Pow!* That loud a sound, you figure that . . . the fucking neighbors and everybody would be running out of the fucking houses."

She thought, I can relate to that. If I killed two people, I would be the one looking all over for my keys. And then I'd hear a siren. . . .

"We were running across the road and a car came around the curve," he was saying, "and we still had the masks on. Shit! The worst! I figured, Well, if the goddamn car stops, I'll kill these motherfuckers."

His laugh made her shiver. Once again he seemed to be savoring the details. Where the hell had the other David gone so quickly? Didn't he realize he was talking about human life? She prodded him by asking if he'd made any mistakes, "one fatal flaw that haunts you."

"The only flaw that haunts me is somebody fucking up and talking," he said.

The statement made her feel sad again. She thought, He's done it to himself. For a bright person, he's such a fool.

He said he didn't think Cindy would be alive in five years. Kim asked, "Are you going to off her?" She flashed on him killing Cindy, killing her and killing himself. In one of his weird moods, it was possible.

"No," he said. "She might actually get better. But she's just too fucked up." He couldn't seem to make up his mind about Cindy. She realized that he never had.

She took one more stab at getting him to take her to Cindy. She apologized for upsetting him about the twenty-five thousand dollars and suggested, "Why don't you go ask Cindy about it tonight?"

He shook his head. "I can sleep," he said. "There ain't nothing going to be different tonight. . . . I'm not so sure I want any of that fucking money anyway." She could see he wasn't going to change his mind.

Once again he brought up suicide. The problem, he said, would be the means. "If I'm already in fucking jail I don't have knives, I don't have guns and I don't have poison and I don't have rope. I could always wait until my exercise time and run headlong into a yard full of goddamn niggers and say, 'All the niggers suck big dick faggots,' ya know?" He seemed to think that was funny. "Or I could stand in the fucking toilet and wet my finger and stick it in a light socket. That might do it."

She asked, "Do you have the balls? Well, obviously, you've killed two people. But could you do it to yourself?" He said he'd only have to have the balls for a second.

He confessed that he'd thought of killing Cindy to keep her from talking. "She's like you are," he said slowly. "She saw, and she just, whew, she stopped, just looked at me, and she said, 'Thinking about maybe killing me, too?' And I said, 'I don't know what to think right now. You're acting fucking stupid.' "

Kim thought, How much of that statement was intended for me? Am I acting stupid? *Was that a threat?*

He was babbling and she was only half-listening. It was time to go. She tried to remember where she was supposed to take him. A 7-Eleven store? A Circle K? A *Safeway?* God, she hoped there was no violence. She'd seen plenty of TV shootouts, but real bullets ripped flesh and killed people. And you couldn't switch the channel.

"Look," he was saying, "if I was so cold-blooded, I would have killed her. She would have had an accident. She would have been raped, stabbed, something, ya know, that would've looked like a street crime."

"How long will it be," she asked, "before you decide to do away with me?"

He looked sheepish. "That's not possible," he said. "For one thing, that's why I didn't want to fucking tell you."

" 'Cause you might kill me?"

"No, because that question would never arise. And it's . . . it's not gonna arise. I've already made up my fucking mind. I'll kill me before I kill you. That's how much power you've got."

He turned toward her with an impish look. "All right, you opened up a full fucking goddamn can of worms here, didn't you? Couldn't fucking leave well enough alone. Couldn't just say, 'Fine now, Dave. I like you, I trust you, ya know?' " He smiled sweetly and patted her hand. "You've seen the other side of me, and that's the way I am."

As she walked to the rest room, she thought, What a dirty deal this is. He's sitting in his corner smiling like a happy little kid. He thinks he's gonna get laid.

On the way to her car he took her arm and said, "See,

what we're talking about here is two different modes. There's the person mode and there's a soldier mode. When I did that, I was in a soldier mode. But I'm a person, and you've seen how sensitive I can be. And if I can't ever just totally relax and love and just be right, then everything's fucked, you understand what I'm saying?"

She understood what he was saying. He was making his move, and he didn't want to come across as a brutal murderer. He said, "It's like I've got to retain that romanticism and innocence, ya know? I mean, that's all, that's what you can expect from me."

"Okay," she said nervously. She was recalling how he'd said he wouldn't be taken alive. She didn't think Schultz and the others gave much of a shit about such niceties. She glanced at him and wondered how much longer he had to live.

He smiled and said, "I love you, baby."

On empty Westheimer Road a series of cars materialized behind her and snapped on their lights—one, two, three, four, five pairs. She thought, It's like an old movie. Edward G. Robinson's back there with Robert Stack and Eduardo Ciannelli. How trippy!

"David," she said, "I need cigarettes. Don't let me pass a convenience store."

137

David was feeling a little silly for laying it on so thick. All the tough talk—fuck this, fuck that, fuck the motherfuckers. All that bullshit about starting to kill Cindy and going into "soldier mode" and deciding not to shoot the boys and— what a load! Christ, he hadn't even seen the boys.

Well, he said to himself, give the lady what she wants. *David West, bad-ass hit man!*

She was driving nice and slow. Not like last night. We'll get home soon enough, he told himself. Tonight's the night. Tonight and every night from now on. He realized he was a little drunk. He thought, Whoopee! We'll drink some Ever-clear and go for it. If she keeps jacking me around, I'll say, "Hey, what's the fucking deal? You can't say I haven't been up front with you." Of course she'll spend the night. She's already promised.

He wondered if he was expected to create a romantic mood. Sometimes the old rituals were nice. "You know what I love about you?" he said. "You're strong, you're smart, you're together, you're a modern woman." He knew he sounded like a cigarette commercial, but he plowed ahead. "But you're still feminine enough. You're not *a*feminine, ya know. And you enjoy things, making me feel good. I love it!"

He promised her breakfast in bed. "Wake up to a heavenly smell," he said. "And coming with a tray—"

"—of rabbit stew," she cracked.

They joked back and forth about the sushi dinner. She asked him what the nasty little orange things were called.

"Salmon eggs," he said.

"Ugh! *Très* ugh!"

They talked about Mexican food and he told her she probably wouldn't like menudo because it was really just tripe soup. "You know what tripe is? It's like, uh, intestines, stomach lining."

"No, no, no, no, *no!*" she said. "Don't be so graphic about it!"

She asked him to watch for a 7-Eleven. He thought, That must be the fifth time. She must be having a nicotine fit.

He said that he'd eaten brains once and didn't like it.

"Goddamn," she said.

"I don't like the texture," he said.

She said, "Just the idea of . . . brains."

He said, "Just imagine scrambled eggs that are a little bit on the runny side, and—"

"I don't want to hear it! No, *no!*"

He told her that Orientals ate beetles. "Fucking bugs," he said. "I ain't gonna eat no goddamn bug. I'm sorry, man."

She said he would if he were hungry enough. He wished she would drive a little faster.

138

Kim felt her scalp tighten. The caravan had closed up behind her and she still hadn't found a convenience store on her right. They'd passed three on the left, but the cops had specifically instructed her to pull off to the right, park, and split. Or had they just told her to pull off any old place? She couldn't remember. A clock in a storefront said eleven-three.

Her mind flashed ahead to the end—sirens, lights, gunshots, David's cowlick matted with blood. The Houston PD was trigger-happy; people slapped stickers on police cars: ARMED AND DANGEROUS. "We don't take money," the cops bragged, "and we don't take shit."

David dribbled on about eating. She'd never seen him happier. She steered past St. Luke's with its tall thin steeple bathed in blue-gray light. She spotted an A-Z food store and the Ankar grocery, but they were on the wrong side. Ahead she saw necklaces of ruby lights marking the tops of downtown buildings. Soon she would have to turn toward David's house. Then what? *Where is a goddamn store?*

He pointed ahead and said, "Circle K. Let's go there to get your cigarettes or whatever it is you want."

She slowed. To the left, faded signs said KEYS LOCKS and GARAGE AUTO REPAIR. To the right was a minimall: a laundromat, a clothing store, two gas pumps, and a small market under a big *K* surrounded by an iridescent red circle.

David said, "Don't turn your engine off. These fuckers are real screwy. They'll have all the lights on like that and the motherfucker will be closed."

She said, "Can you tell?" A white sign in the window advised shoppers to TAKE OUR 10-OZ CLASSIC BURRITO TO LUNCH.

"No, I can't tell," he said.

She wheeled into a parking lot. Her breathing was shallow and fast and she wondered if he noticed. She rammed the shift into neutral, looked in the mirror and saw nothing. She swallowed hard and said, "Well, I'll go check."

She desperately wanted to get away from the line of fire. As she clawed at the door handle she thought, Please, God, don't let him be blown to bits. Don't let the guns hurt my ears. Don't let anybody be hurt. She remembered crying at *Mandingo* when they started to boil a man. She thought, This'll be *worse.* She took a deep breath and said, "Watch the car for me."

"Okay," he said as she stepped out and walked quickly away. "I'll lock the door, but I can't—*Goddamn it!*"

She turned at his yell. The car rolled backward a foot or two, then stopped. David's head was out of sight. She realized she hadn't set the brake and he'd thrown himself across the seat to reach it.

A car skidded to a stop and almost knocked her down. The police van pulled in and Raymond White got out. "Police officer!" he yelled. *"Freeze!"* She braced herself.

David said, "Whoa-whoa-*whoa!*" so fast that it sounded like one long word.

"Hands up!"

"Sure thing. Sure thing! *Whoa!*"

"Hands up now," White said. He was wearing a windbreaker and a cap. "Get outa here!"

"Yes, sir," David said. "No prob, no prob! Yes, sir. Yes, *sir!* What's the problem?"

They spread-eagled him across the hood of the car and patted him down. Gil Schultz read him his rights as David said, "There's some mistake." He sounded like a misunderstood schoolkid.

"There's no goddamn mistake," Schultz said. "You're under arrest." He got right up in David's face. "We're talking about the Campbells, *bo-ey.*"

"You guys are making a mistake," David repeated. He kept it up as the other cars pulled in.

Kim didn't want to see him beaten. She retreated behind a parked pickup truck. The driver looked drunk and was repeating under his breath, "Oh, wow, I didn't do anything! What did I *do . . . ?*"

Denise Moseley ran up and said, "Kim, you did it. You did it!"

"Get away from me, Denise!" Kim said. She didn't want company. "You have no idea what the fuck is going on, man." She lit her last cigarette and smoked in angry little puffs, thinking, I don't need her jumping around like a god-damn cheerleader.

A hand touched her shoulder. "Want a beer?" Mike Manela asked. He ducked inside the store and returned with a can of Miller's.

As she took a long swig, she heard David's excited voice. "I don't know what you're *talking* about!"

She peeked around the truck. He was about twenty feet away, backed against the door of the Jetta in the center of a semicircle of drawn guns. She heard him say, "Capital murder? There's a mistake here somewhere!"

The headlights gave his face a chalky look. More cars pulled in, their sirens growling down. Kim squeezed her hair back, the way she always did when she was nervous. David was being handcuffed. He stared at her and she turned away. "I just can't look at him," she said to Mike.

"He's in custody," Manela said. "Don't worry about him."

She felt overwhelmed. She said to herself, I wish you'd never told me, David. *I wish you hadn't done it!* She tried not to cry.

She knew she had to look at him, acknowledge her role. If you don't, she told herself, you're nothing but a punk.

She turned. His eyes locked on hers. He kept watching her till they stowed him in the back of a patrol car. In his face she saw disbelief and hurt. The car pulled out, and she raised her beer can in a toast.

139

David sat in the caged back seat of the patrol car and thought, Don't I know that cop sitting in front? Yes, he'd come to the house with traffic warrants. "Say, aren't you Officer Cavaliere?" he asked.

The cop nodded and said, "How's that pit bull?"

"Max? He ran off."

"Oh. That's too bad." Cavaliere sounded friendly. It was nice to meet someone who didn't hate pit bulls, even if it was a cop taking you to jail.

The handcuffs dug into the small of his back and forced him to arch his body. He thought, That smart-ass detective back at the Circle K oughta try this sometime. *Capital murder,* the jerk had whispered in his ear. *You know what that means, don'tcha?* In a windowless room at police headquarters he found out that the mind-fucker's name was Schultz. His partner Motard seemed okay; unfortunately, he didn't say much.

David tried to get things off to a gentlemanly start. "I gotta hand it to your lady there," he said with a smile. "I never did suspect her. She always acted airhead enough so I wouldn't suspect her."

The one called Schultz said, "Well, she's not working with us. She's private. Hired by the family."

"Oh, really? I'm surprised."

He wished he could figure out exactly what had happened, but he was still too confused and scared to think straight. Obviously there was a connection between his arrest and Theresa, but what? Had she been wired? He thought, Oh, shit, I said too goddamn much. I said it *all.* He wondered why she would betray him. Is she a cop? No way, he decided. That's something I would've picked up on in a second.

She had real feeling for him; he was sure of that. He thought, Maybe I'm a gullible fool, but I don't think it was faked—the way she looked at me, the way we held hands and kissed. His head swam, trying to make sense of things. He realized that she'd been trying to get him drunk all night. Well, he thought, it worked. He'd knocked off just about the whole bottle of wine and talked his stupid head off.

Schultz said, "We really don't want a confession, West, 'cause you're gone anyway. The D.A.'s office won't offer you a deal 'cause you're the triggerman. What we want you to do, we want you to call Cynthia now and let us plug in the tape and see if she'll make an admission. We can't promise that it'll do anything for you, but if we're asked by the defense, we'd be compelled to say you cooperated."

David said he wanted a lawyer.

"You don't believe me, do ya?" Schultz asked. "Lemme let you talk to the assistant D.A. on the case."

A few minutes later a thickset, balding, bespectacled guy walked in and started talking like a hall monitor at a military school. "Look, we're not offering you *nothin'!* I don't even want you to give us a statement because somebody might think that's showing remorse, and it might keep you from getting the needle."

David thought, It must feel good to be able to talk so tough. The gun in his belt helps.

"The only thing we're offering you," the guy went on, "is a chance to not go down alone. Do the right thing and help us get Cynthia."

"I got nothing to say," David replied. "You could break my thumbs and I wouldn't call her 'cause I don't know her number."

The A.D.A. left and the detectives trooped back in. Schultz did the old Mutt and Jeff routine all by himself, blustering one minute and cajoling the next, while Motard watched with his soft brown eyes. David wanted to say, Hey, Schultz, save the bullshit. But he didn't.

"The trouble with you, boy, is you've always let pussy run your life," Schultz said. "You let Cindy talk you into killing her parents and then you let Kim Paris talk you into confessing."

"Who?"

"Theresa. The one you had the hots for. I'm ashamed of you, David, letting yourself be led around by your dick."

David thought, Kim Paris, huh? She wasn't even honest about her name. He wondered if any of them knew how the Campbells had treated Cindy—the rape, the beatings. He said, "Didn't you guys hear what I told Theresa?"

"Every word," Motard said.

"Well, then, you know about Cindy's parents."

"We know what *you* said about them," Schultz said.

"It was the truth! They did terrible things to her. Her mama would lock her in the bathroom."

"If I had a nasty-ass daughter that wouldn't bathe or take keer of herself," Schultz said, "I'd lock her in there or I'd take the scrub brush and clean 'er up." He slid his chair closer and said, "Why don't you tell us the whole story?"

David decided he'd said enough. The detectives tried to stare him down, but he kept silent. Someone came in with a tape player and he heard himself talking to Theresa. He was mortified. He thought, How stupid I sound, how childish. Listen to Dumbfuck Dave trying to get into her pants. *Smoooooth.* . . . He wished he could die on the spot.

After another long silence Schultz said, "We heard you abused those children."

"Bullshit!" David said. He couldn't keep quiet about that.

"We know all about it, man."

"I *didn't* fucking abuse those kids. That's a fucking lie and you know it, man."

Schultz shook his head sadly. David thought, He doesn't believe me! He thinks I'd hurt kids! Motard seemed just as dubious. "Hey, listen," David said, "all's I did was take 'em to a restaurant and the kid wouldn't eat his food, ya know?" He explained the whole deal, how he'd bartered with the boy for his own good, how he'd spanked him a little and got him to eat his dinner.

Schultz came back in his pseudo-cool voice, "I guess according to your logic we've got a moral justification for smacking you upside the head with a two-by-four, right? You're saying you had a right to use force in both those situations. Just because her parents mistreated her, you claim you had a moral right to blow 'em away?"

David considered his answer carefully. "I didn't do it," he said, "but yeah . . . they needed to die."

"Well, David," Schultz said, working his jowls like Raymond Burr, "just because they were evil people doesn't mean you're judge, jury and executioner. Lookit this situation right there. We know that you killed 'em, and yet we're not gonna execute you tonight. We're gonna give you a fair chance."

David thought, That's cop logic if I ever heard it. *We'll give him a fair trial and hang him.* He'd first heard that line on "Gunsmoke." "Real nice of you," he said.

"Well, it is!" Schultz said with a smile. "You gotta admit, David, the needle's humane."

"Because you don't see any blood? Personally I'd rawther be stood up against a wall and shot."

"Like the Campbells?" Motard asked.

"The Campbells didn't feel a thing," David said. "It was a humane execution."

Other detectives wandered in to take a look at the animal. One guy got right up in his face, but David turned away and ignored him. It was a weird feeling, all those eyes staring at him, nobody talking, other cops peeking around the door.

Schultz said, "We got hours and hours of taped confession outa you, boy. We're gonna give you the needle sure."

David lost patience. "Well, let's get on with it!" he yelled. "Let's go! *Shit!* Fuck it, ya know? Don't sit here and jack with me all night about it." He was almost screaming now. *"Let's go do it!"*

Schultz told him to take it easy. "David," he said, "just tell us yes or no. We got a buncha people out there hounding after ol' Cynthia Ray. We don't want to bother her if she's innocent. We don't want to be fucking with her unless we're sure. Do we need to be looking for her? Yes or no?"

"Yeah," he mumbled. Anything to get them off his back. What he said didn't make a shit anyway.

They put him in a holding cell with a telephone at one end. He thought, They expect me to tip off Cindy while they listen on the extension. They must think I have an IQ of about eighty.

He dialed his parents. "Hi, Dad," he said. "Put Mom on
the other line."

"She's sleeping, David."

"Wake her up!"

Cecelia said a quavery "Hello."

"Mom, are you awake? It's important. Listen!"

"Yes, yes, *yes!* I'm awake."

"I'm in jail," he said. "I've been arrested for the murder
of Cindy's parents, ya know?"

His mom said, "That's ridiculous."

David didn't want to prolong the conversation. "I need a
lawyer down here quick," he said. "And if you can get in
touch with Cindy, tell her they're looking for her, too." That
would have to do for now.

140

It was 4 A.M.; the prisoner was in his cell and Gil Schultz
was thinking ahead. "We still got Cynthia on the ground,"
he said. "Any ideas?"

Everyone spoke at once: Carl Kent, Paul Motard, D.A.'s
investigator Les Ramsey, A.D.A. Terry Wilson, plus some
graveyard shifters who'd been drifting in and out. The prosecutors insisted that they needed more evidence; Texas law
ruled out a conviction based on the uncorroborated testimony of an accomplice, and that was all they had.

They settled on a plan that took into consideration
Cindy's reclusiveness and paranoia. Schultz summed up:
"Okay, we know she won't talk to just anybody, so we'll put
out a short press release saying that there's been an arrest in
the Campbell case. She'll hear about it and get panicky.
Then Kim calls her on a wired phone. Kim says . . .
Lemme see here." He looked at his notes. "Kim says,
'Cindy, this is David's girlfriend Theresa. He's been arrested
for killing your mother and father. He told me he did it for
you and you were supposed to give him some money. I un-

derstand you got your inheritance. I need the money to get him outa jail.' "

"Or words to that effect," Motard said.

"Then Cindy implicates herself on tape," Schultz resumed. "We bring her and West together and let 'em butt heads. Then"—he sighed heavily—"we get some sleep."

Schultz awoke Sergeant J. C. Mosier at home and asked him to put out the press release. The other detectives catnapped at their desks. At 4:30 A.M. a probable-cause warrant was issued for the arrest of Cynthia Campbell Ray. Kent and his new partner Novak were sent to relieve the Clyde Wilson operatives who were sitting on the Kingston apartment. They reported no signs of activity.

At six A.M. Schultz tuned his radio to the early news and heard, "A twenty-eight-year-old white male has been arrested in the Campbell murder case. Mr. and Mrs. James Campbell were murdered in their beds. . . ." He thought, That oughta stir some shit.

In midmorning Kim Paris arrived with fellow agent Bill Elliott. Schultz briefed her while his office phone was being hooked up to a tape recorder.

She dialed Cynthia's apartment twice with no answer. "What do we do now?" she asked.

"We wait."

Stoked up on caffeine and nicotine and generally pleased with the night's work, the group passed quickly from conviviality to horseplay. Day-shift detectives dropped into the office to ogle the private eye's legs, casually draped over Schultz's desk. Wisecracks became raunchier. One thing about Paris, Schultz said to himself, she can jive with the best.

He put her up to betting a notoriously shy detective five bucks that he was wearing boxer shorts. "There's only one way to prove it," she insisted. "C'mon, c'mon, take 'em down!" Her colleague Bill Elliott walked out.

A few minutes later the phone rang and a loud voice told Schultz, "This is Clyde Wilson. I understand you got my operative up there and y'all are playing grab-ass." He said he'd scheduled an important news conference and needed Kim right away. "Put her on!" Wilson ordered.

Paris took the phone and said "Yes, sir" and "Yes, Clyde" about six times. Schultz had never seen her so respectful. Christ, he thought, that old boy runs a tight ship.

She grabbed her purse and said, "Clyde told me to get my goddamn ass back there."

Schultz said, "You gotta go?"

"Yeah, if I want a paycheck."

He thought, There goes our battle plan. He remembered when J. C. Mosier had brought her to the homicide office, a frightened little gal trying not to cry. She was in over her head and didn't know which way to Mexico. Now she was Clyde Wilson's big star, on her way to a press conference.

Well, he thought, she did her part of the job. One down, one to go. That's what matters. Never underestimate the power of the pussy.

141

Detective Sergeant Carl Kent reported later:

"We went over to Cynthia's apartment and staked it out. A cleaning lady was working. We sat down the street a ways and noticed her looking out the window at us. We were trying to be inconspicuous, but it's not a big wide street and everybody up and down knew we were the law. We were driving an unmarked Chevy Celebrity with a li'l bitty antenna in back.

"The cleaning lady leaves the apartment, comes down to where we're at and says, 'Are y'all the police? What're y'all doing?'

"I said, 'We're trying to locate Cindy Campbell Ray. We have a warrant for her arrest.' "

" 'Well, she's not here right now, but she's supposed to be back later on. Can y'all let me get my money from her before y'all arrest her?'

"Turns out this cleaning lady is the wife of a deputy sheriff. Cindy had hired her to clean and redo the apartments.

"I said, 'Tell ya what. When she comes home, you go

ahead and get your money from her and then come to the front window and give me the high sign and we'll pop her.'

"After a couple hours Cindy drives up in a car with a homosexual named Gay Bob. She's all decked out, but she musta put on eighty pounds since the killings.

"She went inside and the woman waved at us from the window. They came down and saw us. Gay Bob went around the back as though he was nervous. Novak and I thought those suckers might take off on foot.

"We sat there for a few minutes. Then Cindy came out the front door and Gay Bob comes from around the back. I says, 'Let's go pop 'em!'

"Cindy starts hollering, 'I didn't do nothing. I'm not gonna go with ya!'

" 'Yeah you are.'

" 'No I'm not!'

" 'Yes you are!'

"She wasn't screaming, but she was loud enough for people to hear. Ol' Gay Bob says he'll git her a lawyer.

"I says, 'Well, git a lawyer 'cuz she's gonna go to jail.'

"We put her in the car and Gay Bob tries to follow us. We thought we eluded him, but he showed up at headquarters. I hollered to one of the other detectives, 'Don't bend over around that guy!' Gay Bob wanted to know my name and I said, 'Get your queer ass outa here!'

"We didn't tell Cindy the whole thing that we had on her, just told her she was under arrest for murder. She says she had a lawyer and wouldn't talk.

"I said, 'We don't need your damn statement. We got somebody that done snitched off on ya. David West.'

"She put on her innocent act. She's the phoniest baloney you ever saw in your life. Her eyes get real big, staring at ya. We talked to her about an hour. She just set there and stared, said things like, 'I can't believe y'all are doing this. I can't *believe* it!'

"I says, 'That's bullshit! We know you were there when West killed your mom and dad.' I was looking for some kind of remorse or reaction, but she just stared. That woman is cold-blooded, filled with hatred, no remorse. A woman that would do something like that with her kids at the foot of the bed. Just *mean!*

"She refused to believe we had West, so we had to bring him down."

142

> . . . this thing of darkness I acknowledge mine.
> —SHAKESPEARE, *The Tempest*.

David kept thinking, I'm gone. There's nothing I can say or do. There's no way to save me.

He still couldn't figure Theresa. He told himself, If she thought she was after some evil, rotten murderer, then maybe what she did was justified. But one of the cops said she'd been running at Cindy and only nailed him by accident. If so, he thought, she's just another scumbag. If she was willing to say "I love you" for a little side-issue job, well, then, she's got to be some kind of slut. He rubbed his eyes and pondered the morality of the situation.

Around nine or ten in the morning the door clanked open and he was led away in handcuffs. Paul Motard told him, "We got somebody we want you to meet."

In one of the glassed-in homicide offices, Schultz was sitting across a desk from a tearful Cindy. She blubbered, "David, I can't believe this. That's not you on those tapes, is it? That's not your voice?"

"Yeah," he said. "It's my voice." He thought, I might as well admit it. There's never gonna be any doubt it's me.

Cindy was fatter than ever, but he managed to flash some unconditional positive regard with his smile. Tears dampened her long lashes and dripped down her face. Her cheekbones had disappeared again. Her new Modigliani nose had expanded into a Rembrandt. She was smoking and sipping coffee from a Styrofoam cup. He thought, What did I see in

her? Well, for one thing, she never finked on me. She kept
our secret. And she loved me. She was my masterpiece and
she loved me.

He wasn't sure how much time the police would allow
them. "I was really being stupid, Cindy," he said, talking
fast. "They got me. I'm gone." He knew the detectives could
hear. "Look," he said, "keep your mouth shut and do what
your lawyer says, ya know? I'm screwed. You just keep
quiet."

One of the cops spread some pictures on the table. David
saw two blood-spattered figures on a bed. He thought,
That's the Campbells! It was weird to see them as people
and not as aiming points. The mother's hand stuck up. It
looked as though a slug had broken her arm. The man had a
hole in his eye. David thought, That looks *nasty!*

He glanced at Cindy. She'd stopped crying, and her face
was blank. One of the detectives said, "Look at her! No
remorse or nothing! Man, she's cold-blooded!" He pushed a
picture under her nose and said, "Look at it. *Look at it!* You
don't even care, do ya? That's your mama there!"

A tall, overweight cop said, "Man, I cain't understand
how you ever got involved with a fat hog like her. We
weighed her in at two sixty-four."

David thought, They're saying these things right in front
of her! That's goddamn cruel! He was embarrassed for her.
He said, "She used to be beautiful."

"Beautiful?" The cop pointed at her nose. "Lookit that
chancre."

David thought, You son of a bitch, don't you know she's
got self-esteem problems? "She's had that broken blood ves-
sel a long time," he said. "She can't help it. She used to be
beautiful."

"I heard the tape," the same cop said. "So you're an atheist, huh?"

David thought, I've been listening to that shit since the
second grade. Once a Boy Scout troop had called on his
father and demanded an explanation. Jesus freaks, David
thought; I can't stand 'em. "That's bullshit," he said.
"Didn't you fucking hear what I said on the tapes? I didn't

say I was an atheist. I said I didn't believe in organized religion."

"Same thang." The cop paused and said, "You musta really been in love with this Cindy, huh?"

"Yeah."

"You in love with her now?"

"You mean . . . romantically?"

"One way or the other."

He looked across at Cindy. She was rubbing her reddened eyes like a little kid. "Yeah," he said, "I still love her." He thought, In twenty million years I couldn't make you guys understand.

He listened to the slip-slap of her jail sandals as they led her away. He thought, I wonder if I'll ever see her again. He wouldn't blame her if she was annoyed at him.

They took him to a smaller cell, about six by eight, painted in shades of gray, with a mattress the thickness of a doily on a one-man bed built out from the wall. The floor was damp and gritty. Brown stains dotted the inside of the toilet bowl. Spatters of urine had formed rust scabs on the steel wall. Everything stank.

He flopped on the bed and thought about the butt-fuckers roaming the halls. How long would he have to defend his ass on death row? Five or six years, he figured, with automatic appeals and all. He thought, Instant death would be better.

He pictured his mother and father. God, he thought, this'll kill 'em. They'll believe me for a while, but down the line they'll have to drop me. They'll say, Oh, my God, where'd we go wrong?

He thought, Goddamn, that's unfair! They didn't go wrong, *I* did it to myself. They shouldn't have to suffer. But they will. He remembered a talk he'd had with his mom about a Houston boy who murdered a female letter carrier. The boy's parents had refused to testify against their son, and a judge had sent them to jail. Cecelia had said, "I just can't understand those people. if a kid of mine ever did something like that, I'd sure testify."

And DuVal—Oh, man, David thought, he can't possibly stick by me. Not with his West Point sense of honor. He flashed on something that hadn't crossed his mind in years.

Back before his van Good Times had been stolen, DuVal had copied a few of his own favorite music tapes for him. They weren't that bad. Sidney Bechet was no Buddy Holly, but he had talent. And some of the old boogie-woogie stuff sounded a little like rock 'n' roll. He tried to remember if he'd thanked his dad for trying. He guessed he hadn't.

Hey, man, he said to himself, it's too late now. He heard puking sounds, then a hollow silence. He wondered where they'd put Cindy. Somewhere in this same block, he imagined. He wished he could sit with her for a while, tell her how sorry he was about the cruel things her folks had done, tell her that he'd always been able to see through her fat to the good person underneath.

He wondered how many people were already reading the Sunday *Post* and laughing at him. David the nerd. David the sucker for every woman who comes along. He thought, I'm not only locked up for the worst crime in the world, but I look like a buffoon. He thought of the stupid remarks he'd made on the tape. His stomach tightened with shame. He thought, Aw, man! and squeezed himself around the middle.

The idea of dying didn't frighten him. It was the waiting on death row, the loneliness. Goddamn, he thought, that's my idea of torture. He remembered TV shows, true stuff, documentaries, where death-row guards hollered "Dead man coming!" when they escorted an inmate. That's me, he thought. *Dead man coming.* The state of Texas, with its DuVal County named after my dad's people and its Simmons Island named after my mom's—the state of Texas is gonna kill me. He thought, We were always an honorable family. We had a good name. Who disgraced our family tree?

Me.

He'd always hoped for a chivalrous death, or at least an honorable one. In childhood daydreams he'd seen himself laid to rest under an American flag while a rifle detail fired over his casket and his dad and mom bawled.

Nope, he thought. Not this trip. He saw himself full of dope, stretched out on a gurney, drooling and pissing his pants as the IV dripped the poison into his arm. He thought, Who would blow taps for that kind of death? I'd rather go out by my own hand than be put to sleep like a dog at the pound.

He dug into the side pocket of his jeans and pulled out his John Wayne fold-open can opener. He tried cutting his wrists, but the tool was designed for C-rations. Shit, he thought, all I'm doing is bruising myself.

He dismantled his Casio watch. The crystal was thick and blunt. When he tried to sharpen it, the glass sheared off in sections.

He scraped a penny against the steel wall, but the copper was too soft to take a good edge. He thought, Goddamn, man, can't you do *anything* right? He was hacking at his wrist when he heard a familiar gravelly voice far down the corridor.

His heart jumped. "Daddy!" he yelled. "I'm back here!" He covered up the nicks in his skin. He didn't want his father to think he was weak.

Epilogue

After months of discussion and disagreement, David West's lawyers convinced him to plead guilty of first-degree murder and testify against Cindy Ray. Both were sentenced to life imprisonment.

PROVENANCE

Cold Kill is a work of fact, not a so-called "fictionalization." The narrative unfolds through the eyes of some two dozen characters who were interviewed in depth by me or my journalistic colleague, John McCormick Harris.*

The extensive dialogue and interior monologue do not flow from my imagination but from the best memories of those involved, carefully cross-checked and reinforced by trial testimony, police records, and public documents. Available resource material included impromptu tape-recorded conversations among Campbell family members—the murder victims James and Virginia, Virginia's mother, Mrs. Helen Amaya, and the two grandsons, Matthew and Michael.

Personal information about the investigator Kimberly Paris, the killer David West, and his long-suffering parents, DuVal and Cecelia West, was obtained by exclusive arrangement. David West was interviewed over a ten-month period, and some fifty hours of recording tape were logged for him alone. Neither West, Paris, nor anyone else involved in the Campbell murder case exercised any control whatever over the manuscript or was permitted to examine any draft before publication. The final responsibility is mine. Real names are used throughout, except for "Dean Thomas Samuels."

For giving so generously of their time, I acknowledge a special debt to the brilliant Russell Hardin, Jr., assistant district attorney of Harris County, Texas, and his colleague Lyn McClellan, who prosecuted the case with him; Eugene Nettles and James Leitner, the skilled defense attorneys for David West; Betty and Richard Hinds, daughter and son-in-

---

* With two exceptions, the minor characters Jamie Campbell and Maria Bravo Gonzales. Material concerning them came from interviews by police and the district attorney's office, from public records, and from friends and relatives.

law of the murder victims and prime movers in solving the
"unsolvable" crimes; Gwen Funk Sampson, friend of the
murderess Cynthia Campbell Ray and a key witness at her
trials; Sergeants Paul Motard, Gilbert Schultz, Carl Kent,
and J. C. Mosier of the Houston Police Department; police
technicians Ronald Knotts and Raymond White; District
Judge A. D. Azios; Clyde Wilson, proprietor of Clyde Wilson International Investigations Inc., and his top hands Denise Moseley, P. M. Clinton, and Michael Manela; and to
Edward Benson, James Brannon, Alan Bynum, Craig Casper, Martha Cobb, Melanie Edgecombe, Steve Epstein,
Milton Flick, David Garrett, Tissy Hardin, J. Robert Har-
ris, Sue Harris, John Lee, Rory Lettvin, Fred Lewis, Steve
Moore, Chuck Montgomery, Bob Nale, Brenda Palmer,
James F. Rittinger, Lyn Roebuck, John Sampson, Michael
St. John, Robin St. John, Sandra Smith, Patrick Southard,
Donald A. Thiel, Rosemarie Walker, Wickie Randolph
Weinstein, Ron Westphal, Paul Whitfield, Andrew Williams,
and Lane and Laura Winsett.

Thanks also to Allen C. Isbell, attorney for Cynthia
Campbell Ray, to Marian and Fred Rosen, and to Chief Lee
Brown and Captain Bobby Adams of the Houston Police
Department.

Editors Susan Ginsburg and Laurie Bernstein were ex-
ceedingly helpful. My agents, Russell Galen and Scott Mere-
dith, provided their customary literary and financial expertise. Attorney J. Jeffrey Dudley of Seattle beat back several
legal challenges to the privacy and confidentiality of my re-
search notes with his customary scholarship and skill.

As always, nothing would have been accomplished without the loving assistance, support, and forbearance of my
wife, Su Peterson Olsen.

                              —Jack Olsen
                              Bainbridge Island, Washington
                              July 1988